BREAKING
THE SOUND BARRIER

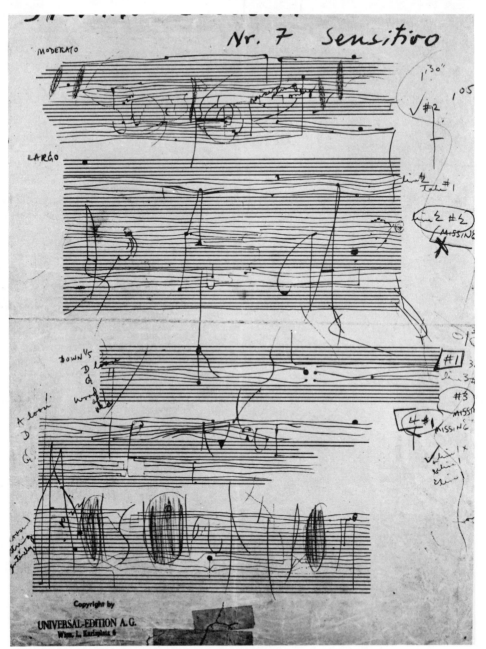

Sylvano Bussotti: Excerpt from composition, c. 1964.

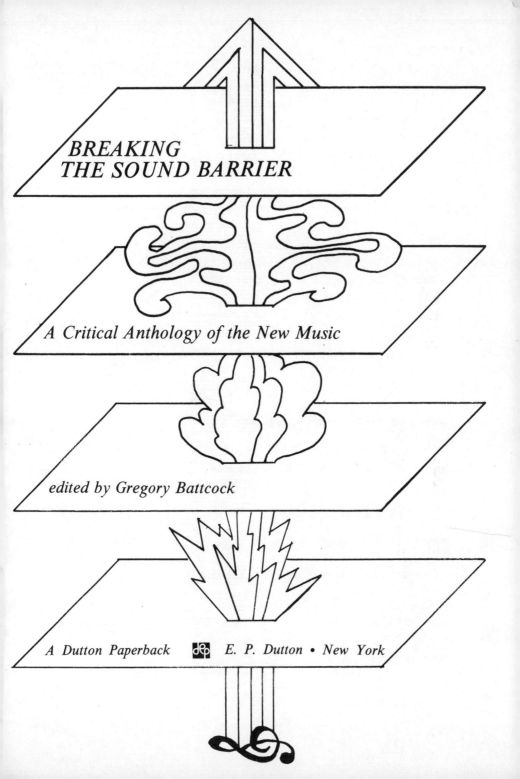

BREAKING THE SOUND BARRIER

A Critical Anthology of the New Music

edited by Gregory Battcock

A Dutton Paperback   E. P. Dutton • New York

For information contact: Elsevier-Dutton Publishing Co., Inc., 2 Park Avenue, New York, N.Y. 10016

Library of Congress Catalog Card Number: 79-53347

ISBN: 0-525-47598-2

Published simultaneously in Canada by Clarke, Irwin & Company Limited, Toronto and Vancouver

Designed by Nicola Mazzella

10 9 8 7 6 5 4 3 2 1

First Edition

Contents

ACKNOWLEDGMENTS   vii

INTRODUCTION: In Search of the Avant-Garde   ix

HISTORY AND THEORY   1

Benjamin Boretz: Musical Cosmology   3

Peter Frank: Fluxus Music   13

Dick Higgins: Boredom and Danger   20

Tom Johnson: Notes on New Music   28

Gaynor G. Jones and Jay Rahn: Definitions of Popular
Music: Recycled   38

Jonathan D. Kramer: Moment Form in
Twentieth-Century Music   53

Rodney J. Payton: The Music of Futurism:
Concerts and Polemics   71

William Wilson: Operational Music   90

COMPOSERS ON MUSIC   95

Earle Brown: Serial Music Today   97

Barney Childs: Time and Music: A Composer's View   102

Brian Eno: Generating and Organizing Variety in the Arts   129

v

Paik and Moorman Perform Cage   142
Steve Reich: Writings About Music   150

NEW TECHNOLOGIES   165
Jerry Davidson: Synthesizers and the Evolution of Electronic
    Music   167
Hubert S. Howe, Jr.: Microcomputers and Electronic Music   174
Allison Knowles: Notations   191
Herbert Russcol: Music Since Hiroshima: The Electronic Age
    Begins   199
Stephen Syverud: Electronic Synthesizers: A Survey   208

CRITIQUE   213
Elaine Barkin: Arthur Berger's Trio for Violin, Guitar,
    and Piano (1972)   215
William Brandt: The Music of Elliott Carter   221
Cornelius Cardew: Wiggly Lines and Wobbly Music   235
Thomas DeLio: Avant-Garde Issues in Seventies Music   254
Ruth Julius: Edgard Varèse: An Oral History Project   272
Richard Kostelanetz: Two Tonal Composers   284
Michel P. Philippot: Ear, Heart, and Brain   300
Josef Rufer: Schönberg—Yesterday, Today, and Tomorrow   316
Elliot Schwartz: Electronic Music and Live Performance   331

INDEX   339

Gallery follows page 164.

Acknowledgments

For her suggestions concerning material, I wish to thank Elaine Barkin. Bob Nickas was most helpful, assisting with research and offering incisive thoughts on musical matters. Furthermore, I wish to acknowledge the cooperation of the Office for Academic Development and Research Programs at The William Paterson College, for which I am very appreciative.

Introduction: In Search of the Avant-Garde

Without doubt, the music of our time may be said to be characterized by its extraordinary variety—in terms of process, style, concept, performance, and aesthetic—in comparison with the music of past epochs. After a long period in which music was generally regarded as an eloquent though relatively stable and formal discipline, the twentieth century has seen the introduction of new forms, sounds, instruments, media, and methods in music, resulting in greater complexity, new meaning, and expanded purpose in all the musical arts.

Some of the new musical developments of the twentieth century have roots that can be traced to ancient periods. Several new composers, including Iannis Xenakis, for example, link musical composition to architecture, a correlation that has been more or less dormant since ancient times. Similarly, the relatively recent development by Schönberg of the dodecaphonic technique is not an entirely new concept, as ancient peoples are said to have been aware of the twelve-tone system.[1]

---

[1] See Fred Fisher, "Music and City Planning," *The Composer* (Spring–Summer 1974), pp. 53–61.

In general, the music of the past was thought to be a cerebral (that is, nonvisual) discipline, playing on tonal responses to sensual, emotional, and perceptual awarenesses. Today it is not uncommon to find experimental and avant-garde composers or performers grounding their musical efforts on concepts based in mathematics, in psychological perceptions, in serial systems, in probability theory, in games, chance devices, improvisation, aleatory sounds, in technological and computer-generated ideas, and "documentary music." Pitched and unpitched percussion—what had been termed *noise* in the past—serves a significant function in the new music, as articulated in the early decades of this century by such composers as Edgard Varèse in *Ionisation* and Erik Satie in *Parade.* Donal Henahan, writing in *The New York Times,* describes an "art of noises" and he claims "music was virtually transformed by this new awareness of undistilled noise."[2] Many of the new systems and forms allow composer-performers to detach themselves somewhat from the music they make, thus ensuring a degree of objectivity and emotional removal that itself has become a characteristic of new music. Just as contemporary artists, from the Constructivists to the Minimalists, have sought a greater degree of detachment in their art through the introduction of technological and mathematical systems, so musicians have sought out a scientific methodology in keeping with modernist reasoning.

In music, as in art, the term *avant-garde* is frequently employed to signify new work. Nevertheless, the meaning of the term is not always clear, particularly in reference to music and composition. What is the musical avant-garde? When did it begin? Is the avant-garde passé? Is it a historical epoch? Or is it a perpetual new wave? Is the term *avant-garde* synonymous with *experimental?*

To take the last question first, we are reminded of Brian Eno's observation in his essay "Generating and Organizing Variety in the Arts" (p. 131), in which he distinguishes between experimental and avant-garde. "Experimental music, unlike classical (or avant-garde) music, does not typically offer instructions toward highly specific results, and hence does not normally specify wholly repeatable configurations of sound." Thus, according to Eno, experimental music is essentially music that may turn out differently each time it is repeated. On the other hand, avant-garde music need not subscribe to this quality.

The answers to the other questions asked above will not be answered

---

[2] Donal Henahan," Clashes, Splashes, and Roars," *The New York Times,* November 23, 1980, Arts and Leisure section, p. 19.

so easily. For in one sense the avant-garde refers to works and concepts introduced very recently, although it should be remembered that many of today's most prominent composers, such as Otto Luening, Samuel Barber, Roy Harris, Douglas Moore, Aaron Copland, Randall Thompson, Elliott Carter, Walter Piston, and Roger Sessions, were in the 1930s or 1940s viewed as part of the musical avant-garde of the period. Although none of these distinguished and, in their time, highly innovative and original composers would be considered part of today's musical avant-garde—although Carter, perhaps because of the difficulties presented by his music, might be an exception—neither would their works be viewed as avant-garde in a contemporary sense. However, such is not necessarily the case with all of the composers and musical radicals of the period. For example, it would be difficult to exclude from the umbrella of the avant-garde a composer such as Edgard Varèse. Similarly, would we rush to exclude from the avant-garde the outrageous proposals made by the Dada and Surrealist artists and musicians of the early years of this century? Similarly, we continue to respect as avant-garde ideas the daring experiments by the Constructivist pioneers in the Soviet Union, who attempted to originate a new music and a new art from scratch, free from the associations and tyrannies of the past in order to communicate totally, swiftly, and democratically. Last, consider the radical propositions in music by the Futurist innovators, discussed at length by Rodney J. Payton in this book. They continue to excite the imagination in a thoroughly contemporary way.

These exceptions aside, works, ideas, and proposals that at one time enjoy avant-garde status sooner or later lose their newness. Usually only temporary solutions to the needs and situations of the times in which they appeared, they often seem to lack permanence when reconsidered. New music simply doesn't stay new. Some new music stays new longer than other new music. Both types are discussed in essays in this book under the headings "History and Theory," "Composers on Music," and "Critique."

If the twelve-tone technique is already part of the history of modern music, how do we place in a historical context the most important event for the world of music of 1948? For in that year the long-playing record was introduced commercially. "We can now demonstrate beyond any doubt that the long-playing record has profoundly altered our conception and perception of music," wrote Robin Maconie.[3] He explained that because of this technological breakthrough our perception of music has gone "from a

---

[3] Robin Maconie, "Stockhausen's *Mikrophonie I,*" *Perspectives of New Music* (Spring–Summer 1972), p. 96.

collective emotional experience ... to an individual, contemplative approach." Thus events that are deemed of enormous importance, sometimes, when viewed from the perspective of another time and place seem to lose their importance. Equally, events that prove historical catalysts may slip by almost unnoticed, only to be recognized as significant years later. Twenty or thirty years ago the contributions of Varèse, Stockhausen, Boulez, and the young Cage were virtually unknown; today they loom as major events in the avant-garde.

In music, as in art, the avant-garde composers of one period can become the great masters of another period. Nevertheless, in the minds of many people, art that is described as avant-garde is a type of art in which "anything goes." According to this viewpoint the avant-garde is synonymous with the outrageous, the undisciplined, and the shocking. However, new music as well as new art is not necessarily without form, not necessarily an arena in which any expression, the more preposterous the better, is encouraged and accepted. New music today possesses form, and the form can usually be identified if not adumbrated. In his essay "Notes on New Music" (pp. 29–31) Tom Johnson identifies six new musical forms that, in his view, have replaced such earlier forms as the symphony, the song cycle, the oratorio, and the cantata. Johnson explains that "Today's music also fits into basic forms," and he suggests that today's forms may, someday, become as rigid as the old forms appear to us.

Encompassing the bulk of today's avant-garde, or "formless," music are the six new forms identified by Johnson. There is the "post-Webern" form of music composed for diverse instruments that is intricate and atonal. The "multimedia" form involves projections and electronic equipment as well as, on occasion, dancers, sets, and props; the Fluxus group (see pp. 13–19) is associated with the multimedia form. The "performer-and-tape" form includes a tape, generally prepared in an electronic studio, that is used to set up a dialogue between humans and machines. There is the "hypnotic" form, consisting of long, extremely persistent, and repetitious sound, which is sometimes referred to as Minimal music.[4] This form would probably include the works of composers from Terry Riley to

---

[4] Not all music writers are satisifed with the term *Minimal music,* although it has become increasingly popular, having appeared in music reviews in publications as diverse as *The New York Times* and *Rolling Stone.* One critic, Alan Rich, writing in *New York* magazine about the music of Philip Glass noted, "Glass, I am told, objects to being referred to as a 'minimalist' composer, and in the sense of other minimalist art, I suppose he's right; the journalist's need for labels embarrasses me no less than it does him." "Fragments of Glass" (March 19, 1979), p. 68.

Philip Glass. Next is the "sound poem," a form that involves the manipulation of words to make music and that probably was first explored in this century by the Futurists. Last, the "performance-art" form in music is, for example, one that has been closely associated with Charlotte Moorman, who, along with the composer and video artist Nam June Paik, is the subject of a photographic essay in this book (pp. 142–149).

All the forms described above, according to Johnson, are linked by a new approach to tonality, in that "the recent music doesn't have much to do with chord progressions." Nevertheless, atonality and dissonance are not, per se, essential to new music, although they seem to have dominated Western classical music in this century. Johnson notes that these both are "very odd phenomena [that] for all their assets and power . . . don't have much to do with music as a whole in the world as a whole."

Some critics would argue that the most significant factors separating new music from music of the past have economic roots, as the sponsors and the audience for new music change from a relatively small elite to a relatively broad-based and economically influential mass. However, such an interpretation, it may be argued, is primarily a sociological one and, for this reason, will not be dealt with here.

A final new form, which has emerged only recently and which involves methods of writing that vary greatly—thus making it difficult to label a school or *genre*—is identified by Johnson as "documentary music." Such music translates facts into sounds and allows the "details of a composition to be dictated by something other than the composer's imagination." This kind of music, which can be expected to be of considerable interest to many new composers, attempts to reflect "some truth, some content, some organizational principle that goes beyond the whims of the composer." Documentary music offers composers the possibility of creating considerable distance between themselves and their music. In this sense it is, perhaps, one of the most thoroughly contemporary of musical forms.

How, then, should electronic music be categorized? Although some writers and musicians have lumped electronic music in a single category, it is probably erroneous to do so. The introduction of electronic devices, from synthesizers to recorders, amplifiers, computer keyboards, and electronic instruments, so pervades all aspects of contemporary musical expression that it can be said that electricity bridges virtually all forms of music. Electronically created sounds are, therefore, a medium rather than a form. Edgard Varèse, in a lecture given at Yale University in 1962 and quoted in *The Musical Quarterly,* noted, "[We] must not expect our electronic devices to compose for us. Good music and bad music will be composed by electronic means, just as good and bad music have been composed for instruments. But, in reality, it is as limited as the mind of the individual who feeds it material."[5] In a similar vein Varèse is also reported to have said, "To me, working with electronic music is composing with living sounds."[6]

It is assumed by some people that the advanced music of our time— the avant-garde—is not authentically new, because it seems that so many new types and forms of composition, performance, and sound are imitative of musical works created during the Dada and Futurist periods after 1910, following the disintegration of triadic tonality. However, an examination of the aesthetic motivations of many composers and performers of today's musical avant-garde will show that even though outward appearance in the form of the sounds themselves are similar to the avant-garde of fifty or seventy years ago, the true motivation, aesthetic intent, and overall concept of such music are quite different. Thus in music, as in the visual arts, the surface impressions and appearances—the sounds—taken alone can be deceptive. In order to determine the real nature of the new, it is sometimes essential to investigate the intentions and content of art of the past. For this reason several essays in this book deal with musical subjects that are not strictly contemporary, such as the examination of the concerns of the Futurist musicians by Rodney Payton (pp. 71–89), a discussion of the early years of electronic music by Herbert Russcol (pp. 199–207), and a critique of works by Schönberg by Josef Rufer (pp. 316–331). Their inclusion in this book may help to explicate the differences in aesthetic and serve to reveal the unique intentions of early twentieth-century musicians.

In his essay "Moment Form in Twentieth-Century Music" (pp. 53–70) Jonathan Kramer suggests that a major difference between today's music and that of the past lies in the concept of *musical continuity,* for such formal continuity no longer characterizes new music. "The consequences of the deposing of musical continuity are enormous. The entire edifice of Western music had been built on the assumption that one event leads to another." Kramer concludes, "To remove continuity is to question the very meaning of time in our culture and hence of human existence."

---

[5] Chou Wen-Chung, "Varèse: A Sketch of the Man and His Music," *The Musical Quarterly,* 52, no. 2 (April 1966), p. 156.
[6] Gunther Schuller, "Conversation with Varèse," *Perspectives of New Music* (Spring–Summer 1965), p. 181.

Thus music, in the company of virtually all the arts, from cinema and video to Abstract Expressionist painting and experimental theatre, can be said to share an involvement in the existentialist values of our time.

Perhaps the greatest single difference separating the early twentieth-century avant-garde—as well as Western music in general—from new composers and performers lies within the concept of *performance* itself. Today, performance is thought of as a serious art form in its own right, not simply one of several factors contributing to a total artistic statement. Performance, all by itself, possesses the complexity and permits the variety necessary to stand alone; herein lies a major preoccupation engaging the imaginations and energies of contemporary performers, artists, and musicians.

The essays in this book have been organized into four sections, dealing with history and theory, composers on music, new technologies, and critiques. These few essays cannot, of course, cover all aspects of new music, its performance, criticism, and theory. Nevertheless, as Benjamin Boretz observes in his essay, "Musical Cosmology," both musicians and scientists "need humanists and journalists to misrepresent us publicly . . . we can share at least the tranquil joys of that impunity which comes uniquely of being thoroughly misunderstood, even by one another."

Humanists and journalists, along with critics, musicians, performmers, and composers, work together in this book, as they do in new music, contributing their efforts and thoughts to the breaking of barriers in the creation of new sounds for our time.

History and Theory

Musical Cosmology*

Benjamin Boretz

The musician and the scientist: Do they approach their work in similar ways, or are there inherent differences in their methodologies? The subject is discussed here by the important contemporary composer and music theorist Benjamin Boretz, editor of the journal Perspectives of New Music.

That I dedicate this occasion to the memory of Werner Heisenberg would perhaps be presumptuous—although you may already identify presumptuousness as virtually the occupational disease, if not indeed the very occupation, of the artist—had I not, in contemplating Mr. Rolf Sinclair's original invitation, thought immediately of Heisenberg's efforts to understand the mutual significance of modern scientific and modern artistic thought. That this effort was in particular oriented toward developments in physics, on the one side, and music, on the other, made it especially attractive for this occasion in particular, as a potential bridging medium across that gulf of mutual oblivion that, in the sheer mental and physical geography of our respective working lives, tends to dissociate our activities and to deprive us, at least overtly, of the cross-fertilizing gifts of mutual awareness and dia-

---

* Reprinted from *Perspectives of New Music* (Spring–Summer 1977), pp. 122–132.

3

lectic encounter. So it is the intrinsically happy appropriateness to our meeting of the invocation of Heisenberg's work that moves me to note also the gratuitously sad appropriateness to it of the invocation of his memory.

Scientists and musicians: we see each other so little that, when we meet, our natural first eagerness is to reassure each other that, really, we're doing the same thing. Music, after all, was "scientific," courtesy of Pythagoras, when science, courtesy of such as Heraclitus and Parmenides, was pretty fanciful: read, "artistic." And music was solidly contained within the medieval quadrivium, while the work of Helmholtz in the nineteenth and Olson and others in the twentieth century seem to keep a lively connection going at least between the ostensible subject matter of physical acoustics and that of music theory. The discourse of speed readers and quick thinkers, moreover, is full of facile imagery assuring us for the assuaging of God knows what spiritual anxieties that art is no less scientific than science is creative. But the comforts of communal indiscernibility, of the neutralization of the sharp particularity of distinct ideas, phenomena, things, or persons—of the erosion, that is, of the very distinctions that particularize and give vivid identity to what there is—are not only denied us both by virtue of our chosen mental occupations but are, insofar as we take them seriously, subversive to the very extra- and interprofessional understanding they are presumably promulgated to promote.

Such intellectual immunity to being homogenized is, perhaps, what we do principally, if not exclusively, share. But even if we were constitutionally able to keep it down, we should have no need to digest such conceptual blandness as a basis for our mutual identification and awareness. For the common cognitive languages in which we speak and symbolize are, alone, all we need to guarantee the possibility of cognitive intercommunication, insofar as those languages are what we all depart from commonly into our increasingly esoteric conceptual worlds; insofar as, too, our own specialized observation languages, so remote from the observation languages of the uninitiated, are still only particular developments of those common languages, which are still, even among our own co-workers, the underlying court of appeal for any claim of intersubjective cognitivity and, indeed, are still the functional delimiters of our capacity to conceptualize and invent freely; and, again, insofar as our creations and subjects are in fact in some significant degree determinate. And when the claim is made, as Heisenberg, along with such contemporary philosophers as Carnap, Reichenbach, and Quine, has made it, that the referential structure, and hence the meaning and significance, of our common languages have been fundamentally transformed by the emergent creations of modern scientific theory, just as when an analogous claim is made on behalf of contemporary music theory, it is still only by a retrograde path along the same linguistic chain that such claims can be imagined. And because the linguistic landscape, however ordered, is flat and indifferent as to direction of flow, the variant revisions of concept and object that emerge within different esoteric pockets such as science and art may flow out not only to the common language but through it to the bowels of any distinct other esoteric pocket as well. So, while the way into, the way out of, and the way across specialized conceptual communities are not directionally the same, whatever Heraclitus would have us think, they are nonetheless functionally interdependent. Hence, when scientists and musicians do meet, rather than celebrating the trivial fact of our common-cultural humanity as perceived through our common logic and our common languages, we might better be concerned to use those as the media through which to elicit and articulate our divergent departures therefrom, offering to each other glimpses both of the worlds our own work enables us to view and of the world views that are shaped thereby, such that each of us may at least share that world which includes the others, and perhaps also that we may enlarge the vision of each of our own specialized worlds by conceiving them compatibly contained within a larger world including both.

The world, or worlds, that the musician's work enables him to glimpse are what I have dared to refer to in the presumptuous language of my title. As I hope you will see, it is an Argus-like glimpse that I am proposing, alternating or merging views from a myriad of perspectives; for even grossly, I am imagining my perspective bifocally onto the worlds that are musical things and out from them to the world as it appears from the perspective of a habitual observer of the worlds that are musical things. Now I do not know the translation value for your world of what there is in mine: that is, of what there is in the world of music, what there is in the world as music might make it appear, and what there is in your world as it appears from the perspective of the world as music makes it appear. But I offer for your contemplation some of the features of the music-cosmological landscape, that is, of some of the remarkable ontological peculiarities of the musical cosmos as they appear to one fascinated musician.

Now if, in the sequel, I use the heuristic device of contrasting musical with scientific matters, that is to be understood entirely in the light, if light it be, of the foregoing. I have no wish, even less any hope, of attaining to an unidiosyncratic characterization of scientific matters, from *your* point of view. No hope, for obvious reasons; no wish, because I believe that the view I afford you of a musician's world and world view might include, even as perhaps its most revealing aspect for you, how your world looks from within it. So it is that which I believe I am conveying when I, rather than you, speak of science, just as it is the complementary view that I discern in the writings of Heisenberg, or Carnap, or Helmholtz, when they, rather than I, speak of music.

Scientific thought, as I suppose it, consists in the construction of theories of which some portions or all of the observable world are models, in whatever inferentially extended sense of "observable." Experimental science seems to arrange linkages among distinct portions of the observable world so that observable events, in the narrower sense, at some given node of such a system, are regarded as determinate data, relative to specific scales of quantization, concerning the behavior of entities of a specific nature as they are defined within a specific theory. One world only is the apparent universe of all, as well as each, scientific theory, and each tenable scientific theory is in principle, as I understand it, supposed to be compatible, cotenable, and indeed coeffective with each other theory conceded to be tenable at a given science-historical juncture. I perceive Heisenberg in this spirit when he speaks of scientific idealization as a way of "understanding the colorful multiplicity of phenomena . . . by recognizing in them unitary principles of form." Elsewhere, he specifies as conditions for theoretical tenability the "crucial precondition for any usable scientific theory that it should subsequently stand up to empirical testing and rational analysis . . . there is an inexorable and irrevocable criterion of value [in science] that no piece of work can evade." Ontological creativity in science is, as Heisenberg points out, entirely the outcome of the painful struggle with empirical anomaly arising within the confines of existing theoretical-experimental systems: How does one make a revolution?, he asks, and answers: By trying to change as little as possible.

Now a good way to elicit the peculiarities of musical things is to notice the oddly inscrutable results yielded by the effort to sustain this scientific perspective in the observation of musical phenomena, which Heisenberg attempts to do. For example, in tracing the history of abstraction in science and in art, Heisenberg is able to suppose that degree of abstractness is a possible relative attribute of musical compositions: witness his remark that "Genuinely abstract art has existed . . . as in Bach's *Art of Fugue.*" To a musician, it seems obscure under what notion of abstraction such an observation can have been made. There is, so far as I can perceive, no relative want of concreteness in the musical entities that constitute the work in question: I do not hear them as classes, generalizations, concepts, or covering laws, but as determinate phenomenal particulars, neither do I find those entities especially indiscernible *as* particulars relative to other particulars, either within the *Art of Fugue* or in other, distinct, musical compositions. Indeed, I can scarcely imagine how to take in any given sounding musical event as more "theoretical" in its sound than any other, any more than I can imagine that the contents of the heavens are more abstract than the contents of my lunch pail, whatever the relative abstractness of the astronomical and gastronomical sciences. And if *abstraction* refers, in Heisenberg's use of it relative to Bach, to some other class of attributes than those comprehended under the familiar relational sense of the term, say, the attribute of being referred to as abstract in the popular print, or the attribute of being complex or relatively inward, in that salient attributes of particularity are relatively less blazoned on the immediate surface, relatively less accessible by virtue of immediate association with extramusical things, and relatively more wholly discernible only as the product of minutely contoured configurations in context, then the word *abstraction* as so applied is a mere homonym of some other word, an epithet rather than a term.

What I discern as the origins of this admittedly rather innocuous confusion are at least two problems of context: first is the question, to which I alluded earlier, of the referential domain, the cosmos, being referred to in observations about something called "music." This we may speak of as the question what is the *object* of focus in speaking of music. Second is the question what aspect of the content, or what content within a given system of activity, or observational complex, is to be regarded as the significant distinguishing characteristic of the individual enterprise or class of enterprises under scrutiny. Thus you might find it odd if someone mentioned as a salient attribute of Heisenberg's uncertainty principle that the brow of Albert Einstein tended to furrow whenever it was mentioned. This question we may speak of as the question of *direction* of focus. Of our two questions, the second is probably the more telling in distinguishing the character of musical from that of scientific activity. But as the question of direction is perhaps subtler and more elusive than, as well as dependent on, the question of object, it is the latter that I will now consider.

I remarked earlier that an adequate view of what is referred to by talk of music would require an Argus-like multiplicity of distinct observational perspectives. I should have mentioned that what is also required is a Cyclopean integrity within each focus: the creature that knows them all together must also know them each as univocally distinct. Music is, then, sometimes the aggregate of musical objects, in which case talk about it is about *all* works of music simultaneously. Or, music is whatever distinguishes anything as music, in which case talk about it is about *any* work of music, equally, but not more than one simultaneously. Or music is the historically ordered set of musical works, in which case talk about music sorts all works of music into proper subsets, with whatever account of the consequentiality and character of the succession of subclass characteristics. Or music may be the name for *musikierung,* music-making, the activity of composing, or perceiving, or performing, or theorizing, or analyzing. The problems that arise in confusing these domains are obvious when we consider another remark of Heisenberg, where he supposes that he finds music in a condition like that of early twentieth-century physics, confronting "the helplessness when faced with the question of what to do about the bewildering phenomena, the lamenting over lost connections, which still continue to look so convincing . . . ," and so forth. Now what he is remarking on is, in fact, a conditon that may have been true of persons attempting to compose and perceive music, and, thus, a true condition of thought *about* music. But it is scarcely scrutable as even a possible condition of any musical composition or group thereof, that is, it is merely incoherent as a report of thought *within* music. Because thought within music is only discernible by virtue of the successful projection of specific attributes, or images, there can only be "bewildering phenomena" in one of only two senses: phenomena that have a determinate feel, hence a distinct identity, but cannot be characterized by any extension of existing descriptive resources. Or, phenomena that appear to purport to be musical, but cannot be so received, and hence are received as noise. In both cases the indeterminacy is not of the phenomena but of the theory. "The theory," too, is two distinct theories: the first of which we may call the *descriptive* theory, the second the *attributive.* And the fact is, that the crisis in music that people talk about as having occurred at the end of the nineteenth century may be understood as the moment when the inadequacies of existing descriptive theory were brutally exposed by the faltering of available attributive theory: composers like Schönberg were finding it difficult to proceed beyond brief passages, or to proceed coherently from any work to a successor. The relativity of musical systems that emerged as the solution to the crisis was not only, or even primarily, a revolution in composition, or in the theory of contemporary music, but was in fact a revolution in the theory of musical foundations, the any-musical theory to which I referred earlier. By having to understand their own music, both descriptively and attributively, musicians of Schönberg's generation and the next were forced to understand the nature of musical systems, beyond the attributes of particular systems, and thus to become able to perceive any given system not as a musical universal but as a musical choice.

From their work, it was possible for some more recent musical thinkers, myself among them, to observe that in fact each work could be observed to create its own system, rather than merely instantiating it, that is, that from any work, given only a large enough any-musical theory to begin with, the particular lexical and grammatical background for that work could be inferred from the theoretically interpreted perceptual characteristics of the data alone, without the intervention of assumed conventions; this was the subject of a large prose work of mine called *Meta-Variations*. But still further, it appeared from the confluence of both systematic relativism and ontological creativity that the variable ontology emergent from within different systems was not restricted to distinct works; that in fact, a system was a mode of cognition rather than an invariant attribute of data complexes, and that hence, music theory was ipso facto creative, and that the effective result of musical description was the intersubjectively determinate transformation of what was experienced.

But to be a specific musical entity is to have a determinate feel—that is, to be perceived as having a *sound* distinct from that of every other musical entity. Musical things are thus truly phenomenal things, not only because, as we have observed, what musical thing something *is* is variable relative to an attributive theory, but because it *is* that thing only *as* perceived, and—even further—may be *experienced fully* as a determinate feel without *being* sensorily perceived: as, that is, *thought,* without the intervention of any physically measurable atmospheric perturbations in the receptive environment of any sense organs. This notion of determinate feels, then, may be an essential extension of our epistemology: for however mentalistic, determinate feels are as intersubjective as thoughts, correlating in no uncertain or indeterminate way with perceivables.

Here arises a still more peculiar ontological observation: consider the sound of a given musical moment, say the lowest pitch of a line of ascending pitches. Clearly, to be the lowest note of that particular ascending line of pitches is a salient aspect of musical thinghood, according to my earlier remarks. But the question arises: *when* is that pitch the lowest note of that ascending line? Obviously, it is dependent on both antecedent and subsequent events to acquire such a character: the pitch preceding it must not have preempted its lowest-ness, and the pitches following must follow in a certain relative height, such that the "ascending line" as a whole is entified by the observation of at least one pitch *subsequent* to its completion, when a "change of direction" isolates it as a specific string. So *chronology* becomes an aspect of *identity* within a musical structure. A datum sounds a certain way at its moment of assertion by virtue of its predecessors, then becomes a progressively distinct entity by virtue of its successors: it sounds different first as the lowest of two, then of three, then of four, then of five successive notes, and to sound different is, as we have noted, to *be* different. The sound of a musical work is then the cumulative sound of the cumulative chronology of its components. And because to be in a given place in a given chronology is to have a unique sound, and because to have a unique sound is to be a unique thing, we may truly suppose that no two musical entities can be alike, that musical qualities, as elicited by attribution through a common theory, are all ontologically distinct, rather than repeatable in the sense of *qualia*.

But if musical qualities within a piece are nonrepeatable because of chronological dependency, are musical compositions themselves nonrepeatable—or, in other words, have I committed myself to a reductio ad absurdum of particularism on top of my imminent peril of solipsism? The answer, I hasten to assure you, is no. Beethoven's Fifth survives intact, and I am as relieved as you are to know it. But it does so only by a further ontological twist, this time in the character of musical time. For the significant chronology within which musical entities arise is within *a piece,* not, I believe, within *pieces.* That is, a musical entity is piece-time, but not world-time, dependent. Piece-time, like piece-pitch-position, is a location within a mental landscape and has a repeatable determinate feel in auditory or thought experience. Just like a particular juncture in a conversation, carried only by a mental act of bounding, the feel of such a moment of piece-time, outside of the determinate feel of a given place in a chronology, may be evoked even in the absence of the rest of the chronology on any given occasion: this happens whenever I write the next note of a piece, knowing just where I am in the time structure, without rereading all previous notes; and it happened to me last week when I turned on the radio, heard one C-major chord, and unhesitatingly perceived it as the last sound of the Beethoven *Coriolan* Overture—correctly, as it turned out, but, as you may by now suspect, I'm not sure whether that indicates that I, or Beethoven, or the piece, or anyone, was thereby passing one of those inexorable tests that none of us can rationally evade.

So the world of musical compositions begins to appear, most favorably, not as an aggregate world but as an aggregate of worlds; each possible as a model of an any-musical theory, but mutually incompatible in that the ontology of predication (the values of the variables that predicate quality) is not even wholly uniform within, much less between, given works. And it is here that we may observe that the *direction* of musical focus diverges from that of science.

For it seems that the principal desideratum of all musical activity is the multiplication of ways for entities to be distinct: the very act which Heisenberg assured us was exceptional and painful for science, regarding which scientists wish to be preternaturally parsimonious, is the one regarding which musicians seek to be limitlessly prodigal. The data yielded by the scientific experiment support or disconfirm the theory. The theory applied to the data of the musical experiment is supported by the richness of identity it thereby confers on the data. The scientist wishes to make it unnecessary to know each in order to know all; the musician wishes to make it impossible to know all without knowing each. In science one seeks to learn, if possible, how new entities are really old ones. No one is interested in creating musical entities that merely duplicate entities already created; and to learn to hear a unique thing as a categorical thing is a net loss for musical experience. If there are "natural" laws of musical hearing, if some given relation of fundamentals to the partial spectrum is more closely in conformity to a natural norm than other relations are, then composers are likely to seek to re-compose nature rather than conform to it, to de-naturalize musical sound and produce empirical reality out of natural anomaly. The qualification, hence, of the *individual* is the devolution point of all musical thought, for whose sake alone the class generality—all the way out to the term *music* itself—is reified; whereas the individual entity within the individual observation complex is specifically valued by the sciences insofar as it can reliably be regarded as instantiating a class of phenomena or objects. Thus induction, and thus what seems, at least, a radical divergence in the nature of the inductive process as between what we may call musical knowing and scientific knowing. Musical thought is not, as Heisenberg thought, in a less happy position than that of science, because it lacks that "inexorable and irrevocable criterion of value that no piece of work can evade," for it has as its modus operandi the no less exigent demand for precision of identity, unique, determinate, and—consequently and for no gratuitous other reasons than those of clarity and specificity—inordinately complex.

And perhaps it would not be altogether surprising if, out of valuing our art for the coexistence of a virtual incompatibles that it enables, there might emerge as a world view a kind of pacific philosophical anarchism, wherein one would seek the means to regard as permissibly within one's world as wide a divergence of views and behavior as possible, without feeling obliged to adopt, accept, emulate, or approve, in order to permit cohabitation within the commonwealth of sentient existence.

You may have noticed that here, as from the outset of this paper, I have been making observations heavily loaded toward the personal—both private personal and social personal—signification of our respective activities. I do this because of the intellectual conviction that this is the nodal perspective out of which the most revealing aspects of the structures I observe will emerge. I also do this because I, personally, am keenly conscious of the particular complexion of this occasion as a confluence of customarily nonconfluent minds and because, especially under that idiosyncratic condition, it looks like the likeliest avenue to mutual communication. Now whether communication is possible or not may depend crucially on whether we can make apparent the *commensurability*—rather than the sameness, or compatibility—of our respective world views, however much in principle—because of their common common-languages origin—we know them to be so commensurable. So it may be of some value right here to take note of the fact that scientists and artists—if I may add being presumptuously categorical to being presumptuously personal—exhibit what seem to me to be interesting and perhaps even eloquently revealing differences in public professional behavior.

Thus, by now, I expect I have sufficiently persuaded you of the irrepressible presumptuousness of the artistic character—at least as it is embodied in one of its immediately observable avatars. But I also see a certain complementarity of presumption across the amniotic social fluid as I look toward my scientific brethren. You, I find, are arrogant by virtue of your apparent modesty in claiming that you merely seek and uncover that which is true about that which truly exists. We, on the other hand, are modest in virtue of our arrogant insistence on constructing and making palpable that which we acknowledge to be wholly fictitious.

We, in other words, presume to decide and create what reality is to be, while you presume that what you decide and create is what reality is and must be. Ladies and gentlemen—metacolleagues—I submit that we are both at the very least insufferable and share a common stake in concealing from the innocent world our social unsavoriness. That, in fact, is why we both need humanists and journalists to misrepresent us publicly, as if we had permissible manners and redeeming social value. Lord help us all if they ever turned on us the sharp critical tools of our own methodologies, in place of the nice soft soap they have been accustomed to use. Until that fearful juncture, at any rate, we can share at least the tranquil joys of that impunity which comes uniquely of being thoroughly misunderstood, even by one another.

Fluxus Music*

Peter Frank

The loosely organized group known as Fluxus championed mixed-media work in the arts beginning in the late 1950s and lasting until the 1970s. Generally oriented toward the visual arts, the group involved numerous musicians, including John Cage and La Monte Young, dancers, sculptors, and electronic artists. Avant-garde music, dance, Happening, and performance art were all forms pioneered by Fluxus, under the casual leadership of George Maciunas.

Involving artists and musicians such as Nam June Paik, Joseph Byrd, Philip Corner, Earle Brown, and Simone Forti, Fluxus, ". . . with its humorous and serious sides, its eloquence and diffidence, its populist availability and near-invisibility, has endured to this day," according to Peter Frank.

A widely published art critic, Frank has written extensively on forms of new art and has lectured throughout the United States.

Among the music-artists fabricating sound-producing structures, incorporating songs and instrumentals in performances, realizing visual "performances" of pre-extant music, and creating graphic notation for visual

* Reprinted from *Journal: Southern California Art Magazine,* no. 22 (March–April 1979), pp. 18–20.

impact *and* musical interpretation, there are artists—and musicians, the line blurs between them—who seek the melding of the very contexts of art and music. That is, the work they make is as much—or as little—music as it is art. It seems equally in or out of place in galleries and in concert halls, workshirt and overalls, tux and tails, in time and in space. The remarkable flexibility of this work's context results from its formal derivation out of many previous contexts. This art-and-music work, while demonstrably descended from the visual and musical traditions, depends neither on visual nor on musical standards. It does not even have to be viewed or performed; to know it is to experience it, and often just to know *of* it is to experience it. While its secondary media are visual and sonic, its primary medium is verbal, or perhaps ontological; while its secondary interpreters are those who realize it visually and/or sonically, its primary interpreters are those who merely read it in its statement form or somehow know the nature of its gesture(s).

Although such an aesthetic of disembodiment, paying no heed to the dividing line between two art forms, may strike one as the *ne plus ultra* of Western aesthetic development, it already has a respectable, if brief, history. (Good news: we reached the vanishing point decades ago.) The more sensate combinations and superpositions of art and music can trace their lineage back as far as primitive ritual, and in the context of modernist aesthetics, as far back as the Symbolists and Futurists. In the context of *post*-modernist aesthetics, however, the art-music aesthetic of disembodiment has the beat on everything else. In fact it serves as a significant facet of postmodernism's initial phase. The best label to hang on this disembodied aesthetic is Fluxus. The participants, steady and occasional, in the loosely knit Fluxus movement make up the majority of this aesthetic's innovators and theoreticians.

In the late 1950s the reaction against the new orthodoxies of modernist art—Abstract Expressionism, the International Style of twelve-tone composition in music, Theatre of the Absurd, academic and (to a lesser extent) antiacademic (for example, Beat, New York "surrealist") schools of poetry—was worldwide and shared some common sources, living and dead. One decision that seems to have taken place simultaneously in New York, California, Germany, France, Italy, Japan, and other places was to work in between the art forms, to combine them, to blend them, or (best yet) to formulate new modes that obviated the distinctions between them. Gutai in Japan, le Nouveau Realisme in Italy and France, dance-and-music-as-ritual in the Bay Area were all tendencies in which creative individuals coming from discrete disciplines not only pooled talents but exchanged formal and attitudinal methodologies.

In New York, where Fluxus began, John Cage—himself a product of unrigid West Coast thought in the 1930s and 1940s—exercised increasing influence over younger thinkers and devisers in all the arts. This influence was made possible by Cage's own responsiveness to work in various arts, a responsiveness brought about by involvement with Merce Cunningham's dance company, summers spent at the Black Mountain School (where all the arts were taught), and study of Zen Buddhist thought and practice. In 1956, and for two subsequent years, Cage taught a course in new music composition at the New School for Social Research. In this course several younger artists, musicians, writers, filmmakers, and others were led, or were encouraged to lead themselves, to means of escaping the restriction of given media and modes of thought. Allan Kaprow devised the first Happenings immediately after attending Cage's class. Classmates of Kaprow, including George Brecht, Dick Higgins, Philip Corner, and Al Hansen, broke through mediumistic boundaries with Cage's encouragement and example in mind.

But, despite the friendships and aesthetic alliances that began in that class, there were divergent sensibilities. The complex, heavily theatrical, and painterly format of the Happening favored by Kaprow, Hansen, and others who came on the scene was eschewed in favor of more restrained, reflective modes by such as Brecht and Robert Watts. Higgins, who was unusual in his ability to work with equal comfort on grand *and* minuscule levels, recalls that, after the flurry of excitement shared by Cage class alumni at the advent of Happenings (and related forms in Europe), a contrasting interest arose

> in the music that was what Bengt af Klintberg calls *"mellan vatten ochsten,"* between the water and the stone. Naturally, if the needs of a particular work seemed to dictate it, it was realized in a purely musical or painterly fashion. But the alternatives were considered. This approach seemed more positive than the purely iconoclastic approach, in which the main context was an absolute denial of experience and the traditions which one had built up, even for oneself.[1]

This growing interest in work—music or otherwise, performance or otherwise—that was not iconoclastic/bombastic led to the creation of pieces in which the economy of form and gesture was dramatically severe. The performances themselves were gesturally (if not chronometrically) minimal to

---

[1] Dick Higgins, Publisher's Foreword to *The Four Suits* (New York: Something Else Press, 1965), pp. xi–xii.

the point of near-inactivity, and quite often their scripts or notations were similarly spare. This sparseness can be read as a Zen inflection introduced by Cage. Such an inflection was redoubled by the influx into New York of artists, musicians, dancers, writers, and others around 1959–1960 from Japan and from the San Francisco Bay Area. A unity among creators in (or, more accurately, from) the various arts had been forming in these places, a unity based on directness and simplicity and on the questioning of limits: where does one art stop and the next begin, and why there? Where does interest end and boredom begin, and why there? Where does tolerance end and outrage begin, and where are the Dadaists to ask, "why there"?

The West Coast, Japanese, and sporadic European contingents merged with the New York group, attended one another's loft performances, and began putting it all into words, into verbal instructions and position papers, into cards, flyers, and books. By the end of 1960 La Monte Young, a Cage disciple from the Bay Area, had edited *An Anthology* of work participating in the new sensibility. In the version of the book finally published in 1963:

> George Brecht published card events;
> Earle Brown published excerpts from his *Folio,* the first graphically notated compositions;
> Joseph Byrd published a piece for wind quintet comprised of cards with single or paired notes, the cards to be played and repeated in random order (a very early modular composition);
> Cage declared that "Eventually everything will be happening at once ... ";
> Walter de Maria proposed an "Art Yard"—an *ur*-earthwork—talked about "Meaningless Work," and contributed several intimate activity pieces (*Beach Crawl, Surprise Box*);
> Henry Flynt defined, outlined, and gave examples of "concept art" (" 'Concept art' is first of all an art of which the material is 'concepts,' as the material of, for example, music is sound.");
> Yoko Ono published a visual poem;
> Dick Higgins published instructions for two events;
> Ray Johnson and James Waring published a laugh poem;
> Jackson MacLow published poems and stories determined by chance operations, to be read and sung by eye and mouth;
> Simone Morris (now Forti) published early examples of her ordinary-movement dance pieces and notations.
> Nam June Paik gave the background to his *Symphony for 20 Rooms;*
> Terry Riley published verbal and graphic scores;
> Diter Rot (now Dieter Roth) included an unbound page riddled with holes;

Emmett Williams published serveral of his modular poems;
La Monte Young published fourteen compositions from 1960.[2]

One of Young's compositions bears resemblance to traditional musical notations: a fifth interval, B-natural and F-sharp, "to be held for a very
long time." Another composition consists entirely of the direction, "Draw
a straight line and follow it." Another: "The performer should prepare any
composition and then perform it as well as he can." Another: "This piece is
little whirlpools out in the middle of the ocean." The *Piano Piece for David
Tudor* no. 3 reads: "Most of them/were very old grasshoppers." *Composition 1960* no. 9 consists of a small card with a straight line on it, enclosed in
an envelope on which the following is printed: "the enclosed score is right
side up when the line is horizontal and slightly above center."[3]

The concision and poetry of Young's formats, the wide range of interpretation they encourage and the availability of their language—anyone
can realize a Young composition at any time, with no concert hall, instrument, training, or even effort necessary—attracted other artists of the new
sensibility, especially those whose performance scores were evolving toward a simplicity of form and statement anyway. George Brecht, Robert
Watts, Yoko Ono, Dick Higgins, Allison Knowles, and George Maciunas,
the designer of *An Anthology*, achieved new brevity, partly through
Young's model.

Maciunas, a former architecture student, was so taken with the whole
aesthetic—not just Young's refined directions, but the increasingly "conceptual" work of Young's friends in New York—that he set out to do a series of his own anthologies modeled on the first one (which he also intended to publish). The series was to be called *Fluxus,* indicating the
protean nature of the work. Financial problems nipped the project in the
bud, but the groundwork laid for Maciunas's anthologies did provide a ru-
bric for the new sensibility and something of a focus for future activities,
that is, around Maciunas, who became the loose-knit movement's prosely-
tizer, publisher, and theorist. "FLUX ART," in Maciunas's definition, is

> nonart—amusement forgoes distinction between art and nonart, forgoes
> artists' indispensability, exclusiveness, individuality, ambition, forgoes all
> pretension towards a significance, variety, inspiration, skill, complexity, pro-
> fundity, greatness, institutional and commodity value. It strives for nonstruc-

---

[2] La Monte Young, *An Anthology* (New York: La Monte Young and Jackson MacLow,
1963; 2d ed., Heiner Friedrich, 1970), unpaged.
[3] *Ibid.*

tural, nontheatrical, nonbaroque, impersonal qualities of a simple, natural event, an object, a game, a puzzle, or a gag. It is a fusion of Spike Jones, gags, games, Vaudeville, Cage and Duchamp.[4]

The Fluxus sensibility, with its humorous and serious sides, its eloquence and diffidence, its populist availability and near-invisibility, has endured to this day, the precursor of nearly every *dematerialization* (to use Lucy Lippard's term) and *intermedia* art (to use Dick Higgins's term) realized in the postmodernist context.

Where does music fit into Maciunas's definition? Where does music fit into Fluxus praxis? Music fits where all the other individual arts fit into Fluxus—into a process of de-definition that robs music and the other arts of their unique, segregated status, fusing them into a general field of intermedia that is itself not easily distinguished from the rest of life. But there is a musical bias to Fluxwork. In the performance scores and directions realized in the Fluxus mode and context, musical referents and formats abound—parodistically, perhaps, but undeniably. Musical instruments are the focuses for (often wildly destructive) Fluxus actions; ensemble presentations often follow concert-hall style and are given in full formal dress; works are structured in burlesque variations on compositional forms (for example, sonata form, the concerto); performance notations often refer to pitches, even incorporating (traditional) pitch notation.

Philosophically, this musical bias can probably be attributed to the nature of music as the most abstract, least palpable of the arts. No pictures, no objects, no human motion is necessary in the musical experience. Even literature emphasizes text and talk equally; music does not stress both sound and score, but just the sound. With the advent of electronically-produced music in the early 1950s the musical performer—and the whole mystique of musical performance and interpretation (which is the object of Fluxus's parodic stagings)—was rendered potentially superfluous. Fluxus took over from there.

In actuality, the musical bias of early Fluxus probably resulted from the musical identity of its most readily identifiable progenitor, John Cage, and the musical interests of his students and other followers. Even artists who came to Fluxus from visual, verbal, dramatic, or choreographic backgrounds tended to have some interest in music. Fluxus can be seen, in fact,

---

[4] Adrian Henri, *Total Art: Environment, Happenings, and Performance* (New York: Praeger Publishers, 1974), p. 159.

as providing these nonmusicians with a way of absorbing their *violin d'Ingres*—their secondary and perhaps embarrassingly amateur involvement in music—into their art.

Of course, Fluxus also gave, and still gives, musicians the opportunity to absorb *their* particular side or co-interests into their music—and then to make that intermedial result widely available and easily comprehensible to anyone armed with three insights: some familiarity with the contemporary context of intermedia and concept art, curiosity, and patience.

Boredom and Danger*

Dick Higgins

Boredom, repetition, and redundancy have been major characteristics found within modern artistic documents. Dick Higgins considers the phenomena as they are found in modern music and cites examples from several composers beginning with the early compositions of Erik Satie and including the work of John Cage and developments within the visual arts.

Higgins notes that "in the context of work that attempts to involve the spectator, boredom often serves a useful function: as an opposite to excitement and as a means of bringing emphasis to what it interrupts, causing us to view both elements freshly."

Mr. Higgins is a composer and founder of Something Else Press in New York City. His compositions include the Danger Musics *series (1961–1964) and* Graphis *(1958–). In 1967 he made an autobiographical movie,* Men & Women & Bells. *He is the author of* Jefferson's Birthday/Postface *and* A Book About Love & War & Death, Canto One.

Boredom was, until recently, one of the qualities an artist tried most to avoid. Yet today it appears that artists are deliberately trying to make their

*Reprinted from *The Something Else Newsletter*, 1, no. 9 (December 1968), pp. 1–4, 6. Copyright © 1968 by Something Else Press, Inc.

work boring. Is this true, or is it only an illusion? In either case, what is the explanation?

There was a time, not so very long ago, when music was considered a form of entertainment, perhaps on a higher level than some other forms, but still part of the same world as theatre, vaudeville, circuses, etc. Similarly, apart from religious art and purely functional art, the fine arts were basically used for decorative purposes. But with the rise of the idea that the work of art was intended first and foremost as an experience, that its function could be spiritual, psychological, and educational, the situation began to change. Kandinsky's view of art as a means of deepening one's spiritual life is a landmark along this way. The musical parallel to this conception is found in Arnold Schönberg's writings, in the letters and in *Style and Idea.*

But it is still a very long way from musical expressionism, which merely denies that entertainment values are at all to the point, to the situation in which boredom and other, related feelings might actually play a part. In music the key personality in this development, as in many others, is Erik Satie. Satie composed a piece shortly before World War I, *Vieux Sequins et Vieilles Cuirasses,* a characteristically programmatic piece in which he spoofs the military and the glories of nationalism. At the end of the piece there appears an eight-beat passage evocative of old marches, and patriotic songs, but which is to be repeated 380 times. In performance the satirical intent of this repetition comes through very clearly, but at the same time other very interesting results begin to appear. The music first becomes so familiar that it seems extremely offensive and objectionable. But after that the mind slowly becomes incapable of taking further offense, and a very strange, euphoric acceptance and enjoyment begin to set in. Satie appears to have been fascinated by this effect, because he also wrote *Vexations* (published in John Cage's article in *Art News Annual,* '58), an utterly serious thirty-two-bar piece (although the bar lines are not written in) intended to be played very softly and very slowly 840 times. Today it is usually done by a team of pianists, and lasts over a period of roughly twenty-five hours. Is it boring? Only at first. After a while the euphoria I have mentioned begins to intensify. By the time the piece is over, the silence is absolutely numbing, so much of an environment has the piece become.

During the 1950s many artists and composers felt a growing dissatisfaction with the conventional relationships between the spectator and the work, and it became increasingly important to them to experiment with the possible relationships. Robert Rauschenberg included mirrors in some of his early combines, with startling results. Allan Kaprow included audience relationships in his collages on an increasingly intense scale, until his collages began to become performances and he formalized the idea of the Happening. Not even stopping there, he has continued to experiment with audience relationships, and his recent Happenings have no passive spectators, only participants. John Cage also made many investigations into and out of music, and found that some of the problems he was considering had been dealt with also by Satie. Much of the present interest in Satie is due to Cage's calling him to our attention.

If it can be said that Satie's interest in boredom originated as a kind of gesture—there is a certain bravura about asking a pianist to play the same eight beats 380 times—and developed into a fascinating, aesthetic statement, then I think it can be said with equal fairness that Cage was the first to try to emphasize in his work and his teaching a dialectic between boredom and intensity. I recall a class with him at the New School for Social Research in the summer of 1958, in which George Brecht had brought in a piece that simply asked each performer to do two different things, each once. When each participant had done two, the piece was over. Cage suggested that we perform this piece in the darkness, so as to be unable to tell, visually, whether the piece had ended. This was done. The result was fascinating, both for its own sake and for the extraordinary intensity that appeared in waves, as we wondered whether the piece was over or not, what the next thing to happen would be, etc. Afterward we were asked to guess how long we had been in the dark. The guesses ranged from four minutes to twenty-five. The actual duration was nine minutes. The boredom played a comparable role, in relation to intensity, that silence plays with sound, where each one heightens the other and frames it.

The point that we have been coming to, then, is that in the context of work that attempts to involve the spectator, boredom often serves a useful function: as an opposite to excitement and as a means of bringing emphasis to what it interrupts, causing us to view both elements freshly. It is a necessary station on the way to other experiences, as in the case of the Satie.

The arts in which boredom has been a structural factor have been predominantly the performing arts (as emphasized in Cage's class), and the kind of performances in which boredom has been most structurally implicit and useful are the events (miniature Happenings) associated with the Fluxus movement. Fluxus was an attempt to provide a coordinating rostrum for a large body of Happenings and events activities that were not oriented toward the visual arts and were therefore unable to effect continuity of information through the art galleries, as the visual Happenings did. Just to indicate the variety of backgrounds of the participants, among the original Fluxus members were George Brecht, the maker of small art objects and early Minimal art; Jackson MacLow, the poet; La Monte Young, the composer; myself, a composer and poet; and ten or twenty others of similarly disparate original concerns. (A detailed history of Fluxus can be found in my own 1964 essay, "Postface.")[1]

The Fluxus performance arose from a feeling that the best of the performing arts should not be entertaining neither should they inherently even be educational. It was felt they should serve as stimuli that made one's life and work and experience more meaningful and flexible. The use, in Fluxus format works, of boredom became not so much a structural factor as an implicit factor, as, for example, when Jackson MacLow proposed a project, a film that, for financial reasons, was not executed (but that was widely published). The film was to be made of a tree on which the camera would be trained from the start of light to the end of light in the course of one day. This film would clearly have been more environmental than entertaining, cinematic, or educational. Once would relate to it in direct proportion to the ability to look with concentration at it. Boring? Of course; if one were to ignore the more intense activity involved, which we might call "super boring," and which took one beyond the initial level of simple boredom. This has very much to do with the Satie idea.

In the same vein, La Monte Young composed a musical piece that consisted of a B- and F-sharp, to be played simultaneously on as many instruments as available with as little variation as possible. But the performed result established a drone over which, although it was intended to have the most neutral, blank character possible and was therefore made of plain, open fifths; one would begin to imagine all kinds of goings-on. In fact, most of La Monte Young's most recent performances have consisted of the playing of just such fantastic patterns over a similar drone.

In a parallel spirit, I tried to achieve a similar effect in a series of pieces by using "blank structures," in which I simply established a rule matrix for the performance, and gave neither explicit clues to my intentions nor any working materials, apart from the matrix, to the performers. What they or the audience contributed became both subject matter and perceptible form. At a Fluxus performance in Copenhagen in 1962 the extremes of this kind of work were tested—with the excitement inseparable, again, from the boredom. During my *Second Contribution* each performer chooses something in the environment of the performance to cue him to perform an action, which he has also determined. The poet Emmett Williams and the composer Eric Andersen each chose to do his action when he

---

[1] New York: Something Else Press, 1964.

became the last person on stage. The resulting hours of waiting to see which would break became very exciting. Each stood motionless. The audience became bored, impatient, and upset. But the word began to circulate, through those who knew the piece, about what had happened. And then the audience quieted down and became fascinated. Very few left. The end of the performance came by accident—one of the performers, offered a drink by someone, misunderstood and thought he was being ordered off stage. It was a very fortunate misunderstanding, for both Williams and Andersen are sufficiently tough-minded to be there still today, six years later, if necessary.

This, then, was the way boredom was used in the event pieces associated with Fluxus. The environment would become part of the fabric of the piece and vice versa. This environmentalism was implicit in most of the work. Fluxus today, of course, is mainly the name of a very interesting publisher of editions of art objects, run by one of the founders, but at that time Fluxus was actually a movement, not so much exploring the frontiers of art as implying them. Most of the early Fluxus pieces could, conceivably, have been executed as absolutely conventional music or theatre simply by ignoring the more extreme possibilities of the structure and by filling in very conventional materials. This last, incidentally, one of the former Fluxus artists, Nam June Paik, the composer, had been doing in recent years, with very interesting results.

But many later pieces were built to avoid this possibility. They became very specific about what object was to be used, and how. This is true of many of the Japanese Flux people (Takehisa Kosugi, Chieko Shiomi) and of many others, including Tomas Schmit and the early work of Eric Andersen, who, however, has more recently been using blank structures. Both are originally composers, and their work pushes this kind of piece about as far as it can be taken.

Tomas Schmit's pieces tend to be extremely private, basically incapable of public performance. For example, there is a piece called *Zyklus*. To perform this piece a circle of Coca-Cola bottles and one performer ideally are used. One of the Coca-Cola bottles is filled with water. The water is poured into the next bottle as carefully and with as little loss as possible, then into the next, and so on, around the circle, moving always in one direction, clockwise or counterclockwise. When all the water has been spilled (as slowly as possible, of course), the performance is over, unless, as one can only imagine, all the water should evaporate first. A performance of this piece can last for two hours, five hours, maybe even twenty-four. The longest performance that I know of is one that Schmit did himself in New York in 1964, which lasted six hours.

Eric Andersen's pieces, on the other hand, are so involved with the simple concept that it is sometimes impossible to discover if a piece is taking place at all. He not only takes blank structures to their logical extreme but Minimal art as well, which results in his establishing interesting new orders of boredom. For example, there is the following piece:

Opus 48: which turns anonymous when the instruction is followed out

It comes through the mail with a piece of cardboard that reads:

place the chosen tautology

So one chooses a tautology and hides it and has a secret. Only the sender and those he tells know what became of it, so it really does become both anonymous and private, making the title observation true. The public performance of a piece like this is unnecessary, however, by its nature. Still, the act is somehow boring and, through this, interesting. But we have now reached the point where performance art merges into nonperformance art, which brings us to the visual arts, among other things.

In our society the visual arts have a problem: they are essentially being produced for sale. For a work to be attractive enough for someone to buy it, it must be appealing and therefore the artist must take into consideration the audience factor, even if only unconsciously. He may think that what he is doing is done as a free agent, but this is seldom the case. More often, he is doing it, I think, because it seems "important" or because it seems to him something he can do well. He tends always to be preparing for an exhibition of some kind ultimately. Therefore, the visual artist is not as free as the performance artist to produce private pieces. The only time I know of such work being done is in the early sculptures of Walter De Maria, described in his short essay "Useless Art,"[2] in which, for example, he describes a small gold ball being placed in a concealed spot on one of his objects. No one but he knows it's there. But here we have the visual art equivalent of boredom and its projection, private art. Again, presumably anyone who buys a large Robert Morris construction, one that *can* be rearranged in many ways, is going to do so, and nobody except Morris will know which was the first intended way of arranging this work.

---

[2] La Monte Young and Jackson MacLow, *An Anthology* (New York: Something Else Press, 1962).

There is still another aspect of what lies behind boredom and private art, which I have suggested are interrelated, and that is danger. In order to build intellectual excitement into work, there must always be the sense that it was a near-miss—a near-failure. I think this has always been true. The opening few measures of the last movement of Beethoven's Ninth Symphony are as close as one could come, within the harmonic concepts of the day, to simple hysteria, and they work because they take the risk of degenerating. The same could be said of many of Mahler's most ambitious works. In the past, then, a great deal of work was exciting because it was so colossal and attempted so much that it was in danger of becoming utterly banal or preposterous. Today there is little point in trying to work as *large* as possible, so the challenge tends to lie in the other direction. And, a sense of risk is indispensable, because any simple piece fails when it becomes facile. This makes for all the more challenge in risking facility, yet still remaining very simple, very concrete, very meaningful.

Also, the composer is perfectly well aware of the psychological difficulties that his composition may produce for some, if not all, of the audience. He therefore finds excitement in insisting on this, to the point of endangering himself physically or even spiritually in his piece. To point up this effect, I wrote a series of compositions called *Danger Musics,* each of which emphasized one spiritual, psychological, or physical danger that seemed appropriate to the general aesthetic means I was using. Again, Robert Whitman, in doing a Happening around 1962 at Bennington College, is said to have turned in a performance so violent that the performance area was covered with blood—his blood. In the course of one of Al Hansen's improvised Happenings in 1962 a young lady fell through a glass roof and was very badly hurt. But her involvement in the piece caused her to do this, almost consciously, and it became incorporated in the intensity of the piece. Most spectators thought it had been planned. In a world in which there isn't so much overt *physical* challenge as formerly, it is very tempting sometimes to see not how much one can get away with but how much one can use the challenges that *are* there. Therefore it becomes extremely attractive to the artist to use danger, *hazard.* This is not the same as *chance,* of course, which is quite a different sort of idea and which ultimately becomes either a technical means of realizing a set of values and textures or, if one is using it spiritually (that is, for the philosophy of the piece), of creating a chaos that suits one's sense of anarchy and of embodying one's views.

In the visual arts there has not been very much work that uses danger in a pure way. One of the few examples I can think of are some works by the Japanese sculptor Ay-O. Ay-O has constructed many small boxes into which one places one's finger or one's hand. In each of these boxes is an object or substance to be touched. Most are relatively soft and safe. For example, some may contain flour, water, tacky glue, perhaps some marbles or some cotton. But others contain razor blades, knives, broken glass. The freshness with which one approaches the boxes (and not all of them are presented as boxes, some are presented as feeling holes in the bodies of cutouts), not knowing if one will be delighted or hurt, develops the intensity and graciousness of experiencing them. This, I would say, is another expression of the same motivation that attracts composers, performers, and, to some extent, the visual artists.

To sum up, it has become almost a hallmark of our mentality to accept the possibility of boredom and danger; a work that is without these possibilities only decorates life and so is merely a commodity; the most intense art is necessarily involved with these things, boredom and danger, not as a new mode, but because they are implicit in the new mentality of our time. This mentality is one in which total success is impossible, total victory inconceivable, and relativism axiomatic. Ours is a mass society, and, although we do attempt to do what we do with maximum quality, quality has for us become one among other indications of integrity. Today we do not equate quality alone with the value of a work. Most of the interesting works of our time are works that shed light on our mentality without necessarily trying for the same standards of success as works, say, of twenty years ago. It is simply not our intention, although we are perfectly capable of achieving the old standards.

The intention is more to enrich the experiential world of our spectators, our coconspirators, by enlarging the repertoire of their overall experience. These values cannot be achieved by emotional impact alone, and such impact has become, for the new artist, merely a language tool, a way of communicating that we can draw on when necessary. I said earlier that we do not want to overwhelm. This is not quite true. We only want to overwhelm when to do so seems a positive factor. There was nothing more overwhelming than Hitler's speeches as staged by Goebbels. There has been a great deal of that in our world and one way to avoid it is to use more sophisticated values in our own work, and the acceptance of boredom and danger as valuable is indispensable to this end.

Notes on New Music:

New Forms for New Music
The New Tonality
Facts Become Sounds*

Tom Johnson

The following article, in three parts, deals with several problems and ideas in music. First, Tom Johnson discusses several morphologies that have arisen in recent years. While such forms as the cantata or the symphony have fallen into disuse, other, newer forms have replaced them, including multimedia forms and the performance-art forms, hypnotic or Minimal forms, and the post-Webern form. Yet another form, still too vague to be firmly identified, is documentary music, in which composers "do not attempt to do everything by themselves but are content to accept a little outside material and leave a few things as they are," which the author analyzes.

Following the discussion of new forms, the author writes about "The New Tonality," in which clean shifts from dominant to tonic chords are not to be heard, thus differentiating the new tonality from the essence of traditional European tonality. According to Johnson, the new tonality arose not through admiration for Beethoven or Mozart but, rather, "because the younger composers began studying ragas, listening to scales from Africa, Indonesia, . . . and observing that there were a whole lot of good ways of writing music with simple scales and tonal centers."

---

* These essays are all reprinted from *The Village Voice:* "New Forms for New Music," September 4, 1978; "The New Tonality," October 16, 1978; "Facts Become Sounds," November 27, 1978.

Tom Johnson is the composer of The Four Note Opera *and the music critic for* The Village Voice. *He has written music criticism for* The New York Times *and other publications and he is author of* Imaginary Music *and* Private Pieces: Piano Music for Self-Entertainment.

NEW FORMS FOR NEW MUSIC

Whatever happened to the symphony? the tone poem? the song cycle? the oratorio? the cantata? the sonata? the prelude? the rondo? One might occasionally run across a composer who still turns back to one of them, but by and large these forms are dead. They were supposed to die. We killed them, and we were glad we did. As music made its brash way through the twentieth century, we decided we didn't need standard forms anymore. We were going to be emancipated from all of that. The twentieth century, or at least the second half of the twentieth century, was to be wide open. Composers could still write string quartets, concertos, operas, and sets of variations occasionally, as those forms were not quite worn out yet, but there was really no need for any of it. The new music could now break all the rules, make up its own forms, and do whatever it wanted.

It was a nice idea, but it wasn't very realistic. Composers, like other groups of human beings, always seem to fall into standardized procedures of some sort. Of course they don't know they are falling into standardized procedures. Artists never do. For example, it was not until composers had been writing sonatas for a century or so that anyone ever completely defined *sonata form.* Today's music also fits into basic forms, and eventually someone will be able to define them all, and the new forms will probably turn out to be at least as rigid as any of the old ones. It is premature to lay down any hard-and-fast rules, but when I sat down to try to make a list of today's standard forms, I was surprised to discover that I could already delineate six of them fairly specifically.

The post-Webern form. Post-Webern pieces are generally scored for ensembles of diverse instruments and last from six to twenty minutes. As in the works of Anton Webern, from which the form was derived, the music involves careful manipulation of intervals, usually with the help of a twelve-tone row. The music must be intricate and atonal, with new variations appearing constantly, and little or no repetition. Major chords, strong rhythmic pulses, and lyrical melodies must be carefully camouflaged, if they occur at all. This is probably the most widely used of all twentieth-century musical forms and it completely dominated contemporary music series, especially in America, throughout the 1960s. It has declined gradually in popularity in the 1970s.

The multimedia form. This spectacular contemporary form always involves projections and electronic equipment as well as instrumentalists, and usually dancers as well. As much of the activity as possible must be presented simultaneously. Normally such performances call for a large cast and take place in gymnasiums, ballrooms, or other open spaces. Usually a sociopolitical message is conveyed. Multimedia pieces were most frequent and most spectacular during the late 1960s, although they are still encountered occasionally in less frenetic variations.

The performer-and-tape form. This form generally calls for one to six performers and lasts about ten to fifteen minutes. The tape is prepared in an electronic music studio, and the main concern is to set up a dialogue between humans and machines, usually with dramatic tension between the two. Both must have more or less equal time. In many early examples the electronic sounds and the instrumental ones were sharply contrasted, but as electronic equipment became more sophisticated, the tapes began to blend with the instruments and sometimes imitate them. The form began almost simultaneously with the advent of purely electronic pieces, but it soon proved to be far preferable for concert-hall presentations. The genre has never been particularly popular but it has held remarkably steady, with new performer-and-tape pieces continuing to crop up every season.

The hypnotic form. Hypnotic pieces may be written for almost any instrumental ensemble, but they must always be rather long, extremely persistent, and highly repetitious. The tempo must be rather fast and must remain exactly the same throughout. The main concern is to lull the listener into a sequence of melodic or rhythmic patterns that shift very gradually as the music progresses. The form sprang up rather suddenly in America in the late 1960s, when Terry Riley's *In C* became widely known, and several composers launched successful careers writing hypnotic pieces. Hypnotic pieces in this strict form are not written so often today, although less well-defined types of repetitious or minimal music crop up constantly.

The sound poem. This form involves making music by manipulating words. In most cases speech sounds are recorded, altered, mixed, collaged, and otherwise made into prerecorded tapes. In other instances sound poems may be performed live. The most important requirement is that the piece be a genuine sound expression and not merely a translation of words that could be conveyed effectively on the printed page. Many early precedents can be found, such as the *Ursonata* of Kurt Schwitters, although the form was not explored with any regularity until the late 1960s and early 1970s, when a number of poets became more interested in public performance than in publication, and a number of musicians became interested in working with speech sounds. Sound poetry still accounts for only a tiny percentage of the new music launched every year, but the genre seems to be gradually growing in popularity, particularly in California.

The performance-art form. The main requirement in this form is that composer-artists perform the pieces themselves. The works may involve instruments, sound effects, talking, singing, theatrical devices, or all of these things, but they must be presented by the artist, with or without assistants, and must be highly individualistic. The content is usually autobiographical, conceptual, or comic, and the performance often utilizes highly developed vocal skills, or other individual performing skills, that only the particular artist can execute. Works in this form must not be addressed specifically to a musical audience, however, as most of the performance outlets for this genre are in museums and galleries. Little songs, dances, or jokes, which would be considered frivolous in most other art forms, are often acceptable in performance art. The genre evolved in the early 1970s and now flourishes, particularly around New York.

Of course, the genres I am calling today's "forms" may not seem parallel to the "forms" of the nineteenth century. But that is only natural, because the music itself is so different. The rules that defined nineteenth-century forms pertained largely to the relationships between themes and the ways in which a composition was to be divided into sections. Now the concerns are different, and the rules are about other things. Of course, many contemporary works turn out to be hybrids, just as many nineteenth-century works turned out to be crosses between symphonies and tone poems or between sonatas and rondos. And occasionally someone like Erik Satie comes up with something that defies all of the categories. But these are only exceptions to the networks of rules that determine the vast majority of music. Ultimately every age is left with a rather small collection of generally accepted procedures.

THE NEW TONALITY

The new ECM release of Steve Reich's *Music for 18 Musicians* arrived in the mail the other day. This is not my favorite Reich work, neither am I convinced that the long fade-out at the end of side one and the fade-in at the beginning of side two do much to enhance what otherwise sounds like a live performance. But there are certain advantages in listening to music at home. In this case there was a piano nearby, and as I listened to the album, I became interested in picking out the pitches Reich was using and attempting to figure out how the piece worked harmonically. This pastime proved most interesting, and I began pulling down other recordings that seemed relevant. By the end of the evening I decided that the Reich work is in a special kind of D major, that Frederic Rzewski's *Coming Together* moves in a very different kind of G minor, that Brian Eno's *Discreet Music* sits in another type of G major, and that one could easily find twenty or thirty other composers working in similar ways, and that the new tonality can be defined as a general phenomenon. I figured I ought to write something about how the new tonality works.

The greatest difference between the new tonality and traditional European tonality is that the recent music doesn't have much to do with chord progressions. You don't hear clean shifts from dominant to tonic chords in the new tonality. You seldom even hear those major and minor chords that are the essence of traditional European tonality. Instead, you hear, basically, a scale, and the chords and melodies that arise may be any combinations of notes from this scale. As there is no concern for the chord progressions that propelled traditional European music and that continue to propel most pop and folk music as well, there is no need for a strong bass line to carry the progressions. There is often, if not always, a tonal center, but this is usually just the note that comes up most often and at the most important points. It does not have much sense of finality. And when this tonal center changes or modulates, it is usually just a question of shifting the emphasis from one note to another, rather than bringing in a whole new set of chord progressions, as Beethoven would have.

Reich shifts the tonal center frequently and quite craftily in *Music for 18 Musicians.* According to Reich's program notes, the piece follows a slow sequence of eleven chords, but I hear it as a sequence of tonalities. The first main section of the piece sits on a D-major scale, and the music really does feel like D major to me, even though there are no actual D-major chords. Most of the time most of the scale is present, and this makes for sappy harmonies, which in combination with the overdressed instrumentation of clarinets, strings, voices, and mallet instruments makes the piece as a whole awfully lush. But other things are going on underneath the lush. After a while, the weight shifts toward major, and eventually to a bright E-major feeling. By the end of side one, we drop into C-sharp minor. Side two takes us from C-sharp minor back through E major, A major, F-sharp minor, and eventually all the way back to D major. Of course, this is not a triumphant return to the tonic, the way it would have been in a nineteenth-century symphony. The music just drifts back. It's a return, but no big deal.

Of the many recordings of new music that are almost totally unknown, Frederic Rzewski's *Opus One* album (op. 1–20) is about the finest one that I happen to know about. When I run into listeners who feel that avant-garde music is too insular or too intellectual, or just irrelevant, I try to find a chance to play this album for them, because it changes their minds almost every time. I've listened to it many times, been touched by its political messages, felt its rhythmic power, and strained my concentration to the hilt trying to follow its melodies as they gradually grow longer and longer, but this time I began thinking of Rzewski's music as a case of the new tonality. Of the three pieces on the album, *Coming Together* is particularly interesting in this way. Here the sound is basically G minor, although it uses only five of the seven notes normally occurring in the G-minor scale and might be more properly considered a mode. The scale is simple and it works well, but the really interesting thing comes toward the end, as one of the melodic progressions gradually winds itself into a corner, where it begins to produce a whole lot more B-flats than Gs. The shift is gradual but, in this limited context, crucial. The music begins to feel like B-flat major, seems bright and optimistic, and fits the climax of the text perfectly. It also fits Rzewski's rigid melodic system, which gradually eases the music back to the G-minor realm.

Brian Eno's *Discreet Music* is not quite so crafty, and like many overdubbed electronic works, it sometimes falls slightly out of tune, but it is a good example of the new tonality and a good piece to mention here, as it is relatively familiar. Here the scale is G, B, C, D, E, and because either G or D is generally present in the bass register, the music has a simple, relaxed G-major feeling. Listening carefully for shifts in the scale, however, I began to think I was occasionally hearing the pitch A in the upper register. I never really could hear it, and concluded that I was picking up an aural illusion or overtone of some sort. But then, toward the end of the piece, there it was. A little line with an A in it. Eno had kept this note practically inaudible until the very end, and then, finally, let us have it. That may not seem like a big deal, but in music this clean and simple, the addition of one new tone can be a major event. It is in this piece, at least if one is tuned in on that frequency.

These are only a few examples of how the new tonality works. A few weeks ago I reviewed a David Behrman album that is a particularly sophisticated and successful case in point, and there are many others, including quite a few that are generally considered to be jazz. For so much music to return to old-fashioned keys after fifty years of dissonance and atonality might seem to be a reactionary development, and I doubt that anyone would have predicted this ten years ago. It is not really reactionary, however. The new tonality did not arise out of any particular respect for Beethoven and Mozart. It came about primarily, I think, because the younger composers began studying ragas, listening to scales from Africa, Indonesia, and other parts of the world and observing that there were a whole lot of good ways of writing music with simple scales and tonal centers. Considering music from a cross-cultural point of view, one has little choice but to conclude that the dissonance and atonality that have dominated Western classical music in the twentieth century are very odd phenomena and that, for all their assets and power, they just don't have much to do with music as a whole in the world as a whole. It is understandable that young composers in the 1960s would have wanted to find a more universal musical language that related to the larger picture. Being trained in Western music, they have generally stuck with the Western tuning system and Western instruments and they have evolved a kind of tonality that does relate back to European music of the eighteenth and nineteenth centuries. But only partly. When Terry Riley titled one of his early works *In C,* he didn't mean "in C major" exactly, and he certainly didn't mean that he was working with tonic and dominant chords again. He was really working "in C something else." It was a new tonality.

FACTS BECOME SOUNDS

Little, if anything, has been said about "documentary music," but it seems to me that there is a lot of it going around these days. I don't mean to define a specific school or category and I certainly don't mean to suggest any exact parallels between what composers are doing and the activity in documentary films or documentary art. I simply mean that a great deal of recent music is documentary in a general sense. Most music is totally creative, totally a figment of some personal imagination or process, but documentary music merely records some pattern or event found in the real, nonimaginary world. It translates facts into sounds. This is a new idea. The closest nineteenth-century and early twentieth-century composers ever came actually to documenting anything would be those operas or tone poems that claimed to re-create some legend or historical incident.

I'd been familiar with *The Sinking of the Titanic* by Gavin Bryars in its

Obscure Records version for some time. And after hearing Bryars's live presentation at the Kitchen on November 11, which included live piano music and a number of projections related to the *Titanic,* I decided this would be a good place to begin describing documentary music. Bryars's work is essentially a sound collage, running about twenty-five minutes, consisting largely of sustained string music along with fragments of piano and barely audible speaking voices. The piece has a solemn quality and is an effective historical memorial, but it is much more than that. It is actually a detailed reconstruction of the incident. The string music consists of the specific hymns reported to have been played by the *Titanic*'s musicians as the ship was sinking, the instrumentation is exactly that of the ship's orchestra, and the voices are actual statements of observers. The complete score, published in *Soundings* magazine in 1975, includes thirty-four pages of other details Bryars took into consideration in composing the work and even suggests that the piece is to be corrected at the dictates of future research. "The piece is an open one," the composer explains, "and materials subsequently found are included in it and are integral parts."

A few weeks ago I heard another arresting case of documentary music when I attended a rehearsal of New York's own gamelan ensemble, Son of Lion. One of the works I heard that evening was a new composition by Philip Corner called *The Barcelona Cathedral.* Corner was conducting in big slow beats that fell heavily once every few seconds. With each beat about ten mallets fell onto the metallic percussion instruments with a tremendous clang. A variety of pitches resulted, and the general effect was much like a big church bell. The piece went on for nearly half an hour, always with that same relentless beat but with slightly different effects. A church bell never rings exactly the same way twice, and in Corner's work too the attacks would vary slightly, and my ear would be drawn to different details as the clangs decayed. Later on some members of the group inserted little upbeats, which sounded almost accidental and clearly reflected the accidental little sounds that clappers often make on bells in between their serious strokes.

Corner had not done any library research in this case, but he had obviously done a good deal of ear research during his recent visit to Barcelona, because this was not simply a fantasy on the sound of church bells. It became quite clear that Corner was actually trying to actually create the actual sound of the actual church bell he had actually heard and that he had actually pulled it off.

The difference between documentary music and other music often reminds me of the difference between photography and painting, and *The Barcelona Cathedral* is a particularly clear example of the photographic approach. Like a photographer, Corner was basically just trying to capture a perception, get it in focus, and convey it to an audience. Of course, many elements of personal taste ultimately enter in. Why did he choose a bell as his subject? Why this particular bell? Why did he decide to re-create the experience with the gamelan ensemble instead of with an orchestra or a synthesizer? But that is like asking why Diane Arbus liked to take pictures of abnormal humans and why she took them in black and white instead of color. Such questions are relevant, of course, and clarify that basic artistic choices are still at stake, but they do not negate the fact that, essentially, both Corner and Arbus were simply documenting perceptions.

The methods used to create *The Sinking of the Titanic* and *The Barcelona Cathedral* are by no means the only ways of composing documentary music. Many other composers have done it in many other ways. One of my favorite examples is Annea Lockwood's *River Archives,* which consists entirely of recordings she has made of rivers, streams, and creeks around the world. This is basically a kind of catalogue, but unlike Messiaen's rather freely elaborated *Catalogue d'Oiseaux,* for example, this one allows nature to speak without human intervention. Other composers have taken a different approach by writing melodic lines that follow the precise contour of a mountain range, the Manhattan skyline, or other lines found in the nonmusical world. Most of Petr Kotik's melodic lines are literal translations of patterns taken from graphs that are themselves documents that record the movements of experimental rats. John Cage's music documents star charts, the flaws in pieces of paper, drawings of Thoreau, tunes from the American Revolutionary period, and numerous other significant and insignificant bits of information that have interested him over the years. The list could go on and on. One might even suggest, without stretching the point too much, that any reasonably strict form of chance composition is a documentation of how the dice fell on a particular occasion.

The methods of writing documentary music vary greatly, as do the results, which is why I should not want to consider this an actual category or school. But they all have something important in common. They all allow the details of a composition to be dictated by something other than the composer's imagination. They attempt to reflect some truth, some content, some organizational principle that goes beyond the whims of the composer.

There is a certain modesty in the approach, and I like that, just as I have always liked the modesty inherent in photography. Documentary composers do not attempt to do everything by themselves but are content to accept a little outside material and leave a few things as they are. It's OK to let the sounds of the Barcelona Cathedral just be themselves. It's OK simply to listen to a river. It's OK just to express the facts of what happened on the *Titanic*. Coming on the heels of an era in classical music when composers were expected to express only themselves, I find the idea most refreshing.

Definitions of Popular Music: Recycled*

Gaynor G. Jones and Jay Rahn

Just what is popular music? Many definitions have been offered to explain the term, but, as the authors of the following article point out, the definitions are frequently concerned with one specific type of popular music to the exclusion of others. The authors explain the problem as a "result from the hyperbolic style that much of contemporary popular music encourages."

Although the authors do not provide the final word on the subject, they do point to many of the problems encountered in attempts to define popular music and they offer several suggestions concerning possible definitions. For example, they offer three major characteristics that all popular music seems to share. These include the emphasis on aural transmission, the entertainment function of such music, and a relatively passive method of listening to it. And they go on to offer twelve criteria for determining the popularity of any type of music.

In the main, popular music shares numerous features with classical music. And the authors recognize that "any music has elements that may be considered folk, popular, or elite to a certain extent." Nevertheless, it is important to search for a definition of popular music, particularly today as the

---

* Reprinted from *The Journal of Aesthetic Education,* 11, no. 4 (October 1977), pp. 79–92.

gap between popular and classical seems to widen, and research into popular music intensifies.

Gaynor G. Jones teaches music history at the University of Toronto. She has published articles and reviews in numerous journals, such as International Review of the Aesthetics and Sociology of Music *and* Current Musicology, *as well as written record reviews and articles in popular magazines.*

Jay Rahn teaches courses on popular music at Laurentian University and York University (Canada). He has published articles in Perspectives of New Music *and* In Theory Only, *as well as in other music periodicals.*

Is it surprising that there is no generally accepted definition of popular music when one considers the range of subject matter that the term embraces and the diversity of approaches that scholars in various fields have taken to study it? Types of popular music studied today range from Renaissance songs, broadsides, parlor music, and more recent dance tunes to Muzak, film scores, and pop in the industrialized countries—in addition to high-life, calypso, and revolutionary opera in the third world. The people who study it may be folklorists, sociologists, psychologists, historians, literary scholars, historical musicologists, or ethnomusicologists. Wiser scholars have prefaced their attempts at defining popular music with reflections on the difficulties of the task and on the small return such definitions yield. For example, in the 1950s Howard Brown wrote: " 'Popular' is admittedly a difficult word. Everyone knows what it means and yet no one can define it quite precisely."[1] In the 1960s Robert B. Cantrick—in a discussion of popular music that ranges more broadly than previous studies, which ignore non-Western music and the historical past—similarly observed that "everyone talks about popular music but no one knows what it is."[2] Most recently and most vividly, Serge Denisoff pointed out that "Popular music is like a unicorn; everyone knows what it is supposed to look like, but no one has ever seen it."[3]

Even special genres like rock or pop seem to elude fruitful definition. To Carl Belz, "Any listener who wants rock defined specifically is probably unable to recognize it,"[4] and Tony Jasper asserts, "Pop refuses definition.

---

[1] Howard Brown, "The *Chanson Rustique:* Popular Elements in the 15th- and 16th-Century Chanson," *Journal of the American Musicological Society,* 12 (1959), pp. 17–18.
[2] Robert B. Cantrick, "The Blind Men and the Elephant: Scholars on Popular Music," *Ethnomusicology,* 9 (1965), p. 100.
[3] Serge Denisoff, *Solid Gold: The Popular Record Industry* (New Brunswick, N.J.: Transaction Books, 1975), p. 1.
[4] Carl Belz, *The Story of Rock* (2d ed.; New York: Harper & Row, 1969), p. vii.

To say it means popular music conveys little. As a term it bears comparison with 'life' as far as difficulty of interpretation goes. Once you think you know, you're already half-dead."[5] On the one hand, popular music is not easy to define—"Fools rush in where angels fear to tread"; on the other hand, everyone seems to know intuitively what is meant by the term. If "You don't need a weatherman to know which way the wind blows" (Bob Dylan), then "Most people don't need us to tell them what popular culture means to them—especially when it is usually completely removed from their common sense or the creative world."[6]

Yet there are reasons for arriving at a workable definition of popular music. Pragmatically, such a definition might facilitate discussions among students of different types of popular music.[7] On a loftier level, reevaluation of definitions could well change the face of research into, and talk about, popular music.[8] Thus it is still useful to consider those definitions of popular music that have survived.[9] Before summarizing them, some general observations on the types of definitions that have been offered to date are in order.

Attempts to define popular music have suffered from three shortcomings. First, they reveal a narrowness of vision, which one does not expect in so broad a field. When one reads beyond the initial paragraphs of most books on popular music, one discovers that the writers are really talking about a special type of popular music, such as pop songs, broadsides, Tin Pan Alley tunes, or urban blues.[10] This often seems to result from the hyperbolic style that much of contemporary popular music encourages, but even scholars in the past, such as Theodor Adorno and David Riesman, have been guilty of calling a part by the name of the whole.[11]

---

[5] Tony Jasper, *Understanding Pop* (London: SCM Press, 1972), p. 10.
[6] Denisoff, "Content Analysis: The Achilles Heel of Popular Culture?," *Journal of Popular Culture,* 9 (Fall 1975), p. 460.
[7] See John G. Cawelti, *Popular Culture Programs* (Bowling Green, Ohio: Bowling Green University Press for Popular Culture Association, 1970), p. 1, on the need for a common basis for interdisciplinary research into popular music.
[8] See David F. Gillespie, "Sociology of Popular Culture: The Other Side of a Definition," *Journal of Popular Culture,* 6 (Fall 1972), p. 298, on the effects of a definition on the type of research that ensues.
[9] Throughout this paper, our emphasis is on those aspects of definitions that have survived. An account of all the unfruitful attempts would fill another article and to little avail.
[10] See Cantrick, "Blind Men and Elephant," on the myopia of much past research into popular music.
[11] Theodor Adorno, "On Popular Music," *Studies in Philosophy and Social Science,* 9 (Spring 1941), pp. 17–48; David Riesman, "Listening to Popular Music," in Bernard Rosenberg and David Manning White, eds., *Mass Culture: The Popular Arts in America* (Glencoe, Ill.: Free Press, 1950), pp. 408–416.

A second failing is the tendency of many writers to make categorical, "black-and-white" statements: this is popular music; that is not. A more flexible approach would stress that certain types of music are more or less popular than other types.[12] Furthermore, there appear to be several criteria by which a given type of music might be considered popular.[13] Thus many variables, each of which can assume many values, should be considered in assessing the popularity of any music.

Third, the application of even the potentially most useful classification of popular culture, Ray B. Browne's view of popular culture as the middle of a horizontal rather than a vertical continuum, should be modified when applied to popular music.[14] Browne's linear scheme is superior to previous vertical models in that it removes the tendency to attribute good, bad, and harmless values to elite, popular, and folk music. It is also useful for grouping together various types of music, play-party songs have more in common with bubblegum music than with the *Lieder* of Hugo Wolf, and the symphonic poems of Richard Strauss are closer to film music of the 1930s than to the tunes of peasant ensembles. Yet this linear ordering breaks down when one is confronted with criteria according to which the outer members, folk and elite, appear to be closer to one another than to popular music, for example in their proximity to ritual functions and in their relatively small audiences. The outer edges of the linear continuum may bend around to form a circular pattern in which folk and elite music are closer to each other than they are to popular music. If, in the circular model, folk and elite music are grouped around twelve o'clock and popular music around six o'clock, then the grouping together of folk and elite might be termed relatively *esoteric,* in contrast to the more *exoteric* popular forms.[15]

As a corollary to these observations, any music has elements that may be considered folk, popular, or elite to a certain extent.[16] Admittedly, cer-

---

[12] See Russel B. Nye, "Notes for an Introduction to a Discussion of Popular Culture," *Journal of Popular Culture,* 4 (Spring 1971), pp. 1,031–1,038, on the need to recognize degrees of popularity.

[13] On the dangers of one-dimensional approaches to popular music, see Serge Denisoff and Mark H. Levine, "The One-Dimensional Approach to Popular Music: A Research Note," *Journal of Popular Culture,* 4 (Spring 1971), pp. 911–919.

[14] Ray B. Browne, "Popular Culture: Notes Toward a Definition," in *Popular Culture and the Expanding Consciousness,* Ray B. Browne, ed. (New York: John Wiley & Sons, 1971), pp. 14–22.

[15] See Denisoff, *Solid Gold,* pp. 31–35, for the distinction between esoteric and exoteric as applied to elite and popular music.

[16] See John Blacking, *How Musical Is Man?* (Seattle: University of Washington Press, 1973), for an interesting view of the folk nature of elite music and Browne's insistence

tain genres (such as middle-of-the-road) are emphatically popular, whereas others (such as the string quartet) are only slightly popular. A workable definition of popular music should embrace all genres of music that are already recognized as popular. It should be more flexible than some current definitions so as to allow for varying degrees of, and criteria for, popularity. Finally, it should allow for both a linear and a circular arrangement of the current folk, popular, and elite categories.

One difficulty that must be confronted in any attempt to define *popular music* is that the term itself does not have a determinate meaning in the same way that *carbonation, right angle,* or *dominant seventh* can be precisely defined. It is a part of a living language, not a strictly technical term. Accordingly, the referents of the term *popular music* are bound to change with the culture in which it is embedded. Some languages do not have an equivalent for the term, thus further confounding the issue. For example, the French *chanson populaire* includes both popular song and what is now termed the *chanson folklorique.* The German *volkstümlich-* and *Volks,* although close to the English popular and folk, respectively, possess special, Teutonic connotations. In Iran there is no synonym for popular music, yet there is a phenomenon that, as Bruno Nettl demonstrates, clearly parallels that of Euro-American popular music.[17] In India, it is more appropriate to discuss film or "folk" music.

Nevertheless, the meaning of the term *popular music* is not so vague as to render it useless. This paper, although specifically geared to popular music, does follow the approaches to popular culture of scholars such as Russel Nye and Ray B. Browne.[18] Although some difficulties of definition are peculiar to music, the specialized area of popular music provides a good testing ground for theories of popular culture. A number of connotations have surrounded popular music, and these elusive associations must be specified if the term is to be useful. Fortunately, a number of perceptive writers have already managed to ferret out some of the connotations that

---

on keeping the lines of demarcation that separate the three categories of culture as mobile as possible.

[17] Bruno Nettl, "Persian Popular Music in 1969," *Ethnomusicology,* 16 (May 1972), pp. 218–239.

[18] See Browne, "Popular Culture," and Nye, "Notes for an Introduction." Nye selects six approaches to popular culture: (i) the means of transmission; (ii) differences in the production of its artifacts; (iii) its function; (iv) popular culture viewed as inclusive of "everything not elite" (Marshall Fishwick); (v) the kind of taste that popular culture reflects (Abraham Kaplan); (vi) Ray Browne's view of differences among cultural levels being those of degree, where the scale is a horizontal not a vertical one.

serve as a background to our everyday and professional uses of the term; thus we shall attempt to construct a composite picture of those features that seem generally associated with popular music. Unfortunately, we must rely heavily on examples from Western music, as studies of non-Western popular music have been few and exploratory rather than comprehensive and definitive.

An obvious criterion for a music's popularity is the number of people who experience it: the more people involved, the more popular the music.[19] In this sense children's songs, national anthems, organ renditions in baseball parks, and Muzak are more popular than most progressive rock.[20] To a certain extent, this criterion can be applied to determine the popularity of historical repertoires. For example, unaccompanied French song of the early sixteenth century appears to have reached a far wider audience than French polyphonic song of the time, which in turn was more widely known than polyphonic songs in German, Italian, Spanish, or English.[21] In general, however, it is impossible to determine from historical documents how many people listened to a certain repertoire of music in the past.

A simple application of numbers can prove misleading; various groups of people cultivate certain genres within a popular idiom. Throughout history, professionals and tradespeople such as lawyers, miners, and masons have patronized special repertoires of their own.[22] Much the same could be said of today's popular audience, which can be divided into smaller and demographically more homogeneous taste groupings based on age, sex, social class, race, education, and geography.[23] Frequently, social class alone is invoked in defining popular music. For example, Swanwick and Spaeth distinguish between "democratic" and

---

[19] See Edward Lee, *Music of the People: A Study of Popular Music in Great Britain* (London: Barrie & Jenkins, 1970), p. ix, for a definition in numerical terms.

[20] See Tim Souster, "Rock, Beat, Pop—Avant Garde," *World of Music,* 12, no. 2 (1970), pp. 32–43, on the proximity of progressive rock to the music of the classical avant-garde.

[21] See Jay Rahn, "Melodic and Textual Types in French Monophonic Song" (Ph.D. diss., Columbia University, 1978).

[22] See Ernst Klusen, *Volkslied: Fund und Erfindung* (Köln: Hans Gerig, 1969). Although Klusen equates his "group songs" with folk songs, they appear to be more popular than folkloric in character. Cf. Walter Wiora, "Reflections on the Problem: How Old Is the Concept Folksong?," *Yearbook of the International Folk Music Council,* 3 (1971), pp. 23–33.

[23] See Denisoff, *Solid Gold.*

"plebeian" music on the one hand, and "aristocratic" music on the other.[24] However, as Russell Lynes long ago demonstrated, taste does not necessarily correlate with social status.[25] Rather, it would seem that complexes of social, educational, and other factors explain listener preferences better than an isolated variable such as social class.[26]

In line with this view is the observation that music that is relatively popular tends to have not only a heterogeneous audience but also one that is unpredictable.[27] If this seems paradoxical compared with the generally accepted notion that popular audiences are homogeneous, one should remember that each homogeneous group of listeners contributes to the more heterogeneous whole. Although there appears to be no parallel to this fickleness of audiences in folk communities, much of the classical music of the past reflects the capricious taste of courtly patrons.

The vastness of the audience for popular music leads to another criterion for defining it: the size of the business that produces and transmits the product. One can only hazard a guess at the number of minstrels, hawkers, dancing masters, etc., who have plied their trades, as well as the volume of pedagogical materials, broadsides, and sheet music that they have disseminated throughout Europe and North America in the historical past. Reliable records of them are few, and cheap prints tend not to survive; yet there has been a substantial "music business" since the sixteenth century. With the advent of electronic media and an increase in the standard of living, the economic importance of popular music has swelled enormously. Generally, the more popular forms have been not only the most widely but also the most cheaply transmitted. Pulp magazines of lyrics, 45 rpm records, and AM radio have been the mainstays of recent popular music, just as single-sheet broadsides and inexpensive chapbooks served popular music from the Renaissance onward. The more popular genres appear to seek out the more efficient means of transmission.[28] Because things are transmitted

---

[24] Keith Swanwick, *Popular Music and the Teacher* (Oxford: Pergamon Press, 1968), pp. 7–22, and Sigmund Spaeth, *A History of Popular Music in America* (New York: Random House, 1948), pp. 6–8.
[25] *The Tastemakers* (London: Hamish Hamilton, 1954). See also Nye, "Notes for an Introduction," p. 1,035.
[26] See Cantrick, "Blind Men and Elephant," p. 112, on the oversimplification resulting from an approach based merely on social class.
[27] As Denisoff points out (*Solid Gold*, p. 32) : "The larger the exoteric taste group the less stability and predictability."
[28] Ilse Storb, "Apropos Pop Music," *Melos,* 37, no. 5 (1970), pp. 187–190, emphasizes the massiveness of production and consumption in her definition of popular music.

more efficiently in cities than in the countryside, this may explain the frequent equation of popular music with urban music. But to put the emphasis on geography rather than on economic factors seems to be placing the cart before the horse: efficient transmission encourages an urban milieu, not vice versa.[29]

Despite its long involvement with printers and publishers, popular music, like traditional folk music, seems to be preeminently an aural form. In contrast to elite music, popular pieces have been transmitted largely by word-of-mouth, or some electronic extension thereof (recordings, tapes, films, or radio). Notation plays a secondary role; used for pedagogical purposes or as aide-mémoire, scores are typically eschewed in popular performance. Stemming from the rise of the virtuoso performer in the nineteenth century, classical instrumentalists and conductors now tend to perform from memory like their popular counterparts in order to show a similar talent for memorization. The ragged rhymes, grammatical infelicities, and unnotatable performance mannerisms for which popular music has been derided in the past seem to stem from this aural rather than visual approach to music-making. On the other hand, according to this criterion, assiduous readers of Beatles' lyrics and opera librettos would appear to be peers in a relatively elite audience, if only because of their involvement in the printed text.[30]

The overriding cultural function that popular music has served is entertainment. The rubrics of Elizabethan ballads are instructive: "to be sung in merry pastime by Bachelors and Maydes," "a pleasant jigg," "a pleasant new song," "a merry discourse." All of these point to pleasure and amusement as the desired aims.[31] There is a vividly secular appeal to popular music. This is even the case with popular devotional song, which, although religious, has been cultivated privately and domestically in an extraliturgical setting.

---

[29] See John Storm Roberts, "Popular Music in Kenya," *African Music*, 4 (1968), pp. 53–55, who, along with other writers, equates popular music with the music of the cities—again an oversimplification.

[30] The literate aspects of such lyrics as those of the Beatles should not be overlooked. Thus, those who argue against taking popular music seriously, as do Richard A. Peterson, "Taking Popular Music Too Seriously," *Journal of Popular Culture*, 4 (Winter 1971), pp. 590–593, and Tracy Strombom, "Another Boring Article About Music," *Journal of Popular Culture*, 8 (Winter 1974), pp, 637–643, are avoiding characteristics of the subject matter itself.

[31] See Charles Read Baskerville's classic study, *The Elizabethan Jig and Related Song Drama* (New York: Dover, 1965), pt. II: "Texts." On the other hand, Denisoff, *Solid Gold*, p. 423, points out that "Listeners rarely find Louisiana twelve-bar blues progression a happy motif."

With regard to the aesthetic object itself, Swanwick characterizes popular music as easier to grasp and more readily intelligible than "art" music.[32] Another way of looking at this issue is that popular audiences might have passive methods of listening.[33] Adorno, writing of Tin Pan Alley in the 1930s, said that listeners to popular music did not interpret popular hits, but merely recognized them: "That's the hit 'Night and Day.' "[34] Using this criterion, recent rock hermeneutics such as those surrounding the old Beatles' albums would be a more elite phenomenon than the auditory philistinism of many symphony patrons.[35]

With regard to the individuality or identity of a piece, David Riesman observed in the 1950s that followers of classical music identified works by their composers, whereas popular music fans identified them by their performers.[36] Along much the same lines, Adorno points out that idiosyncratic musical devices of performance or arrangement aid the popular listener in attributing the work to a given performer.[37] This would have to apply not only to Elton John but also to Glenn Gould. And, following this reasoning, symphonies of the Mannheim school, with their orchestral rockets and other trademarks, would have to be considered more popular than much of the anonymously arranged and performed Muzak of our day.

According to Adorno, the need for trademarks in popular music arises from standardization: stereotyped forms dominate the larger structural units of strophes and stanzas, and formulas permeate the smaller parts. Restricted deviations from these brief formulas provide the music's appeal, so that the trademarks are transitory rather than enduring.[38] Much of Baroque and preclassical music and Middle Eastern court music, then, would be popular by virtue of their stock forms and semistandardized ornaments.

In accord with Adorno's view of popular music as a standardized product subject to variation, Howard Brown asserts that a popular piece

---

[32] Swanwick, *Popular Music,* p. 4.
[33] See Serge Denisoff and Mark H. Levine, "Brainwashing or Background Noise: The Popular Protest Song," in Denisoff and Richard A. Peterson, eds., *The Sounds of Social Change* (Chicago: Rand McNally, 1972), pp. 213–221.
[34] Adorno, "On Popular Music," p. 34.
[35] See also James E. Harmon, "Meaning in Rock Music: Notes Toward a Theory of Communication," *Popular Music and Society,* 7 (Fall 1972), pp. 18–32, on the importance of local events such as individual words for the popular listener's appreciation of a piece.
[36] Riesman, "Listening," p. 416, n. 4.
[37] Adorno, "On Popular Music," p. 26.
[38] *Ibid.,* pp. 21–24.

retains its germane characteristics despite considerable de___ns from the
original version.[39] Rearranging and improvisation play a la___ole in popular music. This range of variability is probably related to a___ transmission and to the audience's and performer's lack of concern a___ the composer's intentions.[40] In this regard, popular music resemble___aditional
folk music, which has also circulated in an oral tradition and ___ose composers have largely been forgotten. Groups such as Liverpool, ___ich imitate Beatles' arrangements note for note, are closer to classical per___mance
practices than to those that we usually associate with popular mus___

Finally, standardization seems to result in the conservative qua___y of
popular music discussed by James E. Harmon. Nothing is new; rath___,
everything is a slight variation on the old.[41] However, because styles do
change, Henry Glassie's distinction between truly conservative and nor-
mative cultural elements is applicable here: popular styles are seldom as
experimental as those of elite music or as static as those of folk music, but
they are always current.[42]

When writers talk of the historical perspective on popular music, they
generally concentrate on its ephemeral nature:[43] the issues of its texts grow
out of date, although it takes longer for the inherently musical qualities to
seem old-fashioned, because so much depends on standardization. However, a song may survive even when its original implications might no
longer be valid—as in the case of several political songs that have survived
as nursery rhymes.[44] And, although it is exceptional, there is a degree of
the ephemeral in classical music. The music of Ives and Scriabin—even of
J. S. Bach—suffered oblivion at one time or another.

There are at least twelve criteria by which one can determine the pop-

---

[39] Brown, *"Chanson Rustique,"* pp. 19–20.
[40] For an early comment on the relative anonymity of popular pieces, see Frank Sidgwick, *Popular Ballads of the Olden Time* (London: A. H. Butler, 1903–1912), I, xxi.
[41] Harmon, "Meaning in Rock Music."
[42] Henry Glassie, "Artifacts; Folk, Popular, Imaginary and Real," in Marshall Fishwick
and Ray B. Browne, eds., *Icons of Popular Culture* (Bowling Green, Ohio: Bowling
Green University Popular Press, 1970), pp. 103–122, especially pp. 104–105.
[43] See *International Conference on the Role and Place of Music in the Education of Youth
and Adults: Music in Education* (Paris: UNESCO, 1955), p. 190, for an extreme characterization of popular music as ephemeral.
[44] See Cantrick, "Blind Men and Elephant," p. 107, on the oversimplification of attributing an ephemeral quality to all popular music. Although Cantrick's examples of
popular songs that have survived in one form or another are suggestive, they represent
exceptions rather than the rule.

ularity of any
homogeneity
ers; (4) size
breadth an
mission; (
thetic obj
dardizati
these cha
appli

n music: (1) number of people involved; (2) combined heterogeneity of audience; (3) unpredictability of listeners; (4) size the business that markets the product; (5) efficiency (that is, eapness) of transmission; (6) aural rather than visual transmission; cular or entertainment function; (8) simplicity of the aesthetic obj (9) emphasis on performer rather than composer; (10) standardizati (11) range of variability; (12) degree of ephemerality. Each of these characteristics should be prefaced by the word *relative,* and each is applicable to all types of music.

This is not a neat definition that puts popular music in some convenient cubbyhole. Such compartmentalization is precisely what one should avoid with popular music, for one must consider its transmission, its relationship with its environment, and its creator.[45] What constitutes popular music changes in relation to the changing society of which it is a reflection; for example, distinctions based on social class that might prove valid for music of the *ancien régime* are inapplicable today.

When asked for a definition of folk music, blues musician Big Bill Broonzy apparently replied, "I guess all songs is folk songs: I never heard no horse sing 'em."[46] In a sense, one can extend Broonzy's answer: all music is popular music to a certain extent. If this seems to leave us where we started— that is, without a definition—two points should be considered. First, most music is either folk, or popular, or elite within a given cultural and historical context. Yet the context of a given music can change considerably. For instance, Playford's country dances were popular in the context of seventeenth-century English culture as we know it, but are now the preserve of an elite minority. In the same vein the popular ballads of the same period survive only in folk communities and in scholars' libraries. Similarly again, the opening measures of Beethoven's Fifth Symphony have become "A Fifth of Beethoven." The same piece can change position from time to time, but its position at any given time and within a given cultural grouping is relatively clear.[47]

The second point is that a highly flexible, relativistic definition is of

[45] Denisoff, "Content Analysis: The Achilles Heel of Popular Culture?," p. 460. See also Ray B. Browne's definition of popular culture as comprising "all those elements of life which are not narrowly intellectual or creatively elitist and which are generally though not necessarily disseminated through the mass media."

[46] "Folk Singing—Sibyl with Guitar," *Time* (November 23, 1962); quoted in Charles Keil, *Urban Blues* (Chicago: University of Chicago Press, 1966), p. 37.

[47] Nye, "Notes for an Introduction," p. 1,031, on the tendency of cultural items to cross borders.

great heuristic value. If one looks for popular features in music that is usually considered elite or folk (or vice versa), unexpected aspects of the subject matter emerge. An example of this procedure appears in Carl Belz's *Story of Rock,* where the view of rock music as a folk idiom is consistently maintained and leads to the discovery of aspects of the music that might otherwise have been overlooked.[48] One need not deny that a given genre is relatively popular in order to describe its folkloric or elitist features; on the other hand, to assert from the outset that a certain type of music is only folk, or popular, or elite would be to force it into a Procrustean bed.

Admittedly, the twelve criteria need refining. Certain of them, however, can be grouped together. For instance, relative simplicity and variability go hand in hand with the preeminently aural nature of popular music. An aural approach is compatible with the entertainment function of popular music, which in turn seems to encourage large numbers of people to patronize it or participate in it. Large audiences lead to unpredictability of taste, resulting in the ephemeral nature of popular music.

Depending on the type of popular music studied, some criteria will appear more important than others and will need to be expanded. For instance, relative homogeneity of audience would include taste, which is a salient variable. In this regard, Denisoff's definition of popular music depends not so much on the features of the music as on the fact that *"Popular music is the sum total of those taste units, social groups and musical genres which coalesce along certain taste and preference similarities in a given space and time.* These taste publics and genres are affected by a number of factors, predominantly age, accessibility, race, class and education."[49] Denisoff's definition of popular music is broad enough to embrace all types of popular music, past and present; it is also more manageable than our proposed model. That both viewpoints do not have precise limitations may to a certain extent appear dangerous: all music could be said to be popular to some degree because people play or listen to it or support it.

More important than the criteria themselves are the questions and hypotheses that might be investigated. Is it true that simpler music is orally transmitted more frequently than more complicated music and therefore tends to accumulate more variants? This certainly holds for folk music and for monophonic song of the past. Do standard forms tend to persist in the repertoire longer than more experimental forms? Is it easier to remember

---

[48] Belz, *Story of Rock.*
[49] Denisoff, *Solid Gold,* p. 39.

simple tunes in standard forms such as ABA and AABA (set strophically with or without refrain) than to recall more complicated or experimental ones?[50] How many listeners can recall the melodies of pieces written in the form of a palindrome? Is it surprising that most of the popular music of the past that has survived (relatively little, compared to what was sustained by wealthy patrons of the church or court) is either vocal or dance music, and that dance music by nature demands strongly defined and relatively simple rhythmic patterns? Do the types of music that function as entertainment tend to be ephemeral and topical?

As the aural nature of popular music appears to be a central criterion, perhaps a digression is in order here. Popular music lacks the reliance on the printed score that elite music has. Simplified sheet music arrangements exist largely to copyright words, melody, and chord changes, rather than for the performers. Compared with this, the classical musician today shows concern for the *Urtext* edition. Obviously this has not always been the case with elite music; for centuries the manuscript scores that survived used almost a musical shorthand to be elaborated on in performance, and only after the Baroque period did composers take care to indicate all their intentions precisely. Since then there have been exceptions—as in the case of Paganini, who cared relatively little about having his music published because he wanted to dazzle his audiences without giving away the secrets of his technical exploits. (He even cultivated a mystique of the diabolical: his appearance as some sort of devil figure is comparable to the gimmickry of some contemporary rock groups such as Kiss and the New York Dolls. Classical music, both in its star system and in its distancing of the performer from the audience, thus shares further features with popular music.)

The variability of popular music is also echoed in much elite music of the past. The nineteenth century especially saw a proliferation of transcriptions and arrangements of works that were popular among elite audiences. More people knew symphonies through four-hand pianoforte ver-

---

[50] Examples of songs with AABA form within the strophe include the sixteenth-century chorale "Was mein Gott will" by C. de Sermisy, arranged by J. S. Bach in the eighteenth century and appearing in the *Harvard Hymnal* in the twentieth century; "Sally in Our Alley" used in English ballad operas of the eighteenth century; Beethoven's setting of Schiller's "Ode to Joy" in the Ninth Symphony; George T. Root's Civil War song "Still upon the Field of Battle"; "The Marine's Hymn" based on music by Offenbach; Jimmy McHugh's Tin Pan Alley standard "I'm in the Mood for Love"; Duke Ellington's "Take the 'A' Train"; Lennon and McCartney's "Love Me Do."

sions than from hearing them in the concert hall. Catalogues list thousands of instrumental transcriptions of works for various combinations, in addition to sets of variations on, and potpourris of, favorite operatic themes. In this century listeners to orchestra, pianoforte, saxophone quartet, jazz vocalise, and Moog synthesizer versions of works by J. S. Bach still compare them, whether intuitively or deliberately, with the originals in a way in that most listeners of cover versions and arrangements of contemporary pop music do not. There is nothing sacred or fixed or superior about the original in popular music. Unlike the snobbism of elite music, part of the concern is for which rendition is most effective with audiences. Elvis's version of "Wooden Heart" would be considered superior to (and sell more records than) the original folk version.

Hypotheses about the aural nature of popular music could be extended. Often the harmonies of popular music are deemed simple and repetitious, as in three-chord rock-and-roll or in much nineteenth-century band music. Yet instrumentalists have often found unusual and colorful progressions that happen to lie well under the hands. Thus tactile as well as aural approaches serve to distinguish popular music from elite music.[51] Tablature is the preferred notational system for folk and popular guitarists, whereas classical performers play from staff notation. Renaissance lute tablature might also be considered in this context, as the lute was used to accompany secular entertainments.

Questions such as whether or not simple genres encourage more aural and less visual transmission and thus are more subject to variability can only be answered if similar types of music patronized by similar groups of people are considered. The range of hypotheses that might be investigated is as broad, culturally and historically, as the range of popular music, culturally and historically. The discipline *ethnomusicology* was once called *comparative musicology*. We are not advocating a special discipline called *comparative popular music studies.* However, if certain limitations are set up in order to compare genres within a given temporal and cultural milieu, refinements of the criteria suggested here would emerge and would suggest further studies.

Definitive studies already exist for certain genres of popular music, such as protest songs and urban blues. But where are the studies of songs inspired by similar literary rather than social themes, or of appearances of

---

[51] See Blacking, *How Musical Is Man?*, pp. 13–19, for a non-Western instrument that generates its own tune: the *mbira*.

the same or similar musical ideas in various genres or historical periods, or the social studies that provide evidence for the popularity of one genre over another within a given period, or studies on the role of improvisation in popular music?

Yes, our model resembles an octopus, and its tentacles will undoubtedly grow longer as society and its taste change and as the body of music to consider increases. There are several ways in which it can run into dangers or even strangle itself. Yet it will encourage interdisciplinary studies such as those advocated by Denisoff, Nye, Cantrick, and Cawelti rather than discourage them. Musicological and literary criteria are necessary to establish the degrees of complexity, standardization, and variability in different kinds of popular music. Evaluations of the functions of various genres and the makeup of their audiences require the expertise of social scientists. Far from being a futile exercise, defining popular music—or continually redefining it—promises to clarify many of the issues that confront us today.

Moment Form in Twentieth-Century Music*

Jonathan D. Kramer

Twentieth-century music is viewed as a movement away from continuity to a condition of moment form. Moment-form music "consists of a succession of self-contained sections that do not relate to each other in any functionally implicative manner," explains Jonathan Kramer.

Music has always relied upon continuity of compositional elements. Such continuity was itself an essential characteristic of music until challenges to triadic tonality appeared in 1910. However the idea of moment form was not formally analyzed until 1960 when Stockhausen wrote an article explaining his compositional procedures.

In this essay moments *are defined by the author as "self-contained entities, capable of standing on their own, yet in some sense belonging to the context of the composition." Referring to the works of La Monte Young, Igor Stravinsky, Olivier Messiaen, and Karlheinz Stockhausen, the author gives numerous examples of moment form in music and theory.*

* Reprinted from *The Musical Quarterly*, 64, no. 2 (April 1978), pp. 177–194. Part of the research for this essay was done at the School of Criticism and Theory at the University of California, Irvine, in 1976, under a grant from the National Endowment for the Humanities. This essay is extracted from a book-length study titled *Stravinsky and Darmstadt: A Study of Musical Time.*

Jonathan D. Kramer studied composition with Karlheinz Stockhausen, Roger Sessions, and Leon Kirchner. He has served as program annotator of the San Francisco Symphony Orchestra and is currently associate professor and director of electronic music at the College-Conservatory of Music of the University of Cincinnati. His compositions have been recorded widely and his theoretical articles have appeared in numerous journals.

Discontinuity is a profound musical experience. The unexpected is more striking, more meaningful, than the expected because it contains more information.[1] The high value I place on discontinuity is a personal prejudice (surely it is a culture-bound opinion—discontinuity is not, for example, what Indian music is about); the musical experiences that are most memorable are the magical moments when expectation is subverted, when complacency is destroyed, and when a new world opens. The power of discontinuity is most potent in tonal music, which is the music par excellence of motion and continuity. Harmonically defined goals and linear priorities for voice-leading provide norms of continuity against which discontinuities gain their power. Tonal discontinuities, when pushed to extremes, create new experiences of time—time that is not linear and not one-dimensional.[2]

The dissolution of triadic tonality after about 1910 removed the a priori of continuity. The early post-tonal composers were forced to extreme lengths in order to create contextually a sense of goal-directed motion, because continuity was no longer a given of the system. The solutions of Schönberg, Berg, and Bartók, for example, are often powerful and convincing, but they are nonetheless constructs. Once continuity became an option, other composers attempted to create music that minimized it. Such a composer is Stravinsky (as well as Ives); his *Symphonies of Wind Instruments* (composed in 1920) is an extreme expression of discontinuity.

The consequences of the deposing of musical continuity are enormous. The entire edifice of Western music had been built on the assumption that one event leads to another, that there is implication in music: Western composers have believed for centuries in the metaphor of musical motion. The decline of tonality contained the seeds of destruction of this myth; the temporal discontinuities of certain early twentieth-century works

---

[1] Leonard B. Meyer, "Meaning in Music and Information Theory," *Music, the Arts, and Ideas* (Chicago: University of Chicago Press, 1967), pp. 5–21.
[2] Jonathan D. Kramer, "Multiple and Non-Linear Time in Beethoven's Opus 135," *Perspectives of New Music,* 12, no. 2 (Spring–Summer 1973), pp. 122–145.

confirmed that motion is not absolute; by the 1950s some composers were able to write music that in no way assumed continuity or motion. (Many composers, of course, have continued to create continuous languages for their pieces, often with considerable effort. The struggle against the crumbling of continuity lends great strength to the most successful of these pieces. I have in mind such composers as Sessions, Carter, Gerhard, and Henze.) The crisis for the listener is extreme; it is no surprise that discontinuous contemporary music is often not understood by its audience. To remove continuity is to question the very meaning of time in our culture and hence of human existence. This questioning is going on all around us, and its strongest statement is found in contemporary art. By dealing with the resulting apparent chaos of this art, we are forced to understand our culture and thus to grow.[3]

I have written elsewhere about the correlation between discontinuous life-styles and contemporary art.[4] Since writing that article, I have found it increasingly difficult to experience musical continuity comfortably. There is something artificial, something otherworldly, about the idea that one musical event can actually progress to another. Even listening to the most innocently linear tonal music involves some sense of contradiction. The conflict is not in the music; the conflict is between how the music uses time and how a contemporary listener understands time. Recent music that deals with time in new ways has sought to solve this conflict, and in so doing, it has struck a nerve center in our culture. I refer to antiteleological music (for example, some works of John Cage), which presents static, endless Nows; to process pieces (for example, some works of Steve Reich), which move inexorably through well-defined gradual changes (Is this a desperate attempt to recapture continuity?); and to moment-form pieces (for example, some works of Karlheinz Stockhausen), in which the music consists of a succession of self-contained sections that do not relate to each other in any functionally implicative manner. However, composers of moment forms have not given up continuity entirely; that would be a fiction, because implication is still possible and the discomfort of continuity can be used positively. But implication is now localized because it has become but one possibility within a large universe; continuity is no longer part of musical syntax, but rather it is an optional procedure. It must be created or denied anew in each piece and thus it is the material and not the language of the music.

---

[3] Morse Peckham, *Man's Rage for Chaos* (New York: Schocken Books, 1967), pp. 25–40.
[4] Kramer, "Multiple and Non-Linear Time," pp. 132–141.

The concept of *moment form* was first articulated by Stockhausen in his 1960 article "Momentform."[5] This article is an explication of compositional procedures in *Kontakte* (composed in 1959–1960), Stockhausen's first self-conscious moment form. His ideas were expanded and slightly modified a year later in "Erfindung und Entdeckung."[6] The procedures that are crystallized in these two articles can be traced back through several earlier articles and compositions; but they derive ultimately from the practices of Debussy, Stravinsky, Webern (particularly in his variation movements), Varése, and, above all, Messiaen. The philosophical basis of Stockhausen's thought reflects aesthetic ideas implicit in twentieth-century visual, literary, and filmic arts as well. Stockhausen writes:

> Every present moment counts, as well as no moment at all; a given moment is not merely regarded as the consequence of the previous one and the prelude to the coming one, but as something individual, independent and centered in itself, capable of existing on its own. An instant does not need to be just a particle of measured duration. This concentration on the present moment—on every present moment—can make a vertical cut, as it were, across horizontal time perception, extending out to a timelessness I call eternity. This is not an eternity that begins at the end of time, but an eternity that is present in every moment. I am speaking about musical forms in which apparently no less is being undertaken than the explosion—yes—even more, the overcoming of the concept of duration.[7]

Because moment forms verticalize time, render every moment a Now, avoid functional implications between moments, and avoid climaxes, they are not beginning-middle-end forms. Although the piece must start for simple practical reasons, it may not begin; it must stop, but it may not end.

> I have made a strict difference between the concepts of "beginning" and "starting," "ending" and "stopping." When saying "beginning," I imply a process, something that rises and merges; when saying "ending," I am thinking about something that ends, ceases to sound, extinguishes. The contrary is true with the words "start" and "stop," which I combine with the concept of caesurae which delineate a duration, as a section, out of a continuum. Thus

---

[5] *Texte zur elektronischen und instrumentalen Musik*, 3 vols. (Cologne, 1963–1971), I: Aufsätze 1952–1962 zur Theorie des Komponierens (hereafter *Texte I*), pp. 189–210.
[6] "Invention and Discovery," *Texte I*, pp. 222–258, but especially pp. 250 ff.
[7] *Texte I*, p. 199, trans. Seppo Heikinheimo in his book, *The Electronic Music of Karlheinz Stockhausen* (Helsinki, 1972), pp. 120–121.

"beginning" and "ending" are appropriate to closed development forms which I have also referred to as dramatic forms, and "starting" and "stopping" are suitable for open moment forms. This is why I can speak about an infinite form even though a performance is limited in its duration because of practical reasons.[8]

A proper moment form will give the impression of starting in the middle of previously unheard music and it will break off without reaching any structural cadence, as if the music goes on, inaudibly, in some other space or time after the close of the performance. These ideals are difficult to realize compositionally, especially the start that does not sound like a beginning. Several compositions that for other reasons deserve to be considered moment forms do not achieve this ideal of an endless eternity.

The compositional idea of endlessness is richly suggestive. Stockhausen writes:

> For me, every attempt to bring a work to a close after a certain time becomes more and more forced and ridiculous. I am looking for ways of renouncing the composition of single works and—if possible—of working only forwards, and of working so "openly" that everything can now be included in the task in hand, at once transforming and being transformed by it; and the questing of others for autonomous works just seems to me so much clamour and vapour.[9]

In his recent book on Stockhausen, Robin Maconie writes in a more craft-oriented vein about the implications of closing off endless forms:

> Ending a permutational form is nearly always a matter of taste, not design. While the listener may be satisfied with a sensation of completion, the composer knows that though a series of permutations may eventually be exhausted, it does not automatically resolve. The ending's essential arbitrariness has to be disguised.[10]

This description applies to Stockhausen's earlier, nonmoment permutational forms (in this case the reference is to *Kontra-Punkte,* 1952–1953); the

---

[8] *Texte I,* p. 207, trans. Heikinheimo, pp. 121–122. Heikinheimo retains the original *Anfang, Beginn, Ende,* and *Schluss* for which I have substituted respectively "beginning," "starting," "ending," and "stopping."

[9] Quoted in Karl H. Wörner, *Stockhausen: Life and Work,* trans. Bill Hopkins (Berkeley: University of California Press, 1973), pp. 110–111.

[10] *The Works of Karlheinz Stockhausen* (London: Oxford University Press, 1976), pp. 143–144.

advent of moment form came about through the celebration, rather than the disguise, of the arbitrariness of closing a permutational form. By abruptly stopping rather than artificially ending, Stockhausen makes overt his reference to eternities. Maconie's description also applies aptly to Stravinsky's *Symphonies of Wind Instruments:* the C-major chorale that tonally closes this otherwise nontonal work is the means by which Stravinsky disguises the arbitrariness of ending a piece that has dealt with neither tonality nor foreground motion, but rather with permutation.

Moments are defined as self-contained entities, capable of standing on their own, yet in some sense belonging to the context of the composition. They may comprise a static entity, such as a harmony, that lasts throughout the moment, or they may contain a process that completes itself within the moment. If a static state or process defines the self-containment of the moment, the order of moments should not matter. That the order actually be arbitrary is an extreme requirement; in many moment-form pieces complete mobility[11] (or even any partial mobility) of form is avoided. Nonetheless, the order of moments must *appear* arbitrary for the work to conform to the spirit of moment form. This apparent arbitrariness even applies to the return of previous moments. Stockhausen forbids return in his articles, but it is to be found in *Kontakte*[12] and more overtly in his other works. There should be no reason that a previous moment cannot return, provided such a return is not prepared by a structural upbeat (this would render the return a recapitulatory goal of the previous moment, thereby destroying its self-containment). For, if no moment ever returned, the requirement of constant newness would in itself imply a kind of progression, because the listener could predict that the next moment would always differ from from all previous moments. And progression is impossible in a pure moment form.

If moments are defined by internal consistency, it follows that they can be of any length[13] (practically speaking, from a few seconds to several minutes). Thus proportions are indeed important in moment-form pieces. Global coherence cannot come from progression or even, in most cases, from order of succession. Neither can the statistical totality of moments necessarily be highly meaningful in those pieces that really do suggest themselves as fragments from an ongoing eternity. But the nature of moment form suggests proportional lengths of moments as the one remaining

---

[11] In a mobile form there are several possible orders of succession of the sections from which to choose for a given performance.
[12] Heikinheimo, *Electronic Music*, p. 208.
[13] *Ibid.*, p. 192.

principle of formal coherence. It is no surprise, therefore, that Stockhausen at times laid out his proportional schemes prior to deciding with what music to fill these empty forms. (Interestingly, his proportional layouts often depend on the Fibonacci series, which approximates both a golden ratio and a 3:2 ratio.[14]) Consider, for example, *Adieu,*[15] *Telemusik,*[16] *Klavierstück IX,*[17] *Mikrophonie II,*[18] or *Hinab-Hinauf.*[19] Whether or not a moment-form composition is formally satisfying depends to a large degree on the proportional lengths of moments.

Two questions thus arise:

1. Can durational proportions be perceived? It is safe to say that, when there is no large internal activity within sections, the objectively measurable durations correspond to the perceived proportions. However, I am reluctant to discuss relative proportional weight in two sections of a tonal piece, because those sections will undoubtedly be filled with various kinds of motion—middle-ground motion of voices, rates of harmonic change, varying degrees of harmonic stability, dissonance resolutions, the whole network of structural upbeats and downbeats. This complex of kineticism influences (one might say distorts, although surely in a positive way) our perception of time units. Furthermore, as I have shown,[20] tonal motion is not necessarily temporally linear at all. The whole question of proportions in tonal music *as perceived* is too complex to be dealt with by objective measurement. But if there is no motion, the problem evaporates. The measurable length of one static section relates to that of another.

2. Is musical staticism an experiential possibility? The archetypal static moment—a prolonged unchanged sound—is almost never really encountered. (La Monte Young's *Composition 1960,* no. 7, which prolongs B and F-sharp "for a long time," is a somewhat special—although not unique— reductio ad absurdum.) But would even this sound be experienced as static? How long must it go on before the listener gives up expectation of change and enters a static mode of perception? The answer seems to depend on the richness of the unchanging sound; experiments with students have suggested a threshold of static perception at somewhere be-

[14] Kramer, "The Fibonacci Series in Twentieth Century Music," *Journal of Music Theory,* 17, no. 1 (Spring 1973), pp. 114–118.
[15] *Ibid.,* pp. 125–126.
[16] Maconie, *Works,* p. 207.
[17] Kramer, "The Fibonacci Series," pp. 121–125.
[18] Jonathan Harvey, *The Music of Stockhausen: An Introduction* (Berkeley: University of California Press, 1975), p. 96.
[19] Maconie, *Works,* p. 263.
[20] Kramer, "Multiple and Non-Linear Time, *passim.*

tween two and three minutes. But this is a trivial case. More common are nondifferentiated yet subtly changing sound worlds: Iannis Xenakis's *Bohor I* is a prime example. We soon understand the very narrow limitations of its sound world and we stop expecting change beyond those limits. There is motion, but it somehow does not matter—it is not perceived as change. I am not saying just that changes are nondirectional—there are pieces that involve directional changes that do not really matter, so that the experience is static (*Les Moutons de Panurge*, 1969, by Frederic Rzewski is a good example). A large part of the answer has to do with the absence of phrases, of alterations of density, or of rhythmic events that might appear cadential. But I am also saying that it is a question of degree. The threshold of staticism depends on context: if there are large contrasts between sections, a higher degree of internal motion will not disturb the perceived staticism as it would in situations where the contrasts between sections are small. This threshold ultimately depends on the rate of flow of information. In a given context a certain amount of new information per unit time creates a static sensation, while more information produces motion.[21]

My assertion that staticism is relative to context is supported by stylistically eclectic music, such as William Bolcom's *Frescoes* (1971), some of the music of Peter Maxwell Davies, George Rochberg's Third Quartet (1972), or, to go back to the source, several works of Ives, such as the two piano sonatas, *Putnam's Camp,* or parts of the Fourth Symphony. In all of these pieces, there are tonal sections alongside nontonal passages. Tonality is heard as a possibility of the particular composition, but surely not as its universe of discourse. The result is that the tonal sections are rendered static by contrast with the various nontonal surroundings. Tonality is robbed of its inherent kineticism, but it retains its associations, so that we experience a moment of history frozen in the middle of a contemporary sound world. It is impossible to enter the world of tonality when it occurs in such a context; it is also impossible to experience tonality as a system, because we encounter it in a world that has different laws. Tonality becomes a foreign object, and thus one tonal passage in an eclectic work relates to another simply because the two are tonal, which can hardly be claimed of a truly tonal composition.[22]

If we grant that relative staticism can be experienced and that the

---

[21] For a very interesting and rather different discussion of musical staticism, see Thomas Clifton, "Some Comparisons Between Intuitive and Scientific Descriptions of Music," *Journal of Music Theory,* 19, no. 1 (Spring 1975), pp. 96–105.

[22] The Rochberg quartet, by the way, plays on the dual nature of tonality—system versus material—in a way that emphasizes my argument. The middle movement is a fif-

proportional lengths of static sections in a moment-form composition can be a perceptual force governing the global form, then it is meaningful to calculate actual durational proportions. To find consistent proportions in the music of Stockhausen or in that of some of his Darmstadt colleagues and disciples would hardly be surprising, given their predilection for establishing the lengths of sections as a first act of precomposition. However, there are interesting proportions in earlier moment-form constructions, most notably in what is probably the first moment-form piece ever composed: Stravinsky's *Symphonies of Wind Instruments*. In *Symphonies* the music is not really static, of course, but the major progressions take place between rather than within moments, and motivic consistency and tempo consistency support this self-containment of the moments, guaranteeing their relative staticism. The elegance of the temporal form is created by a system of proportions that functions only because the moments are self-contained. This system is not exact, and hence probably was not consciously derived, but within the limits of perception it does operate.[23] The system has to do mainly with the ratio 3:2. This proportion pertains to many important relationships. To demonstrate this, I have tabulated the durations of the moments and submoments of the first half of the piece.[24] (The bracketed numbers refer to rehearsal numbers in the printed score.)

---

teen-minute set of variations in A major. We almost forget, we try to forget, that the quartet lives in the expanded world of atonality-plus-tonality; the movement tries to lure us into the world of tonality-as-system, but the comfortable associations of tonality—continuity, progression, goal-direction, resolution—are never quite as comfortable as they would be in a real tonal quartet because the language of the variation movement can never completely erase that of the two earlier movements (a language that is to return in the final two movements). There is therefore a contradiction between movements 1, 2, 4, and 5, in which triadic tonality is used as musical material, and movement 3, in which it is the system, the bounded world, of the music. This provocative and haunting paradox lends the quartet its special appeal; the piece really probes the consequences of stylistically eclectic music. It seeks to reestablish tonality as the music of kineticism despite its tendency to behave statically in an atonal context.

[23] I know of no psychological data that would determine what degree of approximation of a given duration proportion of moments is tolerable. There is, however, a perhaps not irrelevant study by C. Douglas Creelman that demonstrates experimentally that a ten percent or less deviation of duration in two compared sounds is not perceived. Creelman uses durations only up to 2 seconds; the shortest moment in *Symphonies* is 3.61 seconds. Possibly the ten percent limit also applies to greater durations; I have kept my approximations all well within this limit. See C. D. Creelman, "Human Discrimination of Auditory Duration," *Journal of the Acoustical Society of America,* 34 (1962), pp. 582–593.

[24] Durations, shown in seconds, are calculated from the first attack of a section to the first attack of the next section. Stravinsky's metronome markings are the basis of the calculations. The fermata value is averaged from several recordings. The decision about what constitutes a moment or its subdivision, a submoment, in this music was made on the basis of degree of change in tempo, harmony, and melodic material, with supporting

MOMENTS:		SUBMOMENTS:	
[0]— [6]	49.58	[0]— [1]	7.92
[6]— [8]	12.22	[1]— [2]	12.92
[8]— [9]	7.78	[2]— [3]	5.21
[9]—[11]	14.17	[3]— [4]	3.54
[11]—[26]	80.00	[4]— [6]	20.00
[26]—[29]	22.50	[11]—[15]	26.11
[29]—[37]	35.28	[15]—[26]	53.89
[37]—[38]	9.58	[40]—[41]	8.61
[38]—[39]	7.50	[41]—[42]	7.49
[39]—[40]	10.83		
[40]—[42]	16.10		

A useful proportion with which to start this discussion is that between [15] — [26] and [29] — [37], as the latter moment is a condensation of the former (both go through the same material, except for certain key omissions in [29] — [37]); this condensation is in an interesting relationship because the ratio of the durations of these two sections approximates 3:2 = 1.50.

$$[15] — [26]:[29] — [37] = 1.53$$

Similarly the subdivision at [15] of the moment [11] — [26] approximates 3:2 because

$$[11] — [26]:[15] — [26] = 1.48$$

Consider also the internal subdivisions of the first moment, up to [6]:

$$[4] — [6]:[1] — [2] = 1.55 \text{ (similar submoments)}$$
$$[1] — [2]:[0] — [2] = 1.63 \text{ (adjacent submoments)}$$
$$[0] — [1]:[2] — [3] = 1.52 \text{ (similar submoments)}$$
$$[2] — [3]:[3] — [4] = 1.47 \text{ (adjacent submoments)}$$

A still more impressive utilization of the 3:2 proportion is between rather than within moments. Consider, first, the two types of moments first heard at the beginning and at [11]:

$$[11]—[26] : [0]— [6] = 1.61$$
$$[0]— [6] : [29]—[37] = 1.41$$
$$[29]—[37] : [26]—[29] = 1.57 \text{ (adjacent moments)}$$

---

data from timbre and texture. Only the first half of the piece is analyzed here; the second half uses a different proportional system, less economical and less elegant, but nonetheless appropriate to moment form.

$$[26]—[29] : [9]—[11] = 1.59 \text{ (similar moments)}$$
$$[9]—[11] : [37]—[38] = 1.48 \text{ (similar moments)}$$

These proportions include all instances of the opening fanfare moment except its final appearance in [39] — [40], which is in a 3:2 ratio with its surrounding moments.

$$[40] — [42]:[39] — [40] = 1.49 \text{ (adjacent moments)}$$
$$[39] — [40]:[38] — [39] = 1.44 \text{ (adjacent moments)}$$

The only moments in the first half of the piece not yet included in a 3:2 proportion are [6] — [8] and [8] — [9].

$$[6] — [8]:[8] — [9] = 1.57 \text{ (adjacent moments)}$$

Therefore every moment in the first half of the piece is involved in a meaningful 3:2 approximation (meaningful because of adjacency or because of similarity of moment type), and almost every moment containing submoments is partitioned according to 3:2. I find the pervasiveness of this ratio impressive. It accounts for the formal balance of the first half of the piece. I do not of course claim that we listen and say, "Aha! A 3:2 piece." But we surely do hear something consistent and elegant in the way the proportions relate, and the persistence of 3:2 explains such an impression.

Stravinsky clearly discovered something important and it received its purest statement in *Symphonies.* The techniques of this piece are both a culmination of Stravinsky's earlier methods and an anticipation of the radically nonlinear procedures of a younger generation, in whose music moments are truly independent both of each other and of an underlying progressive logic. Stravinsky subsequently did not abandon his explorations of proportioned staticism, any more than he abandoned radicalism after *Sacre,* as is often charged. The techniques achieved in *Symphonies* suggest the procedures, although not the materials, of neoclassicism. Stravinsky was now ready to embrace the music most deeply involved with kineticism. He was able to strip tonal sounds of their kinetic implications and to freeze them in motionless nonprogressions.[25] Still there is a background

---

[25] For an obvious demonstration of the process of neoclassic staticism, compare Stravinsky's 1956 "orchestration" of Bach's *Vom Himmel hoch* variations with the original. Bach's version is contrapuntally dense, yet the goal-directed harmonic motion is unmistakable. Stravinsky, considering triadic tonality as a violable possibility rather than the entire universe of musical discourse, was able to add new melodic lines, stylistically consistent in themselves yet obscuring the triadic orientation of the verticalities. The

motion at work—the neoclassic pieces have beginnings, middles, and ends, although these gestures are created by other than tonal-triadic means. The music of neoclassicism is like that of *Symphonies* with an added complexity: the material implies a motion that never (or at least rarely) occurs *on its own level*. There is irony in this music: the tonal materials suggest movement, but they do not move; in the background the pieces do move, but by nontonal means.

Therefore Stravinsky's move into neoclassicism was in no way a retreat from his temporal explorations. He may have adopted the outlines of forms that originally dealt with kineticism, but he often used them as assemblages of static, or at least self-contained, sections. In his use of sonata form, for example, he transformed the traditional kinetic sections into moments. Because of the reference to classical style, the resulting music is less aggressively discontinuous on the surface than *Symphonies*. But the sections do tend to be defined by bounded processes or by static harmonies. To take one of many possible examples, consider the first movement of the Sonata for Two Pianos (1943–1944), an unjustly neglected work. Here we find Stravinsky's typical verticalizing of tonal functions (the opening, for example, superimposes lines simultaneously outlining I and V^7 chords), with the result that the harmony is a static complex (such writing used to be called pandiatonic). The texture remains as constant as the harmony, until the bridge section begins abruptly. This section is a new static harmonic area, arriving with minimal preparation; its texture is also new and unprepared. Just as suddenly, the second theme arrives, which is static by virtue of ostinato figures. The exposition section, then, is really a series of three apparently unrelated and unconnected moments (there are really half-hidden relationships, as there are in *Symphonies*). The development section is also a series of moments (of lesser duration so that the increased rate of succession of static moments functions analogously to the increased harmonic rhythm of the classical sonata's development), as is the recapitulation. The gentle nature of this movement precludes extreme discontinuities like those of *Symphonies,* but it is nonetheless a product of the same time consciousness.

The composers working in Darmstadt in the late 1950s did not realize

---

new lines, it would seem, should increase the polyphonic density and thus complicate the music, but in fact they almost freeze the harmonies and thereby simplify the situation. With harmonic direction no longer a prime factor, there is actually less information. Similar additions are made to the originals (thought to be by Pergolesi) in *Pulcinella*, Stravinsky's first neoclassic effort, composed just prior to *Symphonies.*

that Stravinsky's neoclassic music continued the striking temporal achievements of his Russian period. The misguided scorn that they heaped upon Stravinsky fortunately had no impact on either his or their music. The Darmstadt musicians did not even realize the importance of the overtly experimental *Symphonies* to their aesthetic. Their writings praise *Sacre* as the source of permutational and cellular rhythms, yet they turn to Debussy's *Jeux* (written in 1912) as the source of moment form. This work, in contrast to *Symphonies,* was seminal to the Darmstadt composers. Stockhausen pays homage to it in "Von Webern zu Debussy (Bemerkungen zur statischen Form)";[26] Herbert Eimert analyzes it in "Debussy's *Jeux*";[27] Boulez conducts it; and references to it are scattered throughout the Darmstadt literature.

The often fragmentary nature of the material, the frequent changes of tempo, the nondevelopmental form, the transformation of material, the discontinuities—these were the appealing features of *Jeux.* But it is really not a moment-form piece. It is highly sectionalized, to be sure, but the sections are as often in motion toward other sections as they are static. Because motion is usually to or from some place not immediately heard, the piece works as a nonlinear progression. The sections are not self-contained, because they point toward goals (or come from sources) not within their boundaries; that these goals (or origins) do not appear in adjacent sections, and may not appear at all in the piece, renders the temporal world of *Jeux* complex and fascinating. But to move into the realm of moment forms was another huge step, one that Debussy never took. This development was taken up by Stravinsky and later by Messiaen.

Olivier Messiaen began his compositional maturity under the influence of Stravinsky and Debussy, and he eventually wrote music of a sufficiently arresting originality to become the father figure of the Darmstadt school. His music, then, is a link, perhaps an all too convenient link, between early Stravinsky and the Stockhausen circle.

In his early years Messiaen toyed with the sonata but, like the neoclassic Stravinsky, he approached the form as a static object rather than as a self-motivating process. As Robert Sherlaw Johnson says in his comprehensive book on Messiaen, "He is thinking of the sonata sectionally rather than organically, and, as a result, the forms he derives from it have very

---

[26] *Texte I,* pp. 75–85.
[27] *Die Reihe* (1959), trans. Leo Black (1961), V, pp. 3–20.

little to do with its real spirit."[28] Later on, his sectionalized forms became
more organically coherent.

> In his later works the musical thought often *demands* a sectional treatment.
> The stark juxtaposition of ideas in earlier works eventually becomes sophisti-
> cated in the '40s with superimposition as well as juxtaposition being involved.
> The eventual outcome is a refined collage structure such as used in *Couleurs*
> *de la Cité céleste* [1963], where not only melody and harmony but also rhythm
> and timbre interact to form the total collage.[29]

These sectionalized collages (in our terminology, moment forms) suggest a
species of musical time quite different from that of classical tonality:

> He arrives at a position which is analogous to Eastern music because of his
> attitude to harmony as a static element. A sense of time, marked by an evolv-
> ing texture, is fundamental to Bach and Beethoven, but it has always been
> Messiaen's aim to suspend the sense of time in music (except in those works
> which are based on birdsong in relation to nature), in order to express the
> idea of the "eternal"—in which time does not exist—as distinct from the tem-
> poral.[30]

Embryonic moment forms, adulterated by occasional goal-directed passages but becoming progressively more pure, can be heard in such pieces as
L'Ascension (1931–1935), *Visions de l'Amen* (1943), *Turangalîla-Symphonie*
(1946–1948), and *Cantéjodayâ* (1948).

Written in 1960, virtually concurrently with Stockhausen's *Kontakte,*
Messiaen's *Chronocromie* is the work in which the composer most fully
confronts moment form. Gone are the recapitulations, cadences, and structural downbeats of the earlier pieces. Moments stop rather than conclude,
and they are juxtaposed without mediating transition. They are defined by
a rich palette of textures, instrumental colors, compositional techniques,
and in addition the use or avoidance of various birdcalls. Proportions are
important in the form, as are the placement of particularly long and especially short moments. And the placement of returns contributes to the
overall coherence, although there is no feeling of prepared recapitulation.
The formal division into movements is minimal, as they are played without
pause and some movements contain but one moment, while others contain
many.

---

[28] *Messiaen* (Berkeley: University of California Press, 1975), pp. 22–23.
[29] *Ibid.,* p. 24.
[30] *Ibid.,* p. 183.

The first movement includes several moments; some are only a few seconds in length, but none is long. The second movement is internally undifferentiated and it is static. Despite its greater duration (eighty-six seconds), it, too, is a moment. The placement of the long moment after a series of shorter ones is satisfying. (This is one of the first pieces in which Messiaen uses metronome markings, indicating perhaps a greater sensitivity to the importance of exact proportions in an extended moment form.)

The longest moment (the sixth movement) comes late in the composition and thereby serves as the major focal point. Although theoretically a moment form is antithetical to the idea of climax, in practice composers gave up the dramatic curve with reluctance.[31] We find remnants of it here in the placement of this weightiest moment at the traditional climax point; we find it also in *Symphonies,* whose climax occurs in [46] — [56]. It remained for the younger generation to write totally antidramatic music that is faithful to the moment-form idea. The nonclimactic nature of a piece like Stockhausen's *Momente* (1960–1972), for example, makes difficult listening for someone brought up on art that respects the dramatic curve. Of course the dramatic curve is peculiar to Western art; it is not a universal of mankind, as Eastern music readily demonstrates.[32] Hence we should not lament its passing; its time has come and gone. Still, our expectation of finding a dramatic curve is strong, and listening to a pure moment form requires an effort, a commitment, a belief. This weighty three-minute and thirty-six-second moment in *Chronocromie* is a dense texture of birdsongs, with little internal differentiation of the texture; there are no phrases (phrase structure, which had proven to be the most tenacious relic of tonality, is overthrown), and the moment finally breaks off rather than comes to any conclusion. It is a most obvious self-contained moment, and quite static; an undifferentiated block whose main formal significance is its duration and its placement within the whole.

The close of *Chronocromie* is a rather short moment that does not cadence but rather drops away: an open ending, fully appropriate to a moment form, although on the background level there are ample reasons to conclude with this moment—reasons having to do with pacing of moment returns and placement of moment durations within the span of the piece.

---

[31] For a discussion of the dramatic curve in music and its demise in the twentieth century, see Barney Childs, "Time and Music: a Composer's View," *Perspectives of New Music,* 15, no. 2 (Spring–Summer 1977).

[32] For an interesting discussion of temporality in certain non-Western music, see Richard Saylor, "The South Asian Conception of Time and Its Influence on Contemporary Western Composition," a paper read to the American Society of University Composers, Boston, *Proceedings of the Annual Conferences,* February 29, 1976.

The power of moment forms such as Messiaen's *Chronocromie* or Stockhausen's *Mixtur* (1964) comes from the power of discontinuity, which is discussed at the beginning of this essay. Extreme discontinuities became readily available with the advent of the tape recorder. A simple splice can transport the listener instantaneously from one sound world to another. Discontinuity is heightened by the unpredictability of precisely when a splice might occur or into what new world it might send the listener. Not all tape music, of course, avails itself of the potency of extreme discontinuity, but the possibility is there to be used or not used. Stockhausen must surely have realized the implications for musical form of the new technology when he was working in the *musique concrète* studio in Paris in 1952 and in the electronic studio in Cologne in 1953–1956.[33] A composer's involvement with electronics tends to influence any subsequent return to purely instrumental media. Although Stockhausen's early tape pieces (*Etüde, Studie I, Studie II,* and *Gesang der Jünglinge*) are not cast in moment form, *Kontakte* (for tape with or without instruments) was the work that opened the door for such further explorations in moment form as *Carré* (written simultaneously with *Kontakte*), *Momente, Mikrophonie I* (1964), and *Mixtur*—none of which uses tape.

Of course, the splice did not originate with the invention of the tape recorder. The technology of the film is intimately linked with new time conceptions. According to art historian Arnold Hauser,

> the agreement between the technical methods of the film and the characteristics of the new concept of time is so complete that one has the feeling that the time categories of modern art have arisen from the spirit of cinematic form, and one is inclined to consider the film itself as the stylistically most representative . . . genre of contemporary art. . . . In the temporal medium of a film we move in a way that is otherwise peculiar to space, completely free to choose our direction, proceeding from one phase of time into another, just as one goes from one room to another, disconnecting the individual stages in the development of events and regrouping them, generally speaking, according to the principles of spatial order. In brief, time here loses, on the one hand, its irreversible direction. It can be brought to a standstill: in close-ups; reversed: in flash-backs; repeated: in recollections; and skipped across: in visions of the future. Concurrent, simultaneous events can be shown successively, and temporally disjunct events simultaneously—by double-exposure and alternation;

---

[33]Maconie, *Works,* pp. 30–40.

the earlier can appear later, the later before its time. This cinematic conception of time has a thoroughly subjective and apparently irregular character compared with the empirical and the dramatic conception of the same medium.[34]

The language and conventions of the film depend on the splice, just as the discontinuities of tape music are creations of the razor blade. The profound temporal experience caused by the simple act of splicing deeply altered the consciousness of all composers, not only those who work with tape. And the power of the film splice—juxtaposing standstills, flashbacks, flash-forwards, successive simultaneities, double exposures—scrambles the hitherto orderly and inviolable succession of time. Time is thus redefined as a malleable Now, as an arbitrary succession of moments. This new concept, born of technology, reverberated in all art forms during this century. Thus Stravinsky's 1920 masterpiece is not an isolated experiment; he was responding to new concepts of time that were deeply affecting the meaning of human existence, at least in Western Europe. To what extent other composers who came to compose moment forms were influenced by Stravinsky's radical statement hardly matters. They, too, were reacting to increasingly potent new currents in Western thought. New concepts of musical time were well enough assimilated to have been articulated verbally by 1960, the year of Stockhausen's first article on moment form. His polemical stance may sound as if he is proposing an original musical form, but he is in fact providing a rational framework within which to deal with a species of musical time that had been practiced for some forty years. Stockhausen makes clear, as do the most successful moment-form compositions, that that species of time deals with the isolated moment as an eternal Now. As Arnold Hauser has aptly said:

> The time experience of the present age consists above all in an awareness of the moment in which we find ourselves: in an awareness of the present. Everything topical, contemporary, bound together in the present moment is of special significance and value to the man of today, and, filled with this idea, the mere fact of simultaneity acquires new meaning in his eyes. . . . Is one not in every moment of one's life the same child or the same invalid or the same lonely stranger with the same wakeful, sensitive, unappeased nerves? Is one not in every situation of life the person capable of experiencing

---

[34] *The Social History of Art,* 4 vols., trans. Stanley Godman (New York: Vintage Books, 1958), IV, pp. 239, 241.

this and that, who possesses, in the recurring features of his experience, the one protection against the passage of time? Do not all our experiences take place as it were at the same time? And is this simultaneity not really the negation of time? And this negation, is it not a struggle for the recovery of that inwardness of which physical space and time deprive us?[35]

[35] *Ibid.,* pp. 243, 245.

The Music of Futurism: Concerts and Polemics*

Rodney J. Payton

Very often contemporary musical compositions appear surprisingly similar to works composed during the early years of this century by Dadaists, Constructivists, Futurists, and Surrealists. This is not to say that such works were created with the same intentions or for the same purposes. The similarities in sound may betray enormous differences in aesthetic. Therefore it seems especially important to investigate the intentions of the early experimentalists.

In general, works by musicians associated with the early twentieth-century schools do, in many ways, anticipate contemporary developments. The Futurists seemed particularly active, although as Rodney Payton points out, much work that was labeled "futurist" by critics was not, in fact, truly linked to Futurism. In this essay the compositions and manifestoes of Luigi Russolo, and Francesco Balilla Pratella are placed in the Futurist context, and the organizing role of Filippo Tommaso Marinetti, the central Futurist artist, is discussed.

Rodney Payton is a graduate of the University of Chicago, where he studied in The Committee on History of Culture. He is associate professor of liberal studies at Western Washington University.

* Reprinted from *The Musical Quarterly*, 62, no. 1 (January 1976), pp. 25–45.

For a number of years before World War I and in the period immediately after, the Futurist movement both entertained and amazed the European intellectual community. Yet unaccountably, although Futurism is a mine of art and polemics rich in cultural insights into the European scene, the history of the movement failed to capture the imagination of either the general art public or the scholarly community in America until very recently. With The Museum of Modern Art show in 1961, however, the situation began to improve, and now we possess much information about the Futurist painters. But the movement was more than painters. It was originally a literary group, and its poetic and dramatic experiments foreshadowed much that is fashionable today in literature. Even less known is the musical side of the movement, yet the Futurists were just as daring in music as they were in the visual arts and literature. During the years 1911–1912 the two Futurist musicians, Francesco Balilla Pratella and Luigi Russolo, published their radical manifestoes, gave many concerts, and invented a number of new instruments that are spiritual ancestors to the very latest synthesizers. Today Pratella and Russolo are largely forgotten; a few journal articles, an occasional passing reference, are all they have received from scholarship. They deserve better. In their own time their experiments were no less an affront to contemporary sensibility than *Le Sacre du Printemps,* and until their efforts are recognized and evaluated we cannot say we have an adequate picture of the early twentieth century or understand how deep are the roots of some of our contemporary artistic expression.

William W. Austin, in *Music in the Twentieth Century,* makes a comment that reflects the general state of scholarship as it relates to Futurist music:

> The art of noises, now called "bruitisme," was introduced by Marinetti into the group of painters and poets that rallied in 1916 with the slogan "Dada" whence its fame reëchoed in histories and dictionaries. No composers were directly associated with Dada. The terms "futurism" and "Dadaism" have been loosely applied to composers as staid as Richard Strauss. They are seldom illuminating in talk about music.[1]

Now Futurism and Dadaism were actually separate things. Dadaism did indeed originate in 1916, in Switzerland, and Futurism dates from 1909 in

---

[1] William W. Austin, *Music in the Twentieth Century* (New York: W. W. Norton, 1966), p. 30.

Italy, where Marinetti was its founder. But in 1916 the Futurist leader, an ardent patriot who was then an officer in the Italian army, had other concerns than the international group of war resisters who called themselves "dada." As for the term *Futurism,* it may seem to lack usefulness because, rather than being used to refer to the efforts of the musicians of the Italian movement, Pratella and Russolo, it has, as Mr. Austin reports, often been used as a catchall term for almost any avant-garde effort.

It would appear that quite early in the course of the movement, even before Russolo published his 1913 manifesto, the term *Futurist,* as it defines a musical movement, was used in English to describe almost any composer whose works could be considered "difficult." Thus, in May 1912 the *Literary Digest* printed "Futurists Breaking Out in Music," by Thomas J. Gerrard. This title refers not to the Italians, but to a Schönberg concert given in London.[2] The article sets the tone for most popular commentary throughout the 1920s, when the term was still often used; writers of that decade refer with monotonous regularity to the Futurism of Schönberg, Stravinsky, Scriabin, or Ornstein.

In *The Musical Quarterly* of January 1916 the term *Futurism* appears. "Futurism: A Series of Negatives," by Nicholas C. Gatty, disparages the destruction of traditional musical values by "modern" composers, but does not refer to any individuals by name. The article concludes with the following paragraph:

> On the face of it, their productions are little more than studies in musical noises, and it is perhaps quite in keeping with the inner logic of things that they do not adapt their ideas for musical instruments but seek to obtain more stimulating effects with specially constructed machines.[3]

This reference might indicate that Gatty knew of Russolo's *intonarumori* concert of 1913–1914 or had at least read of his experimental instruments. There is no way to be sure of this, of course, but it is difficult to imagine to what else he is referring (unless it is to the widely publicized attempts of Dr. Thaddeus Cahill to introduce his "Dynamophone" to the city of New York in 1906).[4]

---

[2] Thomas J. Gerrard, "Futurists Breaking Out in Music," *Literary Digest* (May 28, 1912), p. 517.

[3] Nicholas C. Gatty, "Futurism: A Series of Negatives," *The Musical Quarterly*, 2 (1916), p. 12.

[4] Ray Baker, "New Music for an Old World," *McClure's Magazine* (May–October 1906), p. 291. Yet it seems unlikely that Dr. Cahill's machine would have offended Gatty's sensibilities, since it was an experiment in the mechanical reproduction of traditional music.

After the article in 1916 there is one other mention of Futurist music in the pages of *The Musical Quarterly*. This occurs in a 1920 article by Georges Jean-Aubry, who was then the editor of the *Chesterian*. Pratella's *Musica Futurista per Orchestra,* performed in 1913, and his current composition, *L'Aviatore Dro,* are there deemed worthy of further study.[5]

The *Chesterian* itself sometimes carried articles by Italian composers and critics. Two articles in the December 1920 issue point, each in its own way, to the passing of musical Futurism, properly defined. "A Letter from Italy," by Guido M. Gatti, mentions Pratella's opera *L'Aviatore Dro* favorably but calls Pratella a less attractive composer than the others mentioned in the article.[6] The other article, "Some Reasons Why a Futurist May Admire Rossini," by Alfredo Casella, is an explanation of why a modern composer may admire the past. The word *Futurist* in the title refers not to the original group but to Casella himself. By 1920 evidently the term *Futurist* had acquired somewhat different connotations even in Italy.[7]

One possible reason that the title *Futurist* should have escaped the Italian group, in the field of music at least, is that Pratella's and Russolo's primarily nationalistic concerns had kept the two from being generally recognized by an international public. But how had composers themselves reacted to the Futurist stimulus? The trail begins with the publication of Busoni's essay "Futurism in Music" in *Pan* in September 1912. Busoni quotes Pratella's 1912 musical manifesto and reacts favorably to it: "That is right. It pleases me, and I stood on this side long ago, if only as a theorist." He concludes by wondering if the Futurists have the talent for the task.[8] Because of the resistance of conservative circles to the radical fringe, this article created some resentment. In 1917 the Austrian Hans Pfitzner published his *Futuristengefahr,* which accused Busoni of *being* a Futurist.[9] Busoni was moved to defend himself.[10]

Other composers were at least aware of the Futurists, and some have left their comments and opinions. One of these, Igor Stravinsky, who heard the music of Russolo and Pratella in 1915, recalled the encounter some forty years later:

---

[5] G. Jean-Aubry, "The New Italy," *The Musical Quarterly,* 6 (1920), p. 54.
[6] Guido M. Gatti, "A Letter from Italy," *Chesterian* (December 1920), p. 373.
[7] Alfredo Casella, "Some Reasons Why a Futurist May Admire Rossini," *Chesterian* (December 1920), p. 321.
[8] Ferruccio Busoni, *The Essence of Music and Other Papers,* trans. Rosamond Ley (London, 1957), p. 28.
[9] Hans Pfitzner, *Futuristengefahr, bei Gelegenheit von Busoni's Ästhetik* (3rd ed.; Leipzig, 1921).
[10] Busoni, *Essence of Music,* p. 28.

On one of my Milanese visits Marinetti and Russolo, a genial quiet man but with wild hair and beard, and Pratella, another noisemaker, put me through a demonstration of their "futurist music." Five phonographs standing on five tables in a large and otherwise empty room emitted digestive noises, static, etc., remarkably like the *musique concrète* of seven or eight years ago (so perhaps they were futurists after all; or perhaps futurisms aren't progressive enough). I pretended to be enthusiastic and told them that sets of five phonographs with such music, mass produced, would surely sell like Steinway Grand Pianos.[11]

Francesco Cangiullo, a poet associated with the movement, remembered the incident in greater and somewhat different detail.[12]

That evening in the salon of Marinetti—Casa rossa, Corso Venezia, Milan—there was a meeting of the Futurist musicians, all of whom were present: Luigi Russolo, Balilla Pratella, Igor Stravinsky (who came especially from Lucerne), Prokofiev, Diaghilev (director of those Russian ballets that had become a choreographic epidemic), Massine (first ballerino), an exceptional Slavic pianist whose name construe who can, made up of difficult consonants, neither known nor written nor pronounced; there entered Boccioni, Carrà, the brother of Russolo, Ugo Piatti, the Visconti di Modrone, Buzzi, the female Bohemian painter Rongesca Zotkova (neither is this name a joke), and, naturally, the dynamic owner of the house, and the Neapolitan undersigned. Who else . . . Decio Cinti. I do not remember others.

The composer of *L'Aviatore Dro,* Balilla Pratella, stout, heavy though still young, with a top hat with a large brim and a pendant on a chain, had come to Milan—a city that he did not take very well—from his Lugo di Romagna, looking very bored, like a farmer who had descended to market and made bad deals. Actually, though, for a plate of mutton *alla livornese* he was always willing to go from Lugo to Livorno.

On the other hand, Diaghilev. This person arrived from Paris, by express, very fresh, rosy, with powdered face, but very modernly dressed; unfortunately, he looked like an eccentrically dressed vertical hippopotamus. In his buttonhole he had an enormous chrysanthemum, unraveled and drooping like the mane of Leoncavallo; his head of hair was parted in the middle, the mop well combed, half white and half black, similar to a hard piece of lemon and coffee. The specimen had a very short turned-up nose, with out-looking nostrils, the teeth white as ivory, the upper jaw receding, the protruding lower jaw nearly trapping two little mustaches, colored with velvety tint; his snob-

---

[11] Igor Stravinsky with Robert Craft, *Conversations with Igor Stravinsky* (London, 1958), p. 93.
[12] According to Boris Kochno, this incident took place in the fall of 1914. See Boris Kochno, *Diaghilev and the Ballets Russes,* trans. Adrienne Fouke (New York: Harper & Row, 1970), p. 101.

bish and decadent mask was completed with a great monocle encircled with black tortoise shell; the pupils were little, and they always met at an angle, in ambush, under the long eyelids which were always lowered. They love to look so, but never looked at a woman; is it clear? Stravinsky is slightly built, blondish, and near-sighted. In compensation he has a nose of great caliber that supports the bicycle of his eyes. . . . Ugo Piatti, docile mechanic, collaborator with Russolo in the construction of the *intonarumori*, was doomed to accept with humility the frequent rebukes of the hysterical inventor who could have used some opposition. . . .

. . . the major attraction was Luigi Russolo with his twenty *intonarumori*. Stravinsky wanted to have an exact idea of these bizarre new instruments and, possibly, insert two or three in the already diabolic scores of his ballets. Diaghilev, however, wanted to present all twenty at Paris in a clamorous concert. He had also come to hear the compositions of Pratella. . . .

On the contrary, the swan of Romagna arrived at Milan expecting to find hospitality or, in the worst hypothesis, to not sound a note! Not even a demisemiquaver! Except, man proposes, God disposes, he was dragged to the piano by the hair and forced to sing and play his music with a mouth that had had aspirations toward a fish soup, with his fingers similar to ten sausages that he would more willingly have thrown in the frying pan in order to eat them rather than place them on the piano.

. . . eight or nine *intonarumori*, peaceful quadrupeds expecting a sign from their trainer who nervously waited for conversation to die down. This happened, and it was then that Russolo turned a magic crank.

A "crackler" crackled with a thousand sparkles like a fiery torrent. Stravinsky gushed, emitting a syllable of crazy joy, leaped up from the couch of which he seemed a spring. Then a "rustler" rustled like petticoats of winter silk, like leaves of April, like sea rending summer. The frenzied composer tried to find on the piano that prodigious onomatopoeic sound, in vain proved the semitones of his avid digits while the ballerino moved the legs of his craft.

These gentlemen remained enchanted and called the new instruments the most original orchestral discovery.[13]

Thus musical Futurism knew, and was known by, composers from all of Europe. In general, its history followed the lines of development of Futurism itself, thanks to the magnificent organizing abilities of the *caposcuola* Filippo Tommaso Marinetti (1876–1944). Officially, Futurist music celebrated the new urban environment with its speed, noises, and machines. The actual course of musical Futurism can be charted by studying its two composers' different responses to this idea. Luigi Russolo (1885–1947) was a true believer in this aesthetic. Francesco Balilla Pratella

---

[13] Francesco Cangiullo, *Le Serate Futuriste* (Milan, 1961), p. 245.

(1880–1955), on the other hand, while subordinating himself for a time to these ideals, retained his own original personality and lived out an artistic history that goes beyond that of Futurism. Born at Lugo di Romagna, Pratella remained an enthusiastic proponent of Romagnese culture all his life—notwithstanding his Futurist period.[14] By 1909, when Pratella was twenty-nine, he had written two operas on traditional Romagnese themes, *Lilia* and *La Sina d'Vargöun,* both of which won prizes in competitions and were produced. *La Sina,* in particular, attained some critical notice, and it was the work that attracted Marinetti's attention. Aleco Toni, writing in *Rivista Musicale Italiana,* said of the work:

> *La Sina d'Vargöun—scene della Romagna bassa, per la musica* is what Pratella has called his work. It is animated by the breath of folklore which breathes out of every scene, in the constructive element of poetry, in the faithfully introduced music of popular songs. The color of the environment has a truly living part, a major part, in the explication of the drama. Every scene is a realistic reconstruction of the life of Romagna. Customs and costumes come to life. Every sentimental manifestation of the characters has its determinant in the popular soul of the region. The drama, thus, is *localizzato* and does not draw on the universal motives of life.[15]

Pratella met Marinetti on August 20, 1910, at Imola during a concert in which some of Pratella's music was played.[16] By that time, of course, *Il*

---

[14] Information about Pratella's early life is to be found in Alba Ghigi, *F. B. Pratella* (Ravenna, 1930). This seems, in the section about Pratella's youth, to be an expanded version of Alfredo Grilli, "La Musica di un Giovane Romagnolo," *La Romagna,* 6, fas. 7, ser. 3 (June 1909), which was extracted and reprinted. The copy of this reprint in the collection of The New York Public Library bears Pratella's autograph, and it is possible he paid for the reprinting. Also useful are: Claudio Marabini, "Per una Storia del Futurismo: Balilla Pratella, Music e Futurismo," *Nuova antologia,* 98 (1963), and Pratella's own *Autobiografia.* The Marabini article appeared eight years before the *Autobiografia* and served as the basis for my research. Having seen the *Autobiografia,* I have rechecked this research, and I shall give parallel citations to the *Autobiografia* whenever I cite Pratella from the Marabini article: for example, for p. 86 in Marabini, "Per una Storia," cf. F. Balilla Pratella, *Autobiografia* (Milan, 1971), p. 140. The *Autobiografia* was written in 1953, but not published until 1971, when it was released by Pratella's daughters Ala and Eda. Marabini evidently saw the work in manuscript, for he refers to it as "Sinora rigorosamente inedite." Marabini, "Per una Storia," p. 68.

[15] Aleco Toni, " 'La Sina d'Vargöun' di F. B. Pratella," *Rivista Musicale Italiana,* 17 (1910), p. 196. The nationalism that Toni admired in Pratella's work, indeed, that moved him to praise it in spite of defects, is one of the strongest characteristics of music in the early days of this century. What Toni calls drama *localizzato* is part of the same stream that is the source of Bartók's attempts at Hungarian national opera in *Duke Bluebeard's Castle* (1911), of Stravinsky's *Firebird* (1910), and even of Rimsky-Korsakov's *Golden Cockerel* (1907).

[16] Marabini, "Per una Storia," p. 67 (cf. *Autobiografia,* p. 100).

Primo Manifesto del Futurismo, Il Manifesto della Pittura Futurista, and *Il Manifesto Technico della Pittura Futurista* had already been published, and to judge from the tone of these documents, all inspired by Marinetti, the subject of the opera certainly would not have been attractive to the Futurists. (In fact there is one conclusion of the *Manifesto Technico* that would seem to label *La Sina's* plot as definitely *passatista:* "Against the nude in painting, as nauseous and as tedious as adultery in literature.)[17] However, Pratella's reforming zeal made him attractive to the Futurists and the Futurists attractive to him. In his memoirs Pratella says: "The condition of my art at that time and my particular state of mind, so to say, predisposed my spirit to abandon itself to the persuasive fascination of promises and salutary liberation which the ideas and practical actions of the Marinetti group emitted."[18] The actual introduction of Marinetti and Pratella was accomplished by Luigi Donati, a journalist of Oriani, who knew both Marinetti and Pratella, the latter because of the success of *La Sina.* The conversation was evidently amiable. Pratella records in his memoirs: "From then on we were faithful friends, and so we have remained. We reciprocally tolerate one another, notwithstanding the changed times and events and the evolution of ideas and principles."[19]

More immediate evidence of the agreement between the two can be ascertained from the fact that by September 28 Pratella's *Il Manifesto dei Musicisti Futuristi* was in Marinetti's hand. Marinetti immediately put his editorial oar in:

> I have received your kind letter and your beautiful proclamation. I am enthusiastic, I will work on it tomorrow, since it might be possible to make some cuts in the printer's proofs that seem necessary to me: not of *ideas* or of violence, but of simple phrases, and this to stay within the proportions of a manifesto, easily reproduced by newspapers. I will send you the proofs as soon as they arrive and you yourself judge these cuts.[20]

By October 8 the manifesto was circulated. Marinetti now addresses Pratella as "tu."

> 8–11–10: In great haste, I have sent the manifesto to all your addresses. Five thousand copies have been sent to good addresses, and more than one thousand copies have been distributed by hand.[21]

---

[17] Joshua C. Taylor, *Futurism* (Garden City, N.Y.: Doubleday & Company, 1961), p. 127.
[18] Marabini, "Per una Storia," p. 67 (cf. *Autobiografia,* p. 100).
[19] *Ibid.*
[20] *Ibid.,* p. 69. This letter and the next cited do not appear in the *Autobiografia.*
[21] *Ibid.,* p. 70.

Much later, after World War II, Pratella was to complain of Marinetti's editing:

> In the field of music I tend to recreate the world humanly and never to go against humanity and therefore against nature. I must say that some affirmations, of a polemic and others of a theoretical nature, which one can read in my *Manifesto*, refer to a rapport between music and machine. These were neither written nor even thought by me and often are in contrast to the rest of the ideas. These inventions were added by Marinetti arbitrarily and at the last moment. I was then astonished to read them over my signature, but the thing was already done.[22]

Il Manifesto dei Musicisti Futuristi was quickly followed by *Il Manifesto Technico della Musica Futurista,* on March 11, 1911, and by *La Distruzione della Quadratura* on July 18, 1912. These three works form the backbone of Futurist musical polemic and have very much the flavor of the other Futurist manifestoes, in particular those signed by the painters connected with the movement.[23] This unanimity is probably due to the iron editorial fist of Marinetti, who maintained considerable control over the polemics of the movement.[24]

The three manifestoes form the basis of a complete musical aesthetic program. *Il Manifesto dei Musicisti Futuristi* is a dramatically written attack on the *passato* of contemporary Italian composers and their tendency to perpetuate the musical forms of the past rather than attempt what is new and truly creative. *Il Manifesto Technico* places the blame for Italy's unprogressive attitudes on conservatories and teachers who inhibit experimentation for their own benefit and explains that the new Futurist music will be rhythmically free and microtonal. *La Distruzione della Quadratura* presents Pratella's notational system, designed to free music from repeated rhythmic pulses.

By the time of the publication of *La Distruzione della Quadratura* Pratella's theoretical program was substantially complete. What was needed now was an example of music composed to conform to the program, and Pratella was not long in providing it. *Inno alla Vita, Musica Fu-*

---

[22] *Ibid.,* p. 85 (cf. *Autobiografia,* p. 103).
[23] These manifestoes are all available in English. For a selection, see Michael Kirby, *Futurist Performance* (New York: Dutton Paperbacks, 1971). For complete texts of the musical manifestoes, see Rodney J. Payton, "The Futurist Musicians: Francesco Balilla Pratella and Luigi Russolo" (Ph.D. diss., University of Chicago, 1974).
[24] Payton, "The Futurist Musicians," pp. 14–16.

turista per Orchestra[25] was first performed in February 1913 and again in March. Pratella tells of both occasions in his *Autobiografia:*

> My first true direct contact with the public, as a Futurist musician, took place at the Teatro Costanzi di Roma on two evenings, February 21 and March 9, 1913, with the first and second performances of my *Musica Futurista* with the great orchestra of the Teatro Costanzi itself under my direction.[26]
>
> The first performance on February 21, reserved by the Mocchi firm of impressarios for season ticket holders and those who were invited, went off fairly well: applause, ironic comments, discussions in a loud voice, but nothing more, and these were reserved for the aggressive and polemic addresses of Marinetti, Boccioni, Carrà and Russolo.
>
> At the second performance on March 9 pandemonium broke loose. . . .
>
> The spectacle was opened by me with my *Musica Futurista per Orchestra,* which proceeded to the end amidst an infernal clamor, made up of whistles, applause, cries, acclamations, and invectives. The public seemed driven insane, and the frantic mass boiled and from time to time exploded in rage resembling a mass of burning lava during a volcanic eruption. Some threw upon the orchestra and also on me, the conductor, an uninterrupted shower of garbage, of fruit, of chestnut cakes; others shouted themselves hoarse crying every kind of thing; some protested not being able to hear; some became exalted, others infuriated, some laughed and enjoyed themselves, others quarreled and started rows, with frequent blows between friends and enemies.
>
> Finally, as if God willed the music, without which most people would not even have heard it, I turned towards the public, made a beautiful smile of thanks to friends and of mirth to enemies, and then went up to the stage where I found Marinetti, who was pronouncing in a loud voice some strange formula of exorcism to which he attributed a great mystical power like a magical mascot, and woe to anyone who contradicted him.[27]

These performances evidently supplied the impulse that brought Luigi Russolo onto the Futurist musical scene. Russolo, flamboyant inventor of the *intonarumori* and other marvels, painter and eventual mystic, would be precisely the sort of disciple Pratella and Marinetti might have wished for. Where Pratella could promote real reform with subtle polemic,

---

[25] Pratella, *Musica Futurista per Orchestra, riduzione per pianoforte* (Bologna: F. Bongiovanni, Editore, 1912). This is the only published form of this work and includes Pratella's three manifestoes.
[26] Pratella may mean his first contact as a *composer*. There exists a sketch by Boccioni published in *Uno Due e . . . Tre* on June 17, 1911, of a Futurist performance that shows a portly man conducting an orchestra who might well be Pratella. See Taylor, *Futurism,* p. 10.
[27] Pratella, *Autobiografia,* pp. 114–116.

Russolo could truly *believe*. A brilliant man, he faced the world pragmatically; if a program like that described in Pratella's manifestoes existed, it existed to be acted on. A little ingenuity would make it all a reality. The scope of his vision was staggering. Witness this passage from the conclusions to his manifesto *L'Arte dei Rumori:*

> 8. Let us therefore invite young musicians of genius and audacity to listen attentively to all noises. . . . Our increased perceptivity, which has already acquired futurist eyes, will then have futurist ears. Thus the motors and machines of industrial cities may someday be intelligently pitched, so as to make of every factory an intoxicating orchestra of noises.[28]

Born on May 1, 1885, at Portogruaro, a small town north of Venice, Russolo was the son of the local cathedral organist, who was also the director of the local Scuola Filarmonica. The father's most cherished ambition was fulfilled when his two elder sons, Giovanni and Antonio, graduated from the conservatory in Bologna.[29] Luigi, too, was from the first interested in music and began the study of the violin, but soon announced that he wished to learn to draw. This desire was indulged by his father, who said he did not wish to fail to be of help to his children.[30] When Luigi's family moved to Milan, he stayed behind with an aunt in order to finish the *ginnasio*. At the age of sixteen he joined his family in Milan and continued to study painting, although he did not enroll in any school. From 1901 to 1909 he seems to have worked as a painter in Milan. In 1910 he joined Marinetti and the Futurist movement and with Carlo Carrà, Giacomo Balla, Umberto Boccioni, Arnoldo Bonzagni, and Romolo Romani signed the *Manifesto della Pittura Futurista*. Russolo's career as a Futurist painter continued until 1913, when he issued *L'Arte dei Rumori* and officially joined Pratella in musical Futurism.[31] The document is in the form of an open letter:

> My Dear Balilla Pratella, Great Futuristic composer:
>   In the crowded Costanzi Theater, in Rome, while I was listening with my futurist friends Marinetti, Boccioni, and Balla to the orches-

---

[28] Russolo, "The Art of Noises, Futurist Manifesto," trans. Nicholas Slonimsky, *Music Since 1900* (4th ed; New York: Charles Scribner's Sons, 1971), pp. 1,298–1,302. From Slonimsky's helpful book one can, with the aid of the index, construct a fairly accurate picture of the Futurists' activities at least through 1921. The appendix reprints two manifestoes.

[29] Maria Zanovello Russolo, *Russolo, L'Uomo, L'Artista* (Milan, 1958), p. 542.

[30] *Ibid.,* p. 1,720.

[31] For a discussion of Russolo's career as a painter during the years 1909 to 1914, see Taylor, *Futurism*.

tral performance of your overwhelming MUSICA FUTURISTA, there came to my mind the idea of a new art: The Art of Noises, a logical consequence of your marvelous innovations.[32]

Thus was the concept of *rumorismo* presented to the public, but it is important to note that while Russolo proclaims the "art of noises" to be a logical outcome of Pratella's efforts, Pratella himself does not specifically advocate any such innovation in any of his manifestoes. Indeed, it is tempting to speculate that the appearance of *L'Arte dei Rumori* was conceived and masterminded by the *caposcuola* himself, F. T. Marinetti. This speculation is prompted by Pratella's specific denial of any interest in "a rapport between music and machines."[33] In addition, there exists a letter from Marinetti to Pratella that seems to indicate that the *intonarumori* were Marinetti's passion, not necessarily Pratella's.

> Work with great confidence. Do not hold back, not forgetting that all, absolutely *all extravagances are obtainable* by you. I will mention, almost insist on, the necessity of confusing everyone and always going forward. Not forgetting, moreover, your most important intention, it seems proper to me, to introduce into the orchestra of your *Aviatore Dro,* two, three, four, or five or even more of Russolo's *intonarumori.* This is of enormous importance, I think, because while Russolo prepares a complete orchestra of *intonarumori,* you absolutely must, it seems to me (in one part of your new work, perhaps best in the finale of the second act), create the first example of a mixed orchestra or, better, of a *conventional orchestra enriched with intonarumori.* Think about all this. I believe this innovation is absolutely necessary to your work, from your personal point of view as an innovator and from the point of view of Futurism. One would then be able to frankly define you as the first musician who has with his genius revolutionized the orchestra, courageously leaping the gap that separates Futurism from *passatismo* in music. You know that I see exactly, and that I am armed with great discernment.[34]

Whatever the source of Russolo's innovations and the ideas for the applications of this theory, his own dedication to them is not subject to debate. He continued to work on various noise instruments, occasionally giving concerts until the 1920s, when he turned to Eastern mysticism.

L'Arte dei Rumori, dated March 11, 1913, agrees theoretically with

---

[32] Slonimsky, *Music Since 1900,* p. 1,298.
[33] See note 22.
[34] Marabini, "Per una Storia," pp. 70–71.

Pratella's manifestoes, in that it views the history of music in terms of a purely melodic art that only gradually evolved the idea of vertical organizations:

> The Middle Ages . . . [regarded] music from the point of view of *linear development in time.* . . . In a word, the medieval conception of music was horizontal, not vertical. An interest in the simultaneous union of difficult sounds, that is, in the chord as a complex sound, developed gradually, passing from the perfect consonance, with a few incidental dissonances, to the complex and persistent dissonances which characterize the music of today.[35]

One of the problems faced by the composer or theorist seeking to renovate the art of music, according to Russolo, is that the circumstances surrounding the birth of music were such that a mystic character was assigned to the art:

> *Noises* being so scarce, the first *musical sounds* which man succeeded in drawing from a hollow reed or from a stretched string were a new, astonishing, miraculous discovery. By primitive peoples musical sound was ascribed to the gods, regarded as holy, and entrusted to the sole care of the priests, who made use of it to enrich their rites with mystery. Thus was born the conception of a musical sound as a thing having an independent existence, a thing different from life and unconnected with it. From this conception resulted an idea of music as a world of fantasy superimposed upon reality, a world inviolate and sacred. It will be readily understood how this idea of music must inevitably have impeded its progress, as compared with that of the other arts.[36]

As the machine has proliferated and added noise to the environment, says Russolo, human response to sound itself has changed: ". . . the machine today has created so many varieties of noise that pure musical sound—with its poverty and its monotony—no longer awakens any emotion in the hearer."[37] Russolo is careful to note that not all noises are by

---

[35] Slonimsky, *Music Since 1900,* pp. 1,298–1,299.

[36] *Ibid.* This is another area of apparent agreement between Pratella and Russolo, an agreement that might be attributed to the editorial efforts of Marinetti. In an article "Musica Futurista e Futurismo," dated May 4, 1914, Pratella makes the following assertions: "Music, until today, has been judged as the abstract art *par excellence:* the gift of the gods, the sublime, the intangible, the ethereal, the otherworldly. . . . [But] its major appeal depends on other factors, not its pretext of immateriality." —Pratella, *Scritti Vari di Pensiero* (Bologna, 1932), p. 117.

[37] Slonimsky, *Music Since 1900,* p. 1,299. Further excerpts, given below, from *L'Arte dei Rumori* are also taken from Slonimsky, pp. 1,299–1,301.

any means disagreeable: "I need scarcely enumerate all the small and delicate noises which are pleasing to the ear." Modern man needs more and more complex sounds, and this is a need that can be met by Futurist musicians, as Russolo states in his conclusions:

> 1. Futurist musicians must constantly broaden and enrich the field of sound. This is a need of our senses. Indeed, we note in present-day composers of genius a tendency towards the most complex dissonances. Moving further and further away from pure musical sound, they have almost reached the noise-sound. This need and this tendency can only be satisfied *by the supplementary use of noise and its substitution for musical sounds.*

In order to use the richness of noise creatively, noise must be controllable. This can be accomplished by determining the predominating pitch or pitches of a given noise:

> Every noise has a note—sometimes even a chord—that predominates in the ensemble of its irregular vibrations. Because of this characteristic note, it becomes possible to fix the pitch of a given noise, that is, to give it not a single pitch but a variety of pitches, without losing its characteristic quality—its distinguishing timbre.

That the modern ear requires more complex sounds (noises) is important, but more important is an assertion relating to the very function of music:

> Every manifestation of life is accompanied by noise. Noise is therefore familiar to our ears and has the power to remind us immediately of life itself. Musical sound, a thing extraneous to life and independent of it, . . . has become to our ears what a too familiar face is to our eyes. Noise, on the other hand, which comes to us confused and irregular as life itself, never reveals itself wholly but reserves for us innumerable surprises. We are convinced, therefore, that by selecting, coordinating and controlling noises we shall enrich mankind with a new and unsuspected source of pleasure.

However, in spite of the fact that noise reminds one forcefully of life itself, Russolo categorically moves beyond mere programmatic imitation of natural sound: ". . . the Art of Noises must not limit itself to reproductive imitation. It will reach its greatest emotional power through the purely acoustic enjoyment which the inspiration of the artist will contrive to evoke from combinations of noises." Russolo lists the six families of noises proper to the Futurist orchestra: booms, whistles, whispers, screams, percussive sounds, and the voices of men and animals.

Russolo must have been working on these instruments, which were to be called *intonarumori,* by the time of the manifesto's publication or immediately thereafter, since the first demonstration of a single *intonarumore* was held at the Teatro Stocchi in Modena on June 2, 1913, only three months after the publication of *L'Arte dei Rumori.* The instrument demonstrated was a *scoppiatore* (crackler), which, according to Russolo's "Gl'Intonarumori Futuristi," imitated the sound of an internal-combustion engine.[38] In his article Russolo takes the opportunity to state again the aesthetic considerations behind the art of noises in response, he says, to the lack of understanding of his program by the foreign press.[39] He proceeds to a description of the workings of his machines:

It was . . . necessary . . . that these instruments, *intonarumori,* be as simple as possible, and it is in precisely this that we[40] have succeeded perfectly. It is enough to say that a single stretched diaphragm, correctly positioned, will produce by variations in tension a scale of more than ten whole tones with all the divisions of semitone, quarter tone and of even smaller fractions.

. . . Varying, then, [the manufacture and] the way of exciting the diaphragm, one obtains yet a different sound *as to type and as to timbre,* always preserving, naturally, the possibility of varying the pitch. So far we have used four different means of excitation and have already completed the relative instruments.

The first makes the *scoppio* [explosive] sound like an automobile engine; the second makes the *crepitio* [crackling] sound like rifle fire; the third makes the *ronzio* [hum] sound like a dynamo; the fourth makes different kinds of *stropiccii* [stamping, shuffling of feet].

In these instruments the simple movement of a graduated lever suffices to give the noise the pitch that one wants, even in the smallest fraction. Just as easily regulated is the rhythm of every single noise, making it easy to calculate the beat, be it equal or unequal. . . .

Research is already complete to obtain noises (always, understand, tunable)—of the first series listed in the *Manifesto,* the *rombi* [rumbles], the *tuoni* [thunderers,] and the *scrosci* [crushers]; of the second series, the *sibili* [whistlers]; of the third, the *gorgoglii* [gurglers]; of the fourth, the *stridoni* [screamers], and the *fruscii* [rustlers]. For these noises the instruments are already being built: *rombatore, tuonatore, scrosciatore, gorgogliatore.*[41]

---

[38] Russolo, "Gl'Intonarumori Futuristi," *Lacerba,* 1, no. 13 (July 1, 1913), pp. 140–141. This article is dated May 22, 1913, was published on July 1, 1913, and is about a concert that was held on June 2.

[39] *Ibid.,* p. 151.

[40] The "we" in this passage refers to Russolo and Ugo Piatti, his assistant.

[41] Russolo, "Gl'Intonarumori Futuristi," p. 141.

Russolo concludes the article by emphasizing again that the music of the *intonarumori* is not to be merely imitative.[42]

During the period between the printing of "Gl'Intonarumori Futuristi" and the first concert given at Teatro del Verme in Milan on April 21, 1914, Russolo published two more theoretical articles in *Lacerba.* The first of these, "Conquista Totale dell'Enarmonismo Mediante gl'Intonarumori Futuristi,"[43] seconds Pratella's assertion, in *Il Manifesto Technico,* that *"enarmonia* gives us the possibility of rendering the natural and instinctive intonations and modulations of enharmonic intervals presently impossible, given the artificiality of a tempered scale which we wish to overcome."[44] Russolo believes not only that, when the sounds of nature change pitch, they invariably do so by "enharmonic gradation" but that the world of machines is no different:

> Equally, if we pass from natural sounds into the infinitely richer world of the sounds of machines, we again find that all the sounds produced by rotary motion are in their crescendo or diminuendo constantly enharmonic . . . examples: the dynamo and the electric motor.[45]

Furthermore, the human ear is quite capable of hearing these microintervals, even those as small as one eighth of a tone. Since these sounds exist and are natural, and since they are easily perceptible to the ear, it behooves Futurism to enlarge the field of music with them "as it has enlarged the field of painting with *dinamismo,* poetry with *immaginazione senza fili* and free words, music with *antigrazioso* and the abolition of any rhythmic system."[46] The *intonarumori* are the means by which Futurism will accomplish this task:

> In fact, in the construction of the *intonarumori* we have attempted not only the possibility of changing the sound-noise by whole and half steps but also by any gradation between one tone and another.

---

[42] "The noise must become a prime element to form the work of art . . . though the resemblance of the timbre to the natural sound imitated is attained by these instruments almost to the point of deception, nevertheless, no sooner one senses that the noise changes in pitch than one perceives that it loses its uniquely, episodic, imitative character. . . . And thus, liberated from the *necessity* that produced it, we dominate it, transforming at will the pitch, the intensity and the rhythm, we quickly feel it become anonymous malleable material, ready to be transformed by the will of the artist, who transforms it into elements of emotion, into a work of art." *Ibid.*
[43] Russolo, "Conquista Totale dell'Enarmonismo Mediante gl'Intonarumori Futuristi," *Lacerba,* 1, no. 21 (November 1, 1913), pp. 243–245.
[44] See Pratella, *Musica Futurista,* p. xii.
[45] Russolo, "Conquista Totale . . . ," p. 242.
[46] *Ibid.,* p. 244.

We have succeeded perfectly in obtaining any fraction, however small, of pitch.

Enarmonismo is today, thanks to the *intonarumori,* a musical reality.[47]

Russolo's second article in *Lacerba,* which appeared on March 1, 1914, is titled "Grafia Enarmonica per gl'Intonarumori Futuristi."[48] It includes an example from *Rete di Rumori, Risveglio di una Città,* and this seven-measure excerpt is the only available specimen of Russolo's own work for *intonarumori.*[49] In spite of Russolo's seeming determination to embrace all of Pratella's polemic program, the excerpt does not include any rhythmic innovations derived from Pratella. It is somewhat surprising that there is only one instance of a quarter tone in the excerpt.

Russolo's concert in Milan at the Teatro del Verme was given on April 21, 1914.[50] In *L'Intransigeant* of Paris, Marinetti wrote an account of the occasion. He reports on how the Futurists responded to the large number of unruly *passéistes* among the audience.

> For an hour, the Futurists offered passive resistance. But an extraordinary thing happened just at the start of *Network of Noise No. 4:* five Futurists— Boccioni, Carrà, Amando Mazza, Piatti and myself—descended from the stage, crossed the orchestra pit, and, right in the center of the hall, using their fists and canes, attacked the "passéistes," who appeared to be stultified and intoxicated with reactionary rage. The battle lasted fully half an hour. During all this time Luigi Russolo continued to conduct imperturbably the nineteen bruiteurs on the stage. It was a display of an amazing harmonic arrangement of bloody faces and infernal mêlée. . . . The performing artists were suddenly divided into two groups: one group continued to play, while the other went down into the hall to combat the hostile and rioting audience. It is thus that an escort in the desert protects the caravan against the Touaregs. It is thus that the infantry sharpshooters provide cover for the construction of a military pontoon. Our skill in boxing and our fighting spirit enables us to emerge

---

[47] *Ibid.* Russolo concludes with a progress report: "We finally have the sound-noise material, capable of taking on all forms without exception . . . I was convinced of all this during the first private concert of *intonarumori* which I recently directed in the hall of the Direzione del *Movimento futurista*—and especially by the performance of my two *reti* [networks] of noises entitled *Risveglio di Capitale* and *Convegno d'Automobile e d'Aeroplani." Ibid.,* p. 245.

[48] Russolo, "Grafia Enarmonica per gl'Intonarumori Futuristi," *Lacerba,* 3, no. 5 (March 1, 1914), pp. 74–75.

[49] The present author does have in his possession a tape made from a record of 1921 of two compositions for orchestra and *intonarumori* by Antonio Russolo, the brother of Luigi, which he obtained from Fred K. Prieberg of Baden-Baden.

[50] Slonimsky, *Music Since 1900,* p. 238, provides information on the orchestra and the pieces played at this concert.

from the skirmish with but a few bruises. But the "passéistes" suffered eleven wounded, who had to be taken to a first-aid station for treatment.[51]

In the May 15, 1914, issue of *Lacerba* there appeared a short article, "Gl'Intonarumori nell'Orchestra," and a short composition for *intonarumori* and orchestra, *Gioia Saggio di Orchestra Mista,* both by Pratella. The piece is printed in a piano score plus parts for *scoppiatori* and *ronzatori.* In the article Pratella acknowledges his debt to Russolo. He ends his remarks by speaking of the role of the *intonarumori:*

> As one can easily see, the *intonarumori* in practice lose any sense of objective reality; they move from an objective reality, to stand aloof from it immediately, coming to form a new abstract reality—the *abstract expressive* element of a state of mind. Their timbre does not join itself to the other *sound elements* as heterogeneous material, but joins as a new *sound element, emotional* and essentially *musical.*[52]

One has the feeling that the *Saggio* might be the direct result of Marinetti's urgings, but, be that as it may, the two forces in Futurist music were now officially unified, even though no composition was ever produced by the two musicians in collaboration and even though Pratella was to use the *intonarumori* for little more than sound effects in his opera *L'Aviatore Dro,* which was performed only in 1920.

The third concert of Russolo's *intonarumori* took place in the Politeama theatre in Genoa on May 20, 1914. It was evidently held in a more genial atmosphere. Maria Russolo, the widow of the master, quotes him:

> At the Politeama of Genoa, the evening of May 20, 1914, followed a performance with the same orchestra. The conduct of the Genoese public was not as unreasonable and indecorous as that of Milan. . . . The Genoese had the rare good sense *to want to hear.* They did not lack troublemakers, but the majority made them keep silent. Thus the Genoese public could get a general idea of that which is my orchestra.[53]

The chance to hear Futurist music was afforded London audiences on June 15, 1914, at the London Coliseum, where Russolo and his *intonarumori* were presented. This took place during the time when the Futurist

---

[51] *Ibid.,* pp. 238–239.
[52] Pratella, "Gl'Intonarumori nell'Orchestra," *Lacerba,* 2, no. 10 (May 15, 1914), p. 152.
[53] Maria Zanovello Russolo, *Russolo, L'Uomo,* p. 54.

painters were on exhibition at London's Dore Gallery. Little information is available about the concert, as it does not seem to have had the same impact on British cultural life as Futurist polemic implied. The review of the concert in the London *Times* is indulgent, but hardly laudatory:

> . . . the curtain rose upon an orchestra of weird funnel-shaped instruments directed by Signor Luigi Russolo.
>
> It is impossible to say that the first of the "noise-spirals" performed "The Awakening of a Great City," was as exhilarating as Futurist art usually is; on the contrary, it rather resembled the sounds heard in the rigging of a Channel-steamer during a bad crossing, and it was, perhaps, unwise of the players—or should we call them the "noisicians?"—to proceed with their second piece, "A Meeting of Motor-cars and Aeroplanes," after the pathetic cries of "No more!" which greeted them from all the excited quarters of the auditorium.[54]

These six occasions, Pratella's two concerts in February and March 1913, and Russolo's four concerts on June 2, 1913, April 21, and May 20, 1914, and the Coliseum concert (or, possibly, concerts) in June 1914, constitute the Futurists' chief musical exposure in the years before the war. It is hoped that with a knowledge of this record and on the basis of the documentary evidence scholars will recognize that musical Futurism, in combination with the other artistic aspects of the movement, forms an important and fertile part of the cultural history of the twentieth century. It seems particularly significant that the Futurists were the first group to be aware of the possibilities of a larger technological aesthetic. Long before *musique concrète* the Futurists were attempting to enlarge the vocabulary of sounds available to the composer; long before the Surrealists they demonstrated how categorical might be the imperative of *épater les bourgeois* in achieving an artistic objective. Before the Fascists, they showed how to use art as propaganda, and before almost anyone, they practiced an art of violence demonstrating the use of art as a weapon against the past, against the present, in short, violence as art and art as violence. However unhappily, this motive has had its way not only in music, painting, and the other arts but also in the world of political action.

Operational Music

by William Wilson

In his essay on operational music, William Wilson defines music as "less a matter of a special sensibility, a structure, a quality of sound, an image of time, an expression of feeling, or a significant form, than a series of operations with sounds." He notes that "More recently, music has added ordinary sounds and outright noises, until nothing can be defined as in itself musical or nonmusical material."

Hence "music finds a reconciliation between the claims of physical materiality and ideal spirituality in operations that mediate between the concrete and the abstract." Wilson cites, as examples, the works of four composers: John Cage, La Monte Young, Nam June Paik, and Joe Jones.

European music of the last few centuries has emphasized expression, and the materials, instruments, and techniques have served the expression of individual sensibilities. More recently, music has added ordinary sounds and outright noises, until nothing can be defined as in itself musical or nonmusical material.

When nothing is forbidden as a musical instrument, some inaudible things and anything capable of noise can be used in performance. La Monte Young has used the silent flight of a butterfly, and John Cage has used the audience itself as a source of sound. Traditional instruments have been altered or destroyed: Cage has prepared or fixed pianos, La Monte Young has burned a violin, and Nam June Paik has destroyed a piano. What defines a musical instrument and its correct use?

The concept of the performer has yielded as Joe Jones, for instance, has constructed a revolving base with a potted plant on it. "Electric eyes intercept the leaves/branches. From the base are mounted three violins each with its own motor and beaters. A leaf intercepted, energy to a motor, a violin playing, briefly or for a long time—two or three together" (George Brecht). In another Joe Jones piece, a bicycle is outfitted with drums and violins; the piece can be performed by anyone who can ride a bicycle. The use of untrained performers brings in the problem of defining a musician.

The questions about musical materials, instruments, and performers belong with the larger question of what music is. The answer that emerges from some present practice is that music is less a matter of a special sensibility, a structure, a quality of sound, an image of time, an expression of feeling, or a significant form, than a series of operations with sounds. An operation is an abstract art, a piece of abstract work, an exertion of energy uncomplicated by irrelevant emotions, and satisfying or acknowledging standards of simplicity, economy, and efficiency. An operation is an act that exemplifies a principle; it usually is definite, unequivocal, discrete, but capable of combining with other operations. When music is defined operationally, then the operations define what is musical material, idea, instrument, or performer. The first violinist at the New York State Theater, when he was supposed to slap his violin with his hand, knocked on the wood of the orchestra pit and smiled at the conductor. Clearly he prefers the operations he understands to be implied by the violin to the operations prescribed by the composer's notations. A violin does imply some operations, and these have traditionally been subordinated, as technique, to expression of feeling or of a musical idea about time. But when operations assume ascendancy over feeling and time in defining music, then the operation gets to define the instrument, not the instrument the operation.

Ideas that cluster around *operation* include the withdrawal of attention from emotional or dramatic development, with the accompanying feeling of completion and fulfillment. Attention is more likely to be undifferentiated, scattered, or evenly distributed. This fluctuating attention is possible because of the accompanying withdrawal of point of view on the part of the composer. He is unlikely to be concerned with ideals or ideas that can be abstracted any further than operations. So music finds a reconciliation between the claims of physical materiality and ideal spirituality in operations that mediate between the concrete and the abstract.

This equilibrium between facts and ideas in operations turns music away from self-expression and organic necessity, opening up many other possible relations of person to sound. The lack of internal or organic necessity means that criticism must dispense with organic criteria and metaphors. The study of music for the relation of part to part, and for the interdependence of part and whole, is irrelevant in a music of distinctly separate parts, with many possible correlations. The criterion of unity or of wholeness cannot be applied to work which, forgoing organic necessity, gains a feeling of continuing possibility. A music of operations presents not dramatic necessity, but possibilities—some trends, fluctuations, and uncertainties, with many live alternatives to what is actually happening. In such open systems, operations combine with operations, and these cooperations further combine in loose correlations with a suggestion of endlessness. Instead of a composition that starts with *possibilities* that, as choices are made, become *probabilities,* with the probabilities, as alternatives are exhausted, becoming necessities, operational music presents operations that remain possible, sometimes probable. This is a music of possibilities, where necessity is excluded and chance or uncertain correlations are comfortably contained in operations.

Music has often been heard as an image of time. The discovery of operational music is that time has no intrinsic metric and that music has no intrinsic metric. Time can be defined by operations for measuring it. The clock enters operational music as a system of arbitrary coordinates, and the operations of the clock take their place among other operations that define musical time. Once John Cage used the operations of chance to select tempos, but "After that, I altered my way of composing; I didn't write in tempos but always in times." Of his *Theatre Piece* he says, "I might be said to have conducted it; I acted as a clock . . ." The clock provides coordinates, but the musical time here is experienced as the operations that measure the intervals.

When music consists of operations with sounds, then a guide to the orchestra will have to include a guide to operations. If we take a noise and add another noise, we experience addition as well as noise. If we add an amplified noise, then we experience addition and amplification. So sounds can be added, subtracted, multiplied, differentiated, and integrated, and the operation is part of the meaning. Amplification enlarges the randomness or chance in sounds, but within a range of uncertainty that can be given a probability. The role of chance in music has more to do with neutralizing a point of view than with complete noncorrelation. Operational music avoids the opposition between chance and causality by offering an image of the present as neither random nor determined, but as an open system of possibilities. Possibilities can always be amplified to uncertainties, as in reading a meter with a magnifying glass, but those uncertainties are still contained by the operations that reveal them. Because we experience operations as immediately as we experience sound, operational music must be studied as operations with sounds and understood in its own terms as a way of thinking about time as a system of possibilities defined and governed by operations.

Composers on Music

Serial Music Today*

Earle Brown

In this essay Earle Brown writes that "serial music today has come to terms with the necessity of expanding its technical orientation away from horizontality, and that its 'problem' (in the positive sense) is to deal with the performer as a fallible as well as a creative parameter (unserializable)." He writes that an epoch can never be "defined solely in terms of a point of view as confined and self-indulgent, as 'classical' serial music, chance music, neoplastic art, pop art, etc., . . . these are merely the escape clauses of publicists whose powers of assimilation have been overtaxed."

Brown indicates that developments in serial music reveal a parallel between music and the " 'open-reading' of a Pollock, the 'open-reading' of Le Livre of Mallarmé, the infinite environment of Joyce, and the endless contextual, preordained but unforeseeable mobility of elements of a Calder." He is a composer and served as a member of Project for Music for Magnetic Tape with John Cage and David Tudor in New York. He is a former Guggenheim fellow and at present he is Director of the Contemporary Sound Series sponsored by Time Records and teaches at the Peabody Conservatory in Baltimore.

In a recent interview that appeared in Paris, Brown remarked:

---

* Reprinted from *Preuve* (March 1966).

I owe the aesthetic orientation of my music to two American artists: to the sculptor Calder and to the painter Pollock. In the mobiles of Calder I found the organizational precision which I wanted, but more important, I discovered the possibility of a work of art never being the same twice yet always being the same work; some sort of a new dynamism. I found another kind of dynamism in the paintings of Pollock: to the art of painting they brought a new, intensified spontaneity.

I would not say that the development of techniques called "serial" has in any way caused a "rupture" in the continuity of our musical culture. On the contrary, it seems to me to be the one *material* technique most rationally compatible with and relevant to many methods of analysis and synthesis employed by mathematics and the physical sciences today. The serial procedures are also clearly contemporary extensions and developments of musical techniques of the past (although not of the recent nineteenth-century past), such as the time of the quadrivium when music was considered to be one of the mathematical sciences; to me the most explicit connection is to isorhythmic principles of generating and structuring sound materials. Any "rupture" is only the result of very restricted experience and reflection on developments in the history of music and lack of imagination in respect to its probable future. *One* dimension of this future is certainly dependent on further clarification and definition of materials and their combinatorial potential by means of a "clean abstraction" such as enumeration and the manipulative potential of a series rationale. We must not, however, be led to think that this is the *only* dimension to be considered.

The stylistic expression of an epoch is only seen after many years and within a perspective that encompasses *all* of the arts, sciences, and humanities of that epoch. We are not yet at that point in relation to our particular epoch and the most exciting "creative" realization is that *we* (who are trying to do it) never shall be. *The* stylistic expression of our epoch may not be clear for centuries, if ever. As long as it remains unclear, we are free to speculate and search for it rather than to conform to its clear, paralyzing finality. Everything that happens is an expression of the epoch but it may not be the most significant or the least significant, regardless of its "public image" at either time.

The "certainty" that some of the early theoretical serialists exhibited in propagandizing for this point of view as the newfound "stylistic expression of our epoch" had a tendency to shut them off from speculative concern with the non-numerical *effect* that is necessarily produced in the uncertain sound art of music. I don't mean that one should imagine an effect and then produce its cause, only that one must allow cause and effect to coexist in the ambiguous (innumerable) continuum that they actually inhabit. Everything can be serialized except response ... including the response of oneself to the series, the musician to the notation, the listener to the results of all of these, and one's own response to the inevitable differences between what one wants and what one gets. It is always a surprise, thankfully, but "strict" serialism had within itself a principle of total control that, I believe, was contrary to the nature of the art. A Mondrian can be physically what he wants it to be but the physical reality of a piece of music is not its score but its actual sound in time as performed by people.

It is not true of "serial music today" (1965) but it seems that in the early days of serializing, Mallarmé's famous statement, "poems are made with words, not with ideas," was misinterpreted. Serializing sounds is primarily concerned with making something with "words." When the generation of the relationships is automated serially, however, the "words" (sounds) operate in the service of an idea, as an inflexible ideational system. This is perfectly all right of course. No one has to agree with Mallarmé or with my interpretation of him, but it seemed to be a rather closed world in which "relinquishing the initiative to the words themselves" (Mallarmé) was thought to be a matter of "total organization" ... controllable cause and effect ... a good idea but impractical. Now, another "parameter" has slowly come to the surface (always present in the serial works of the overtly "musical" composers), and things are becoming more full, broad, artful, and confusing.

The term *total organization* had within it its own time bomb of absolutism, as does the term *chance music* (not to be confused with *indeterminate music*), and both have exploded. (Valéry: "we still have two things to fear; order and disorder.") Never can an epoch be defined solely in terms of a point of view as confined and self-indulgent, as "classical" serial music, chance music, neoplastic art, pop art, etc., ... these are merely the escape clauses of publicists whose powers of assimilation have been overtaxed.

At a certain point it was difficult to go anywhere (compositionally), with confidence, and exterior automatic justifications seemed necessary merely to proceed. Now, with no more confidence than Webern or Varèse had, a personalization of the abstract language becomes the necessity, but not a justification. To consider *all* things, even the unserializable and the uncontrollable, is now the necessity that will modify serial "purity" and bring it back to a reasonable relationship to the creative insecurity that is the nature of Art ... there is no insurance policy ... who ever said it would be easy?

If I seem to be both positive and negative about serialism, it is because I take it very seriously and both positions are relative to the proportions of reality and infatuation that the conception has produced, both in theory and in practice. The best practical examples within the genre have made the theory obsolete; the seemingly endless theorizing that has gone on has not justified those works that most need it.

Not being European, or having been in Europe during the beginnings of "serial music," I may have a rather warped conception of what a European thinks of it, however, my sympathy with it, in principle, is based on my intimate connection to a very similar way of thinking at nearly the same time as the first European serial work . . . between 1945 and 1950. The "similar way of thinking" was in the techniques of Joseph Schillinger; similar in that it is a "system" of total organization based on the serializing (enumeration) of all sound elements, generating materials by permutation and expansion within arithmetical and geometrical series, generating macroform from very small units (nuclei), concepts of density in strata (fields), and various "statistical" concepts. The significant difference between Schillinger's "abstraction of sound elements" and European developments seems to be that Schillinger did not focus on any one composer as "prototype" and therefore did not produce a primarily *contrapuntal* basis of serial relationships. Webern, as the prototype contrapuntalist from whom European serialism developed its strict ordering techniques, seems to have inspired the extremely complicated horizontal fragmentation, which is not a new point of view but only the continuation of the contrapuntal rhetoric that we have had for centuries. Naturally the texture is dense, tending toward the destruction of appreciable linearity (an effect basically contrary to the "coherence factor" of the row), but never approaching a truly "continuum" equality of sound dimensions and conception. (I speak of serial works written before approximately 1955.)

My closest "prototype" (in America in 1950, not conceptually) was Varèse, who knew but had no close connection to Schillinger. His music seemed to be "explained" by Schillinger principles, and he had, many years before, broken with counterpoint as a technique. His music seemed to me to be dealing with a new concept of rhetoric, which is to say, having a new temporal reality that spoke in a new and fresh way . . . his thinking in terms of "masses, planes, volumes, densities" rather than of a series of *notes* . . . and his term, "organized *sound*" (my italics), imply this. It seemed to me that here, in Varèse and Schillinger, was a starting point for the development of a new dimension of *sound* thinking rather than to go on complicating old forms and attitudes. An entirely new way of speaking and forming was more urgently necessary than an increase of detail specificity.

Not notes but sounds (multidimensional complexes); serialized or merely existing as a "collision" of character, qualities, and quantities; systematically or subjectively (what about *that* parameter?), as you will. Excesses of systems or of subjectivities tend to diminish the objective-subjective complexity that is the richness of art as an open, speculative, ambiguous dream.

It seems to me that serial music today *has* come to terms with the necessity of expanding its technical orientation *away* from horizontality, and its "problem" (in the positive sense) is to deal with the performer as a fallible as well as a creative parameter (unserializable) and with the aesthetic and formal implications of "aleatoric" music, as this music presented the "problem" from 1950 to 1955 in America.

The American aleatorism came about not as a reaction to serialism but primarily under the influence of the strength and freedom and iconoclasm of American painting and sculpture right after the war ... the catalysts of *that* development were people (in America during the war) such as Duchamp, Ernst, Breton, Masson, of course (Calder had already "done it" for himself). Young composers in America at this time were separated geographically and culturally from Webern and the continuity of European systems. The strongest examples of *Art* were in space, and, as you know, radically unsystematic, but beautiful, committed, and full of potential that had the power to make one rethink the entire question of artist-audience-communication responsibility, rather than focus on development of a *technique.*

I am as impatient with "chance" (the nonutilization of choice by the artist) as a "compositional technique" as I am with serialism as a justification. The former producing a pseudo-lifelike entropy and the latter a pseudo-machinelike entropy, at their purest point of self-realization of principles. Both tend to eliminate the possibility of involvement and contextual freedom of action which, it seems to me, should exist at every instant and at a high pitch of creative intensity. This "contextual freedom" is the only freedom that interests me and is the indispensable factor in the equation for any activity and is the most difficult to "control." This point of balance between control and noncontrol is the most urgent matter at hand now ... somewhere "out there" is where serial, atonal, chance, open-form, and all of the challenging "problem" musics are going ... as are all of the other arts, of course. Music is finally catching up with the "open-reading" of a Pollock, the "open-reading" of *Le Livre* of Mallarmé, the infinite environment of Joyce, and the endless contextual, preordained but unforeseeable mobility of elements of a Calder. We can serialize, generalize, mobilize, do anything now ... but with care and responsibility and without needing to be *right.*

Time and Music:
A Composer's View*

Barney Childs

Time as idea and element in music continues to challenge our thinking about music and to affect the nature of music. In the following essay Barney Childs, a distinguished contemporary composer, introduces several thoughts concerning time and traces views about time as they have been molded by such modern thinkers as Marcel Duchamp, John Cage, Morse Peckham, and Benjamin Boretz, among others.

Barney Childs was self-taught as a composer until his late twenties, when he studied with Leonard Ratner, Carlos Chavez, Aaron Copland, and Elliott Carter. He is coeditor of Contemporary Composers on Contemporary Music, *a composer of numerous works, and the author of a number of papers on contemporary musical aesthetics and theory. He is professor of composition and music literature at the University of Redlands, California.*

* Reprinted from *Perspectives of New Music*, 15, no. 2 (Spring–Summer 1977), pp. 194–219. This paper is a thorough reworking of an original prepared at the request of Professor Mario Lavista for the magazine *Talea*, in which it has appeared (2, December–April 1976, in Spanish), and was read at the Fall 1975 regional conference of the American Society of University Composers (region VIII). The present version owes a great deal to extensive critical review and commentary by Jonathan Kramer, David Maslanka, and Gerald Warfield. My considerable debt to them, attested to by the frequency with which they are cited, is for their stimulating and forceful thinking, and I am happy to be able to include some of it here, even if only at secondhand.

I

The composer is of course peculiarly concerned with time; like the poet, dramatist, filmmaker, and choreographer, he is in the business of making structures that require real time to be fulfilled. He is working, however, with material the arrangement of which is very loosely bound by "communicative" strictures, if at all, and these are subject to a variety of interpretation: questions of what music "means" and how, even if it can "mean" at all, are still topics of thorough debate.

As are all other artists, the composer is involved with his development and growth *as* an artist with his continual re-attacking the same evasive problems. His achievement in his art may be seen as a steady and ongoing search for, exploration of, and affirmation of his personal mythos. How we deal with our lives is thus affective of our art; each one's aggregated personal experience over the years clearly shapes his responses, stances, the very flavor of perception and affirmation. Our concern is thus not only with "arrangement in time" in working out the music we write but also the pervasive immediacy of, and uses of, the past, our own as well as "historical," and with immediate response to the present. Much of this has been accultured into us: the models of how we live and react, of how we work, of how we postulate future choices and actions, and those models that we live by and move with, all shape, sometimes indirectly, our responses in and out of art.

Man traditionally searches to "make sense" out of experience, and art provides one means by which he can choose to do this. In time art, he will then be paying attention to a part of his life that isolates and stylizes some of the shapes and rhythms of life, and this stylizing not only "makes sense" to him as he deals with the familiar but may also challenge him with disorder with which he must come to terms. Our training and acculturation generally will not accept certain deformities of expectation, alteration of "natural" happenings, beyond a point we do not wish to pass: It isn't real ... It doesn't sound like music ... It doesn't come out right ... I don't know what it means. Whether or not we wish to deal with these challenges, to "grow and change until these are no longer deformities but rather the very stuff of experience"[1] is our choice, and we will so deal with them in terms of this inherited training and acculturation.

The Western European intellectual and cultural tradition has seemingly found most fundamental a basic structural organization of a work of time art, what might be called a *narrative curve.* Greek tragedy, the "clas-

---

[1] Jonathan Kramer, letter to the author, April 1, 1976.

sic" short story, the television crime drama, the Romantic tone poem furnish examples of this organization, which presumably is held to exist as a
stylized reflection of how the tradition views life itself:[2] "Observed drama
invites us so to participate in an event as if it were lived."[3] Material—characters, musical sound, whatever—is introduced along with elements of
question or tension—archetypally, perhaps, as in the Renaissance tragic
drama, of disordering an ordered universe; actions, relationships, and responses increase irregularly in complexity and intensity; a high point or
revelation or climax or catastrophe or denouement is reached; resolution or
relaxation or "falling action" follows; concluding gesture or comment is
made—again archetypally, the renewal of cosmic order, of course altered
from the original order.[4] Graphically we might represent this narrative
curve thus:

> We who have grown up largely under the influence of [an inherited] Western
> European culture are so imbued with the narrative curve that we readily im-
> pose it on experiences that do not demonstrably contain it. Try playing a
> non-narrative piece of music for a class of non-musicians sometime, and ask
> them to graph its intensity, or their own interest curves. It will be there, even
> though it can be objectively demonstrated that the narrative curve (or any
> other temporal progression) is not in the music. I have tried this (and certain
> colleagues also) with *She was a Visitor, Caritas,* and *Aria with Fontana Mix.*[5]

Whether we are concerned with this in terms of goal-direction, no act
without a reward, or by life as a script that we plan for ourselves and live
out, or by life as a series of stages (as the croquet game analogy, in which
we must go through each wicket in turn before being allowed to go for the

---

[2] Or any of life's organic processes, as the late Richard Maxfield's two-piano composition based on the rise, climax, and relaxation of the sexual act. Fidelity to what we assume to be the processes of life and nature—growth and decay, for example—is usually
held to be a virtue, and this is assumed in some instances to reflect an artistically valuable "harmony" with the natural.
[3] William Sacksteder, "Elements of the Dramatic Model," *Diogenes,* 52 (Winter 1965),
p. 32. We discuss Hamlet and Odysseus as though they had actually lived; hundreds of
listeners write letters mourning the "death" of a TV soap opera character.
[4] Or, for music, as Edward Cone puts it, "introduction, statement, development, climax,
restatement, peroration." ("Beyond Analysis," *Perspectives of New Music* [hereafter
PNM], 6, no. 1, Fall-Winter 1967, p. 37) The question, raised by Kramer, of "how do
the various components of the narrative curve acquire their characteristics? . . . Are
these qualities defined contextually, or are there certain defining attributes of, say, climaxes that make them recognizable out of context?" (letter, p. 2) is particularly intriguing, but I must regretfully declare it beyond the scope of this particular paper.
[5] Kramer, letter, p. 1.

next one), we view time art in a manner that applies this stylizing. The perceiver says, "I'll pay attention to your special chunk of time if what I see and hear happening gratifies me in some fashion," and the artist, "Pay attention and I will gratify your expectations in some fashion." As long as a model of living seems natural to us, even "real" and "right" to us, we shall approach perception of, and making of, works of time art in terms of this model. "Thus our ordinary sense of dramatic time suggests a sequence which stimulates us to ask, 'And then what happened?' "[6] How we use the past, for ourselves and, directly as well as indirectly, in our art, is cast in these terms: we may even plan our "future" by extrapolation from these stylized models.

The concern with models is accompanied by the pervasive assumption that there must *be* a model, an ordered system, to be followed: this assumption presumes that there is a "philosophy of life," a "life-style," which if properly worked out and applied will be successful. With any commonly concerned group, from oil field workers to musicologists, the inevitable development of a specialized language/symbol system, a model for behavior on a smaller scale, affirms the anthropological commonplace that what a culture sees is what its language allows it to see.[7] Confusion can arise in cases in which the symbol system is responded to as though its structures were actuality instead of simply a means of dealing with actuality, the sort of thing indicated by W. H. Whyte's comment that the social sciences may confuse the accuracy of their mathematics with the accuracy of their premises.[8] On a general level, an example could be the growth of children believing that the world as seen on television *is* the real world, not a representation of it. Value judgments can thus be based *on* the properties of a system, not in terms of it, leading in turn, in the arts, to the equating of aesthetic validity with systemic validity. As will be discussed later, these problems inevitably arise in a discussion of musical analysis. An interesting sample of this concern for the necessity of a "logically" operable sys-

---

[6] William Thomson, "Musical Analysis and Evaluative Competence," *College Music Curricula* (1970), p. 7.

[7] Its language may permit it to assume "a position from which it is possible to observe the limits of language." David Maslanka, annotations to previous version of this paper, March 28, 1976. Cf. note, 16ff.

[8] This is of course the concern of Korzybskian semanticists, dramatized in such popularizing works as Stuart Chase's *The Tyranny of Words*. It can, however, reach serious misapprehension in the attribution of validity to any internally "logically consistent" meta-system whose original datum is itself a symbol system: a pernicious example is Osgood, Suci, and Tannenbaum, *The Measurement of Meaning* (Urbana: University of Illinois Press, 1957).

tem is Stanford Evans's article in a recent issue of *Proceedings* of the American Society of University Composers,[9] in which he cites Carnap that "the meaning of a proposition is its method of verification."

For some time now the composer has had available a position from which to challenge the Western European intellectual and cultural tradition. This alternative position is perhaps best developed historically from the work of John Cage and his immediate contemporaries, although this can tend to blur the importance of Marcel Duchamp's contribution. Some implications available to this approach assume the following to be invalid:

the "masterpiece" idea

permanence as aesthetic value

process as subservient to the product it realizes

hierarchical systematized nonrandom ordering

aesthetic validity being partly dependent upon the extensive and careful making of choices

the "responsibility" of the artist

the aesthetic value of historicity and the validity of historical succession

emphasis on the logical, the rational, and the analyzable

the aesthetic response's highest form being feelings of profundity, awe, and the like.

Although this view is nowhere near extensive acceptance, its power to question the suitability of the other view to certain artistic directions combines with its capacity to fill a need for some artists, these almost without exception in the Western Hemisphere, who have felt the earlier view curiously dissatisfying and unworkable, who have felt stirrings that somehow some other position of personal integrity that is natural to them may exist.[10]

Part of this alternative is a reworking of the relationship of life and art. The previously structured and stylized values have been thoroughly loosened up: art may no longer be an assumed imitation of life (mimesis)

---

[9] "The Aural Perception of Mathematical Structures," *Proceedings,* 6 (1971), pp. 46–48. Might one alter the Carnap statement to suggest that the proof of the pudding is in the eating?

[10] I have worked elsewhere with some of this material (cf. the article on musical continuity in *Proceedings* of the American Society of University Composers, 6, pp. 55–64). Dealing with the world in a borrowed language is akin to seeing it with distorting glasses. Much of the history of the arts in America is characterized by a search for something we sensed should be there, something that would be in keeping with our status as a genuinely "new" world, but which turned out to be difficult to find. A good example is the history of the strain of American poetry that begins with Whitman and includes Crane, Williams, Pound, and the "Black Mountain" poets of the 1950s.

but instead may be held to *be* life, and, by corollary, life to *be* art. As Morse Peckham explains, by choosing to become art-perceiver, we see as art that which we have selected so to look at.[11] The implied—and potential—inability to make distinctions between life and art easily—in fact, their very interpenetrating inseparability—may often be confusing to the traditionalist. As such, the composer invoked certain stylized structures, gestures, and musical "language" to repeat the same kinds of narrative shapes, of representations of life. And inherent in this is a musical analysis applied with a near-Byzantine intricacy of concern with the nuances of various levels of a few fairly simple-minded constructs, carrying through post-Baconian man's sententious concern for everything coming out right, all edges tucked in, all squares of the crossword puzzle filled: "the game isn't over until the last man is out." The assumption follows, therefore, that this is most completely self-fulfilling with those musical systems whose rules have been most thoroughly delineated.

But life does not always "come out right," nor need music do so, and just as well too. We can now choose to replace these closed structures (and their accompanying analytic apparatus) with an extensive and complex range of art/life interweavings. Composers have, as well as graphic artists earlier, discovered "confrontation with materials": music can be "about" music, about sound, about itself. Music may now be, at choice, solely the product of a process, as a Jackson Pollock painting is evidence of the process of the action of its having been painted. The nature of the process may be completely predetermined, as is certain post-Webern serialism, or determined only in large-order stipulations, as is much indeterminate music. Music may also explore degrees of relationship involving performers, audience, composer, environment, activity, motive, and so on. Experience may become, untransmuted, the raw stuff of music, as easily as one may wish to set up his tape recorder and turn it on or to ask performer (or audience as performers) to pay attention to (or participate in) any sort of activity or perception. The important "what happens" in the traditional structures may be relocated (Cardew's *Octet '61 for Jasper Johns:* "the piece will be known and remembered [if at all] as 'the piece where something peculiar happens in the middle' ") or may simply never appear. Concern with complex formal (and hence presumably analyzable) structures persists today, of course, especially in postserial developments and such ordering principles as the Fibonacci series and "the threading of pitch and mystical number associations with constructional and ideological affinities."[12] But the

---

[11] *Man's Rage for Chaos* (New York: Schocken Books, 1967), pp. 41ff.
[12] Cf. Richard Witts, "Report on Henri Pousseur," *Contact*, 13 (Spring 1976), pp. 13–22.

most immediate and generally only dependable means of ordering what we hear is still, as it has always been, that order we impose *by* observing, *by* hearing, in the fashion we use in observing our own past and present.[13]

II

It is the person who constitutes time by the relations which he necessarily forms between himself, other people, and objects in the world.[14]

—THOMAS CLIFTON

Whatever uses of the past the composer may choose to make, he is constrained by certain inescapable peculiarities of time. Some of these might be suggested as follows:

It's always now.
Something is always happening.
One thing irrevocably succeeds another.
Something just became "past."

These may seem obvious enough to be regarded as truisms.[15] It may be much less obvious, however, that, to the perceiver, within the limits of the precision and selectivity of his memory, his entire past is equally accessible. He can call to present attention a "historical fact" from that past, whether it be a childhood experience remembered or what he may know of

---

[13] "The responsive listener does not create the composition, but he constitutes it as meaningful for him, and if the composition created by the composer is not quite the same as that constituted by the listener, still it is the listener's composition which counts for him. In short, order is constituted a priori by the listener, not imposed by the composer." Thomas Clifton, "Music and the A Priori," *Journal of Music Theory* [hereafter *JMT*], 17, no. 1. (Spring 1973), p. 81.

[14] "Some Comparisons Between Intuitive and Scientific Descriptions of Music," JMT, 19, no. 1 (Spring 1975), p. 98. Cf. also Richmond Browne's review of Allen Forte, *"The Structure of Atonal Music," JMT*, 18, no. 2 (Fall 1974), pp. 390–415: "Even if we accept a current position from linguistics—that a sentence (piece) does not 'contain' its content, but only provides a way for the listener to make up a content-structure out of his own experience—we must still examine the kinds of strategy employed by the listener (ourselves) in that process, even though we no longer assert that the sentence (piece) 'contains' those strategies" (p. 397).

[15] Kramer, letter, p. 3: "How about a few other temporal truisms:
There are as many different Nows as there are different people.
Each Now has its own individual length.
Hence Nows overlap.
Several events have just become past.
Some events become past by human choice.
All recalled past comes through the filter of the present."

Alexander's tactics at Arbela, with instant facility. And in doing so, all experiences in recall are equally valid (although they may produce different "feelings" for him): in the abstract an event remembered from a dream or summoned up from fantasy is neither more nor less "real" than the vivid event remembered of, say, being stung by wasps in the mountains in 1940. Regarding the past as linear, with one's self as a kind of advancing cutting edge at the now and the past extending ever more dimly behind, can be a misapprehension: a more viable metaphor might involve the analogy in which one is inside a sphere of his total experience, each component of which is the same distance from him, and as easily obtained, as every other component, and instantly cross-relatable and synthesizable with any other. Everything thus accessible "makes sense" in terms that it has "happened," a quality all these retrievables share. Any hierarchies are assigned only by personal ordering. Beyond this, the accessible "makes sense" in terms of one's model of living, that with which he has become acculturated, based on one's interpretation of what has "happened" and how. By "looking back," we observe, consider, and, as we wish, we order.

Obviously all this has application to a discussion of music, but in this case it has some special extensions.

1. In hearing a work of music at any "now," all past parts of the work, and of our experience, within the work and without it, including all potential "futures," are equally accessible to us to blend with what we are immediately hearing and experiencing. The first bars of a piece are as immediately accessible as that part ten minutes later which we have just heard, as well as any other experience. David Maslanka (in a letter to the author, May 8, 1975) says this:

> An alternative to straight-line logic is what I have termed "constellation-logic" . . . meaning that from a given starting point the composer can make the intuitive leap of light-years instantaneously and arrive at a seemingly incongruous juxtaposition that is, nonetheless, appropriate. This suggests that the composer can sublimate his conscious state into a quasi-dream state and make extraordinary connections. Intuitions!

and later, "Our experience moves continually in tangents from each 'point' of time art—that is why each moment of time art must be loaded with triggering devices."

2. An event can be defined for each of us as the total, at a given moment, of our knowledge, our experience, of it. What do we talk about when we talk about a piece of music? A bunch of printed papers? The "actual" sounds made? If so, when? The total of what we have available about it

provides a chunk of response, which we may, if we wish, review and, of course, mix, blend, overlay with other responses. Consider the differences of sort-and-review that go on in each of these cases.

> A green chair.
> The green chair.
> Your uncle Walter.
> Remember when your uncle Walter said. . . ?
> Did your uncle ever wear that kind of hat?
> Imagine your uncle's face when he walks in here tomorrow!

Similarly with music.

> Webern's opus 24
> You remember that place in opus 24 where . . .
> Perhaps the candidate will compare this use of the trombone with Webern's. . . .

Suppose in the first group of examples the response to the latter remarks is "I've never met my uncle Walter" and, in the second group, "I've never heard opus 24." We can, depending upon our familiarity with other Webern works, have some idea about what the piece *might* be like; we can certainly tell what it will *not* be like and we can suggest that this defines a fairly small auditory range over which our experience of the piece can occur.

An even more revealing example is the recently discovered Prokofiev viola sonata. Of course there isn't such a piece, and there never was, but, given Prokofiev's extensive output and our own knowledge, though patchy, of this output—and that a viola sonata is something the composer might well have written—we can, if we believe it exists, come pretty close to inventing it for ourselves.[16]

What about the descriptions in fiction of nonexistent works of music such as Leverkühn's compositions in Thomas Mann's *Dr. Faustus,* or the even more detailed descriptions in Walter Van Tilburg Clark's *The City of Trembling Leaves?* We can discuss works we have never heard; we can mention these fictive compositions, as I have just done, in substantive fash-

---

[16] A delightful illustration: a good friend of mine cited and documented a paragraph from the *Sierra Club Bulletin* in his freshman English term paper. When I protested that no such article had appeared in that issue, he replied that there should have been such an article there, and if there had been, that is what it would have said. Question: does the article exist? if so, how? where?

ion.[17] This direction has, of course, led us to a close analogue of the compositional process; the composer is concerned with inventing and realizing a work originally imaginary.

III

For Hume, it is not licit to speak of the form of the moon or its color: its form and color are *the moon. Neither can one speak of the mind's perceptions, inasmuch as the mind is nothing but a series of perceptions.*[18]

—JORGE LUIS BORGES

We perceive music as a result of our paying our "aural attention (or a silent imagining of such attention)"[19] over any extension of time, usually demarcated by performance limits. The imminence of a performance, or our decision to pay attention, is usually a metaphorical putting on of our music-listening ears (or, as Morse Peckham would put it, we take on the role of music listener). What comes to this special attention we deal with, in terms of our acculturation, as music. The first time we hear a piece we may be so overloaded with new aural data and our own perhaps unpremeditated responses that we are able only to hang on to the isolated detail, to a glimmer of the large-order shape we may seek to find. Experience and familiarity, on the other hand, will have us listening to perhaps such specialized details as, say, the nature of the conductor's interpretation or the oboist's phrasing and tone quality. In any event, we shall begin listening for similarities and relationships, later for divergences from a familiar and established ordering. For we shall most probably attempt to order the increasing totality of what we have heard, and are hearing, as it happens, and this ordering will of course depend on how we wish to regard what we have heard ("It doesn't MEAN anything; it's just a lot of noise."). We listen for what we want to hear. Usually we look for cues and clues that will help us to order and "make sense" in terms of our own culture and experience as we hear events; this preconditioning will more than likely impose the nar-

---

[17] Space here is too limited to move into a consideration of the part played by—and the snares of—language itself in talking or thinking about music. This has been discussed for some Western languages, but what about such verb-centered languages as Navaho? or, more challenging, the fictitious language in Borges's "Tlön, Uqbar, Orbis Tertius": "There are no nouns in the hypothetical *Ursprache* of Tlön, which is the source of the living language and dialects; there are impersonal verbs qualified by monosyllabic suffixes or prefixes which have the force of adverbs." *Ficciones,* trans. Anthony Kerrigan (New York: Grove Press, 1962), p. 23.
[18] "A New Refutation of Time," *A Personal Anthology,* trans. Anthony Kerrigan (New York: Grove Press, 1967), p. 49.
[19] Browne, *"The Structure of Atonal Music,"* p. 397.

rative curve, discussed above, as the rationale for the piece's over-structure.

As suggested in Copland's phrase, "the adventures of a melody," the part of music we tend to be concerned with is usually melodic, although of course harmony, rhythm, texture, density, etc., may be later recognized as contributory. The Western European tradition has since Plato made assumptions that certain musical elements and configurations will produce, in response, predictable feelings and emotional responses.[20] This belief about what music does and is supposed to do has a contemporary analogue in stock response: when we hear certain melodic shapes, turns of phrase, whatever, our accultured response is automatic and predictable. No film producer would normally permit stagecoach music during a love scene or tremolo string-section tritones when the kiddies are romping on the lawn with the cocker spaniel. At the most simplistic, any culturally nearly universal melodic identity may be cited, as , which most readers here will instantly identify as the opening notes of a familiar television and radio theme.[21] As a complete melodic line becomes more familiar during the course of a piece of music, it becomes what I ruefully have to label a *gestalt*—eventually its first few pitches suffice to signal its entirety, bringing on each hearing a denser collection of association ("They're playing our song, dear!").[22] David Maslanka discusses ". . . the

---

[20] Cf. Deryck Cooke, *The Language of Music* (London: Oxford University Press, 1959).

[21] This measure, however, has been taken directly from the Chavez violin concerto (full score, three measures after cue 18). Another example: in this case the first theme of the second movement of Stravinsky's Symphony in Three Movements, not QUITE "Oklahoma!"

[22] "False entry" in a classical fugue (for example, m. 19 of the B-minor fugue in vol. 1 of the *Well-Tempered Clavichord*) exploits this. A contemporary and immediate example, although not unrelated: "In one sense, the communication is perfect—one person has complete trust in the other when he is told that a song holds all the truth of a moment or an experience. They both know it; they both accept the validity of the metaphor. Thus, on a non-verbal, non-visual, level they understand each other and the way in which they both think, and they share the knowledge that only certain people can understand them." (Greil Marcus, *Rock and Roll Will Stand* [Boston: Beacon Press, 1969], p. 22.) The whole business of music, symbol, and metaphor is far too extensive to discuss here. I do, however, share Colin Cherry's distaste for dealing with musical "communication" in terms of structures dependent upon entropy. *On Human Communication* (New York: John Wiley & Sons, 1957).

time-compression phenomenon of music *remembered*—An entire piece of Bach or Beethoven or you or me is recalled in a flash; the fine residual liquor is savored in a manner totally beyond elapsed-time experience."

In much "conventional" music, ordering and development use themes as blocks—the melodic unit is moved around as such, retaining most or all of its identity in each appearance. The brief points of imitation in Renaissance polyphony, the music of the Baroque, the "classical" period of Haydn and Mozart all explore this means, and of course it is still a culturally indoctrinated ordering device, the rationale of such musical structures as rondo, fugue, minuet, sonata-allegro, and the like. Parallel to this is the steady-melody means of construction, whether stanzaic as in troubadour and trouvère songs, or through-composed as in operatic recitative.

Again, short motives may be used either with block themes or replacing them—Beethoven and Wagner furnish examples. Once, however, these motives are regarded as nuclei for organic extension and development, although the narrative curve is probably preserved, the direct gestalt quality is blurred and at a remove. Material thus takes on plasticity, apparently capable of organismlike ability to pursue its own life.[23]

> A tree is there. It's a thing. It's not to be denied. It exists for itself. It has its span, and continues in its life span until something happens to it. Again, everything in my music exists in its own personal life span, you see. And one is very conscious of each individual note's life span as well as the gestalt of the gesture, as well as the opposite of the gesture which almost drowns the gesture, that the gesture is fighting AGAINST that drowning . . . they're repetitions in terms of roots, let's say, which are constantly feeding the flower all the time, giving the sap to the flower that is the gesture itself . . . I preset every single one of these ideas. In some sense they're circular, too; they always come back to themselves, like the yin/yang of Chinese . . . And I know in a sense exactly how far I intend to push against these limitations.
>
> —RALPH SHAPEY, interview, August 1972

The musical gesture is, in variation structures, viewed from many ways. Its identity may be maintained almost completely throughout, or it may be taken through highly various transformations until the only perceptible connection a variation may have with its predecessor is its having succeeded that predecessor in the same composition.

---

[23] Cf. note 2.

IV

> *Each moment we live exists, not the imaginary combination of these moments.*
> *The universe, the sum total of all events, is a collection no less ideal than the sum*
> *of all the horses of which Shakespeare dreamt—one, many, none? between 1592*
> *and 1594.*[24]

—JORGE LUIS BORGES

I cannot remember who once defined *now* as the fringe of recollection tinged with anticipation, but it has stuck in my mind for thirty years as fairly apt. How long *now* is in music has been the subject of varied speculation. Roger Reynolds, for example, says this:

> A *perception,* as opposed to a memory of an expectation, is an experience
> which seems totally in the present (no part of it seems "past" before the whole
> is finished). Its duration is normally 2 or 3 seconds, but in the case of small
> groups of stimuli it may extend to as much as 5 seconds, including, perhaps,
> 25–30 items.[25]

One may get some empirical idea of this in operation if he will, while listening to music, fix his attention on a given musical event, say a chord, as it happens, holding it before his present concentration; he will find that as the surge of events continues, he is probably blurrily jarred away from what he is holding and instantly snapped back to awareness of the immediacy he is "now" hearing.[26] Another interesting experiment involves one's listening

---

[24] "A New Refutation of Time," p. 51.

[25] "It(')s Time," *Electronic Music Review,* 7 (July 1968), p. 12. "If one concentrates on a train of signals, its elements are retained in the brain for approximately 5–6 seconds, while elements of an unattended series remain for only 1–2 seconds." The reader is not told from whence these figures come; some of them seem a little "long" to me. The entire article is of considerable interest. Cf. also A. A. Moles: "The *length of presence,* a sort of 'phosphorescence' from immediate perceptions, varies greatly in extent, from a fraction of a second to several seconds. It functions both to create the presence of sensations and to assume the *continuity of being.* . . . (This instantaneous memory brings about the perception of duration connected with the sensation which fills up time. It *dates* events in our consciousness while the phosphorescence of perception lasts. It makes it possible to perceive form in the course of scanning." *Information Theory and Esthetic Perception,* trans. Joel E. Cohen (Urbana: University of Illinois Press, 1966).

[26] The three *fff* piano chords in the second movement of Shostakovich's First Symphony (at cue 22) are good to practice this with: how does each chord, breaking in on one's thinking *about* its predecessor, alter expectation? alter how one thinks about what has just been heard? Ideally, one should let the experiment continue through cue 23, the altered reprise of these chords, to discover how the mind has instant access to a past event and how, in this case, one's thinking about the event is shifted (and, hopefully, enriched). Cf. also Arthur Layzer, "Some Idiosyncratic Aspects of Computer Synthesized Sound," *Proceedings,* 6 (1971), pp. 34–35.

to someone read and reciting back what he is hearing, verbatim (or playing back verbatim what he is hearing played): there is a fixed time lag between his reception of the information and his repeating it, between now and now, as it were. Of course, there are variables here. "Time" might be said to move "faster" or "slower"—if there is silence after a musical event, the attention stays with that event, allowing itself perhaps to wander from it, to ruminate about it. If, on the other hand, events succeed one another rapidly and seem to be "unrelated," as say the spatters of "grace notes" in a Stockhausen piano piece, attention is so densely challenged that it may back off a step, so to speak, and regard the notes as a single cluster, a group event, as Reynolds suggests above. I am not really concerned here with the various subjective and objective qualifications of time that have been dealt with by several writers. We are involved simply with the now; what we hear now is counterpointed against what we remember, by choice or otherwise, of what we have heard, at that moment. Similarly, we are making guesses, more or less qualified by this present/past mix, at anticipating what is about to happen: the future is defined and qualified, as far as we can define it, by expectation and anticipation, and this is continually being fulfilled or surprised.[27]

The step may be made, unfortunately, from observation of and stylization of sequential events to the attribution of inevitability, determinism, even efficient cause as their animation. The result thus emerges not as "Event B happens after event A" but instead "Event B is the result of event A." And in an art vocabulary that is extensively stylized and whose options are restricted, as well as in an art vocabulary that purports to deal fairly directly with the representation of (or simulacrum of) human activity, this assumption can become dangerously easy ("What motivates Iago, or is he simply evil by nature?"). V^7 does not *cause* I; the composer may, however, feel that by his involvement with V^7 in context he has caused I.[28] "Event A implies event B. During event A, we may suspect that event B might come later; but there are many other possible sequels. Or event A may not give a

[27] I have discussed the expectation matter at length elsewhere: "Articulation in Sound Structures: Some Notes Toward an Analytic," *Texas Studies in Literature and Language*, 8, no. 3 (Fall 1966), pp. 423–445.

[28] Clifton discusses this properly in terms of the *post hoc, ergo propter hoc* fallacy ("Music and the A Priori," p. 105), continuing "But it need not be a fallacy for intuitive thought. In music, we have on hand some simple examples of the validity of this expression, one of which is the function of the "introduction." Now, whether or not the introduction is actually written first or later, its aural impression is that it not only introduces the main body of the work but brings it into existence." The entire passage is of considerable interest.

clue while we are in it to event B. Not the only possible consequence, probably not the most likely consequences."[29]

As we have noted, the listener is searching, as he listens, for order, for narrative dramatism, for "making sense." In music written with a traditionally accultured musical grammar, this ordering process becomes a coherently ongoing process with listening: our expectations become codification and we have, as the piece unwinds, clues and cues to familiarize us with the musical structure we are hearing. The music therefore tends to "come out right"; it satisfies what we have grown up expecting to hear, while also challenging us by alteration and surprise. The more familiar the vocabulary, then the more precise what Gerald Warfield refers to as our "internalized grammar"[30] and the more easily this will be accomplished; similarly, the more easily we are able to limit our range of anticipation of what is to be next and the less often will our expectation be surprised. Such expectation can, as it were, "shadow" the future as we listen: V^7, the second entry of a fugue subject, the 6/4 pre-cadenza cue, even longer-range anticipations such as the return of the A part in a rondo (often by what I believe is called "pattern perception," providing our ability to say, "Oh, it's one of *that* sort of piece.").[31]

A recent article by Jonathan Kramer explores some special cases of time perception.[32] One of these is discussed by Clifton.

The notion of temporal overlap, for example, as it appears just before the recapitulation in the first movement of Beethoven's Third Symphony, seems a

---

[29] Kramer, letter, p. 2.

[30] Unpublished notes on notation, April 1976.

[31] A possible and intriguing line of inquiry is suggested "in a paper by Puthoff and Targ, published as chapter 22 of astronaut Edgar D. Mitchell and John White's anthology *Psychic Exploration* (New York: G. P. Putnam's Sons, 1974). The two authors present their theory that events send out waves that propagate backward in time but decay rapidly. The closer the event to the precognition, the stronger the precognition. . . . The authors believe that the familiar *déjà vu* phenomenon is the most common form of precognition. . . . They are also convinced that awaking just before an alarm clock rings is another familiar instance of precognition. Since that is a 'large, timely, and unpleasant event,' its backward wave in time makes a strong impression on the sleeping mind." Martin Gardner, "Mathematical Games," *Scientific American*, 233, no. 4 (October 1975), p. 115.

[32] "Multiple and Non-Linear Time in Beethoven's Opus 135," *PNM*, 11, no. 2 (Spring–Summer 1973), pp. 122–145. I question as naïve the analogy between contemporary life "without goals, where time is fragmented, where past, present, and future interpenetrate each other, where the order is arbitrary" such that "it is fitting that modern multi-directional music should lack unequivocal goals." I have tried to deal with a similar fallacy in the writing of Leonard B. Meyer, see my article, "The Beginning of the Apocalypse?," *Kulchur*, 15 (Autumn 1964), pp. 48–56.

reasonable candidate for a material temporal a priori. (The future, that is, the rest of the movement, and the past, the development section, momentarily slide into one another.)[33]

The same phenomenon can be observed in the first movement of Beethoven's opus 59 no. 1, in which the first bar of the recapitulation is overlapped with the cadencing last bar of the development. Not only do we have here, then, a case of this "shadowing" mentioned above, we have also a subtle and startling jarring of expectation. Of course music that instantly fills every expectation becomes tedium (turn on your AM radio and try this!), just as music that is endless surprise, in which nothing can be guessable, becomes tedium (as is certain music of the 1950s Darmstadt school). The building and surprising of expectation can of course occur at every level of our as-we-listen ordering, from the next note (the diminished seventh in the first movement of Beethoven's opus 74, which is followed by another diminished seventh half a step higher [m. 93 of the development]) to the macrostructure (the second theme reprised first in the first movement of Prokofiev's Sixth Symphony). The more familiar the acculturated vocabulary, the more definite the listener's imposed order, and hence the more accessible, and apt, the composer will find playing with expectation and surprise.[34]

Benjamin Boretz deals at some length with the uniqueness of musical immediacies and with their interrelation.

> Thus there is a particular kind of commensuration in which distinct things are heard, resonating relative to each other, as exhibiting parallelisms, analogous characteristics—these being discovered, as always, by acts of creative attribution, rather than being qualities that inhere in the data. Because these distinct things must occur in chronological order, the attribution of analogy, or parallelism, amounts to the creation of a retroactive illusion that a fused musical event (fused at its time of appearance, or by a subsequent retroaction) actually harbored distinguishable parts, composed of repeatable qualities. As two things in different chronological positions must be altogether distinct in sound, the sharing of aspects is in fact metaphorical, a particular way of attributing resonance to each at a given chronological juncture; and since time-position is an unsharable aspect, even metaphorically, all degrees

of parallelism up to one-to-one repetition are, even metaphorically, only partial . . . True identity is reserved, as always, for the only repeatable quality in
music: being in the same place in the same piece.[35]

As Warfield points out, any order to be applied to these musical identities can be operable

> . . . on any time span, that is, relatively local "disorders" (surprises such
> as the addition of an appoggiatura in a melody the second time it appears) as
> well as relatively large-scale disorders (such as climaxes). . . . Also, and partic-
> ularly in contemporary music, disorder or surprises can be effected at gram-
> matical level by an abrupt change of the organizational principles or style
> within which a piece is composed . . . In a nutshell, I would characterize dull-
> ness as order to the degree of predictability and interest as higher level order
> that makes sense only in retrospect (i.e., as soon as or immediately after one
> hears it.)[36]

And, finally, vital to the position, "I would think that that which is interesting would be richer rather than poorer, that that which is interesting
would, under investigation, reveal a multitude of relationships."[37] It is this
investigation that, as musical analysis, moves within specifically accultured
models in time-art structures to discover, perhaps to reveal, shapes, analogues, divergences, echoes, and other "relationships," and therefore the
nature of investigation becomes needful of question.

1. You will find exactly what your investigative apparatus permits you
to find: what comes through the filter depends on the nature of its mesh.
One might conceivably analyze a Mozart work with post-Webern serial
criteria or a Gibbons madrigal in terms of late nineteenth-century tonal-
functional harmony: he would not get much, but he would probably get
something.

2. You can reveal anything you wish to reveal by using the apparatus
particularly so suited. We have all been amused at the varieties of proofs

[35] "What Lingers On (, When the Song Is Ended)," unpublished paper (1976), pp.
12–13. Both this and a companion paper, "Musical Cosmology," are of considerable importance.
[36] Warfield, unpublished notes.
[37] *Ibid.* Contrast this with the mainstream party-line position: "What is crucial is relational richness, and such richness (or complexity) is in no way incompatible with simplicity of musical vocabulary and grammar. That value is enhanced when rich relationships arise from modest means is scarcely a novel thesis." Leonard B. Meyer,
"Grammatical Simplicity and Relational Richness: The Trio of Mozart's G Minor Symphony,"*Critical Inquiry,* 2, no. 5 (Summer 1976), pp. 683–694.

invoked by those claiming Shakespeare's work to have been written by someone else, but we are still stuck with no serious refutation much beyond "That's silly; everyone knows that this can't be so" and by affirming our alternate apparatus to be more valid.

3. The most suitable apparatus is implied in the work and by it. The finding of relationships must be done, usually lacking explicit cues from the composer, from the musical text itself, subject to our wish to prove our assumptions and our accrued experience of the work: someone has remarked that we know far more now about the poetry of Eliot than he did when he wrote it.

The next question is of course that concerning music in which some fashion of indeterminacy causes the piece not to be the same twice, in which Boretz's "being in the same place in the same piece" is no longer available. Warfield's terms *syntactical disorder* and *contextual disorder* seem to me extremely useful here. Indeterminacy is generally concerned with some sort of process; the realization of the work in performance affirms the process and leaves a unique record of this affirmation. Judgments may be made about the nature and implications of the process at least as revelatory as those arrived at by any other course. Again, unless some manner of dramatism or meta-information is present, no means of informing the listener of indeterminacy is available, and on first hearing he will presumably deal with the fixity of the performance he hears: once the work has happened it is no longer random.[38]

> Given a random string of something, say notes, as soon as you can "understand" it, it is no longer random. The numbers 14, 18, 23, 34, 42, 50, 59, 66, 72, 79 may be hard to remember and have the appearance of randomness to everyone except those who use the N.Y. west side subway. Now that I understand those numbers as where the train stops they are anything but random. My understanding of the situation is that as soon as one can rise above low-level description ("the first number is a fourteen, the second number is an eighteen, etc.") something is no longer random. (Or, to be very precise, something is no longer *regarded* as being random.)[39]
>
> Given that there are an infinite number of relationships between any two elements, on what grounds do we select some over others? It seems to me

---

[38] Cf. David Behrman, "What Indeterminate Notation Determines," *PNM*, 3, no. 2 (Spring–Summer 1965), pp. 58–73.

[39] Warfield, letter to the author, March 20, 1976. (The example of the West Side New York subway station numbers originated with Milton Babbitt.)

most efficient to describe such a relationship as an embeddiing, i.e., something which happens in conjunction with something else. This does not mean that the second event is predictable. Certainly in music written within a specific style there will be more events predictable than non-predictable, but, in the case of the unpredictable-in-advance, a relationship *can* be established later that is consistent with one's view of the composition and the style within which it is composed.[40]

And I suggest that one's view of the composition depends much on what data from his experience he selects to be aware of at any now, at the hearing of any particular event; this is what I presume Boretz would include as "acts of creative attribution." Of course this can be looked at in the light of the composition process and the improvisation process as well: one is selecting, at a given now, that option that makes best immediate "sense" to him in terms of that selectivity from his total available experience.

To regard the piece, therefore, as a time-extended totality—this perception moving *from* its nature as an accrued succession of events—is almost inescapable to anyone considering it in other than its real-time performance, and of course, as familiarity increases, often even then.

> Within a piece, however, the history of every distinct thing is ultimately its absorption as a component of a complex thing—ultimately the whole piece itself, whose sound is then the cumulative sound of the cumulative chronology of its components. But the retroaction of musical things on each other is not merely replacement by different things—the syntactical landscape is at all times connected, and ordered by the uniform projection of quantized qualities; so that everything possible within a musical landscape at any moment is *commensurable* with everything else.[41]

My point here is that to begin with this end product, *without* seeing it always first as this kind of "cumulative chronology" of now perceptions, can do little to remove one from the traps and redundancies of the first of the two overviews of the nature of music discussed above.

Kramer says, concerning contemporary music in which "the most readily apparent and the most meaningful connections are often not between those events immediately adjacent in clock-time,"[42] music in which anticipation of a coherent total structure, even "goal-directedness" itself, is apparently destroyed:

---

[40] Warfield, critical notes to the original version of this paper.
[41] Boretz, "What Lingers On," p. 11.
[42] "Multiple and Non-Linear Time in Beethoven's Opus 135," p. 142.

We do not progress from one moment to another, but rather each moment provides fresh data concerning a static totality that will be known completely only at its end . . . The whole is defined, but its individual parts are irrational. They have tendencies, they have probabilities, but they are not individually predictable or understandable.

I hope I have been able to show that without a precultured musical language this is bound to happen to the listener: we can feel the same sort of "static totality" about *any* kind of music whose acculturation and tradition are unfamiliar to us: music from non-Western cultures, for example. He continues, "Much of the power in traditional music lies in backwards and forwards hearing—hearing a later event as clarifying an earlier one and hearing an earlier event as implying a later one." Once we have become familiar with a style, we can attribute apparent directionality in its terms. The business about "backwards and forwards" needs clarifying, however, especially in light of Kramer's footnote to this same page: "An important aspect of [Stockhausen's] *Zyklus,* not often mentioned, is that, since the performer may go in either direction around the circle, the piece proclaims the equality of backwards and forwards."[43]

This has been anticipated by Edward Cone: "Thus, for purely instrumental compositions lacking passages where the exigencies of strict note-counting determine the direction of events, forward and backward indeed seem to be indistinguishable."[44] All retrogrades, whether those in the second movement of Webern's opus 21, the reprise of the minuet of Haydn's A-major violin sonata, or the retrograde inversion of the Preludium of Hindemith's *Ludus Tonalis* that forms the Postludium (Cone discusses inversion extensively in his article as well), are equivalent. We are simply, at a recognition point, able to say, "Ah, that's the whatever-it-is backward" or, more accurately, to recognize that the order of a previous collection of musical events has been reversed. Apparently the version we hear first is "forward"; why should the composer not say that the first hearing is the backward of what you'll later hear forward? What Kramer refers to as time-scrambling is actually merely expectation-fooling.[45]

---

[43] I assume as commonplace the perceptibility of "motion in time" being dependent on motion in space. With spatial immobility, especially when the senses of sight and sound are denied (as in solitary confinement in darkness, say), we encounter "losing track of time." Cf. research involving total sensory isolation, a good introduction being Woodburn Heron, "The Pathology of Boredom," *Scientific American,* 190, no. 1 (January 1957), pp. 52–56.

[44] "Beyond Analysis," *PNM,* 7, no. 1 (Fall–Winter 1967), p. 37.

[45] I agree with Kramer's statements "When expectation is fooled, there are consequences. A network of fooled expectations can have profound structural and perceptual

V

Given a fixed structure in familiar terms, in which accultured expectation can generate more or less an analytical hearing, we have a number of ways to move against its apparent linear time extension. One of these is the citation of other material. When Ives cites a familiar tune, it will often be somewhat distorted in rhythmic or pitch relationships, perhaps incomplete or overextended. Not only, then, may we suddenly realize a rich complex of remembrances, with their attendant connotations, but this in turn is being counterpointed against by the expectational surprises Ives has written into the familiar: well-known shapes blur and shift before our attention. George Rochberg's "magic theatre" uses citation to invoke, directly as on the stage of our perception, past experiences and feelings. Sometimes citation may be included to raise the surprise contrast and counterpointing to the satirical, as the clichés from the conservatory piano repertoire collaged in Phil Winsor's *Melted Ears*. In other cases the familiar is repeated, unchanged or only slightly so, to allow us to drift leisurely about in our selection of experience remembered as we listen, for example, as the variations on "The Last Rose of Summer," which make up the last movement of Michael Sahl's *A Mitzvah for the Dead*. In Ives's work the citations function as actual structural determinants, sometimes as *en bloc* themes. Still other composers may move against expected ordering within citations or even disrupt or short-circuit them, breaking our expectation loose from the familiar and reshaping how we view the growing totality of what we have already heard.

I wish to suggest that certain vital moments in a piece of music serve us as focal and organizing, events that in the immediacy of the new so jar our expectation and so alter (and reilluminate) our sense of what we have heard that we regard what we are subsequently hearing in a changed fashion. I have mentioned elsewhere that this is analogous to Ezra Pound's use of the "image"-cum-ideogram in his poetry: "We are aware of cross-references, of clusters of ideograms that (like bees swarming) mysteriously but demonstrably swarm together. Each cluster of ideograms gets *some* of its cohesion because of its polarity to another cluster."[46]

---

consequences, going beyond the 'mere' into the whole essence of musical temporality, as defined in the piece in question at least" (letter, p. 5) only in such cases in which the listener, by previous (sometimes voluntary) familiarity with a specific style, is in a position of generating the "structural and perceptual" for what he hears are not simply different sounds. Cf. Elliott Carter, "Shop Talk by an American Composer," *Problems of Modern Music* (New York: W. W. Norton, 1962), p. 56. The whole problem of what literary critics have termed *stylistics* needs considerable investigation, as such, for music.

[46] Harold W. Watts, cited in Barney Childs, "Indeterminacy and Theory: Some Notes," *The Composer*, 1, no. 1 (Summer 1969), p. 33. The primacy of contextuality in affirming

It is this focusing quality, this polarizing quality both "ahead" and "behind," that redetermines relationships, makes the events in a piece of music relate in supra-"linear" fashion, lifts a piece out of Kramer's "static totality," and provides rationale to the "irrational" individual parts, makes recognizable possible tendencies and probabilities. The past is re-viewed and the expectation redefined. These are the moments at which we suddenly hear differently, maybe the moments at which we say, "Ah, NOW I see what is happening; now I can see what he's getting at." And, although this works most obviously in nonlinear compositions, replacing the conventional narrative curve and tightly structured ordering, it may be seen equally well to happen in "conventionally" made pieces: the opening of the first movement development, in F-sharp minor, in the Mozart G-minor symphony, for example. The expected relationships of a now can be disoriented and redefined in terms of a freshly felt totality.[47]

Another means of expanding the potential of nontraditional musical structure is characterized by David Maslanka:

Attempts to warp straight-line perception—"logical" sequence, "real-time" perception—have been traditionally (and presently) most often concerned with the inducement of a quasi-narcotic state in which the subject is mesmerized by a specific type and quality of sound, e.g., long, sustained sounds, low dynamic, few events, repetitions small and large. This evoked state appears to be non-analytical, that is, analytical function is repressed (which it is normally in most listeners in any case). Information is received

---

uniqueness—"*chronology* becomes an aspect of *identity* within a musical structure"—is developed by Boretz in his two papers previously cited (cf. note 35 above). These special vital moments may not only be related to the sort of embedded hierarchic structure discussed by Thomas Fay, "Perceived Hierarchic Structures in Language and Music," *JMT*, 15, nos. 1 & 2 (1971), but also may establish such an apparent structure in terms of our own listening.

[47] Kramer objects (*ibid.*) on the grounds that "such an event can be felt throughout the whole piece only if it is a progressive (I almost said linear) piece, whose parts are functionally implicative, to use Meyer's term. . . . Consider the pieces I mention in the article: *Klavierstück XI*, Third Sonata [Boulez], Piano Concert, *Cantéjodayâ, Momente*—and let's add a few: *A Rainbow in Curved Air, HPSCHD, Caritas*—there are huge gestures in some of these pieces, even an overwhelming discontinuity in *Rainbow*, but what do these moments mean? They do not define the total past and future of the piece; they cannot because of the nature of the pieces." I forget which jazz musician was given the objection to early bop, "You can't dance to it": his response was on the order of "Maybe *you* can't dance to it." I submit that as any piece is bounded and possessed in our experience, such moments do indeed so define. They may be recognizable in terms of a defined style, as the Mozart example above, and they may also be specially and individually imposed by the listener. In some indeterminate music they may be different with each different performance.

uncritically and the whole process, if successful, results in a sense of dream-state, a suspended time-sense; events are perceived in a different time frame.[48]

The expectational pre-set for many people hearing this music, and proba-bly for some writing it, can be attributed to the current accultured enthusi-asm for "expanded consciousness"—"mind blowing," "trips," psychedelia, interest in the philosophy, and sometimes the music, of "primitive" tribes and of the Far East. Once the effectiveness of the now as a perceiver of sep-arable and potentially orderable musical events has been overruled, atten-tion is able to rummage as it pleases in the vast display of remembering, feeling, etc., making the sort of intuitive "light-year jumps" cited in the previous Maslanka quotation. The now thus appears to be reduplicating and extending itself.

The intent of some composers, however, and no doubt of some listen-ers, is counter to this use of the music. The plan to blur and shift our sense of time "progression," of linear "development," may be in the interest of increased rather than decreased immediacy of listener attention to the music. A premise can be immediately made clear, followed by a micro-altering of relationships and events building up, or by subtle acoustic changes, as in the recent music of La Monte Young. Essentially, however, the concern is with breaking the now loose from its traditional capacity as sequential ordering apparatus, to free it from obvious past associations and gestures, and to make it thus ever unique and freshly felt. This is often ap-proached by casting what is to be heard without obvious rhythmic order-ing, either by elasticizing or otherwise deforming a steady pulse (heard or inferred), or by abandoning it altogether. Clifton discusses one version of the phenomenon as *static succession:*

> . . . a static succession will tend to obliterate not only the distinction but the very idea of rhythmic levels. Instead, what is offered is a simple "pres-ence," a state of sound which does not seem to move but which is rather pas-sively content to be replaced by another sonority. "Static" should probably be interpreted as a limit case, since even a simple sustained sound does not be-have analogously to the color of a wall, but is always in a state of becoming. Perhaps you can think of static succession as a time experience lying some-where between duration and rhythm.[49]

Clifton cites Ligeti's organ piece *Volumina* to furnish examples; as do other American scholarly writers, he seems almost exclusively concerned with

---

[48] Letter, May 30, 1975, as annotated later.
[49] "Some Comparisons," pp. 99–100.

European examples in illustrating music of the last twenty years. For an experience a little nearer home I would suggest some of the music by Pharoah Sanders. In one approach (say, "Let Us Go into the House of the Lord," Impulse S-9199) harmonic progression has been slowed down so thoroughly that we hear each "change" as a sustained sonority field, minutely textured by steady quiet shifting small sounds. In another (say, "Light of Love," Impulse S-9181) we have a steady wall of high-energy sound with the similar microvariables in continuous minute detail.

The fact that a piece is the result of an indeterminate process is apt to lead to erroneous conclusions about the nature of its treatment of musical time. Such a piece may vary enormously from performance to performance, but each single performance will happen as uniquely and irrevocably in its succession of what's presented now as any more "ordered" musical construct. Admitting performer choice to determine order, or improvisation, animates the performer's sense of "right"-ness about what should be played when, but the result is still no less committed to itself than any other piece of music. Graphic or field notation cannot have an analogue in listening; often an audience must be preinformed that indeterminacy is present, or see it dramatized for them during the performance, and its process requirements are as binding and result-directed, in the abstract, as those of any other work. Christian Wolff discusses how the performer, if not the audience, may use his sense of fitness of choice to order within the limits of the score:

> A situation is indicated, but not when one enters into it, nor, necessarily, for how long one is in it. Durations of the individual notes may be indicated as relatively short, long, or free, or they may be determined by the requirements of a situation. . . . The players constantly have options of what to play (say, one of three pitches, any pitch at a fixed loudness, any loudness at a fixed timbre). . . . It's as though you take a walk with a friend or friends, going by whatever way you like, agreeing on the way, with a direction in mind or getting lost or going nowhere in particular, and you are absorbed by this: the landscape in which they walk is what is given.[50]

---

[50] Notes to *Music of Our Time: A Second Wind for Organ* (Odyssey 32 16 0158). Kramer calls to my attention Ives's remarks (in the *Memos*) concerning *Tone Roads* leading by different ways to the same destination, with every traveler going his own way on basically the same journey.

VI

> *For gloss demands*
> *A gloss annexed*
> *Till busy hands*
> *Blot out the text. . . .*[51]
> —J. V. CUNNINGHAM

Richard Witts characterizes as one of the "sides" of Henri Pousseur:

> The intellectual attracted to past creativity ("any human creation is carried in a general motion, a motion of history"), who simply loves "the classics" and detests ascetic puritanism, but realizes that these are products supporting the prevailing means of repression. This can be reconciled through "enriching the last word in the revolutionary thought of mankind . . . bringing about permanent interaction between the experience of the past and the experience of the present" (Lenin). Or in the words of Mao: "Make the past serve the present . . . Weed through the old to bring forth the new."[52]

"A theory," says Thomas Clifton, "ultimately represents a decision to regard objects from a particular point of view."[53] Just as we may impose any ordering we please on what we choose to call to mind of the phenomena in a work of music, so also we may thus impose upon what we select from the events of "past" or "historical" time. To regard as an artifact the collection of perceptions about sound that make up a piece of music is probably less confusing than so to regard a collection of perceptions to make up "history." Linear thinking about time, and our wish to "make sense" of experience, may even lead us to consider our own life as artifact, as a shape or trajectory "moving" from the past into the future, with our attendant efforts to preplan and control that future part "yet to come." In such a "particular point of view" a theoretic can be assumed to serve as an apparatus to deal with events, a dynamic of events (for example, "a motion of history," as above) with prescribed qualities of relationship, predictablity, even inevitability. This presumes further that such an apparatus provide its users with a coherence whose implicit nature as such furnishes not only ordering but also validity and even purpose absolute beyond whatever

---

[51] "To the Reader," *The Exclusions of a Rhyme* (Denver: Alan Swallow, 1960), p. 70.
[52] Witts, "Report on Henri Pousseur," p. 14.
[53] "Training in Music Theory: Process and Product," *JMT*, 13, no. 1 (Spring 1969), p. 63.

analysis or perception may impose. For the adept, therefore, only certain perception schemes can reveal this purpose.

> What should be obvious [in a score by Valentin Silvestrov] is that the dialectical "debate" between the "cultural" [precisely notated] and "mysterious" [indeterminate] and its substructures here reaches a culmination, and that the opposition is no longer tolerable as a dialectical debate but only as a synthesis.

How is this to be understood: as a retreat, a retrenchment, a surrender to possible pressures? Not at all! Let us make the following argument: If classical (tonal) music is regarded as the "text," modern developments (historical inevitability) assume the position of "context" to the "text." In other words, the surge of history from Mozart to Schönberg is the creation of "contextual" music with serialism ultimately viewed as the severest form of criticism of the diatonic aesthetic. *Text* and *context* (a comfortable dualism) was ultimately undone by the phenomenon of John Cage and *4′ 33″*. The result, for Silvestrov, lies in the synthesis of the two—no longer an anathema. Thus, in the dialectical language of avant-gardism, Silvestrov's more recent activities can be viewed as "textual" criticisms of "contextual" activities and *not* a rejection of them. The result, of course, is a new *text,* the merger of the knower and the known.[54]

In light of the position that this paper suggests, the above is not only simply another trap into which linear time thinking may lead us, but is also, because its assumptions from historical inevitability ("the surge of history," etc.) and the dialectic place it within our accultured intellectual tradition and its view of time and history, difficult to override. It provides what may be taken as a self-evident value with which our traditional need for order may be satisfied: the dramatism of the narrative curve is thus seemingly inherent, macrostructural, in cultures and historical eras.[55]

---

[54] Virko Baley, "The Kiev Avant Garde: A Retrospective in Midstream," *Numus-West* (June 1974), pp. 12–14.

[55] Americans seem peculiarly resistant to the political stances concomitant with the ideas in these two previous citations. "Our audience is, first, less political than any European audience. (I am thinking of political theory, not politician's antics.) It lives in a country without serious radical politics, and where the Cold War was waged right down to our last brain cells. The first audience condition combines with the second, our aversion to being the object of 'messages.' Now it is clearly the combination of these qualities that makes the going for socialist or anarchist realism so rough. The first condition makes it necessary to start from scratch, to set the stage, to explain, to redefine all those poisoned political terms. Condition two forbids you to do that, on pain of speaking to an empty hall." Hans Koning, "That Rarest of Birds, a Successful Political Movie," *The New York Times,* June 23, 1974, sec. D, p. 13.

Mr. Baley, in a later footnote to his article, acknowledges his debt to structuralism, the latest European-generated fashion in critical apparatus. This has not been extensively explored in dealing with music, despite the fervor of its disciples, and some of its premises may prove of value detached from the main body of assumptions. Unfortunately, as a catchall, it appears merely to be yet another time- and history-relating manner of organization to produce order, not only in the material to be ordered but in the means of ordering as well. A recent article, one of singular opacity, strikes a note already dispiritingly familiar:

> Our understanding of what is going on is hampered, however, by the speed of the influx of imperfectly digested theories from Europe—theories, having their own text milieu, whose acclimatization on Anglo-American culture will take more time. (One should not assume, even, that they must be acclimatized: quite possibly we can discover, through such thinkers as Peirce or Burke, a native strain of thought that would parallel what challenges us in Europe.)[56]

Our "need" is not, of course, for something that will parallel the import, but that will, in terms of the directions of much New World creativity, furnish a durable and applicable replacement. Knowledge of the process generating a piece of music can be a powerful assistance in dealing with the music, but (1) the process is *not* the analysis and (2) the means of selection we apply to provide whatever makes up the music for us, no matter how developed or structured, can be assumed to be a validation of the music only through misapprehension.

---

[56] Geoffrey Hartman, "Literary Criticism's Discontents," *Critical Inquiry*, 3, no. 2 (Winter 1976), p. 211.

Generating and Organizing Variety in the Arts*

Brian Eno

In this essay Brian Eno, himself a well-known composer of new music, discusses a primary focus of experimental music, which, he notes, "has been toward its own organization, and toward its own capacity to produce and control variety." Concentrating for his example on Michael Nyman's piece, 1-100 (Obscure 6), *Eno suggests in this essay a "technique for discussing contemporary music in terms of its functioning."*

A musical score is a statement about organization; it is a set of devices for organizing behavior toward producing sounds. That this observation was not so evident in classical composition indicates that organization was not then an important focus of compositional attention. Instead, the organizational unit (be it the orchestra or the string quartet or the relationship of a man to a piano) remained fairly static for two centuries while compositional attention was directed at using these given units to generate specific results by supplying them with specific instructions.

In order to give more point to the examination of experimental music

* Reprinted from *Studio International* (November–December 1976), pp. 279–283. Copyright © 1976 by Brian Eno.

that follows, I should like to detail some of the aspects and implications of the paradigm of classical organization—the orchestra. A traditional orchestra is a ranked pyramidal hierarchy of the same kind as the armies that existed contemporary to it. The hierarchy of rank is in this pattern: conductor, leader of the orchestra; section principals; section subprincipals; and, finally, rank-and-file members. Occasionally a soloist will join the upper echelons of this system; and it is implied, of course, that the composer with *his* intentions and aspirations has absolute, albeit temporary, control over the whole structure and its behavior. This ranking, as does military ranking, reflects varying degrees of responsibility; conversely, it reflects varying degrees of constraint on behavior. Ranking has another effect: like perspective in painting, it creates "focus" and "point of view." A listener is given the impression that there are a foreground and a background to the music and cannot fail to notice that most of the "high-responsibility" events take place in the foreground, to which the background is an ambience or counterpoint.[1] This is to say that the number of perceptual positions available to the listener is likely to be limited. The third observation I should like to make about the ranking system in the orchestra is this: it predicates the use of trained musicians. A trained musician is, at the minimum, one who will produce a predictable sound given a specific instruction. His training teaches him to be capable of operating precisely like all the other members of his rank. It trains him, in fact, to subdue some of his own natural variety and thus to increase his reliability (predictability).

I shall be using the term *variety* frequently in this essay and I should like to attempt some definition of it now. It is a term taken from cybernetics (the science of organization) and it was originated by W. R. Ashby.[2] The *variety* of a system is the total range of its outputs, its total range of behavior. All organic systems are probabilistic: they exhibit variety, and an organism's flexibility (its adaptability) is a function of the amount of variety that it can generate. Evolutionary adaptation is a result of the interaction of this probabilistic process with the demands of the environment. By producing a *range* of outputs evolution copes with a *range* of possible futures. The environment in this case is a *variety-reducer* because it "selects" certain strains by allowing them to survive and reproduce, and filters out others. But, just as it is evident that an organism will (by its material

---

[1] This ranking is most highly developed in classical Indian music, where the tamboura plays a drone role for the sitar. I think it no coincidence that Indian society reflected the same sharp definition of roles in its caste system.

[2] W. Ross Ashby, *An Introduction to Cybernetics* (1956; reprint ed., London: University Paperbacks, 1964).

```
——→ sing 8        IF
    sing 5        THE ROOT
    sing 13(f 3)  BE IN CONFUSION
    sing 6        NOTHING
    sing 5 (f 1)  WILL
    sing 8        BE
    sing 8        WELL
    sing 7        GOVERNED
    hum 1
——→ sing 8        THE SOLID
    sing 8        CANNOT BE
    sing 9(f 2)   SWEPT AWAY
    sing 8        AS
    sing 17(f 1)  TRIVIAL
    sing 6        AND
    sing 8        NOR
    sing 8        CAN
    sing 17(f1)   TRASH
    sing 8        BE ESTABLISHED AS
    sing 9 (f 2)  SOLID
    sing 5 (f1)   IT JUST
    sing 4        DOES NOT
    sing 6 (f 1)  HAPPEN
    hum 3(f 2)
——→ speak 1      MISTAKE NOT CLIFF FOR
    MORASS AND TREACHEROUS BRAMBLE
```

NOTATION

——→ The leader gives a signal and all enter concertedly at the same moment. The second of these signals is optional; those wishing to observe it should gather to the leader and choose a new note and enter just as at the beginning (see below)

sing 9(f2) SWEPT AWAY" means sing the words "SWEPT AWAY" on a length of 9 breath note (syllables freely disposed) nine times; the same note each time; of the nine notes two (any two) should be loud, the rest soft. After each note take in breath and sing again.

"hum 7" means: hum a length of a breath note seven times; the same note each time, all soft.

"speak 1" means: speak the given words in steady tempo all together in a low voice, once (follow the leader)

PROCEDURE

Each chorus member chooses his own note (silently) for the first line (if eight times) All enter together on the leader's signal. For each subsequent line choose a note that you can hear being sung by a colleague. It may be necessary to move to within earshot of certain notes. The note, once chosen, must be carefully retained. Time may be taken over the choice. If there is no note, or only the note you have just been singing, or only a note or notes that you are unable to sing, choose your note for the next line freely. Do not sing the same note on two consecutive lines.

Each singer progresses through the text at his own speed. Remain stationary for the duration of a line, move around only between lines. All must have completed "hum 3(f2)" before the signal for the last line is given. At the leader's discretion this last line may be omitted

Cornelius Cardew: *The Great Learning.*

nature) and must (for its survival) generate variety, it is also true that this variety must not be unlimited. That is to say, we require for successful evolution the transmission of *identity* as well as the transmission of *mutation.* Or conversely, in a transmission of evolutionary information, what is important is not only that you get it right but also that you get it slightly wrong, and that the deviations or mutations that are useful can be encouraged and reinforced.

My contention is that a primary focus of experimental music has been toward its own organization, and toward its own capacity to produce and control variety, and to assimilate "natural variety"—the "interference value" of the environment. Experimental music, unlike classical (or avant-garde) music, does not typically offer instructions toward highly specific results, and hence does not normally specify wholly repeatable configurations of sound. It is this lack of interest in the *precise* nature of the piece that has led to the (I think) misleading description of this kind of music as *indeterminate.* I hope to show that an experimental composition aims to set in motion a system or organism that will generate unique (that is, not necessarily repeatable) outputs, but that, at the same time, seeks to limit the range of these outputs. This is a tendency toward a "class of goals" rather than a particular goal, and it is distinct from the "goalless behavior" (indeterminacy) idea that gained currency in the 1960s.

I should like to deal at length with a particular piece of experimental music that exemplifies this shift in orientation. The piece is Paragraph 7 of *The Great Learning*[3] by Cornelius Cardew, and I have chosen this not only because it is a compendium of organizational techniques but also because it is available on record (DGG 2538216). In general I shall restrict my references to music that has been recorded. I should point out that implicit in the score is the idea that it may be performed by *any* group of people (whether or not trained to sing). The version available on record is performed by a mixed group of musicians and art students, and my experience of the piece is based on four performances of it in which I have taken part.

A cursory examination of the score will probably create the impression that the piece would differ radically from one performance to another, because the score appears to supply very few *precise* (that is, quantifiable) constraints on the nature of each performer's behavior, and because the performers themselves (being of variable ability) are not "reliable" in the sense that a group of trained musicians might be. The fact that this does not happen is of considerable interest, because it suggests that *somehow a set of controls that are not stipulated in the score arise in performance* and that these "automatic" controls are the real determinants of the nature of the piece.

In order to indicate that this proposition is not illusory, I now offer a description of how the piece might develop if *only* the scored instructions affected its outcome. I hope that by doing this I shall be able to isolate a difference between this hypothetical performance and a real performance of the piece and that this difference will offer clues as to the nature of the "automatic" controls.

Hypothetical performance. The piece begins with a rich sustained discord ("choose any note for your first note"). As the point at which singers

---

[3] Each paragraph corresponds to one in the Confucian classic of the same title.

move onto their next line and next note is governed by individual breath lengths ("sing each line for the length of a breath"), it is probable that they will be changing notes at different times. Their choice of note is affected by three instructions: "do not sing the same note on two consecutive lines," "sing a note that you can hear," and, if for some reason neither of these instructions can be observed, "choose your next note freely." Now, let's propose that there are twenty singers, and that by some chance they have all chosen different first notes. Presumably one of them reaches the end of his first line before any other singer. As he cannot repeat his own previous note, he has an absolute maximum of nineteen notes to choose from for his "next note." He chooses one, and reduces the "stock" of notes available to nineteen. The next singer to change has a choice of eighteen notes. By a continuation of this procedure, one would expect a gradual reduction of different notes in the piece until such time as there were too few notes available for the piece to continue without the arbitrary introduction of new notes in accordance with the third of the three pitch instructions. With a larger number of singers this process of reduction might well last throughout the piece. So, in this hypothetical performance, the overall shape of the piece would consist of a large stock of random notes thinning down to a small, even, occasionally replenished stock of equally random notes (as they are either what is left of the initial stock or the random additions to it).

Real performance. The piece begins with the same rich discord and *rapidly* (that is, before the end of the first line is reached) thins itself down to a complex but not notably dissonant chord. Soon after this, it "settles" at a particular level of variety that is much higher than that in the hypothetical performance and that tends to revolve more or less harmonically around a drone note. This level of variety is fairly closely maintained throughout the rest of the piece. It is rare that performers need to resort to the "choose your next note freely" instruction, and, except in the case of small numbers of singers, this instruction appears to be redundant.[4] This is because new notes are always being introduced into the piece regardless of any intention on the part of individual performers to do so. And this observation points up the presence of a set of "accidents" that are at work to replenish the stock of notes in the piece. The first of these has to do with the "unreliability" of a mixed group of singers. At one extreme it is quite

---

[4] A number of the score instructions seem redundant; all of those concerning the leader, for example, make almost no difference to the music.

feasible that a tone-deaf singer would hear a note and, following the primary pitch instruction to "sing any note that you can hear," would "match" it with a new note. Another singer might unconsciously transpose a note into an octave in which it is easier for him to sing, or might sing a note that is harmonically a close relative (a third or a fifth) to it. A purely external physical event will also tend to introduce new notes: the phenomenon of beat frequency. A *beat frequency* is a new note formed when two notes close to each other in pitch are sounded. It is mathematically and not harmonically related to them. These are three of the ways by which new material is introduced.

Apart from the "variety-reducing" clauses in the score ("sing a note that you can hear," "do not sing the same note on two consecutive lines"), some others arise in performance. One of these has to do with the acoustic nature of the room in which the performance is taking place. If it is a large room (and most rooms that can accommodate performances on the scale on which this piece normally occurs are large), then it is likely to have a *resonant frequency*. This is defined as the pitch at which an enclosure resonates, and what it means in practice is this: a note sounded at a given amplitude in a room whose resonant frequency corresponds to the frequency of the note will *sound louder* than any other note at the same amplitude. Given a situation, then, where a number of notes are being sounded at fairly even amplitude, whichever one corresponds to the resonant frequency of the room will sound louder than any of the others. In Paragraph 7 this fact creates a statistical probability that the piece will drift toward being centered on an environmentally determined note. This may be the drone note to which I alluded earlier.

Another important variety reducer is preference ("taste"). Because performers are often in a position to choose between a fairly wide selection of notes, their own cultural histories and predilections will be an important factor in which "strains" of the stock they choose to reinforce (and, by implication, which they choose to filter out). This has another aspect; it is extremely difficult unless you are tone-deaf (or a trained singer) to maintain a note that is very discordant with its surroundings. You generally adjust the note almost involuntarily so that it forms some harmonic relationship to its surroundings. This helps explain why the first dissonant chord rapidly thins out.

In summary, then, the generation, distribution, and control of notes within this piece are governed by the following: one specific instruction ("do not sing the same note on two consecutive lines"), one general instruction ("sing any note that you can hear"), two physiological factors (tone-deafness and transposition), two physical factors (beat frequencies and resonant frequency), and the cultural factor of "preference." Of course, there are other parameters of the piece (particularly amplitude) that are similarly controlled and submit to the same techniques of analysis, and the "breathing" aspects of the piece might well give rise to its most important characteristic—its meditative calm and tranquillity. But what I have mentioned above should be sufficient to indicate that something quite different from classical compositional technique is taking place: the composer, instead of ignoring or subduing the variety generated in performance, has constructed the piece so that this variety is really the substance of the music.

Perhaps the most concise description of this kind of composition, which characterizes much experimental music, is offered in a statement made by the cybernetician Stafford Beer. He writes: "Instead of trying to specify it in full detail, you specify it only somewhat. You then ride on the dynamics of the system in the direction you want to go."[5] In the case of the Cardew piece, the "dynamics of the system" is its interaction with the environmental, physiological, and cultural climate surrounding its performance.

The English composer Michael Parsons provides another view on this kind of composition:

> The idea of one and the same activity being done simultaneously by a number of people, so that everyone does it slightly differently, "unity" becoming "multiplicity," gives one a very economical form of notation—it is only necessary to specify one procedure and the variety comes from the way everyone does it differently. This is an example of making use of "hidden resources" in the sense of natural individual differences (rather than talents or abilities) which is completely neglected in classical concert music, though not in folk music.[6]

This movement toward using natural variety as a compositional device is exemplified in a piece by Michael Nyman called *1-100 (Obscure 6)*. In this piece, four pianists each play the same sequence of one hundred chords descending slowly down the keyboard. A player is instructed to move on to his next chord only when he can no longer hear his last. As this judgment is dependent on a number of variables (how loud the chord was

[5] Stafford Beer, *Brain of the Firm: The Managerial Cybernetics of Organization* (London: Allen Lane, 1972), p. 69.
[6] Michael Parsons, quoted in Michael Nyman, *Experimental Music—Cage and Beyond* (London: Studio Vista, 1974).

Michael Nyman: *1–100* for four or more pianos. Allow each chord to fade before playing the next chord. Dynamics should be constant throughout (that is, all *pp*, or *f*, or *fff*) apart from the beginning, when all players should begin together, no attempt should be made to synchronize chords.

played, how good the hearing of the player is, what the piano is like, the point at which you decide that the chord is no longer audible), the four players rapidly fall out of sync with one another. What happens after this is that unique and delicate clusters of up to four different chords are formed, or rapid sequences of chords are followed by long silences. This is an elegant use of the compositional technique that Parsons has specified, not least because it, like the Cardew piece, is extremely beautiful to listen to—a factor that seems to carry little critical weight at present.

Composition of this kind tends to create a perceptual shift in a listener as major as (and concomitant with) the compositional shift. It is interesting that on recordings, these two pieces both have "fade" endings (the Cardew piece also has a fade beginning), as this implies not that the piece has finished but that it is *continuing out of earshot.* It is only rock music that has really utilized the compositional value of the fade-out: these pieces use it as a convenience in the sense that both were too long for a side of a record. But a fade-out is quite in keeping with the general quality of the pieces and indicates an important characteristic that they share with other experimental music: that the music is a section from a hypothetical continuum and that it is not especially directional: it does not exhibit strong "progress" from one point (position, theme, statement, argument) to a resolution. To test the validity of this assumption, imagine a fade-out ending halfway through Beethoven's Ninth Symphony. Much of the energy of classical music arises from its movement from one musical idea to another—the theme and variation idea—and this movement is directional in the sense that the history and probable futures of the piece have a bearing on the perception of what one is hearing at the present.

Experimental music, however, has become concerned with the simultaneous permutation of a limited number of elements at a moment in time as well as the relations between a number of points in time. I think also that it has tended to reduce the time-spans over which compositional ideas are developed; and this has led to the use of cyclic forms such as that in Gavin Bryars's *Jesus' Blood Never Failed Me Yet.* (It is interesting that this piece, Paragraph 7, and *1-100* are all based on "found material"; and in each case the focus of the composer's attention is toward *reorganizing* given material. There is a special compositional liberty in this situation.)

I do not wish to subscribe to the view that the history of art is a series of dramatic revolutions where one idea overthrows another. I have made some distinctions between classical and experimental compositional techniques, and between the perceptual modes that each encourages in a listener, but I do not wish to propose that the development from one to the other is a simple upward progression. I have ascribed characteristics to

these two musics as though they were mutually exclusive, when virtually any example will show that aspects of *each* orientation exist in any piece. What I am arguing for is a view of musical development as a process of generating new hybrids. To give an example: one might propose a "scale of orientations" where, on the right hand, one placed the label "Tending to subdue variety in performance" and, on the left, "Tending to encourage variety in performance." It would be very difficult to find pieces that occupied the extreme polarities of this scale, and yet it is not difficult to locate distinct pieces at points along the scale. A classical sonata, if only by virtue of the shortcomings of musical notation, allows some variety in performance.[7] On the other (left) hand, the most random of *random music* (whatever that term meant) is constrained in its range by all sorts of factors down to the straightforward laws of physics. So we might place the Cardew piece toward the left, but not as far left as, say, a free-jazz improvisation. A scale

---

[7] It is interesting to observe that the sound of a string orchestra results from minute variations of tuning, vibrato, and timbre. This is why electronic simulations of strings have not been notably successful.

Gavin Bryars: *Jesus' Blood Never Failed Me Yet.*

of this kind does not tell us much about the music that we place on it, but its function is to remind us to think in terms of hybrids rather than discontinuities.

Given the above reservation about polarizing musical ideas into opposing camps, I should now like to describe two organizational structures. My point is not that classical music is one and contemporary music the other, but that each is a group of hybrids tending toward one of the two structures. At one extreme, then, is this type of organization: a rigidly ranked, skill-oriented structure moving sequentially through an environment assumed to be passive (static) toward a resolution already defined and specified. This type of organization regards the environment (and its variety) as a set of emergencies and seeks to neutralize or disregard this variety. An observer is encouraged (both by his knowledge of the ranking system and by the differing degrees of freedom accorded to the various parts of the organization) to direct his attention at the upper echelons of the ranks. He is given an impression of a hierarchy of value. The organiza-

---

[8] Beer, *Brain of the Firm*, p. 305.

tion has the feel of a well-functioning machine: it operates accurately and predictably for one class of tasks but it is not adaptive. It is not self-stabilizing and does not easily assimilate change or novel environmental conditions. Furthermore, it requires a particular type of instruction in order to operate. In cybernetics this kind of instruction is known as an *algorithm.* Stafford Beer's definition of the term is "a comprehensive set of instructions for reaching a known goal"; so the prescription "turn left at the lights and walk twenty yards" is an algorithm, as is the prescription "play a C-sharp for quaver followed by an E for a semiquaver."[8] It must be evident that such specific strategies can be devised only when a precise concept of form (or identity, or goal, or direction) already exists, and when it is taken for granted that this concept is static and singular.

Proposing an organizational structure opposite to the one described above is valueless because we would probably not accord it the name *organization:* whatever the term does connote, it must include some idea of constraint and some idea of identity. So what I shall now describe is the type of organization that typifies certain organic systems and whose most important characteristics hinge on this fact: that changing environments require adaptive organisms. Now, the relationship between an organism and its environment is a sophisticated and complex one, and this is not the place to deal with it. Suffice it to say, however, that an adaptive organism is one that contains built-in mechanisms for monitoring (and adjusting) its own behavior in relation to the alterations in its surroundings. This type of organism must be capable of operating from a different type of instruction, as the real coordinates of the surroundings are either too complex to specify, or are changing so unpredictably that no particular strategy (or specific plan for a particular future) is useful. The kind of instruction that is necessary here is known as an *heuristic,* and is defined as "a set of instructions for searching out an unknown goal by exploration, which continuously or repeatedly evaluates progress according to some known criterion."[9] To use Beer's example: if you wish to tell someone how to reach the top of a mountain that is shrouded in mist, the heuristic "keep going up" will get him there. An organism operating in this way must have something more than a centralized control structure. It must have a responsive network of subsystems capable of autonomous behavior, and it must regard the irregularities of the environment as a set of opportunities around which it will shape and adjust its own identity.

---

[9] *Ibid.,* p. 306.

What I have tried to suggest in this essay is a technique for discussing contemporary music in terms of its functioning. I have concentrated primarily on one piece of music because I wanted to show this technique at work on one specific problem and because I feel that the technique can thereafter quite easily be generalized to deal with other activities. I do not wish to limit the scope of this approach to music, although because music is a social art that therefore generates some explicit organizational information, it lends itself readily to such analysis. I have in the past discussed not only the fine arts but also, for example, the evolution of contemporary sporting practices and the transition from traditional to modern military tactics by asking the same kinds of questions directed at the organizational level of the activities. It does not surprise me that, at the systems level, these apparently disparate evolutions are very accurate analogues for each other.

In this book *Man's Rage for Chaos* Morse Peckham writes: "Art is the exposure to the tensions and problems of the false world such that man may endure exposing himself to the tensions and problems of the real world."[10] As the variety of the environment magnifies in both time and space and as the structures that were thought to describe the operation of the world become progressively more unworkable, other concepts of organization must become current. These concepts will base themselves on the assumption of change rather than stasis and on the assumption of probability rather than certainty. I believe that contemporary art is giving us the feel for this outlook.

---

[10] Morse Peckham, *Man's Rage for Chaos* (New York: Schocken Books, 1967), p. 314.

Paik and Moorman
Perform Cage

The cellist Charlotte Moorman and the composer/sculptor/video artist Nam June Paik are well known for their performances of numerous avant-garde musical compositions. They are perhaps the foremost American avant-garde musicians and have performed and interpreted works by many of the leading contemporary composers in America and Europe.

In 1968 Miss Moorman was convicted for her topless performance of Paik's Opera Sextronique at the New York Film-Makers' Cinematheque; the piece has since then come to be regarded as one of the classics of avant-garde musical expression.

Paik and Moorman are noted for their performances of Happenings, concerts, and mixed media in concert halls, art galleries, television shows, radio broadcasts, colleges, and lofts, and open-air performances in city parks, ferryboats, graveyards, churchyards, city thoroughfares, and Venice's Grand Canal.

Miss Moorman was born in Little Rock, Arkansas, received a M. Mus. degree from the University of Texas, and studied with Leonard Rose at the Juilliard School of Music. She was a member of the American Symphony Orchestra under Leopold Stokowski and producer of the annual New York Avant-Garde Festival.

The rhythmic structure. 3;7;2;5;11. is that of
34! 46.776" for a pianist and for the other part
already written for a pianist. All of-these pieces
may be played alone or in combination, and in whole
or in part, the title to be appropriately changed
to indicate time in minutes and seconds and the
instrumentalists involved. The present part may be
played on any 4-stringed instrument or(using parts
indicated by dotted lines) any combination of 2 or more.

The notation is in space, the amount equalling a
second given at the top of the page. Vibrato is
notated graphically. ⌐ or V are the conventional
symbols for bowing. H indicates hair of bow, W,
col legno. B indicates bridge (extreme ponticello);
EN is closer to bridge than normal; NB is closer to
normal than bridge, etc., F indicating extreme sul tasto.
Below these notations is an area where bowing pressure
is indicated graphically, the top being least, the bottom
most pressure (i.e. pianissimo, fortissimo). The 4
strings (e.g. violin EADG) are the lower large areas, the
points of stopping these being indicated. These strings
are in a continual state of changing "tune" indicated
by the words, decrease and increase, i.e. tension. Slides
are indicated by angles and curves, harmonics by 3 lines
connected vertically by dots. Vertical lines connecting
two separate events indicate legato. 4 pizzicatti are
distinguished: ., the normal; ↑ , stopped against fingerboard; x against fingernail; ↳ slide following pluck.
A dotted horizontal line indicates saltando. Manner of
breaking triple and quadruple stops is indicated by arrows.
If no indication is given, the player is free to break
as he chooses. The lowest area is devoted to noises on
the box, sounds other than those produced on the strings.
These may issue from entirely other sources, e.g. percussion
instruments, whistles, radios, etc. Only high and low are
indicated.

The 5 pieces (pg. 34 through 58) were written in 1953 in
NYC and are variously dedicated. The time was originally
indicated in terms of ritardandi and accelerandi, metronome
values given at structural points. Vertical lines
accompanied by the actual seconds have been added (1955).
The triple stop at the end of pg. 33 is the triple stop at
the beginning of pg. 34. The other pages were written at
Stony Point, N.Y., August-September 1955 with assistance
from David Tudor which is gratefully acknowledged. The
whole constitutes a fragment of an unfinished work for
many activities and may be performed with any of those to
be written or otherwise calculated.

*Mr. Paik is a noted sculptor who frequently employs electronic manipu-
lations involving television. He was born in Seoul, Korea, was graduated from
the University of Tokyo, and exhibited at the Galleria Bonnino and the
Howard Wise Gallery in New York.*

*The illustrations that follow are from the artists' copy of a score written
for them by John Cage. Accompanying the illustrations from the score are
photographs of the piece being performed. The score is changeable: no two
performances are alike. As the piece is performed, the artists make notations
on the score, so that it constantly changes, too.*

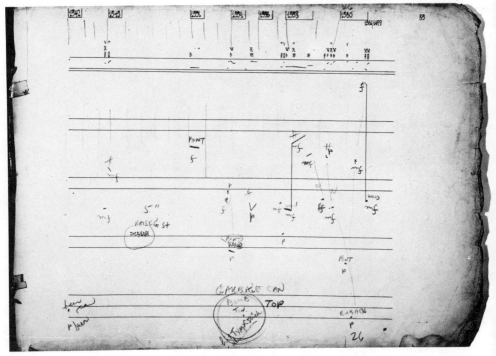

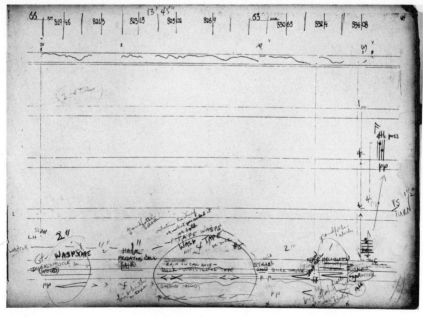

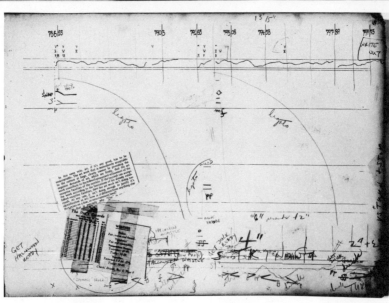

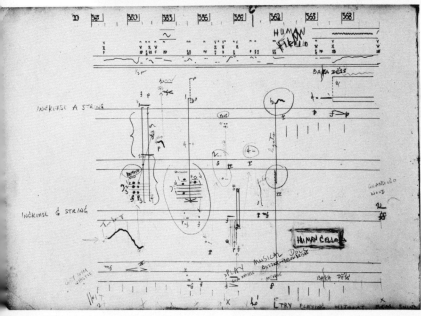

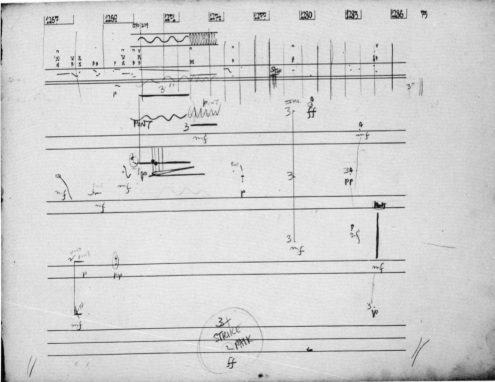

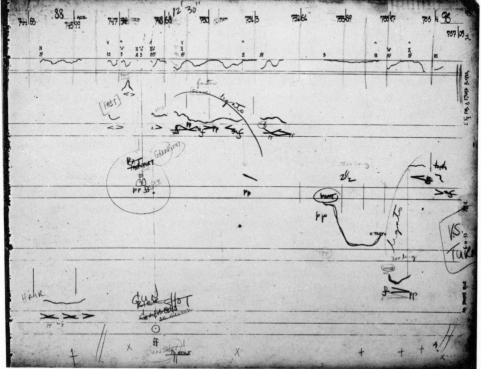

Writings About Music *

Steve Reich

Steve Reich, musician and composer, has been in the forefront of the avant-garde musical world for almost two decades. His works are frequently performed at museums and galleries, including the Guggenheim Museum, Whitney Museum of American Art, and The Museum of Modern Art, to name but a few.

In his works the links between contemporary music and contemporary art are revealed. He has worked closely with visual artists and his work has been discussed by numerous critics and theorists in the visual arts.

In the following notes, Reich discusses process in music, observing that "Material may suggest what sort of process it should be run through (content suggests form), and processes may suggest what sort of material should be run through them (form suggests content)."

The last two sections, dealing with "Gahu: A Dance of the Ewe Tribe in Ghana" and Balinese and African music, are reprinted here because they will remind the reader that many of the characteristics of contemporary music are to be traced to the primitive and anonymous music of ancient cultures, thus

---

revealing yet again that some of the most radical departures typical of new music are, in fact, grounded in unfamiliar traditions.

MUSIC AS A GRADUAL PROCESS (1968)

I do not mean the process of composition, but rather pieces of music that are, literally, processes.

The distinctive thing about musical processes is that they determine all the note-to-note (sound-to-sound) details and the overall form simultaneously. (Think of a round or infinite canon.)

I am interested in perceptible processes. I want to be able to hear the process happening throughout the sounding music.

To facilitate closely detailed listening, a musical process should happen extremely gradually.

Performing and listening to a gradual musical process resembles:

pulling back a swing, releasing it, and observing it gradually come to rest;
turning over an hourglass and watching the sand slowly run through to the bottom;
placing your feet in the sand by the ocean's edge and watching, feeling, and listening to the waves gradually bury them.

Though I may have the pleasure of discovering musical processes and composing the musical material to run through them, once the process is set up and loaded, it runs by itelf.

Material may suggest what sort of process it should be run through (content suggests form), and processes may suggest what sort of material should be run through them (form suggests content). If the shoe fits, wear it.

As to whether a musical process is realized through live human performance or through some electromechanical means is not finally the main issue. One of the most beautiful concerts I ever heard consisted of four composers playing their tapes in a dark hall. (A tape is interesting when it's an interesting tape.)

It is quite natural to think about musical processes if one is frequently working with electromechanical sound equipment. All music turns out to be ethnic music.

Musical processes can give one a direct contact with the impersonal and also a kind of complete control, and one doesn't always think of the impersonal and complete control as going together. By "a kind" of complete control I mean that by running this material through this process, I completely control all that results, but also that I accept all that results without changes.

John Cage has used processes and has certainly accepted their results, but the processes he used were compositional ones that could not be heard when the piece was performed. The process of using the *I Ching* or imperfections in a sheet of paper to determine musical parameters can't be heard when listening to music composed that way. The compositional processes and the sounding music have no audible connection. Similarly, in serial music the series itself is seldom audible. (This is a basic difference between serial [basically European] music and serial [basically American] art, where the perceived series is usually the focal point of the work.)

What I'm interested in is a compositional process and a sounding music that are one and the same thing.

James Tenney said in conversation, "then the composer isn't privy to anything." I don't know any secrets of structure that you can't hear. We all listen to the process together since it's quite audible, and one of the reasons it's quite audible is it's happening extremely gradually.

The use of hidden structural devices in music never appealed to me. Even when all the cards are on the table and everyone hears what is gradually happening in a musical process, there are still enough mysteries to satisfy all. These mysteries are the impersonal, unintended, psychoacoustic by-products of the intended process. These might include submelodies heard within repeated melodic patterns, stereophonic effects due to listener location, slight irregularities in performance, harmonics, difference tones, etc.

Listening to an extremely gradual musical process opens my ears to *it,* but *it* always extends farther than I can hear, and that makes it interesting to listen to that musical process again. That area of every gradual (completely controlled) musical process, where one hears the details of the sound moving out away from intentions, occurring for their own acoustic reasons, is *it.*

I begin to perceive these minute details when I can sustain close attention and a gradual process invites my sustained attention. By "gradual" I mean extremely gradual; a process happening so slowly and gradually that listening to it resembles watching a minute hand on a watch—you can perceive it moving after you stay with it a little while.

Several currently popular modal musics like Indian classical and drug-oriented rock-and-roll may make us aware of minute sound details because in being modal (constant key center, hypnotically droning, and repetitious) they naturally focus on these details rather than on key modulation, counterpoint, and other peculiarly Western devices. Nevertheless, these modal musics remain more or less strict frameworks for improvisation. They are not processes.

The distinctive thing about musical processes is that they determine all the note-to-note details and the overall form simultaneously. One can't improvise in a musical process—the concepts are mutually exclusive.

While performing and listening to gradual musical processes, one can participate in a particular liberating and impersonal kind of ritual. Focusing in on the musical process makes possible that shift of attention away from *he* and *she* and *you* and *me* outward toward *it*.

From Program Notes

Whitney Museum of American Art, New York, May 1969

I am not interested in improvisation or in sounding exotic.

One hardly needs to seek out personality as it can never be avoided.

Obviously music should put all within listening range into a state of ecstasy.

I am interested in music that works exclusively with gradual changes in time.

New York University, Loeb Student Center, November 1971

A performance for us is a situation where all the musicians, including myself, attempt to set aside our individual thoughts and feelings of the moment and try to focus our minds and bodies clearly on the realization of one continuous musical process.

This music is not the expression of the momentary state of mind of the performers while playing. Rather, the momentary state of mind of the performers while playing is largely determined by the ongoing composed slowly changing music.

John F. Kennedy Center for the Performing Arts, Washington, D.C., May 1974

As a performer what I want is to be told exactly what to do within a musical ensemble, and to find that by doing it well I help make beautiful music. This is what I ask of my own compositions, those of another composer, and this is what I looked for and found when I studied Balinese and African music. The pleasure I get from playing is not the pleasure of expressing myself but of subjugating myself to the music and experiencing the ecstasy that comes from being a part of it.

GAHU: A DANCE OF THE EWE TRIBE IN GHANA (1971)

During the summer of 1970 I went to Ghana to study drumming. With the help of a travel grant from the Special Projects division of the Institute of International Education, I traveled to Accra, the capital of Ghana, where I studied with a master drummer of the Ewe tribe who was in residence with the Ghana Dance Ensemble, the national dance company that rehearses daily in the Institute of African Studies at the University of Ghana.

I took daily lessons with Gideon Alorworye and recorded each lesson. Afterward I would return to my room, and, by playing and replaying the tape, sometimes at half or one-quarter speed, I was able to transcribe the bell, rattle, and drum patterns I had learned. The basis for learning each individual instrument was as follows: first I would learn the basic double bell (gong-gong) pattern, which is the unchanging time line of the whole drumming. Then I would learn the rattle (axatse) pattern, which is quite similar to the gong-gong pattern and also continues without change throughout the entire performance. We would then proceed to the drums by my playing the gong-gong while my teacher played one of the drum patterns. We would then exchange instruments and I would try and play the drum patterns while he played the bell. I found that although I could pick up the drum patterns fairly rapidly by rote, I would forget them almost as rapidly. I couldn't really remember them until I could understand exactly what was going on rhythmically between the drum and the bell patterns. This process of understanding was greatly aided and accelerated by replaying the tapes of my lessons until I could finally write down with certainty the relationship between any given drum and the bell pattern. One drum after the other was learned and written down in relation to the bell until an entire ensemble was notated. This method was followed as the result of reading A. M. Jones's *Studies in African Music* (Oxford University Press, 1959). Dr. Jones has been able to make the first full scores of African music (as it happens, of the Ewe tribe) by using his own drum recorder, which consists of a moving roll of paper that is electrically marked each time a drummer touches one of his metal pencils to a metal plate. As Dr. Jones tapped out the bell pattern, an Ewe master drummer would tap out one of the drum parts, and both patterns would be recorded in accurate graph form on the moving paper. This was then transferred to conventional notation. My readings in Dr. Jones's book in 1963 first awoke my interest in African music, and that interest grew through listening to recordings, corresponding with Dr. Jones, and finally having two brief lessons with Alfred Ladzepko, another Ewe master drummer in New York who was working with Nicholas England at Columbia University. Finally, I decided it was important to go to Africa myself and learn some drumming by drumming.

Gahu is an extremely popular dance. It can be performed whenever and wherever the musicians and dancers feel like it. This is in contrast to the court dances, Atsiagbeko of the Ewes and Fontenfrom of the Ashantis, both of which are only performed at the proper formal time and place. All Ghanaian dances are appropriate to particular situations, and Gahu is appropriate to a relaxed informal one.

Gahu is not a purely Ewe dance. My teacher told me that it originally came from the town of Gbadagri (ba-da-gree) which used to be situated in Nigeria between Lagos and the Dahomey border. The Ewes used to go on fishing trips with these people, who were called Agunnas or Guans and had their own language which was neither Yoruba nor Ewe. My teacher did not say how long ago this had been.

In Ghana the name of a piece of music is also the name of the dance that is performed to that music. The two are inseparable. (I once attended an informal recording session outdoors in back of the Institute of African Studies where several musicians were playing directly in front of two microphones. Although they all were quite aware that only sound was being recorded, several people, nevertheless, started dancing the appropriate dance.) Gahu is a circle dance performed by men and women. The basic step is simply alternating the feet in small steps forward (left, left, right, right) while swinging the arms gently to the opposite side of the body (right, right, left, left), all on the basic four quarter notes of the bell pattern. There are many other variations I am not familiar with.

Often in the afternoon, preceding the evening's drumming, the Ewes perform Hatsyiatsya songs, which are sung to the accompaniment of four iron bells: two gong-gongs and two atokes. This accompaniment is a miniature polyrhythmic drumming made of beautiful bell sounds. I became extremely fond of these sounds and asked Gideon to teach me the Hatsyiatsya patterns for Gahu.

This represents a very approximate notation of the pitch of these bells. The high E-flat in the first atoke is actually a bit sharp, while the C in the

Two gong-gongs and two atokes.

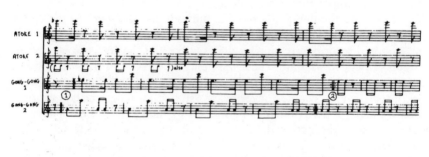

Hatsyiatsya patterns—Gahu. Ewe tribe, Ghana.

second atoke is a bit flat. The E-flat on the first gong-gong is very flat, and, depending on where you strike the bell, is sometimes a sort of minor second with D and E-flat combined. The second gong-gong is about a quarter tone above the A in the notation. The absolute pitch of these kinds of bells varies a good deal, although gong-gongs are usually roughly tuned to octaves or major sixths.

The basic pattern is played by the first atoke who, together with the second atoke, never changes his pattern throughout the piece. The second atoke is free to add two sixteenth notes in place of his single eighth note on any or all beats. The two gong-gongs each have a first pattern only two quarter notes long, so that two of their patterns equals one atoke pattern. Both of them begin their patterns in different places, and neither of them begins on the first beat of the atoke pattern. This, in simplified miniature, is the essence of African rhythmic structure: *several repeating patterns of the same or related lengths and each with its own separate downbeat.* Pattern two for the gong-gongs is a simple alternation of double sixteenth notes on their lower bells, which acts as a sort of changing pattern leading to their third pattern, which for the first gong-gong begins on the last eighth note of the atoke pattern while the second gong-gong begins on the third quarter note of the atokes. There is no hard-and-fast rule about when the gong-gongs will change from one pattern to the next, but they must do so together. Players are also free to reverse the order of high and low bells within a particular pattern. As players are seated, the rests in the gong-gong patterns are created by bringing the large bell directly down on the thigh on each rest, thereby muting it. The atokes are muted on rests by touching the edge of the bell with the thumb of the hand holding it. My teacher mentioned that there were many other patterns, and also said that up to eight gong-gongs could play with the two atokes.

I have not transcribed the songs because, basically, I was not really attracted to them. The accompaniment was what I found to be unique, beautiful, and quite different from anything in Western music. Because I am a composer/performer and not a musicologist, I am passing along the information I believe may be of particular interest to others in situations like my own. Those wishing to see other Hatsyiatsya songs transcribed more completely, with accompaniment and melody, are urged to look at A. M. Jones's *Studies in African Music.*

The instruments used in the full drumming of Gahu are: one or two gong-gongs, at least one rattle though it is common for several people to double the easy rattle part in any Ghanaian drumming, and the following drums: kagan, the smallest; kidi, the second smallest; sogo, the next to the largest; and agboba, the master drum. Those familiar with Ewe music should note that for Gahu, which, as mentioned above, is a dance the Ewes imported from Nigeria, a special drum, agboba, is used in place of the customary Ewe master drum, atsimevu.

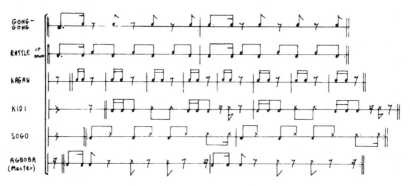

Gahu. Ewe tribe, Ghana.

Unfortunately, because of illness, I was unable to stay in Ghana and complete the preceding transcription, so that only basic repeating bell and rattle parts, together with the beginning pattern in the master drum with the appropriate response patterns in the supporting drums, appear here. The pitch of the drums, which is important although it varies a bit from performance to performance, is also not notated for lack of time. Those interested in the pitch of Ewe drums are again referred to Jones's work. With all these limitations this is, nevertheless, the first and at present the only transcription of both the Hatsyiatsya patterns and the basic drumming of Gahu.

The basic pattern of the whole dance appears in the gong-gong. It is exactly what the first atoke was playing in the Hatsyiatsya patterns. The first time the pattern is played the performer may remind all the other musicians of his downbeat by playing it on his low bell. Thereafter, unless someone loses his place in relation to the bell pattern, the gong-gong player just "rides" his top bell only, ringing out over the whole ensemble. This 4/4 pattern is a bit unusual for Ewe or West African music in general, where one most often finds the basic bell pattern to be in what we would call 12/8, as in the transcription of Agbadza on page 160. When I finally decided that this pattern had to be written as it appears on this page, I wrote to A. M. Jones to ask for his reaction to what I considered to be an unusual pattern. He responded that it was, in fact, quite similar to the basic gong-gong pattern in the Ewe dance Sovu and was, therefore, quite correct. If a second gong-gong is played, it will play the same part as the second atoke in the Hatsyiatsya patterns for Gahu, that is, a simple pulse on each of the four quarter notes of the first gong-gong part, with the option of playing two sixteenth notes instead of one eighth note on any or all of the pulses. The atoke itself is only used for Hatsyiatsya patterns and is not used in the full drumming.

The rattle (axatse) is played in a sitting position, and is struck downward on the thigh and then upward against the open palm or closed fist of the other hand held above it. The downstrokes (notes below the line) exactly double the gong-gong, while the upward movements (notes above the line) simply fill in the rests.

Ewe drums are played both with sticks and by hand. In Gahu all the drums are played with sticks. The Xs in the drum notation indicate muted beats. In kidi and sogo this is played by pressing one stick down on the drumhead while gently striking the head with the other stick. Because of the added tension on the head, the pitch of a muted beat is higher, by about a fifth, than a regular beat. In the agboba the muted beats are played by striking the stick rather sharply against the wooden side of the drum.

The kagan keeps up the same pattern throughout, and in this respect is closer to the gong-gong and rattle than it is to the other drums. This is generally the kagan's role in all Ewe music, and not just in Gahu.

There are many different master drum patterns, and each has a different response pattern from kidi and sogo. I simply did not have time to learn more than this first one. While the master drum makes constant improvised variations on his pattern, which I realistically felt were completely beyond the scope of my short visit to learn and therefore transcribe, the other drums simply repeat their patterns without variation until the master changes. They make the appropriate change then to the proper response pattern and repeat it without variation. In the patterns above the master drum begins a sixteenth note after the gong-gong, and the sogo responds on the second quarter note of the bell pattern, while the kidi answers an eighth note later. All instruments in this particular section have patterns the same length as the gong-gong, except for the kagan, whose pattern is only one quarter note in duration.

Before I became interested in Gahu, my teacher started me off with Agbadza, perhaps the best known Ewe social dance. Although an excellent full transcription of Agbadza, complete with master drum improvisations,

Agbadza. Ewe tribe, Ghana.

appears in Jones's *Studies in African Music,* I offer the following so that readers here may see how the master drum plays a changing signal, changes to a second pattern, and is responded to by the supporting drum. In Agbadza, the master drum is the sogo, which is played with the hands while the kidi and the kagan are both played with sticks. My transcription is not only simpler than Jones's it also differs slightly in the master drum patterns and the kidi responses. This is partly because of the fact that there are many different patterns for Agbadza and also because of the fact that my teacher was about ten years younger and from a different village from the master drummer Jones worked with. Patterns do apparently change in time, and there are also apparently regional differences in performance. Basic patterns, like that of the gong-gong, however, do not change.

The gong-gong pattern in 12/8 here is the most common in West Africa. Again the player will start by playing the first beat on his low bell, but will then continue on his high bell only, unless some musician needs a reminder about where the first beat of the gong-gong is. The rattle once again doubles the bell with his downstrokes while filling in rests with his upward motion. Here, however, he begins his pattern on the second quarter note of the bell pattern. The kagan's pattern is somewhat similar to that in Gahu, and once again four kagan patterns equal one bell pattern. Like the bell and rattle, the kagan continues without change for the entire performance. The first sogo master pattern is only four eighth notes long and begins with the bell. He is responded to by the kidi with a pattern that fills in the sogo's rests while doubling the sogo's beats with muted beats. After many repetitions with ample improvised variation by the sogo, the changing signal of unbroken eighth notes is sounded by the sogo telling all the musicians and dancers that a new pattern will begin. This second pattern is six eighth notes long, and once again the sogo begins with the bell, with the kidi responding on the second quarter note of the bell pattern.

My teacher told me that all drum patterns in Ewe music not only have a series of "nonsense syllables" associated with them to help remember their rhythm but also have a literal meaning. For instance, the gong-gong pattern in Agbadza means "Do mayi makpo tefe mava" in Ewe or "Let me go and witness this myself and return," while the rattle means "Tso, miayi miakpo nusia tefe" or "Stand up and let us go and witness this ourselves." The kagan pattern means "Kaba" or "Quickly," the kidi is saying "Midzo" or "Let us go," and the sogo's first pattern is "Do va" or "Get out and come here." These patterns may refer to the Ewe's hasty departure from Benin in Nigeria sometime probably in the nineteenth century.

When it is remembered that there is no indigenous written language in Africa, and when the talking drums are considered, it may be seen that not only are the dances the choreographic reenactments of important historical events in the history of the tribe but that there is actually a literal recorded history of these people in the drum patterns themselves.

POSTSCRIPT TO A BRIEF STUDY OF BALINESE AND AFRICAN MUSIC (1973)

During the summer of 1973 I studied Balinese Gamelan Semar Pegulingan with I Nyoman Sumandhi, a Balinese musician in residence at the American Society for Eastern Arts Summer Program at the University of Washington in Seattle. During the summer of 1970 I studied African drumming with Gideon Alorworye, a master drummer of the Ewe tribe in residence with the Ghana Dance Ensemble at the Institute for African Studies in Accra. I studied Balinese and African music because I love them and also because I believe that non-Western music is currently the single most important source of new ideas for Western composers and musicians.

Although earlier generations of Western musicians *listened* to many non-Western musics, live or on recordings, it is now becoming increasingly possible to learn how to *play* African, Balinese, Javanese, Indian, Korean, and Japanese music, among others, directly from first-rate African, Balinese, Javanese, Indian, Korean, and Japanese musicians, here in America or abroad. A Western musician can thus begin to approach non-Western music as he would his own; he learns how to play it through study with a qualified teacher, and in that process can also analyze the music he is playing in detail to understand how it is put together. During the process of performance and analysis he will find basically different systems of rhythmic structure, scale construction, tuning, and instrumental technique. Knowledge of these different systems also sheds light on our own Western system, showing it to be one way among many.

It was my personal desire to understand the basic differences between African drumming and Balinese mallet playing on the one hand and Indian drumming on the other. After a bit of reading in Walter Kaufman's books on North Indian music and in Robert E. Brown's Ph.D. thesis, "The Mrdanga—A Study of Drumming in South India," together with some discussions with Indian musicians and students at Wesleyan University, I came to the conclusion that there are three main differences, and that they are closely related. First, *Indian drumming, both in the Hindustani (northern) and Carnatic (southern) traditions, is basically a solo music, while African drumming and Balinese mallet playing are basically ensemble musics.* Second, *Indian drumming is improvised* within a given framework of a particular tala, or rhythmic cycle, *while Balinese mallet playing is composed,* and allows no improvisation. In African drumming all the musicians have fixed parts, with the exception of the master drummer, who improvises on traditional patterns. Third, *the basic rhythmic structure of any tala in Indian drumming, northern or southern, has one main downbeat at the beginning of the cycle,* whereas *African drumming has multiple downbeats,* often one for each member of the ensemble. In this respect, Balinese music is similar to Indian in that it has one main downbeat for the entire ensemble at the beginning of a cycle. It is no surprise then that Indian drumming is for the solo virtuoso, while in African drumming and Balinese mallet playing the individual parts, with the exception of the African master drum, are all relatively simple, and it is in the precise rhythmic blending of the ensemble that the virtuosity lies. Not being a virtuoso, not being interested in improvisation, and being thoroughly committed to my own ensemble that performs music I have composed with repetitive patterns combined so that their downbeats do not always coincide, it may be natural for my interests to run strongly toward Balinese and African music.

Not only African, Balinese, and Indian music but also Javanese, Korean, Japanese, and many others are having a strong effect on Western musicians. This very real interest in non-Western music can be seen now in composers, performers, and even universities, where the interest in electronics, so marked in the 1960s, is gradually giving way to an interest in world music. Along with the obvious benefits of this interest, which include a strong belief in live performance and the aural or rote teaching of music instead of the exclusive use of scores, there are also some problems. The most difficult of these is the problem of Western composers, like myself, absorbing non-Western music. What can a composer do with this knowledge? One possibility is to become an ethnomusicologist, using the talents of analysis that composers often have to transcribe non-Western music into Western notation and analyze it. This is work of the utmost value, producing masterpieces of scholarship like Colin McPhee's *Music in Bali,* but it is not musical composition. Alternatively, a composer can give up composing and devote himself to trying to become a performer of some non-Western music. This will take many years of study and may, even then, only lead to mediocre performing abilities when judged by African, Balinese, Indian, or whatever appropriate non-Western standards. (If the performance of non-Western music were available for musically gifted Western children and teen-agers to study, this would undoubtedly lead to American- and European-born virtuosos of non-Western music.) Lastly, one may continue composing, but with the knowledge of non-Western music one has studied, and this is the case for myself and most other composers in this situation.

The question then arises how, if at all, this knowledge of non-Western music influences a composer. The least interesting form of influence, to my mind, is that of imitating the *sound* of some non-Western music. This can be done by using non-Western instruments in one's own music (sitars in the rock band), or by using one's own instruments to sound like non-Western ones (singing "Indian-style" melodies over electronic drones). This method is the simplest and most superficial way of dealing with non-Western music as the general sound of these musics can be absorbed in a few minutes of listening without further study. Imitating the sound of non-Western music leads to "exotic music," what used to be called "chinoiserie."

Alternatively, one can create a music with one's own sound that is constructed in the light of one's knowledge of non-Western *structures.* This is similar, in fact, to learning Western musical structures. The idea of canon or round, for instance, has influenced motets, fugues, and then, among others, the music of Anton Webern and my own phase pieces. The precise influence of this, or any structural idea, is quite subtle and acts in unforeseen ways. One can study the rhythmic structure of non-Western music and let that study lead one where it will while continuing to use the instruments, scales, and any other sound one has grown up with. This brings about the interesting situation of the non-Western influence being there in the thinking, but not in the sound. This is a more genuine and interesting form of influence because while listening one is not necessarily aware of some non-Western music being imitated. Instead of imitation, the influence of non-Western musical structures on the thinking of a Western composer is likely to produce something genuinely new.

Gallery

William Anastasi: *Broken Jug,* 1966. Sound object, mixed-media construction. In the artist's words: "A one-gallon wine jug is dropped onto an 8″ × 16″ cinder block from a height of 15 feet. The sound of the shattering jug is taped. The cinder block is hung in an open, clear plastic box. The pieces of the jug are gathered into a clear vinyl package and hung from one side of the block. An 8″ speaker is hung from the other side of the block. At intervals the speaker emits the taped sound." Photograph courtesy Dwan Gallery, New York.

William Anastasi: *Beethoven's Fifth Symphony,* 1965.

Bob Ashley: *Private Parts*, 1977. Performance at the Kitchen with Peter Gordon at the Synthesizer.

François and Bernard Baschet: *One-Octave Piano*, 1962. H. 48″. The 13 keys in this sculpture can be played. Photograph courtesy Waddell Gallery, New York.

Bob Bates: Performance with Gail Bates on Bates's instrument Fuser, 1979, in "Sound Performance Series" at Auditorium of P.S. 1, New York. Photograph by Ivan Dalla Tana © 1979 and courtesy The Institute for Art and Urban Resources, Inc. (P.S. 1), New York.

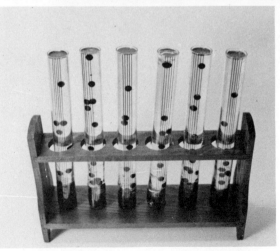

William Hellermann: *Experimental Music—A Solid Score,* 1978. 13″ × 9″. Wood, glass, and resin.

Arthur Frick: *Boat,* 1979. Installation shot from a traveling exhibition of contemporary instruments. Photograph by Ivan Dalla Tana © 1979 and courtesy The Institute for Art and Urban Resources, Inc., New York.

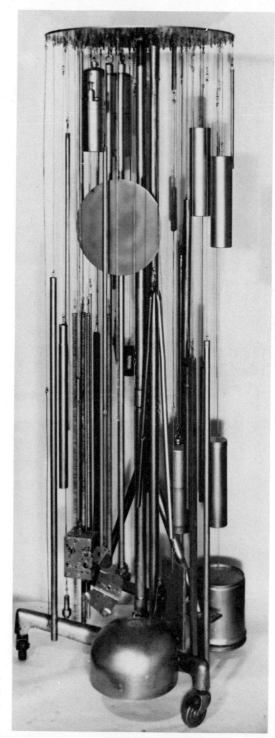

Emil Hess: *Ancient Sounds,* 1969. 73″ × 22″. Photograph courtesy Betty Parsons Gallery, New York.

Tom Johnson: *Nine Bells,* 1978. Photograph courtesy Experimental Intermedia Foundation, New York.

Joe Jones: *Music Plant,* 1964. Leather strips attached to small motors whirl around and slap the strings of violins, causing a continual hum of music.

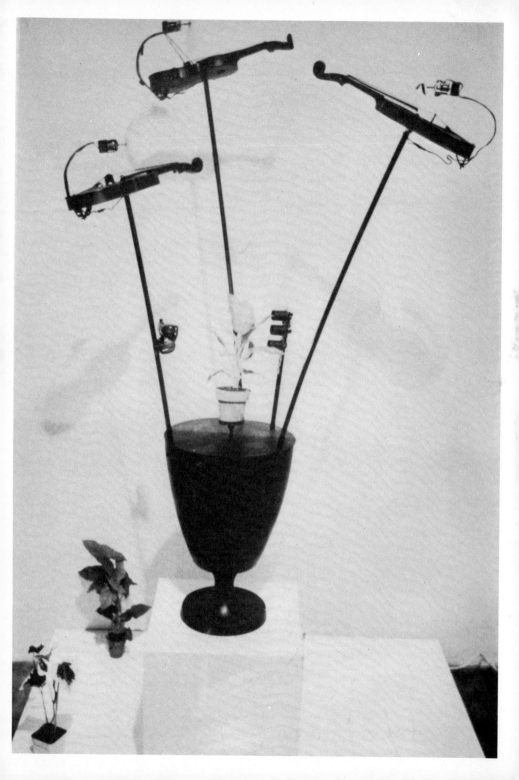

Frederick Kiesler: *The Gong*, 1963–1964. H. 8'6". Bronze and aluminum. Photograph courtesy Howard Wise Gallery.

Jill Krosen: *The Original Lour and Walter Story,* Part III, 1974–1979. Performance in 1979 in "Sound Performance Series" at Auditorium of P.S. 1, New York. Photograph by Ivan Dalla Tana © 1979 and courtesy The Institute for Art and Urban Resources, Inc. (P.S. 1), New York.

Nam June Paik with Charlotte Moorman: *TV Bra for Living Sculpture,* 1969. As Ms. Moorman plays her cello, electronic impulses cause movements and station changing on the two miniature television sets attached to her breasts. Photograph courtesy Howard Wise Gallery, New York.

Bruce Nauman: *Tape Recorder with a Tape Loop of a Scream Wrapped in Plastic Bag and Cast into the Center of a Block of Concrete,* 1969. From the exhibition "When Attitudes Become Form." Photograph courtesy Institute of Contemporary Arts, London.

Robert Rauschenberg: *Soundings*, 1968. 8′ × 36′ × 4′6″. Silk-screened and silvered Plexiglas, lights, and microphones. Exhibited at The Museum of Modern Art, New York, in 1968, the images in this artwork were constantly changed by means of sounds made by the viewers that were picked up by the microphones in the piece, while lights went on and off.

New Technologies

Synthesizers and the Evolution of Electronic Music*

Jerry Davidson

The development of contemporary music has been profoundly altered by the invention and acceptance of electronic keyboards called synthesizers. *In the brief notes that follow, Jerry Davidson introduces new electronic synthesizers and explains their feasibility and advantages for students and performers. He discusses several different types of synthesizers and surveys their use. Following the basic introduction to this important new electronic instrument, Davidson traces the evolution of electronic music.*

As he explains, electronic music of one form or another has been around since 1906. In recent times the author cites three events that have helped mold new electronic music and music theory. These are the 1952 concert of electronic music by Leopold Stokowski at The Museum of Modern Art, the development of Robert Moog's synthesizer, and the advent of computer-motivated musical composition.

Jerry Davidson is a composer specializing in sacred music. He is on the music faculty at Harper College in Palatine, Illinois, and is a Ph.D. candidate at Northwestern University.

SYNTHESIZERS

An electronic music studio presents a fascinating array of equipment to newcomers. Most studios have several different synthesizers, as well as ad-

* Reprinted from *Clavier,* 16, no. 8 (November 1977), pp. 16–19.

ditional oscillators (the devices that produce wave forms at specific frequencies), tape recorders, amplifiers, and playback apparatus.

The synthesizers that are used solely for performance are different from those used in a studio. Performance models involve only a small keyboard, perhaps an internal speaker, and many circuits wired in permanent arrangements.

Many persons have built their own electronic equipment for use at home, connecting a simple oscillator with whatever other devices they can produce and integrate into their systems. Several companies now produce small, inexpensive components that can be easily put together to make a highly gratifying studio for the high school, private teacher, or home. Experimenters can build these components in compatible "modules" that can be strung together as far as the builders' bank accounts will allow.

Production of Sound

The large synthesizers can produce almost any sound but cannot change sounds quickly, whereas the smaller, performance-oriented models don't have as wide a range of sounds but are faster in changing timbres.

In any type of synthesizer the sound production basically requires generation, modification, storage, and reproduction. Generation is accomplished by means of oscillators that produce wave forms. Most oscillators produce one wave form at a time, which may be converted into pitch. These wave forms may be changed in myriad ways by different devices such as filters and ring modulators to vary the sound. These signals can be recorded on tape and later reproduced by amplifiers and speakers.

An interesting comparison may be made between synthesizers and electronic organs. The electronic organ is constructed with sixty-one oscillators, one for each note of the keyboard. A few modifying circuits are arranged to affect all sixty-one oscillators in exactly the same way. No storage is necessary because the organ is designed to produce pitches directly. The organ provides a limited number of timbres but with multiple pitches. On the other hand, most synthesizers use only one oscillator and therefore produce only one pitch at a time, but the modifications that can be applied to it are almost limitless.

As most synthesizers are capable of producing only a single pitch at a time, polyphony is produced by means of layering with tape recorders. (Some newer synthesizers can produce more than one pitch, but the basic layering process is not significantly changed.) One voice of a composition is recorded on tape and then rerecorded together with a second voice from the synthesizer onto another tape recorder. This process is continued over and over until the desired number of voices is recorded together. It is a slow, laborious process, but with good tape-recording equipment it is capable of producing fine results. One person has the potential of creating limitless timbres and layers of sound for any number of polyphonic voices.

Uses of Electronic Music Equipment

There are four major areas in which electronic music equipment is used today. The first is the "classical" studio, usually found in conjunction with a college or university. Most schools today have at least one synthesizer, and many have large, sophisticated arrays of equipment and full-range programs in electronic music. The composers associated with this type of studio do not contribute much music designed for the mass market, but their experimental efforts have greatly influenced the development of contemporary music.

The second use, and by far the most readily apparent, lies in the field of commercial music. Electronic music is used extensively—probably much more than you realize in television and movie sound tracks and on the radio. A person with a synthesizer can easily produce the entire range of unusual sound effects used in even the most bizarre science-fiction film.

A third area is the pop music field, where the synthesizer has become an integral part of most pop rock and jazz groups. These performers use synthesizers that range from the simple solo instruments designed for live performances to complex systems rivaling the most sophisticated equipment used in the recording studios.

We have just begun to tap the fourth area of use for the synthesizer, and this area has the greatest potential for teachers. Synthesizers can be used to explore and reveal the nature of sound. Even the simplest synthesizer can easily demonstrate the harmonic series, microtones, and many other acoustical examples that until now have had to exist in the abstract. A synthesizer can be easily coupled with an oscilloscope to allow students to see how wave forms (and therefore the sounds) change when they alter the controls. Synthesizers can also be a great ear-training aid, as a few schools are beginning to discover. No previous instrument could change timbre so much. The possibilities for exploration in even that one facet of the synthesizer are exciting.

Electronic Music-Making and You

The best way to learn about making music with a synthesizer is to try it. *Seeing* the equipment, hearing what it can do, and having a hands-on experience are an unbeatable introduction to the medium. No amount of reading about the differences between sine waves and voltage-controlled oscillators can equal seeing them on an oscilloscope and hearing what they sound like. In my classes at a community college I have found that a one-hour orientation in which I give a rudimentary explanation of how the synthesizer controls work is sufficient to allow students to begin experimenting. After only a few hours they are able to produce amazing results.

Schools that own electronic equipment are almost always eager to let the public admire it, and it is usually possible to find someone who is willing to demonstrate the equipment to interested people. Junior and senior high schools often have electronic equipment, and inevitably there is some student who loves to show it off. Also, professional recording studios often are cooperative in letting the public see what they do. Even individuals can be persuaded to demonstrate their own equipment. So, get one of the groups to which you belong to organize a tour and lecture, or lead a group of your students to the nearest synthesizer.

THE EVOLUTION OF ELECTRONIC MUSIC

Of all the areas in which a modern-day musician can be involved, few offer a greater source of bewilderment than electronic music. But there are some areas of electronic music that can and should be a part of every musician's store of knowledge. With even a small amount of information it is possible to involve oneself with whatever segment of the entire range is appealing.

The experimental electronic works conceived to find new sounds and combinations of sounds broaden the entire realm of musical awareness. The fine line between our traditional concepts of musical sounds and noise is frequently crossed, and questions of taste are soon raised.

We can perceive electronic music as being organized into the "classical" type, in which electronic sounds are used solely; electronic music on tape used together with live performers; live electronic performances, involving synthesizers and/or amplified instruments; and a mixture of these. In live performances taped sounds can be added to those of conventional instruments with fine results, and many pieces of this type are becoming staples of music literature.

Tape recording provides the best medium for electronic music. It not only gives a simple method of storing and reproducing sounds but also its very nature opens up new possibilities for the manipulation of sound. Tape offers the composer an opportunity to experiment with sound in time. The speed of even the simplest tape recorder can be increased or decreased.

Newer models offer variable time controls that provide an infinity of speeds, some with the fascinating feature of speed change without change in pitch!

Electronic music has been around since 1906, when Thaddeus Cahill was experimenting with a mammoth apparatus he called a *telharmonium*. Its unwieldy size belied its versatility, but it remained for modern-day electronics to provide a degree of practicality in artificial sound production. The *theremin* and *ondes Martenot* were considerably more successful and survive in some musical scores today. The eerie wailings in science-fiction and murder movies from the 1930s and 1940s were nearly always produced by one of these.

Soon after the invention of the tape recorder, many experiments were made in which natural sounds (sounds other than instrumental or electronic) recorded on tape were subjected to simple modifications: running at slower or faster speeds, cutting the tape into short lengths and reassembling at random, and stretching the tape. This process produces what is called *musique concrète* (to distinguish it from purely electronically derived sounds), a technique that was devised by Pierre Schaeffer and his colleagues at the French National Radio in 1948. It is one of the easiest ways for the amateur with little equipment to experiment with electronic sounds. A few hours spent with a tape recorder and tape, some scissors, and a roll of splicing tape can produce results that are both satisfying and a lot of fun. Helpful suggestions for using this technique can be found in Terence Dwyer's *Composing with Tape: Musique Concrète for Beginners*,[1] which is available in a paperback edition.

In 1952 Leopold Stokowski organized a concert of electronic music for The Museum of Modern Art in New York, and the modern age of electronic music performance seemed to spring to life. Twelve years later one of the most significant innovations was produced in the form of Robert Moog's synthesizer, a modular device, little more than a series of various circuits housed together. Prior to Moog (mōg) most studios relied on huge, tube-type equipment setups such as the Columbia-Princeton Synthesizer in New York. These monster synthesizers were (and still are) incredibly sophisticated and sensitive, but Moog's innovation made it possible to have that sophistication in a more compact framework.

In electronic studios some composers now use computers to create

---

[1] New York: Oxford University Press, 1971.

works (calculating relationships in pitch, timbre, rhythm, etc.) and/or to produce the actual sounds that are recorded on tape. When a work is composed by computer, the computer represents sound by numbers on a digital tape, and then the numbers are converted into a voltage that is recorded on audio tape and then played through loudspeakers.

In 1968 Walter Carlos produced his *Switched-On Bach* album so familiar to us all now. *Switched-On Bach* was the first time electronic music had a ring of familiarity to many of its listeners. Its clever jacket illustration, with a man dressed as Bach seated before a synthesizer, fixed in the minds of many the idea that electronics could produce sounds that they might enjoy hearing. *Switched-On Bach* gave a slight aura of legitimation to electronic music to the average person and musician. The popularization created by this recording, however, was often seen as an anathema by the classicists. I view *Switched-On Bach* as little more than a curiosity—something that an instrumental ensemble or organist could (and probably should) do almost as well, or even better.

Today electronic music is as pervasive as it is ubiquitous. How many people realize the amount of it they hear while listening to radio, television, movies, or records? A few years ago I received a gift of a small tape recording from one of my students who was working for a commercial recording studio. I was amazed to find how many of the commercials I had been hearing were made on a synthesizer. The ersatz "brass ensemble" was obviously electronic, but the synthesized "rock band" and other ensembles were difficult, if not impossible, to distinguish from their real counterparts.

Reading about electronic music is one way to become familiar with the field. Unfortunately, many books tend to deal with the more technical electronic aspects that quickly turn off the reader who cannot comprehend schematic diagrams. Two books that I have enjoyed and use frequently are *The Liberation of Sound: An Introduction to Electronic Music* by Herbert Russcol,[2] which deals with the history and development of electronic music as well as giving a good look into its philosophical implications; and *Electronic Music Synthesis,* by Hubert S. Howe, Jr.,[3] which deals with the more technical aspects of electronic music (yet is easily read) and has excellent descriptions of equipment, materials, and techniques. These two books provide complementary views of the world of electronic music and its production.

---

[2] Englewood Cliffs, N.J.: Prentice-Hall, 1972.
[3] New York: W. W. Norton, 1975.

Listening to music is possibly the most important way in which a musician can become familiar with a body of literature. Here are five recordings representative of the different approaches of composers.

Silver Apples of the Moon by Morton Subotnick (Nonesuch H–71174)

Poème Électronique by Edgard Varèse (Columbia MS 6146), a real landmark

Time's Encomium by Charles Wuorinen, which won the Pulitzer Prize for Music in 1970 (Nonesuch H–71225)

Switched-On Bach by Walter Carlos (Columbia MS 7194)

Magical Mystery Tour by The Beatles (Capitol SMAL 2835), especially "I Am the Walrus"

You may also want to try some more contemporary sounds. Ask a teen-ager you know to recommend some favorites, or try some Emerson, Lake and Palmer, Chick Corea, and Herbie Hancock.

Electronic music is still very much in its infancy, and it remains for us to learn its strengths and weaknesses and guide it to a satisfactory role in contemporary music. The balancing act is usually between musicians who lack sufficient knowledge of electronics to be technically effective and electronic technicians who lack basic musicianship, training, and artistic sensitivity. Many colleges and universities are working to correct this imbalance by offering courses in electronic music as both an art form and an electronic medium.

It should not be seen as a threat to live performance but rather as a new medium for expressing musical ideas that cannot be given a voice through traditional instruments.

Microcomputers and Electronic Music*

Hubert S. Howe, Jr.

This essay, which was completed in July 1979 and includes information that was up to date at that time, gives some idea of the creative possibilities of the new technology and electronic music. Computer technology provides an increasingly wide range of compositional possibilities for today's composers. The field is, however, very far removed from the usual compositional paths, as this brief introduction to the technology reveals.

Hubert S. Howe, Jr., received his Ph.D. in musical composition from Princeton University. He has been active in electronic and computer music synthesis and has written several programs for music synthesis, programs designed for several different types of computers. A past president of the League of Composers—International Society for Contemporary Music, U.S. section, Dr. Howe is on the faculty of music at Queens College.

I. BACKGROUND

In the last few years there has been a revolution in electronics and computer technology that promises to have a far greater impact on society than

---

* This essay is an adaptation and revision of an earlier article that appeared in *Interface*, 7 (1978), pp. 57–68.

previous advancements. Since there have always been grandiose claims made about technological improvements, we may be tempted to think that this is more of the same. However, this time I believe that these predictions will be borne out. In order to understand what is different about the present situation, it is necessary to review some recent history.

For several years now, the electronics industry has been converting from transistor technology to integrated-circuit technology. Previously, it was transistor or "solid-state" technology that had replaced the earlier technology of vacuum tubes. An integrated circuit, or IC or *chip*, is a small device usually about one-half-inch long that has several wire pins or "legs" protruding down on opposite sides. Sometimes ICs are called *bugs*. An IC contains an entire circuit for carrying out some function; it is usually a component of some larger circuit, but more recently it has been common to have a whole circuit for a device contained in one chip. Through a method known as large-scale integration (LSI) and, more recently, very-large-scale integration (VLSI), a huge number of electronic components can be packed into a single chip. Sometimes these can include thousands of logic and other elements.

In 1971, the Intel Corporation produced the first chip that contained the entire central processing unit (CPU) of a computer, the Intel 4004. This was soon followed by the 8008, and a few years later by the 8080, which became one of the most popular computers of all time. Soon, several companies were producing microcomputer chips, and now virtually every major manufacturer produces them. These computer ICs are called *microprocessors* and they are at the center of the present technological revolution. Microprocessors are among the larger ICs, usually about an inch and a half long, with forty pins, and most of them sell for *under $20*. Some of them can now be purchased for as little as a dollar. Although microprocessors have several limitations that will be discussed in detail below, many of them are comparable in computing power to the second-generation computers that spawned the great expansion and development of the 1950s. Thus the basic reason for the microprocessors' effects on technology is economic. Today it is possible for people to buy a complete computer system, together with all kinds of fancy peripherals, for less than they would spend on a new car. The number of homes and businesses that own such computers has been increasing tremendously, and the mass-marketing efforts of the major manufacturers have hardly begun.

These developments have been occurring at such a rapid pace that many people seriously interested in computer music have been unable to keep up with them. On the developers' side, the pace has been even more furious: it is not possible for designers to produce a system before it is obsolete in relation to the technology then available. In this essay I shall describe the basic concepts of microcomputers and their possible applications to electronic music and provide the reader with some information on obtaining further details about this ever-faster-growing field.

II. MICROCOMPUTERS

1. *Maxi-, mini-, and microcomputers.* Up to now, the kind of computer that most people are familiar with would be called a *maxicomputer.* These are the large, general-purpose systems manufactured mostly by IBM, but also by Honeywell, Burroughs, Control Data, and Digital Equipment Corporation (DEC). (Honeywell has now taken over lines previously introduced by General Electric and Xerox.) A maxicomputer usually sells for a price measured in millions of dollars. It has many peripheral devices, including card readers and punches, high-speed printers, magnetic tape and disk drives, and a large memory. Its word size is at least 32 bits. It can be programmed in a variety of languages that are suitable for different applications. Maxicomputers require a very large area in which to be located, significant amounts of electric power, and a temperature- and humidity-controlled environment in which to work.

A *minicomputer* is similar in architecture to a maxicomputer, but is much smaller physically and possesses fewer peripherals. The largest manufacturer of minicomputers is DEC, but others include Data General, Hewlett-Packard, Texas Instruments, Interdata, and many other firms. Minicomputers can usually be purchased for between $5,000 and $100,000. Their word size is usually 16 bits, but some of them have different sizes. Their software is not so versatile as that of maxicomputers, but it usually includes both an Assembler and Fortran or Basic. Most minicomputers are purchased for special-purpose applications, such as controlling an industrial machine, but many of these applications are now yielding to microcomputers.

A *microcomputer* is a "computer on a chip." The entire electronic circuitry of the microcomputer, containing the CPU and, in the near future, memory and peripheral controllers, might be mounted on one or more printed circuit cards, thus occupying a very small area and consuming a negligible amount of electric power. Most microcomputers have a word size of 8 bits, but recently some 16-bit microprocessors have appeared. A complete microcomputer system may cost anywhere from $600 to $3,000, but these are base prices not including most of the peripherals, which can add considerably to the cost of the system. Microcomputers generally do not have large cabinets with flashing lights and switches like mini- and maxicomputers. Sometimes the entire computer fits inside the unit containing the keyboard, so that from the user's viewpoint, all he sees is an ASCII keyboard and video monitor (see II.5 below).

In both conceptual structure and architecture the distinctions between maxicomputers and minicomputers on the one hand, and between minicomputers and microcomputers on the other, are getting more and more blurred. Future developments are only likely to complicate this situation further.

2. *Basic microcomputer concepts.* A microcomputer is a computer based on a microprocessor. The microprocessor is the central processing unit, or CPU, of the computer. Over fifty microprocessors are currently being manufactured by different companies in the United States, but the most important ones to date are the Intel 8080 and 8085, the Zilog Z-80, the Motorola MC6800, and the MOS Technology MCS6502. All of these are 8-bit microprocessors and have the capability of addressing up to 64K bytes. A new crop of 16-bit microprocessors is being introduced in 1979, and these are likely to dominate the industry in the next few years because their computing power is comparable to that of minicomputers. These include the Intel 8086, the Motorola 68000, and the Zilog Z-8000. Sixteen-bit microprocessors, and 8-bit microprocessors as implemented on some systems, can address more than 64K bytes of memory.

Microprocessor memories are referred to by the mnemonics ROM (read-only memory), PROM (programmable read-only memory), EPROM (electrically programmable read-only memory), and RAM (random-access memory). ROM has the bits burned into the chip so that they cannot be destroyed. PROM is more versatile than ROM in that it can be programmed by electrical pulses. Once programmed, it is a read-only memory. EPROM is erasable. ROM, PROM, and EPROM contain things like the operating system, which should not be destroyed by random storage errors. RAM is the portion of memory that the user's programs and data employ.

3. *Industry structure.* The microcomputer industry has a different structure from that of mini- and maxicomputers. One group of companies produces the microprocessors themselves together with other components that may be used in the computer, and another group of companies produces computers based on the microprocessors of their choice. Still other

companies make some of the peripherals. There are independent groups, sometimes connected with the microcomputer companies and sometimes not, that sell software for different computers. Many microcomputers are sold at the retail computer stores that have been cropping up across the United States. Finally, there are users' groups that consist of owners of a particular type of microcomputer that share programs, hardware, data bases, information, and experiences at their meetings or in publications that they sponsor.

Many microcomputers are sold as kits by the manufacturer, to be assembled by the user. The cost of a fully assembled unit can be up to fifty percent more than the kit, and some companies do not even sell assembled units. More recently, kits seem to be disappearing in favor of fully assembled units, which are in some cases less expensive than previous kits, reflecting decreases in the cost of components.

Although two given microcomputers may be based on the same microprocessor and have the same amount of memory, they are not necessarily compatible with each other, and it may not be possible to run the same program on both machines. The main reason for this situation has to do with the software that the computers may use, particularly what is provided in ROM. While some companies are interested in such compatibility, in both hardware and software, others are not, primarily because they may think that they can make more money by compelling their customers to buy only their software and peripherals.

One of the largest manufacturers of microcomputer systems today is Radio Shack, whose TRS-80 is based on the Z-80 microprocessor. Other companies making computers based on the 8080 or Z-80 include MITS, Cromemco, Heath, North Star, and Ohio Scientific. Companies making computers based on the 6502 microprocessor include Commodore, Apple, and Ohio Scientific. Computers based on the 6800 are made by Southwest Technical Products, MITS, and others.

It would not be fair to discuss microcomputer manufacturers without mentioning that there are hundreds of companies in the field, many of which are small outfits that may have started out in someone's garage. Some have grown from that status into multimillion-dollar corporations. Many companies have gone bankrupt, not so much because they have produced inferior products—in fact, it is usually quite the opposite—but because they lacked the financing or management needed for large corporations. The companies mentioned above represent a sampling of those whose track record is very good and who are likely to be major forces in the industry in the 1980s.

4. *Capabilities and limitations of microcomputers.* The execution times of instructions on microcomputers are not so fast as those of maxi- or minicomputers, but they are still quite fast. Microcomputer execution times are normally given in reference to a "clock speed," of which typical figures may be from 2 MHz to 4 MHz. In order to derive the cycle time of the computer, it is necessary to divide this value into a billion, thus producing 500 nanoseconds for 2 MHz and 250 nanoseconds for 4 MHz. Most instructions require several cycles in which to be executed, so average instruction times are from about 1 to 4 microseconds. Different computers may use the same microprocessor but with different clock speeds. (A microsecond is a millionth of a second; a nanosecond, a billionth.)

One of the important limitations of microcomputers concerns the types of artithmetic and logical operations they can perform. All microprocessors can carry out the operations of addition, subtraction; logical ands, ors, and exclusive ors; comparisons; and register rotations and shifting. But most of these operations are performed only on one byte at a time; shifting and rotations are performed only one bit at a time. Addition and subtraction of multibyte values require several instructions. Multiplication, division, and floating-point operations are not even part of the basic instruction set, and require a complicated series of the basic operations. Execution times for these operations are thus much longer than for the other operations.

Another limitation of microcomputers is software, although this will undoubtedly improve substantially in the next few years, as more people use the computers and develop programs for them. Many microcomputers can be programmed only in some form of Basic. The next most likely language to be encountered is an Assembler, but often the Assembler requires more than the minimum system to run. Many companies and individuals are currently involved in developing new software, and both languages and application programs can be purchased commercially.

The older companies have a distinct advantage over the younger ones, if only because their products have been in use for a while and people have written programs for them. Also, the older companies are usually in better financial condition simply because they have survived where others have not. In the minicomputer field DEC has the largest users' group and software package available. In the microcomputer field the 8080 enjoys a similar advantage. The instruction set of the Z-80, one of the newer microprocessors, is a superset of the 8080 offering more than twice as many instructions, but still capable of executing any 8080 programs. A similar relation exists between the 8080 and 8086. These are examples of the kind of progress that is likely to characterize future developments.

5. *Microcomputer peripherals.* Peripheral devices include all of the hardware used to get data in and out of the computer quickly and conveniently and for auxiliary storage. Microcomputer companies have developed extensive lines of peripherals that are both convenient for most people to use and inexpensive.

The *ASCII keyboard* is the most common type of input device found with microcomputers, although some of the cheapest micros use calculator-type keyboards. The ASCII keyboard is a standard typewriter keyboard with several keys for special functions. *ASCII* refers to the character set, which is a 7-bit code containing upper- and lower-case characters, numerals, special characters, and control characters.

The *video monitor* is the most common output device, and it usually works in combination with the ASCII keyboard. A video monitor is basically a black-and-white television set that has been modified to accept input from the computer rather than from an antenna. In fact, many companies sell kits that enable you to use an old television and thus save buying the monitor, which is usually more expensive than a television of comparable size. (Standard televisions are not as high in quality as video monitors.) The monitor displays characters that are typed in from the keyboard or output from the computer, and many computers have a limited capacity for graphic displays. Standard displays are of 32, 64, or 80 characters per line, with 16 to 20 lines displayed on the screen at one time. A video monitor with extended graphics can display complicated pictures and graphs, and many of the video games that have appeared over the last few years are based on microprocessors running a simple program. A color video monitor can produce beautiful, dynamically changing shapes, and there is a new crop of video artists whose work consists of programming such devices.

Many microcomputers can be used with a standard *teletype* or printing terminal instead of the combination ASCII keyboard and video monitor, although teletypes are used less often nowadays because they are more expensive.

Most microcomputers offer inexpensive *cassette tape recorders* as input and output devices to the computer. The type of cassette machine employed is usually the least expensive monaural audio cassette used to record speech (not music). Information is recorded on the cassette tape in the form of sounds that represent binary numbers. There are, unfortunately, many different systems for translating sound into bits, so that not all computer cassettes can communicate with each other.

A *floppy disk* is a much more convenient device on which to store programs and data, and almost all major microcomputer manufacturers are now offering them or planning to offer them at inexpensive prices, starting at around $600. The floppy *diskette* is the device inserted into the disk, on which the material is recorded. It resembles a phonograph record, although it is never removed from the square paper holder that contains it and it is flexible like a tape, the data being recorded on it magnetically. There are two sizes of floppy disks in use at present: "mini" disks are 5¼ inches, and "regular" disks are 8 inches. The amount of data that can be recorded on a diskette depends on the formating scheme used and on whether both sides of the diskette can be used. Mini diskettes can hold from approximately 90K to 200K bytes depending on these factors, and 8-inch diskettes from 200K to 500K. Data-transfer rates are very fast, enabling entire programs or long data strings to be stored or retrieved in just a few seconds. Because floppy diskettes are cheaper than an equivalent amount of paper to hold the data, their use is becoming widespread for many different applications.

A floppy disk has the advantage that the diskette can be removed and stored in a safe place. *Hard disks* or *fixed disks* lack this characteristic, but compensate for it by holding a much larger quantity of data. Their capacity is measured in *megabytes* (millions of bytes), and systems are now available that may hold from 10 to 29 megabytes. Soon these disks will be mass-produced, and their use will become widespread.

A *hard-copy printer* is a printer that prints on paper, as opposed to the video monitor, which displays the same information but not on paper. The printers offered for microcomputers are usually quite slow, on the order of electric typewriters. Printers are the most expensive of the microcomputer peripherals, except for the hard disks, which are not generally available yet. Inexpensive printers can be purchased for under $1,000, but good ones are in the $3,500 range.

A *modem* (modulator/demodulator) is a device that allows the computer to transmit data to another computer or to a storage device by means of sound. Just as with the audio cassettes, bits are translated into a sequence of tones, but in this case there are usually more standard methods employed. The rate at which data are transmitted is referred to as *baud*, which means bits per second. (Thus, "baud rate" is a frequently used redundancy.) Standard rates are 110, 150, 300, 600, 1,200, 2,400, 4,800, 9,600, and 19,200 baud. Slow-speed modems can be connected to a standard telephone line, allowing the computer to be used as a terminal to another computer (usually a maxicomputer).

Input sensors are real-time controls, such as joysticks, that are operated by the users of the computer to get data into the machine in a manner that is more convenient than the keyboard. At present, the widest use of input sensors is for computer games, where the input sensor represents something like the steering wheel of a car racing across the video monitor, but many serious applications in fields such as medicine also exist.

Finally, it must be mentioned that additional *memory* itself can usually be purchased for the computer, just like a peripheral device. Most microcomputers are originally sold with only a minimum amount of memory, such as 4K RAM and 4K ROM out of the possible 64K. The price of memory has been dropping steadily as new chips are being manufactured that have a greater density of bits on the chip. In the near future microprocessors with built-in memory are sure to appear.

These are the standard peripherals currently offered for microcomputers. Other devices, such as magnetic tape drives, are common on minicomputers but rarely available for micros because of their significant cost. On the other hand, there are several companies that offer a variety of low-cost peripherals for musical applications, such as electronic music and speech synthesizers. Other unusual devices include clocks, model railroad controllers, fire and burglar alarm systems, functioning and mobile robots, and various and sundry other items.

6. *Applications of microcomputers.* At the present time there are several areas in which microprocessors have already been used considerably, so that one can purchase complete systems geared to special purposes.

One of the largest areas of microcomputer applications is that of *business systems,* although these are usually for small businesses because large ones would have maxicomputers. Microcomputers can handle the payroll, accounting, and inventory of a complete business of moderate size. Related applications concern the keeping of economic statistics, monitoring stock market activity, projecting sales, and the like. Many companies specialize in equipment and software for these purposes.

Another extensive microcomputer application is in a *word-processing system.* A word-processing system is basically a microcomputer together with a typewriterlike printer. A secretary can type in a letter, or any document, and edit it directly on the video monitor before anything is printed. When it has been completely proofread and corrected, the document is printed, perhaps in multiple copies. Form letters can be written where the name and address of the recipient is changed on each copy, thus "personalizing" the letter.

Another popular group of microcomputer applications is in *computer games.* Computer enthusiasts have already developed extensive collections of games that can be purchased in books, copied out of magazines, or purchased directly on software cassettes. All kinds of games are available: games that pit you against the computer as opponent; games that you play with an opponent, controlled by the computer, like the video games seen in many amusement areas now; board games; gambling games; puzzles; and many others that can provide hours of enjoyment.

Another large area of applications is in *household management.* This includes not only such purposes as budget management and checkbook maintenance but also the keeping of files of addresses and telephone numbers, diet and nutrition analysis, and the filing of medical and health records.

Another large area of microcomputer applications is in *education,* of course, ranging from programmed and tutorial instruction to the monitoring of a student's perceptions and responses to stimuli. Recently the undergraduate curriculum at Harvard University was revised so that all students will receive basic training in computers. The only way that institutions will be able to provide the facilities needed for this type of instruction will be through increased reliance on microcomputers.

Many people have purchased microcomputers to be used purely as terminals for time-sharing systems. When a microcomputer is used in this way, it is called an *intelligent terminal.* In conjunction with a text-editor program, permitting a data file to be typed in and edited under the control of the microcomputer, an intelligent terminal can reduce the amount of time spent on-line to the time-shared computer, thus saving money.

Even within the limitations mentioned above, microcomputers are still amazingly powerful and can perform many different tasks efficiently. For many types of computing a microprocessor is sufficient. Because they work so well for these applications, there has not been much pressure for manufacturers to develop new processors to overcome these limitations; rather, the new processors are being developed in order to compete with minicomputers.

7. *Software.* As the microcomputer industry is still young, the main interest of most users has been in getting them up and running. In the long run, however, attention will focus on the uses of the systems, with software becoming of crucial importance. The equipment is likely to be evaluated in

terms of its performance for specific applications, whether or not these make full use of the capabilities of the computer.

Software includes all of the features needed to develop and run programs: languages, operating systems, monitors, and application programs. Most software available for microcomputers at present is inadequate. Almost all manufacturers provide some form of Basic with the computer, but everything else must be purchased, sometimes at high prices. Several companies, the best known of which is Microsoft, specialize in the development of software for microcomputers. Excellent progress has been made recently in the development of new software, and this is likely to increase in the future because of the expansion in the number of users and in the applications for which microcomputers are used. Intelligent programmers are pushing for new languages such as Pascal, which make it easier to write programs and to alter them once they are written. Some efforts are being made toward the probably hopeless task of standardizing Basic.

These developments represent the positive side of the software scene. On the darker side, there are innumerable charlatans who are selling worthless products for high prices, often going out of business when their customers catch up with them. Although there have also been such shenanigans on the hardware side of the industry, they are more numerous with software because the products are more elusive, and comparisons cannot be made until after the programs have been purchased.

III. MICROCOMPUTER APPLICATIONS IN ELECTRONIC MUSIC

Although there are many nonserious applications of microprocessors in electronic music from the standpoint of a professional musician, microprocessors promise to have a profound impact on the areas of computer-controlled synthesizers and computer music synthesis.

1. *Computer-controlled systems.* The use of microprocessors for process-control systems has been increasing in recent years. While there have been several previous experiments with computer-controlled synthesizers using minicomputers (such as Bell Telephone Laboratories' GROOVE system), microprocessor systems are now appearing with great profusion. There are now over fifty companies that manufacture electronic music synthesizers in the United States, and many of them employ computer technology or hardware in various stages of the design and production. Synthesizer kits or components can be purchased to fit into the cabinet containing the microprocessor and driven as one of the output devices of

the computer. Alternatively, there are interfaces to other equipment such as voltage-controlled synthesizers, for which the computer can be regarded as just another voltage source.

Most products currently available do not work with the "old-fashioned" synthesizers of the 1960s. Often the operation of the system may depend on the particular electronic or logic structure of the synthesizer hardware, which may be partly digital internally. This is not at all surprising in view of the increasing reliance on standard chips available today. Nobody who sets out to design a synthesizer now would have to tackle the problem of designing an oscillator circuit; books full of circuits can be purchased commercially. It is very easy for a designer to employ a half-dozen or so ICs that can be assembled into a complete module with a minimum of labor. The system will depend on employing certain standard voltages and other characteristics used by the computer. It is in the area of cabinetry and power supply that most microcomputers differ from each other, even when based on the same microprocessor, although several companies do manufacture compatible hardware.

Much confusion now exists over what may be called a *synthesizer*. In advertisements, which are often the only places where equipment is described, devices range from boards that plug into the computer cabinet that can play a monophonic melody over a built-in speaker to polyphonic modules that can play four or more voices in real time. As long as the equipment is controlled by the computer, it is no drawback that the music-generating hardware consists only of a bank of oscillators and filters, because both the pitch and amplitude of the oscillators and the operating characteristics of the filters can be determined independently with enough speed and accuracy to satisfy most musical requirements. More difficult limitations concern the amount of hardware available, for each device must be purchased separately, and often there are limits to the number of devices that can be driven without degrading the system.

Computer-controlled systems for electronic music are sure to profit from current developments in sound-studio technology. Many sound studios are now employing fully automated mixing consoles and other devices that are operated by microprocessors. The type of control that these devices require is exactly the same as electronic music synthesizers. There could be much greater interaction between commercial sound studios and electronic music studios. Standard studio techniques such as overdubbing on multitrack tape recorders are essential for electronic music and will continue to be. As commercial studios possess the financial ability to pay for these advancements, electronic music studios can only benefit.

The greatest problem with these systems at present seems to be the lack of adequate software to enable the best use to be made of them. Some software allows only tempered pitches to be produced, even though the oscillators are capable of a greater range of frequencies. The basic reason for this problem is that, in the present situation, people are more concerned simply with getting a system up and running than with refinements. Furthermore, the result that people desire at this time is better described as a "dazzling commercial sound" than what serious composers would think of as electronic music. Equipment is capable of playing melodies with fancy percussive effects, or silly little computer renditions of popular songs, but going beyond this stage requires special efforts.

Such problems are really the result of the fact that the field is too new, so products have not been around long enough for the users to acquire adequate experience with them. In view of the great strides that have already been made in just a few years, it is clear that these difficulties can be ironed out in the future. An encouraging sign is that several manufacturers are now or soon will be offering electronic music synthesizer modules for microcomputers. The low cost and expected versatility of these devices may well render much present equipment obsolete.

2. *Computer music synthesis.* Computer music synthesis is the production of sound by generating samples of the sound wave, which is converted to sound by means of a digital-to-analog converter (DAC) and a smoothing filter. In the past much effort has been expended in developing adequate software for these systems, which has been accomplished in programs such as Music 4BF, Music V, and Music 360, for example. Much electronic music that is serious in intention has been produced using these programs.

It is clear that microcomputers are capable of carrying out the operations necessary for the production of electronic music according to this method, but at the present time there are two serious limitations: the lack of adequate mass-storage devices, and the need for faster and more powerful arithmetic calculations. Less serious problems concern the need for large quantities of memory and DACs of adequate quality.

All of these limitations are likely to be overcome within the next decade, making it feasible for a complete system to be assembled at low cost. Fixed disks will be the mass-storage devices of these systems, and the 16-bit microprocessors will perform the necessary arithmetic calculations at a speed commensurate with the rest of the system.

Computer music synthesis is likely to profit from the new digital recording techniques that are currently being introduced. Digital tape recorders are now being produced for audio applications in sound studios, and they are likely to spread to commercial products for home use during the 1980s. Digital recording uses the same methods employed by computer music synthesis for the recording and playback of music on audio tape. It is likely that companies developing digital recorders, such as 3M and Sony, will also develop microcomputer-controlled sound-processing systems.

Computer music synthesis techniques are also being employed in a whole new range of musical instruments that are currently being developed. One of the first such instruments is the *Synclavier*, made by the New England Digital Corporation in Norwich, Vermont. The instrument contains a 16-bit microprocessor and allows the performer to store information on a floppy disk in parametric form. During a performance, the information on the disk is read and generated in real time together with what the performer inputs. Although the instrument is limited to a form of FM synthesis, it is still one of the most powerful musical instruments that has yet been produced, and there are already other such instruments being designed by other manufacturers.

As in synthesizer control, the most serious limitation of microcomputer music synthesis is likely to be in the software, in this case not the programs so much as the languages available. Even though music synthesis can probably be programmed in Basic, that is certainly inconvenient. Assembler languages with macro capability would be more suitable, but these would require greater sophistication on the users' part. Best would be a combination of an Assembler and Basic, or one of the newer languages such as Pascal or APL.

3. *Other musical applications.* All areas in which computers are used for musical applications are likely to be affected by the microcomputer revolution. Systems for educational instruction are currently being developed for use with maxi- and minicomputers, and many of these could easily be switched to microcomputers. Special-purpose applications such as music printing might be significantly less expensive if controlled by microprocessors.

Applications in musicology, analysis, and bibliography that require large data bases are likely to continue to use maxicomputers, if available, although possibly under time-sharing systems communicating through intelligent terminals. Many programs have been written in higher-level languages that are not yet available for most micros, such as PL-I, APL, or Snobol, or that require significant amounts of memory exceeding the 64K limitation.

4. *The future.* How microcomputers will affect the future cannot really be known, of course. Undoubtedly much will depend on the economy. What can be observed at the present time is that this industry has experienced phenomenal growth since 1977, and that so much powerful equipment is now available so inexpensively that it is worth serious consideration by persons in electronic music and related fields.

The growth of the industry has not been without certain pains, however. Several microcomputer companies have gone into bankruptcy, leaving users and equipment stranded. The maxi- and minicomputer companies have retaliated against the microcomputers by cutting prices and selling their equipment in the same retail stores that sell micros. IBM has introduced a new line of small computers, the 5100 system. DEC has allowed the CPU of its most successful mini, the PDP/11, to be marketed in kit form by Heath and other manufacturers.

The ideal that microcomputer companies are striving to attain is to have every American household include a computer. If you compare the fantasy of home computers to what has already happened with electronic calculators, the picture is encouraging. A few years ago calculators cost over $100, and they were rather expensive toys. Now they can be purchased for as little as $5.00, and nearly every household has one if not several. When you think about it in these terms, owning your own computer is not really such an unusual idea after all.

IV. BIBLIOGRAPHY

Developments in both electronic music and microcomputers have been occurring so rapidly that few books have been written that describe the current state of knowledge. The best information can be obtained from the latest issues of the magazines listed below, which are full of advertisements from computer companies as well as book publishers. Many of these magazines are not widely known and are sold mostly to subscribers or in retail computer stores. Most microcomputer magazines have existed only a few years, or months.

One cautionary note about these magazines is in order: the packaging is not necessarily a guide to the value of the articles or to the features they describe. Many articles have catchy titles but report little of substance. The same is true of advertisements. A thorough familiarity with the products is necessary to understand and evaluate them.

1. Computer Music
Computer Music Journal. Published by People's Computer Company, Box E, 1263 El Camino Real, Menlo Park, California 94025. Includes a special "Products of Interest" section describing new equipment, which has much information about microprocessors.

2. Electronic Music
Contemporary Keyboard. Published by Keyboard Players International, Box 907, Saratoga, California 95070. A combination of serious and pop music related to the keyboard, including electronic keyboards. Mainly of interest for columns by David Burge, Tom Rhea, Patrick Gleeson, and a column by the staff on synthesizer basics.

Synapse. Published by Synapse Publishing Company, 2829 Hyans Street, Los Angeles, California 90026. Mostly devoted to pop music, but contains much information on synthesizers.

3. Microcomputers
Magazines
BYTE. Published by Byte Publications, Inc., 70 Main Street, Peterborough, New Hampshire 03458. Monthly. The largest publication in the field. Back issues are collectors' items. Articles are on a high level, and issues often collect several articles on one subject.

Creative Computing. Published by Creative Computing, P.O. Box 789–M, Morristown, New Jersey 07960. Monthly. Oriented toward computer applications and software. Contains special features on computer games.

Interface Age. Published by McPheters, Wolfe & Jones, 13913 Artesia Boulevard, Cerritos, California 90701. Monthly. Oriented toward home and business applications.

Kilobaud Microcomputing. Published by 1001001, Inc., Peterborough, New Hampshire 03458. Monthly. Articles are on an introductory level. Oriented more toward home applications and hobbyists than the other magazines.

on Computing. Published by on Computing, 70 Main Street, Peterborough, New Hampshire 03458. Published four times a year. A new magazine, written on an introductory level for personal applications.

Personal Computing. Published by Benwill Publishing Corp., 167 Corey Road, Brookline, Massachusetts 02146. Bi-monthly. Oriented to applications and software.

Books

Barden, William, Jr. *How to Buy and Use Minicomputers and Microcomputers.* Indianapolis: Howard W. Sams & Co., 1976.

Solomon, Leslie, and Veit, Stanley. *Getting Involved with Your Own Computer: A Guide for Beginners.* Short Hills, N.J.: Ridley Enslow Publishers, 1977.

BITS, Inc., 25 Route 101 West, Peterborough, New Hampshire 03458, is a bookselling service that carries practically every publication available in the industry.

Osborne & Associates, Inc., 630 Bancroft Way, Berkeley, California 94710, publishes a whole series of books on microcomputing, from elementary to advanced levels.

Notations*

Allison Knowles

The reading or memorizing of something written in order to play music is an Occidental practice. In the Orient music by tradition is transmitted from person to person. Teachers of music require that students put no reliance on written material.

Western notations brought about the preservation of "music," but in doing so encouraged the development not only of standards of composition and performance but also of an enjoyment of music that was more or less independent of its sound, placing the qualities of its organization and expressivity above sound itself.

Furthermore, as the permissions to reprint in this book testify, music, through becoming property, elevated its composers above other musicians, and an art by nature ephemeral became in practice political.

In any case, until recently, notation was the unquestioned path to the experience of music.

At the present time, however, and throughout the world, not only most popular music but much so-called serious music is produced without

* Reprinted from *Notations,* sel. John Cage, ed. Allison Knowles (New York: Something Else Press, 1969). Copyright © 1969 by John Cage.

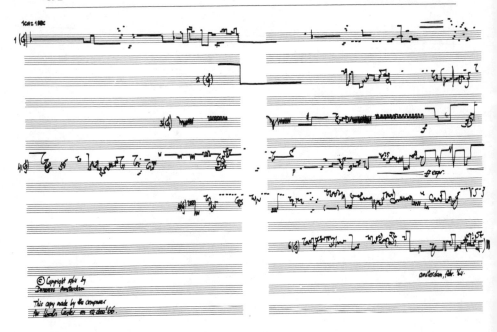

Louis Andriessen: *A Flower Song II.* © 1966 by Donemus, Amsterdam, Holland. All rights reserved. Printed by permission of Donemus.

recourse to notations. This is in large part the effect of a change from print to electronic technology. One may nowadays repeat music not only by means of printed notes but by means of sound recordings, disc, or tape. One may also compose new music by these same recording means and by other means: the activation of electric and electronic sound systems, the programming of computer output of actual sounds, etc. In addition to technological changes, or without employing such changes, one may change one's mind, experiencing, in the case of theatre (Happenings, performance pieces), sounds as the musical effect of actions as they may be perceived in the course of daily life. In none of these cases does notation stand between musician and music or between music and listener.

Asked to write about notation, André Jolivet made the following remark: "One hundred and fifty years ago, Western musical writing acquired

István Anhalt: Sketch from *Symphony of Modules.* Printed by permission of the composer.

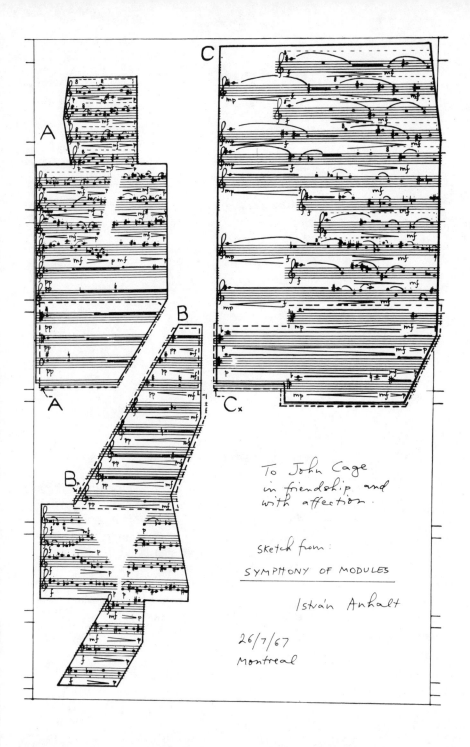

To John Cage
in friendship and
with affection.

Sketch from:

SYMPHONY OF MODULES

István Anhalt

26/7/67
Montreal

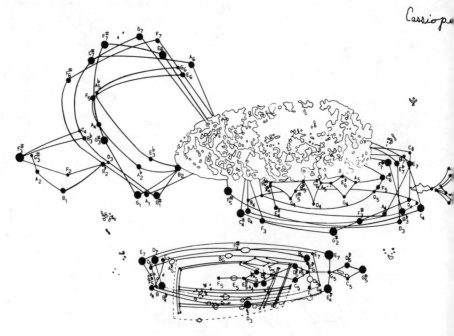

George Cacioppo: *Cassiopeia*. Printed by permission of the composer.

such flexibility, such precision, that music was permitted to become the only true international language."

François Dufrêne, replying to a request for a manuscript, wrote as follows: "I am not in a situation to give you any kind of score, since the spirit in which I work involves the systematic rejection of all notation. . . . I 'note' furthermore that a score could only come about after the fact, and because of this loses from my point of view all significance."

This book, then, by means of manuscript pages (sometimes showing how a page might leave its composer's hand in its working form, sometimes how it looked in its working form as he used it, sometimes finished work) shows the spectrum in the twentieth century that extends from the continuing dependence on notation to its renunciation.

Franco Donatoni: *Babai* (1963). Copyright © 1967
by Edizioni Suvini Zerboni. All rights reserved. Reprinted
by permission of Edizioni Suvini Zerboni.

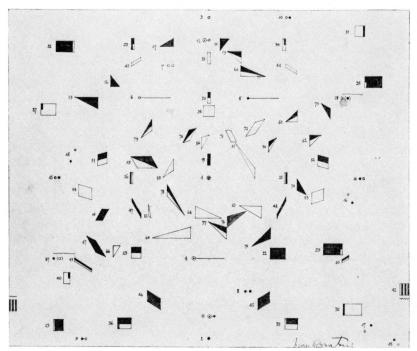

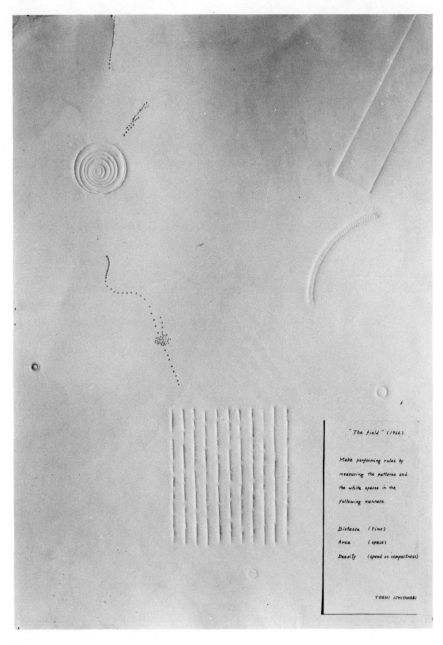

Toshi Ichiyanagi: *The Field* (1966). Printed by permission of the composer.

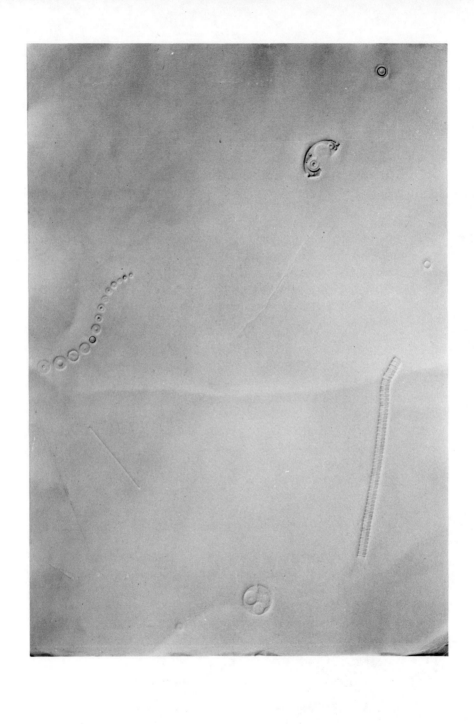

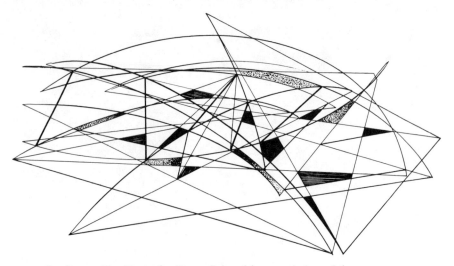

Joe Jones: *Five Pieces for Piano.* Printed by permission of the composer.

Jōji Yuasa: *Cosmos Haptic.* Printed by permission of the composer.

Music Since Hiroshima: The Electronic Age Begins*

Herbert Russcol

Although it is probably impossible to pinpoint the exact date for the beginning of modern music, Herbert Russcol suggests that the search for new materials in order to create new sounds began with the Italian musicians associated with the Futurist movement. (Rodney Payton traces the development of music in the Futurist movement in the essay, "The Music of Futurism: Concerts and Polemics," pp. 71–89.) Experiments in painting were closely related to musical innovations, indicating that music had an interdisciplinary morphology and has retained it, for many discoveries in new music are closely related to experiments in other media.

In arguing the cause of new music, Russcol asks, "why must a composer be constricted to narrow arbitrary assumptions laid down centuries ago?" and he ends his survey of mechanization in music by indicating that electronic music writing may "become the basis of a new art form altogether." Russcol emphasizes the social implications of new musical forms and points out that "Hiroshima is a convenient, dramatic date that marks the dying of one music and the birth of another." In surveying the growth and development of electronic music the author stresses the rationale and motivation that necessitated it.

* Reprinted from *The American Scholar*, 39, no. 2 (Autumn 1970), pp. 289–293. Copyright © 1970 by the United Chapters of Phi Beta Kappa.

Herbert Russcol has written articles on music for numerous publications. His books include Introduction to Electronic Music *(1970). He plays the French horn and has been a member of the Pittsburgh Symphony, the Boston Pops Orchestra, and the Israel Philharmonic.*

The moment man ceased to make music with his voice alone the art became machine-ridden. Orpheus's lyre was a machine, a symphony orchestra is a regular factory for making artificial sounds, and a piano is the most appalling contrivance of levers and wires this side of the steam engine.

—Jacques Barzun

The composer of electronic music flips a switch and programs the dimensions of a sound he has in mind: volume, timbre, duration, articulation. He faces a remarkably sophisticated machine, which can cost from $3,000 to $150,000 and can produce any acoustical event known to man. He flips another switch, and the machine obliges at once with the requested sound. If the composer, who is also part physicist and trained mathematician, is dissatisfied, he can reprogram. Or, he can alter, transfigure, or refine the sound down to mathematically precise gradations. When he is pleased, he flips another switch and easily superimposes, or "patches," his one specific sound onto combinations of layers of other sounds, which he has fixed permanently on the storage medium of tape.

Eventually, after months of laborious splicing, the composer walks out of the studio with his new opus under his arm on a reel of tape. He has been in full control of his musical intentions to a degree undreamed of a generation ago. He knows exactly what his new piece is going to sound like, because he has been his own copyist, proofreader, publisher, conductor, and orchestra; and his orchestra consists not of strings and winds but of the entire spectrum of sound possibilities. What is more, he can dispatch his creation at once, to anywhere in the world, to anyone who cares to hear it, more easily than a painter crates a canvas.

This, in a nutshell, is what electronic music is all about. For the first time in history, composers work directly on the medium, on a material form, and can establish the fixed and final form of their music on a simple storage device, and without the expensive and usually unwilling aid of interpreters. This development has with good reason been termed the "revolt of the composers"; it brings to a close the 350-year-old epoch in which composers could only give approximate indications of their music on a manuscript and then go hat in hand to search for performers who would turn the paper indications back into music. This is the most staggering breakthrough in the art of music since the invention of counterpoint, and may prove to be of more far-reaching significance. Whether or not it can produce a Bach or a Beethoven remains to be seen.

Running parallel with this revolution is another musical revolution, more difficult to grasp. The availability of electronic sound-making machines has spurred the longing of composers to break out of the musical straitjacket—C-major scales, time signatures, tonality, violins, pianos, and everything else connected with what Western music lovers have regarded as almost divine laws of musical creation. For the last fifty years, the era dominated by Stravinsky and Schönberg, composers have sought new roads instead of the old well-trodden paths. Schönberg with his twelve-tone system of serial writing proposed a new grammar for music; it wouldn't do, a whole new language was urgently needed. As the English critic Peter Heyworth has pointed out, we now can view Stravinsky and Schönberg not as anarchists but rather as men who tried desperately to hold the old order of music together somehow, to keep the mainstream of music flowing *somewhere*. But, "by postponing the break they inadvertently built up the pressure behind it."

That "pressure" was yearning for release from the ironclad traditional concept of what was acceptable musical sound. It was also a new, growing awareness that the art of music could encompass and control *the entire range of aural possibilities.* If a writer may use any word, or nonword, a painter draw any line or sign, why must a composer be constricted to narrow, arbitrary assumptions, laid down centuries ago, of what are "acceptable" sounds that may be employed to make music? Is not a Bach fugue a novel, peculiar organization of sound? And who is to say what is an acceptable sound, anyhow? What about the intriguing, subtle sound discriminations of Eastern music?

There is no definition of music that forbids a composer from using the sound of a steam shovel, or of an electronic machine, if it so pleases him. You may agree with the description of music as "the art or science of arranging sounds in notes and rhythms to give a desired or pleasing pattern or effect," or you may care for the definition once given by the eighteenth-century Polish philosopher Hoene Wronski, who decided that *all* music was "the corporealization of the intelligence that is in sound." Neither puts electronic music out of bounds.

The composer of electronic music is indeed very much searching for "the intelligence that is in sound." He is an artistic primitive and is feeling his way, groping for new ways and means of musical expression. Electronics has presented him with a God-given tool. The new music (of which electronic music is one part, along with music for live players) accepts any sound, produced by any means, as valid raw material to be worked artistically. Often the new composer substitutes the beauty of mathematical order for "inspiration," and it is no coincidence that Boulez, Xenakis, Stockhausen, and Babbitt, formidable names in the new music, are all expert mathematicians.

Thus, it is our good fortune to be living in the midst of the twin revolution that rages today in music: the discovery of a material storage device for musical thought; and a tearing down of the old limits and rules of the game, and the substitution of an entirely new aesthetic that sets the limits of music at *whatever the human ear and human intelligence are able to perceive.*

The rupture in musical thinking that faces the contemporary composer, it is generally agreed, had its seeds in Wagner's *Tristan and Isolde,* and Debussy's *Afternoon of a Faun* and ballet *Jeux.* The quest for the broadening of *sound materials* began with the Italian musicians associated with the Futurist movement in painting, as early as 1910. Around this time, the composer-pianist Ferruccio Busoni wrote enthusiastically about a crude progenitor of today's synthesizers,[1] the *Dynamophone.* The 1920s and the 1930s saw such exotically named electrical contraptions as the *Trautonium,* the *Dynaphone,* and the *Theremin,* among others, all of which passed on to the dustbin.

These early attempts were frustrated because the available sounds were limited, and because it is one thing to be able to make weird sounds on an electronic instrument and an entirely different matter when you can get these sounds down permanently on tape, and shape them as you will into a new kind of music. But as early as 1922 Edgard Varèse, a composer whose influence on electronic music has been profound, wrote, "What we want is an instrument that will give us a continuous sound at any pitch. The composer and the electrician will have to labor together to get it." In 1937 John Cage, that Beckett clown and granddada of us all, stated prophetically what became the credo of the new music: "The use of noise to make music will continue and increase until we reach a music produced

---

[1] A system of generators, modifiers, and controllers that is designed to enable the construction of sounds in a general and logical way.

through the aid of electrical instruments that will make available for musical purposes any and all sounds that can be heard."

Then the tape recorder came along, and in the late 1940s, the first "school" of tape music, *musique concrète,* was founded in Paris. Pierre Schaeffer and others achieved what was essentially a series of noise montages of naturally produced sounds gathered from traffic noises, birdcalls, foghorns, the human voice, and whatever. These "junk sounds" were altered on tape and artistically shaped into a structural unity.

At the same time, a group of musicians of the West German Radio at Cologne rejected the *musique concrète* idea of working with prerecorded sound and experimented not in the *re*production of sounds by electronic means, but rather in the *production.* Accomplished theoreticians and acousticians, they set out to design electronic equipment that would drive a loudspeaker or magnetize a tape to produce any sound at all. They followed the basic theorem in acoustics that any tone consists of a combination of simple tones called *sine* or *sinusoidal* tones. These tones can be produced on a loudspeaker or a tape by an ordinary alternating current and later combined as the programmer-composer desires on the remarkable invention, tape.

In America the electronic age in music was casually ushered in on October 28, 1952, at New York's Museum of Modern Art, in a concert led by Leopold Stokowski. (The vision and restless interest of Stokowski in electronic developments in music have never been fully recognized, by the way—he can be seen today as a musical Marshall McLuhan.) The opening pieces of the concert required live performers; then after the intermission all instruments, chairs, and stands were removed, and a large speaker mounted in a cabinet was placed in the center of the bare stage. The audience was left rather uneasily face-to-face with the speaker, which then electronically reproduced music made by Columbia University experimenters on a machine that produced electronic sound, and there went a 350-year-old tradition. Music and music-making would never be the same.

It is significant that the electronic era in music—a cultural period as distinct and all-encompassing as the Renaissance or the Baroque—coincides with the atomic age. The threat of thermonuclear holocaust, the dread reality of Us-It, drove artists to a new sensibility and a search for a new tongue in which to utter the unutterable. The late 1940s and early 1950s saw young composers everywhere seeking to discover and nourish new kinds of music that might express our transfigured world.

There was also a revulsion on the part of young musicians against staid concert halls and performers in white ties in a world that produced the bomb. Red-plush seats, white-maned conductors, and well-fed audiences waiting for a soothing musical massage: all the fixtures and symbols of the well-kept garden of music—you needed a confidence in order and man's status to be part of that establishment. Little wonder that electronic music never sounds like a revelation of faith; it is more likely to be creepy sounds and glissando yelps, and rather absurd.

I do not suggest that the bomb fell and composers lined up to study voltage control and wave forms rather than harmony and counterpoint. Rather, Hiroshima is a convenient, dramatic date that marks the dying of one music, and the birth of another. The entire modern period in music, from 1900 through Schönberg, was cast overnight into the past and its violent arguments and theories made academic.

It is more than fortuitous that after 1945 young composers, especially the Germans, found themselves without a valid past and embarked upon radical innovation; that the Cologne studio was founded in 1950; that Boulez issued his famous rallying cry, *"Schönberg est mort!"* (Read: Anything goes), in 1952; that this period saw Cage's first experiments in random music, and also Babbitt's new concept of music, which would have bemused Johann Sebastian Bach, "totally organized" music of mathematical exactness.

The new composers were fascinated with modern physical theory. Many new musical terms were directly inspired by physics—composers spoke of "space-time relationships," as well as parameters, random choice, time fields, periodicity, formats, and the like. Iannis Xenakis, a brilliant new composer, explained his *Pithoprakta* as "a confrontation of acoustical continuity and discontinuity . . . dense clouds of sound-atoms . . . the law of large numbers," and so on.

The bomb, as the kids say in pop music, was a New Sound. If a composer of the atomic age was to express the sound of his time, he needed new tools, new language, new sounds.

Electronic music has been with us for a generation now, and it is interesting to take a close look at how the boys are doing. The boys are the new breed of musicotechnocrats who think in the new language of frequencies and oscillators and random generators. Not for them the old-fashioned, imprecise indications to an interpreter—crescendo and diminuendo; they speak of "attack and decay" of a tone, and control it themselves, thank you, on a synthesizer and with exquisite precision.

Most of their writing is abstract, in the sense that paintings by Mondrian (controlled) or Pollock (random) are abstract. They are overwhelmed with the rank fecundity of the machine, to paraphrase Lewis Mumford. Just about every young composer of any worth in the world today (including Russia, where they seem to be quasi-underground) has accepted the principle of writing electronically as well as writing for live musicians. In America, quite possibly because American composers have always suffered an inferiority complex vis-à-vis the awesome European composers and because Americans are born tinkerers, young composers have plunged into electronic writing like happy ducks. New, smaller, easily operated machines, of which the Moog Synthesizer of *Switched-On Bach* record fame is the most successful, sell for a few thousand dollars. Colleges and universities all over America have ordered their Moogs, which will soon be as universal and taken-for-granted a campus fixture as the chapel organ. Hundreds, perhaps thousands, of eager would-be composers can hardly wait to get started on the Moog, and it is certain that in the next five or ten years we are going to be deluged with more and more electronic music.

In the scathing words of the liveliest music critic of our time, the octogenarian Igor Stravinsky, "Electronic music . . . has moved into and conquered academe. The young musician takes his degree in computer technology now, and settles down with his Moog or his mini-synthesizer as routinely as in my day he would have taken it in counterpoint or harmony (see dictionary) and gone to work at the piano."

Nevertheless, the availability of synthesizers will bring about a profound change in how we learn about music and what we regard as valid sound materials for the art of music. At the new University of California San Diego campus at La Jolla, the music department teaches music appreciation not with records and diagrams of music history but with tape recorders and synthesizers, and students learn both the performing and creating of music as a basic element of the arts curriculum.

One fascinating aspect of electronic music is that it has been enthusiastically welcomed by young audiences. This is astonishing. Ours has been the first era that hates to hear new music; for us, music is an evasion of life, and almost all of us want to close the gates and be curators.

But the kids have embraced electronic music, along with rock, as their very own. They reject serious jazz as "adult music"—which may dismay over-thirties who once excitedly went to hear Louis Armstrong and Duke Ellington as the very essence of bold youthful music—but they buy recordings of electronic music by the armload. *Switched-On Bach,* an unnerving reconstruction of Bach on a Moog, soared right up there on the best-seller record charts.

James Kunen, the young author of *The Strawberry Statement,* is quoted as saying, "I don't read much, it's easier to go to a movie, and let it all wash over you." With the same philosophy, the most exciting place to hear new music in New York these days is not at Lincoln Center, where electronic music is rarely heard (the kids often despise Lincoln Center, as the symbol of all that's wrong with the musical establishment), but at such unlikely places as the Electric Ear concerts at the Electric Circus, and at the Free Music Store, both in the middle of hippieland. Music is not treated here like a Ming vase under a glass bell. There are no ushers, no dressing up, no chairs. You sit on the floor or walk around and smoke, and let it all wash over you, and I for one am a fervent convert.

The kids have new ears. They are children of the unblinking electronic eye; in Susan Sontag's terms, they are cool, emotionally neutral, free from prejudice about what music should sound like, and utterly lack cultural suppositions. They have been flipping TV channels since childhood and have been exposed to a fantastic sound spectrum of folk, classical, pop, rock, and commercials; their nervous systems are extended to receive messages from every corner of Mr. McLuhan's global village and they groove with electronic music, the true voice of our "technotronic" age.

Of course, the ready acceptance of electronic music by young audiences does not mean it is good music. On the contrary, one cannot avoid the suspicion that so many composers turned on because their music written in the conventional medium was godawful. For them, electronic music is nothing but a cop-out, because they shrink from battling it out with Stravinsky, and the ghostly competition of the old masters.

Is this controlled chaos, these "wild clumps of jagged sound, blips, squeals," "tonal ruptures and utter boredom," "this aural nightmare," in the words of a host of outraged critics, really here to stay? It seems that the answer is emphatically yes. We emotionally refuse to believe it, especially the music lover who adores Mozart and has just made his peace with Bartók. But the aural nightmare is upon us, along with the bomb, and just won't go away.

It is clear that we have entered the postmodern period in music. We cannot unring bells. Rather wistfully, we realize now that all the passionate arguments about Hindemith, Bartók, Schönberg, Stravinsky et al. are now passé. The question that really haunts music today is whether the "electronic postmodern period" is just that, or whether it marks the end of the entire epoch of what we know as serious music.

Walter Sear, a composer who has written striking electronic music, as well as old-fashioned hand-model symphonies, regards the synthesizer merely as a fascinating new instrument—much as the new pianoforte, after the old harpsichord, fascinated Mozart and Beethoven. On the other hand, prophets are not lacking who cannot accept electronic music as part of the orderly flow of the mainstream of music, as we see Brahms as the successor to Beethoven, and Richard Strauss as the inheritor of Wagner. These prophets are convinced that the end has come.

I believe that it is too early to announce that the entire epoch has been brought to a close. Electronic writing may veer off through the mixed-media phenomenon and become the basis of a new art form altogether. Already, in the postmodern period, creative art is bristling with an undisciplined intermingling of disciplines.

It is the beginning of a beginning. We shall have to give up most of our cherished notions about what is off limits in music, open our ears, and learn to live, however unwillingly, with the new music. But after all, music lovers have been complaining about *ars nova* since the fourteenth century.

Electronic Synthesizers: A Survey*

Stephen Syverud

Most electronic music is created with synthesizers. Although not true "instruments" in the usual sense, synthesizers can be separated into three categories, which, as the author of the following essay explains, are studio models, portable models, and kits. Some basic information concerning synthesizers, their development, and their use are explained by Stephen Syverud, who teaches music at Northwestern University where he also conducts the contemporary music ensemble.

In the past decade, various types of commercial synthesizers have become available. Most of these synthesizers are voltage-controlled systems that include one or more of the following items: sources—oscillators and random-sound generators; modifiers—filters and amplifiers; and controllers—keyboard, ribbon, sequencers, and envelope generators. In many synthesizers these parts are connected to each other by patch cords, switches, volume controls, or matrix panels.

Because of its flexibility, the synthesizer should be seen only as a

---

*Reprinted from *The Instrumentalist*, 30, no. 8 (March 1976), pp. 85–87.

sound source, a way of modifying the controlling sound, not as "an instrument." Consider the piano for a moment—the quality of an attack and the decay of a tone are restricted to only a few possibilities; the timbre can be changed only slightly; and volume is limited. The piano is "an instrument," unique, identifiable, limited. Another problem is the persistent notion that the synthesizer is a keyboard instrument. The inclusion of an organ keyboard in the synthesizer "package" helps perpetuate this belief. But the keyboard of the synthesizer is not truly polyphonic and can only produce one or two pitches at a time. Still, the concept of keyboards is so ingrained in our minds that the presence of a keyboard controller limits the use of other controllers, and is often used only to control pitch.

Synthesizers can be divided into three categories: studio models, portable models, and kits. Although many manufacturers produce both studio and portable models, module and complete synthesizer kits are generally not produced by these companies.

STUDIO MODELS: HISTORY

In the 1940s and early 1950s, when electronic music was in its beginning stages, electronic studios were located primarily at radio stations. Early electronic music studios were simply collections of equipment designed for various uses other than the creation of electronic music. The equipment often included filters, oscillators, amplifiers, mixers, and tape recorders. In the late 1950s and early 1960s voltage-controlled devices were constructed solely for composing music. With these units, the pitch, timbre, and volume of a tone could be changed suddenly or gradually, depending on the characteristics of the applied voltage. In addition, a sequence of events could be remembered by a series of predetermined voltages.

The 1960s

During the early 1960s Robert Moog developed a line of commercially available modules, some of which were voltage-controlled. The modules could be grouped together in a cabinet and interconnected by patch cords to form a synthesizer. These early synthesizers were similar to the first electronic music studios of the late 1940s and early 1950s but they had keyboard controllers, voltage-controlled modules, and the various devices in a single cabinet.

About the same time Donald Buchla pioneered a modular synthesizer similar to the Moog systems. The "Buchla Box" (now called the Electric

Music Box) made use of sequential controllers, rather than keyboard controllers. The early Buchla keyboards were touch-sensitive devices that bore little resemblance to an organ keyboard; and sequential controllers enabled the synthesizer to be programmed for particular events that could occur automatically and be repeated.

The Present

Shortly after Moog and Buchla began producing their modules, other manufacturers entered the field. ARP and Electronic Music Studios, now considered major manufacturers of studio-model synthesizers, attempted to interconnect modules without using patch cords. Now both companies use matrix patterns to minimize the effort involved in altering a sound. The ARP model 2500 employs a system of matrix switching, and the Synthi 100 from Electronic Music Studios uses a large version of the pin-matrix panel (developed for the early portable Putney VCS) also used in the Synthi AKS.

All studio-model synthesizers currently on the market have several things in common.

1. They can be expanded through additional modules, making the possibilities for altering the sound virtually limitless.

2. Although there are several systems available from all companies producing studio-model synthesizers, most systems are custom designed for the user and, because of the modular design, can be updated and expanded.

3. Studio-model synthesizers are generally expensive (beginning around $5,000) and are not particularly compact in size.

4. Manufacturers seem to be turning away from the concept of the studio-model synthesizer in favor of smaller, less expensive, nonmodular units designed primarily for the individual involved in popular music. These portable-model synthesizers tend to be restrictive in terms of sound modification. Space-age electronics and miniaturization will enable new, smaller studio synthesizers to be manufactured with computerized controls, so that complete sections or compositions can be programmed and remembered.

PORTABLE MODELS

During the late 1960s manufacturers began producing nonmodular, small portable synthesizers. They were designed so that the sound could be easily modified—patch cords were kept to a minimum and switches were common. Because these systems are organized so that several or all of the devices are on a single circuit board, they cannot be altered. The standardization of some aspects of the system design and the simplification of interconnection between devices have made portable models useful for live-performance situations.

One of the first available portable models is the ARP 2600. Connections between various devices are made by slider volume controls that can be bypassed with patch cords. The only synthesizers similar in price to the ARP 2600 (around $3,000) are the Moog model 12 and the small Electric Music Box System 101. (Moog and Buchla both use modules from their larger studio models.) Other portable models include the Synthi AKS (second generation of the Putney VCS), the ARP systems (Odyssey, Soloist, and Axxe), the Moog systems (Sonic Six, Minimoog, and Micromoog), the Buchla Music Easel, and several ElectroComp units (models 101, 200, and 500). Prices range from $800 to $2,500, and many of the systems include sequential or random voltages and keyboards that will produce two or more simultaneous voltages.

KITS

PAIA and Aries have complete synthesizer kits, as well as individual module kits, while Eμ Systems and Total Technology only have the individual module kits. Useful circuits can be found in *Electronotes, Popular Electronics,* and *Radio Electronics.* In recent years integrated circuits have been packaged, and many times only hardware and a power supply are needed to construct extremely stable devices. One integrated-circuit chip (8038) is a voltage-controlled oscillator that produces sine, pulse, and triangular wave forms for about $3.00. Another chip (4046) contains six voltage-controlled amplifiers and sells for about $1.00.

Critique

Arthur Berger's Trio for Violin, Guitar, and Piano (1972)*

Elaine Barkin

The following notes about Arthur Berger's Trio for Violin, Guitar, and Piano represent an attempt to put into words the sensual, musical, and aesthetic realities of the composition. Reflecting the freedom and independence characteristic of new musical approaches, the essay is both a critique as well as a type of accompaniment to the music.

Arthur Berger was until recently professor of music at Brandeis University and a composer of chamber, piano, and orchestral music. Elaine Barkin is professor of composition and theory at the University of California, Los Angeles, and an editor of Perspectives of New Music.

A lingering short-circuited gapped stream coursing an indeterminate landscape, gurgling, momentarily surging, swelling, ceasing, slipping back, picking up, twitching, flexing, spreading out, limberly and lithely stretching across and over, dipping into and pulling out of, elegantly poised above, as if never to alight, as if always to rebound, yields an advancing sensation of imminences that, once hinted at, dematerialize, only to be re-

*This essay, coupled with detailed analytic commentary, first appeared in *Perspectives of New Music,* 17, no. 1 (Fall–Winter 1978), pp. 23–37.

claimed as new familiar presences, retwittering as it infolds implodingly and abruptly discontinues.

As the Trio begins, it seems unable to distinguish among successive similar-sounding shapes or between sounds of violin and those of guitar—despite their registral incongruities—as they intertwine in shapes resembling those of solo piano, whose high first ring is the start of a continually reinterpreted "piano sound": a mix of crisply and softly articulated flourishes, muted plucked plunks (far too low for violin? far too muffled for guitar?); percussive attacks ("prepared" notes which occasion, even as they distort, metallic, not quite guitarlike twangs); loud, fast, heavily pedaled sweeps; subdued chordal presences; soft, slow, heavily pedaled resonating expanses; dappled leaps; (and more).

As the Trio replays, its samethingness remains implacable; yet it becomes aware of bunched parts protruding from the twittering ramble; and replaying itself over again, it retracts the bunches into and merges them with the leisurely, but never still, streamscape. Samethingness itself is at first continual disjointment, but disjointment manifoldly presented: jagged contours of short tunes and long sweeps; pauses between successive sweeps and longer stretches; patches of mixed durations within single sweeps and patches of similar durations between successions of durationally mixed sweeps; timbral blends and minglings; and those single-tone reutterances where activity immobilizes as sound actively continues to emit. Eventually, as the Trio assiduously plays itself over and over again, fluidity and connectedness imbue it, soft-edge its disjointments, and delicately curve its lines with a cantabile lilt.

As the Trio begins, so is it then as though to begin again; but then no longer is it beginning, rather somewhere en route (where to? shifting in and out of [how to?] focus). A sense of going somewhere, of being expressly led along some path to some place, seems not to be the point. Still, once some there is arrived at, it is instantly recognizable, but as having emanated out of some former there. For no there is ever prepared for as previously it has been prepared, neither is it succeeded as previously it has been succeeded, nor is it ever in the same shape or of the same duration or of the same color; yet a sense of sameness lingers: as if parts of before have been dipped into, scooped out, reclaimed, reimaged: reaffirmed.

For the Trio, timbres are sounds of textures as textures are sounds of timbres, as distinctive wisps of texture retain vividness, resonating whenever and wherever they occur, singly or together, however interlocked, each sound chosen to project a particular texture, each texture designed to environ each sound. Rarely does it find itself inappropriately encumbered with a color, a time, a space (in time, in register), an onset (plucked, struck, muted, clanged, sustained). Eventually, even timbrally indistinguishable sounds feel at home.

Out of each pitch-to-pitch twitter and shape-to-shape stretch arises an unevenly rearticulating, semitonally textured harmony, radiating and rotating, never within a limited registral field, always defining and enveloping a broad field; unfolding slowly (ex. 1); bubbling rapidly (ex. 2); singly timbred (ex. 3); doubly timbred (ex. 4); triply timbred (ex. 5); heard not as going; heard as there.

That pitch sound emerges felicitously seems to connect with the fully chromatic, semitonally stretched incessancy—as if the embodiment of a world inhabited by continual chromatic presences is something that the Trio is about. Yet another world inhabited within the Trio is one of implosion: a world of expansion by contraction, development by self-arrest, of things checking themselves in midstream, reining in, repressing, withholding, remembering and restating their history, their origin. For to go

Ex. 1. Arthur Berger: Trio (mm. 112–114) "... unfolding slowly ... Copyright © 1974 by Boelke-Bomart, Inc., Hillsdale, New York. Used by permission.

Ex. 2. Arthur Berger: Trio (mm. 58–59) "... bubbling rapidly ..." Copyright ©
1974 by Boelke-Bomart, Inc., Hillsdale, New York. Used by permission.

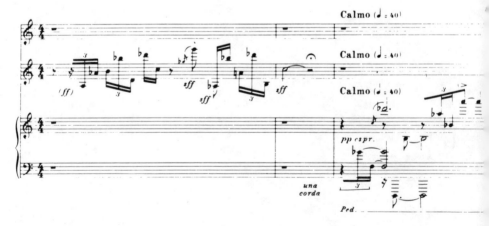

Ex. 3. Arthur Berger: Trio (mm. 165–167) "... singly timbred ..." Copyright ©
1974 by Boelke-Bomart, Inc., Hillsdale, New York. Used by permission.

Ex. 4. Arthur Berger: Trio (mm. 89–93) ". . . doubly timbred . . ." Copyright © 1974 by Boelke-Bomart, Inc., Hillsdale, New York. Used by permission.

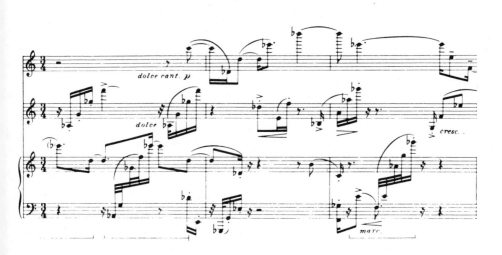

Ex. 5. Arthur Berger: Trio (mm. 21–23) ". . . triply timbred . . ." Copyright © 1974 by Boelke-Bomart, Inc., Hillsdale, New York. Used by permission.

forward is to further accumulate a reserve of such experiences and thus to have more of the past to ruminate on and to recollect.

The Trio's piecehood emerges, simply, from the plausibility of every direction taken, of every corner turned, as every (re)shaped twist and (re)twisted shape refers to within itself, neither growing nor going but turning inward, regenerating its own unmistakable flavor and feel as it both pursues and submerges—catching up with and dipping into—without ever really preparing us (but without never preparing us) for what is next to come. Nor for what does not come next. The Trio ends, plausibly and unpreparedly, like all that has preceded; (it stops: we wait).

A lingering short-circuited gapped stream,
coursing an indeterminate landscape,   gurgling,   momentarily surging,
swelling,   ceasing,   slipping   back,   picking up,   twitching,   flexing,
spreading out,   limberly and lithely stretching across and over,
dipping into and pulling out of,   elegantly poised above,
*   (as if never to alight,   as if always to rebound)*
advancing sensations of imminences that, once hinted at, dematerialize,
*   (only to be reclaimed as new familiar presences)*
retwittering,   infolding,   abruptly discontinuing.

The Music of Elliott Carter*

William Brandt

Of the many important contemporary composers, only a handful are discussed in detail in this book. It is not the purpose of this volume to cover the entire field of modern musical composition and composers but, instead, to give the reader an idea of the scope, vitality, and direction of contemporary music.

In the following article William Brandt discusses the work of Elliott Carter. Although such well-known American composers as Aaron Copland, Roger Sessions, Virgil Thomson, and Charles Ives have each been composing music for over half a century, Carter's first important piece appeared in 1945. Since that time his works have been characterized as having a "strong sense of the continuation of music tradition," thus putting him in a completely different category from such antitraditionalists as Edgard Varèse or John Cage.

As Brandt points out, "Carter's career and education have made him aware of both the problems and the mission of music in the twentieth century." William Brandt is a composer and author of The Way of Music *(1968). He teaches at Washington State University in Pullman, where he is, in his own words, "happily engaged in teaching and writing."*

*Reprinted from *Music Educators Journal*, 60, no. 9 (May 1974), pp. 25–32, by permission. Copyright © 1974 by Music Educators National Conference.

Elliott Carter's music has grown steadily in importance and influence since the Sonata for Piano appeared in 1945. He is now recognized as a major composer not only by responsible American critics but also by those outside our borders. There are sound reasons for this recognition: not only does his music communicate to the listener a sense of freedom and vitality and passion but also, in achieving this, he has offered solutions to some problems of technique and style posed by the developments of twentieth-century music.

During the years before World War II, it seems, in retrospect, composers were trying either to deny or to continue the music tradition of the nineteenth century. Neoclassicism was the predominant style, and its followers sought to revitalize the forms and techniques of pre-Romantic music, while expressionism, followed by twelve-tone serialism, grew out of late nineteenth-century harmonic usages and expressive aims toward a completely abstract language of music. Neoclassicism offered no long-range answers to the problems of grammar and syntax in post-tonal music; it merely marked time, but it did produce what seem now to be some genuine masterworks. In the compositions of Anton Webern and later in the totally serialized works of his followers in the 1950s, a consistent language of music was created, one in which the form, the contents, and the syntax created a unity of the strictest kind. Perhaps this strictness and complete control worked to the disadvantage of the composers, however, for the concept became mechanistic, and the twelve-tone theorists devoted their energies to finding ways to escape the rigidity of the system. The challenge did produce some exciting music, but strict serial technique seems now to have reached an impasse—although some composers will continue working in it for some time.

Experimental and aleatoric music, although frequently stimulating, offer no solutions. These approaches produce works that are beyond criticism because each one is unique and cannot be repeated and thus belongs to no body of composition for which criteria may be set up. What has been needed is a music language that springs from the culture of the second half of the twentieth century—one that consists of a grammar and a syntax that can be employed with integrity, clarity, and consistency.

Elliott Carter's answer to this predicament seems to be one of the most significant, although it is too soon to tell if it will remain his exclusive property or if it can be used by others without their becoming mere imitators. Carter's work has a strong sense of the continuation of music tradition, and the listener who penetrates its complexity finds that Carter's solutions are extensions of the past, not merely reevaluations of that past.

If art expresses the culture of its time, what are the characteristics of the middle of the twentieth century that can be expressed in music? Simultaneity and complexity; confrontation, struggle, and partial resolution; the interrelation of successive events, perhaps with no unifying factor perceptible in them; the sense of time passing, now slowly, now more rapidly until the time is used up; passion and intellect; and finally, a sense of humanity, of common plight and common victory or defeat.

Certainly, complexity is immediately apparent, for Carter's music moves forward without reference to key, and only attentive listening reveals that short melodic patterns, often created out of simple intervals, provide the fabric. The music is nonrepetitive in its larger structures, always moving onward toward a dimly perceived goal through variations of the smaller units. This procedure might not seem complicated were it not for the fact that in a typical work several unlike strata are sounded simultaneously and the "harmony" produced by this process is not really harmony in the accepted sense of vertical simultaneities, but is rather the less important byproduct of the tones of the strata coinciding in time. In addition, each of the strata has a sharply differentiated rhythmic flow that emphasizes its individuality, separating it from the others rather than allowing it to blend. It is much the same feeling one gets from listening to some of the music of Charles Ives, but with that music most listeners allow the effect of hearing familiar tunes in different keys and wholly novel juxtapositions to deflect their attention from the aesthetic basis for the composition. Ives realized both the complexity and the simultaneity of human experience; he also saw that in many ways the two are not independent of each other, but fused. The effect would not be at all the same if the tunes were strung end to end, and certainly the meaning would be less true, for human life consists of simultaneous experiences, often very small, together with a person's reactions to them.

Carter has taken the same point of view and refined it, but instead of using quotations as Ives does, he gives each strata a thoroughly considered and original character, a facet of experience, if you will, that, with its fellows, contributes to the whole at every moment. One might suggest that this is simply counterpoint in which several melodic entities are combined, but this is not exactly true. The word *combined* implies a fusion of the parts, which does not seem to be either true or important in Carter's music. In traditional counterpoint the parts agree amicably and complement each other, even when such disparate points of view are being expressed as in the *Rigoletto* quartet, but in Carter's music, the parts are intended to confront and challenge each other. This is not really counterpoint, although that convenient word is often applied for lack of a better one. And yet, not all the strata are equally important:

> ... the feeling of experience is always the synthesis of our awareness of half-a-dozen simultaneous different feelings and perceptions all interreacting together, with now one and now another coming into the main focus while the others continue, more or less in the background, to influence it and give it the intellectual and affective meaning it has.[1]

To emphasize the individuality of the strata, Carter treats the instruments in his ensembles as characters in a drama, each according to its timbre, idiom, and technical capabilities. To each is also assigned typical melodic gestures, specific intervals, and rhythms and rates of speed in terms not only of metronome tempos but also of note values. Let us use two works of rather different levels of complexity to illustrate this—the Sonata for Cello and Piano (1948) and the String Quartet no. 2 (1959). In the sonata the cello, cast as an emotional, rhapsodic voice, is assigned a flowing, rhythmic part full of triplets (in 4/4 meter), small anticipatory syncopations, and various kinds of tied notes over integral beats of the measure, often to or from triplets, to characterize its affective nature. The cello part contains many thirds and sixths, somewhat fewer fourths and fifths, and some connective tissue of seconds that become more important when inverted to sevenths. The piano in the first movement is rhythmically metronomic, although this effect is alleviated by shifts of the beat from time to time to equidistant syncopated notes. Its melodic character is more rigid, less singing than that of the cello, written more idiomatically for the keyboard. The cello maintains its character throughout the work, but the piano loses some of its rigidity, especially in the second movement in which frequent syncopations in the rapid tempo create a nimble, rather elusive effect and in the third and fourth movements where groups of rapid notes lend more fluidity to the part. Its intervallic character is much like that of the cello, but seconds seem to predominate over thirds. In addition, the wider range and chordal capabilities of the piano are used to contrast it with the cello. The sonata is the first work by Carter in which these tech-

---

[1] Allen Edwards, *Flawed Words and Stubborn Sounds* (New York: W. W. Norton, 1971), p. 100. Copyright © 1971 by W. W. Norton & Company, Inc.; used by permission.

niques are clear; in the second quartet, they have become intensified and developed.

In the quartet, the first violin is cast as a witty and fantastic Paganini, exhibiting "the greatest variety of character, sometimes playing with insistent rigidity (where indicated) but more often in a bravura style."[2] The second violin is more moderate in character, maintaining a regular rhythm and mediating among the other three. The role of the viola is suited to its darker, richer tone, expressive and somewhat melancholy, especially in the cadenza that connects the first and second movements. The cello is again romantic and rhapsodic. In regard to the intervals assigned to each instrument, the first violin part is replete with thirds and fifths; the second violin part, with thirds, sevenths, and tritones; the viola part, with many tritones and sevenths; and the cello part, with fourths, sixths, and some sevenths. The work is rhythmically complex as a result of the interaction of the strata and their characteristic flow. Indeed, rhythmic complexity is a hallmark of Carter's music, but the net result is vital and directed movement that perhaps substitutes for the traditional chord progression in advancing toward rhythmic cadences of less density and complexity.

Carter has used the same approach in his later works, not in the sense of repeating himself but rather as a principle that allows different solutions according to the medium and the materials, and, as in drama, the varying situations created by the interaction of the characters. For these compositions are *dramme in musica,* akin to the Wagnerian music dramas in that they employ a kind of leitmotif—the intervallic and rhythmic individuation—that, combined with the sonorous identity and manner of each instrument, characterizes and reveals its particular personality as it plays its part in the drama. But Carter provides his music dramas with no exterior program: the action is innate to the music and obeys its own dramatic laws as directed by the material and affective content. In the Double Concerto for Harpsichord, Piano, and Two Chamber Orchestras (1961), the dramatic experience is projected not only by the interaction of the strongly differing timbres of the solo instruments and their idioms but also by the sonorities of each of the chamber orchestras, which are designed to reflect and complement the solo timbres. Thus the piano is associated with oboe, clarinet, bassoon, horn, violin, cello, and various kinds of drums; the harpsichord, on the other hand, is the leader of a group composed of flute, horn,

---

[2] Elliott Carter, *String Quartet No. 2* (New York: Associated Music Publishers, Inc., 1961), p. ii.

trumpet, trombone, viola, double bass, and metallic and wooden percussion instruments. The separation in timbres is further emphasized by the seating arrangement, and each ensemble has its own repertoire of harmonic and melodic intervals, rhythms, and tempos. A similar tripartite design is used in the Concerto for Piano (1964–1965), in which the piano and a concertino group of flute, English horn, bass clarinet, violin, viola, cello, and double bass act, as the composer states, in the manner of Job's friends who "sympathize, comment and offer irrelevant suggestions as to how the music ought to go on."[3] The Concerto for Orchestra (1969–1970) is organized around the four string groups and wind-percussion associates that resemble them in color and range; each has, as in Carter's other works, its own material and expressive character. His String Quartet no. 3 (1971, premièred 1973) is made up of a pair of duos, the first violin and cello versus the second violin and viola. The term *versus* is used advisedly, because the first pair plays in the familiar rhapsodic manner (the "written-in rubato") throughout the work, while the second pair moves in strict time; this structure allows a contrast in flow between the groups, much as in the Sonata for Cello and Piano.

In these works the various subensembles interact in a manner similar to that of characters in a drama, or in a way that suggests the contesting struggle implied by one meaning of the word *concerto*. This interaction creates the form and content of the music, and its inner and outer structure and the affective profile are the direct result. As music moves only through the dimension of time, the way in which it flows has an important bearing on the form, the contour of which is revealed to the listener moment by moment and event by event. In developing his concepts of musical flow, Carter began to question the traditional modes of presenting music in which "first you do this for a while and then you do that." He said,

> I wanted to mix up the "this" and the "that" and make them interact in other ways than by linear succession. Too, I questioned the inner shape of the "this" and the "that" . . . as well as their degree of linking and non-linking. Musical discourse, it became obvious to me, required as thorough a rethinking as harmony had been subjected to at the beginning of the century.[4]

This questioning led Carter to formulate means for controlling the simultaneities of strata, their interrelations in rhythms of action-rest, tension-re-

[3] Michael Steinberg, liner notes for Carter's Concerto for Piano (RCA LSC-3001).
[4] Edwards, *Flawed Words*, p. 91.

lease, and condensation and rarefaction of the sound mass as the music unfolds through time. As in drama, which is a directed and heightened representation of life, Carter's music scenarios are formed out of acts of confrontation and conflict, agreement and disagreement, not as isolated events but rather as the result of motion toward and away from them, all organically related to each other. This began to become important to him, he said, around 1944,

> when I suddenly realized that, at least in my own education, people had always been consciously concerned only with this or that peculiar local rhythmic combination or sound-texture or novel harmony and had forgotten that the really interesting thing about music is the time of it—the way it all goes along. Moreover, it struck me that, despite the newness and variety of the post-tonal musical vocabulary, most modern pieces generally "went along" in an all-too-uniform way on their higher architectonic levels. . . . In considering constant change-process-evolution as music's prime factor, I found myself in direct opposition to the static repetitiveness of much early twentieth-century music, the squared-off articulation of the neo-classics. . . .[5]

It is useless, therefore, to seek resemblances to "standard" forms in his music written after the Sonata for Piano (1945–1946), which includes a fugue. Hence, it would seem that a new music grammar has been established, one that reflects the simultaneity and complexity of the present time as well as aspects of its violence and hope, without implying a calculated process and therefore the possibility of a petrified technique, as seems unfortunately to have happened with dodecaphonic serialization. There certainly is the danger, however, that this mode of composition may be uniquely Carter's own and that other composers will create only a host of sterile and obvious imitations.

The concept of the *change-process-evolution* of music movement is apparent both in the larger aspects of Carter's music forms and in the details. For example, most of his compositions are divided into movements, but beginning with String Quartet no. 1 (1950–1951), Carter found means to obscure the seams or to link the sections together so that to the listener there is continuous music narrative rather than the go-and-stop of traditional movements, separated by disturbing pauses filled with audience noises and orchestral tuning. In the Concerto for Piano the first movement's final chord is rearranged to become the opening chord of the sec-

---

[5] *Ibid.,* pp. 90, 91.

	Meter	Tempo	Subdivision
1.	$\frac{3}{4}$	♪=70	Thirty-second note sextuplets—each thirty-second note has the speed of 6 × 70, or 420.
2.	$\frac{3}{8}$	♪=70	No change in speed.
3.	$\frac{6}{16}$	♪=70	Each sextuplet group becomes an integral, normal subdivision of the meter, hence one metric modulation has been completed.
4.	$\frac{9}{16}$	♪=70	Sextuplet subdivision retained in three groups of six thirty-second notes each—each ♪ = 6 × 70 = 420.
5.	$\frac{21}{32}$	♩=420	Three groups of thirty-second note septuplets; the measure is thus divided into three ♩.., hence the new note value of the integral beat is 420 ÷ 7 = 60 = ♩...
6.	$\frac{2}{8}$	♩.=♩= 60	The previous value of the integral beat is now equated to the new beat, ♩, and the modulation is complete.

ond. The movements of String Quartet no. 1 are linked by cadenzas, and the material of each movement is prepared in the preceding movement. The "pauses" occur not at the ends of the movements, but rather during the movements themselves.

Within the unique forms created by the interaction of the "character strata," the motion is also controlled to give an improvisational effect. This is accomplished by meter changes, groupings of five and seven notes equal to one or two beats of the measure, and by "metric modulation," a process by which the music may be accelerated or retarded smoothly according to the gradual shifting of the metronomic durational values of the notes. An example of this process occurs in the second movement of the Sonata for Cello and Piano, where the eighth note, equal to MM 70 at the beginning, is slowed to MM 60 during the course of eleven measures through two metric modulations. The following music example and the table above show the process (the circled numbers in the music example correspond to the subdivisions listed).

Although it would seem that metric modulation could be performed most easily by small chamber music groups, Carter has also applied it in works for larger ensembles, notably in his Concerto for Orchestra. In this composition the structural basis of two of the variations consists of the controlled increase and decrease in motion.

In works from the Sonata for Piano onward Carter has revealed an absorbing interest in rhythmic counterpoint; polyrhythmic combinations, syncopations, and anticipations abound in his writing. In the string quartets, for example, there are many measures in which no tones of the four

Excerpt from Sonata for Cello and Piano. Copyright © 1951, 1953 by Associated Music Publishers, Inc., New York. Used by permission.

instruments coincides exactly. This creates a density and a textural involvement of such intensity that concentrated listening is required. Such music is also difficult to perform because it requires of the players the same concentration plus the ability to employ varied playing techniques. Yet, formidable as these works look on the page, they *can* be performed—with rewards for both player and listener. Carter commented on these difficulties:

> Well, I worked up to one crucial experience, my First String Quartet, written around 1950, in which I decided for once to write a work very interesting to myself, and to say to hell with the public and with the performers too. I wanted to write a work that carried out completely the various ideas I had about that time about the form of music, about texture and harmony—about everything. This work became very much admired, which was quite unexpected because I really didn't think anybody would ever understand it at all, and also I didn't think it could even be played. Now obviously I didn't write it deliberately "so that it would be unplayable"; I wrote it always with the idea of practical performance in mind, but from my experience it was beyond any practical performance that I had ever aimed at before.[6]

This was the work that won the prize at the Liège festival; it has since been an important factor in the respect that Carter's music is accorded in Europe and the United States. Concerning the difficulties of this music, Arthur Cohn commented that "complications are not applied to the music; they are inherent in the climate of the aesthetic; none is twisted in for the sake of effect—one can propose that technical violence and textural involvement are *natural* parts of Carter's temperament."[7] The truth of this statement becomes clearer after repeated listenings to Carter's music. The music is organic, and any surprises that occur are the result of the natural processes of the music—they are not artificially introduced. In a letter to a pianist who had performed his piano sonata, Carter commented on the implications that his music was contrived:

> There are also many devices of close-knitting of ideas and of much more allusive and "metaphoric" relationships. There is an attempt to produce an increasing sense of crystallization of ideas and techniques—a clearer focusing of material as the work progresses and then its final disintegration at the end.

---

[6] *Ibid.,* p. 35.
[7] Arthur Cohn, "Elliott Carter's Piano Concerto," *The American Record Guide,* 34, no. 10 (June 1968), p. 945.

No part of my music is ever "freely composed" but at the same time no part of my music is ever completely dictated by a rigid, mechanical preestablished routine or technique followed without regard for its musical effect. It is never controlled in the way that many twelve-tone compositions are, nor does it accept classical forms like the fugue or sonata form without some specific musical reason, cogent to the material at hand, and ends up usually by transforming these forms into something quite different from their original uses, if it uses them at all.[8]

In spite of the fact that Carter's music is written in the post-tonal idiom, he has found ways to make chords functional and structural. In the polyphonic movement of the strata, certain moments occur that require presentation of new material, articulation, or summation. These are accomplished through the use of "framing chords" that present in chordal shape the intervals out of which the linear material will be formed, a process similar to the twelve-tone "verticalization of the row." The Concerto for Piano illustrates the use of this technique. The material used by the solo and concertino group is derived by dividing a twelve-tone chord into six three-note chords. The orchestral material is similarly obtained from a different twelve-tone chord. These "triads" are inverted in various ways during the course of the work, and out of each a characteristic interval is chosen for special emphasis. Each triad is assigned a particular tempo or tempos, and each has its own rhythmic pattern; as each ensemble deals with material derived from a triad, it adopts that triad's tempo and rhythmic characteristics. The harmonic identities of the various triads are clearly heard. The first movement of the concerto exhibits the resemblances between the materials of the solo and those of the orchestra, whereas the second demonstrates their differences. The full twelve-tone chords act as goals from time to time and hence as articulations of the form created through the confrontations of harmonic-melodic material and timbres. This process may sound fearsomely intellectual, but it is not more so than most compositional modes in today's music. It also has the advantage to the listener of allowing him to hear these factors in the music. They are not purely intellectual devices, like Webern's canons, which are aurally invisible. The form and its explication are inherent in the music itself. Carter said, "The form I seek is Coleridge's 'form as proceeding,' and I try to avoid 'shape as superinduced.' "[9]

---

[8] Elliott Carter, unpublished letter to Jerry Bailey, May 6, 1958; used by permission of Mrs. Jerry Bailey.
[9] Edwards, *Flawed Words*, p. 101.

The composer's main intention, then, is to create music drama whose protagonists and antagonists create the structure of the piece through the rhythmic and simultaneous interactions of their various temperaments and characteristics. As the drama progresses, the individuals change in many ways, and the end is not always a solution of the problems posed, although Carter has said that "in my music it is always the still small voice that wins out."[10] Although there is no guarantee that the application of such concepts will yield genuine music, in Carter's case they seem to work. He has repeatedly won prizes based on the judgment of recognized critics, he is acclaimed by fellow composers, and he is one of the very few currently active American composers deemed worthy of notice in European music circles.

Carter's career and education have made him aware of both the problems and the mission of music in the twentieth century. Born in New York City in 1908, he started piano lessons as a matter of course at the reluctant age of most children, but he never became really involved until he entered high school and came into contact with people who were active supporters of modern music. Through their influence he attended many concerts during the early 1920s, when New York was full of new music. He met Charles Ives, among others, who frequently invited his young friend to join him in his box at Carnegie Hall. Carter probably heard few of Ives's compositions during those years except perhaps songs or similar pieces. On the other hand, he heard *Le Sacre du Printemps* and other new works that the Boston Symphony Orchestra played under Serge Koussevitzky at the Saturday afternoon concerts. Young Elliott's father also took him to Europe frequently, where he had opportunities to hear much new music and to purchase or examine scores by Schönberg, Berg, and Webern that were unavailable in New York. During this period, he also became acquainted with the music of the Chinese opera in New York and of the Arabs in Tunisia, where he spent a summer. The stimulation of these music experiences and his curiosity about them made him want to compose. Ives encouraged him and wrote a recommendation to Harvard on his behalf. Once at Harvard, which he chose so he could be near the adventurous Boston Symphony concerts, he discovered that the teachers disliked "that modern stuff," regarded Koussevitzky as a dangerous man, and excluded anything that smacked of contemporary music from the curriculum. Carter therefore decided to major in English literature and was graduated in 1931.

---

[10] Steinberg, liner notes.

During his years at Harvard he was able to supplement the courses in nine-teenth-century literature with readings in modern poetry, modern novels, and philosophy. He gives considerable credit to the lectures of Alfred North Whitehead and to the ideas of fellow students James Agee, Harry Levin, and Lincoln Kirstein for his understanding of modern concepts of art.

During the year following his graduation Gustav Holst was visiting professor of composition, and Carter studied with him and with Walter Piston, completing his M.A. in music in 1932. In that year he went to Paris to study with Nadia Boulanger, who provided the strict disciplines not found in most American music schools. Carter also benefited from her penetrating insight into contemporary music and from her inspiration. After completing his work in France, Carter returned to the United States and subsequently became music director of Lincoln Kirstein's Ballet Caravan. He wrote two ballets for this company—*Pocahontas* in 1938 and *The Minotaur* in 1946. The style of these was individual within the larger context of neoclassicism and showed able handling of rhythmic techniques and dramatic characterization. In the music he wrote during the 1930s, he sought to present an American profile, making him one of a number of composers who tried to capture the elusive American spirit. In 1940 Carter accepted a position at St. John's College in Annapolis, Maryland, where music was taught as part of the liberal arts curriculum, not as a "professional" course. He was also involved there with the history, language, and culture of the Greek and Roman eras and with acoustics and mathematics.

In 1942 he left St. John's College to spend more time composing. He lived in New Mexico for a year, during which he composed his Symphony no. 1. Despite the environment in which it was written, the symphony reflects rural New England, as he intended, with somewhat the same atmosphere as Copland's *Appalachian Spring*. In this symphony, which consists of three movements, Carter employed the technique of continuous development, which he has retained in his later style. It is a pleasant, quite uncomplicated work and it gives a clear picture of the composer's skill and imagination at that time.

During World War II Carter was Music Consultant for the Office of War Information and also taught for a time at the Peabody Conservatory. He later taught at both Columbia University and Queens College in New York, and at Yale. In 1946 he finished his Sonata for Piano and one of his most frequently performed works, the *Holiday* Overture for orchestra. It was in the piano sonata that Carter's later style first began clearly to emerge. The sonata was immediately hailed by critics as a significant work—individual and powerful, conceived in a bold idiomatic piano style, and holding out hope for the future of the piano sonata in the twentieth century. This composition was followed by the Sonata for Cello and Piano and the Woodwind Quintet (1948), the Eight Etudes and a Fantasy for woodwinds and the String Quartet no. 1 (1950–1951), and the Sonata for Flute, Oboe, Cello and Harpsichord (1952), commissioned by the Harpsichord Quartet of New York. In 1955–1956 he wrote the *Variations for Orchestra* on a commission from the Louisville Symphony Orchestra under their program for the stimulation of contemporary orchestral music. String Quartet no. 2 was finished in 1959; it won both the Pulitzer Prize and the New York Music Critics Circle Award in 1960 and the UNESCO First Prize in 1961. The latter year also saw the completion of the Double Concerto for Piano, Harpsichord, and Two Chamber Orchestras. In 1964–1965, he wrote Concerto for Piano, dedicated to Igor Stravinsky on his eighty-fifth birthday. The Concerto for Orchestra was written in 1969 and performed in January 1970 on the occasion of the 125th anniversary of the New York Philharmonic. String Quartet no. 3, composed for the Juilliard String Quartet in 1971, was first performed by them in 1973. This is a total of eleven important works in twenty-six years, omitting *The Minotaur* and *Pocahontas,* the two ballets that were written prior to Carter's mature period. It is not a bad average for a contemporary composer and is better than that of many, because these are all major compositions that represent Carter at his best.

Elliott Carter's reputation has risen steadily on both sides of the Atlantic among serious listeners as well as professional musicians—enough so that during 1973, the year of his sixty-fifth birthday, a festival was mounted in New York. During the 1973/74 season The New York Public Library has exhibited some of Carter's manuscripts, letters, and photographs, and the Double Concerto has been performed by two different orchestras; early in 1974 Pierre Boulez held a discussion, illustration, and performance session devoted to the Concerto for Orchestra. The recognition is well deserved. Carter is a unique figure in our part of the twentieth century: a composer who has gone his own way with integrity, clear vision, and imagination to create an individual language of music. This language is notable, in a technological and mechanistic culture, for its humanity and, in a time of stylistic multiplicity, for its development of a vital syntax that is neither restrictive nor hermetic.

Wiggly Lines and Wobbly Music*

Cornelius Cardew

Throughout this book there are numerous illustrations of graphic music, new scores that eschew the usual musical notation symbols in favor of various lines, squiggles, and dots. In this essay Cornelius Cardew discusses the new notation and gives some ideas about how such scores might be read and interpreted.

Without wishing to turn this essay into a personal statement, I have to say at the outset that I was engaged throughout the 1960s in writing—I should say drawing—and performing so-called graphic music. I also wrote essays that contributed to the speculation that grew up around the genre (on which academics and students are still feeding) and attempted to provide it with theoretical justification or at least interest. Then in 1971 the ripples of a new revolutionary political movement upset this fragile coracle (as far as I was concerned) and tipped me out into the maelstrom of the class struggle. A period of "settling accounts" with my avant-garde activities followed, and I detected (as have previous generations of artists who wanted

---

* Reprinted from *Studio International* (November–December 1976), pp. 249–255.

to serve the people) a clear antagonism between the bourgeois (artistic) avant-garde and the proletarian (political) vanguard, that is, the revolutionary party of the working class. In 1972 I was asked to speak at a conference on problems of notation in Rome, and spoke of my own composition *Treatise* as a particularly striking outbreak of what I diagnosed as a *disease* of notation, namely the tendency for musical notations to become aesthetic objects in their own right. Today, four years later, such problems have been largely displaced (as far as I am concerned) by more pressing ones, such as how to produce and distribute music that serves the needs of the growing revolutionary (political) movement.

I may as well confess that this essay springs from no "inner necessity." I was asked to write it, and accepted because of a certain "external necessity" with which I am sure most readers are familiar. My opinions on graphic music are no longer those of an active participant, in fact they are quite detached, in that I attempt to view it as a phenomenon (among other phenomena, all interrelated) of a particular historical juncture. I want to go beyond opinions and arrive at an objective assessment of the role played by graphic music as one strand among many in the postwar musical avant-garde. And because the artistic avant-garde is a component—and an ideologically active (should I say virulent?) component—of the superstructure of Western imperialist society (it's no accident that many of the composers I'll be talking about are American), and hence helps to protect that society against radical social change, the assessment is bound to be negative in the overall political sense. What it boils down to is that graphic music "proper" (we'll go into that in a moment) was a constellation of misconceptions and mystifications that contributed to confusing the basic issues facing musicians in bourgeois society, namely: the question of content in music, how music expresses and embodies ideas, and whose interests does it serve.

Casting about for a point of entry to the subject: What do people mean by the term *graphic music?* Can one draw a picture of a sound? Are there aural equivalents of visual effects? What led people to think of "drawing" music instead of writing it? What is the importance of the graphic aspect of ordinary musical notation? What does it mean when visual artists and critics talk about drawings and paintings in musical terms (loud colors, etc.)?

All our sense organs transmit information to the brain. The very fact that the brain can *distinguish* visual from aural from tactile from olfactory stimuli implies that it can also *relate* them to one another. Any new stimulus is also related to the stored experience of a lifetime of social practice. So there can be no purely aural, or purely visual, let alone purely musical (as Stravinsky would have us believe), or purely aesthetic experience. Even though there are areas of the brain that specifically deal with certain stimuli (visual, aural, etc.), these areas are not closed off from one another. They often interfere with one another. *Synaesthesia* is the name for a condition in which the brain jumbles up stimuli of different sorts. If a man watching a solar eclipse finds it so loud that he blocks his ears instead of closing his eyes, then his eyes may be damaged, and we would consider this a result of a malfunction of his brain. But some degree of synaesthesia is present in everyone, and can be developed from a less conscious to a more conscious level. It's this faculty that allows us to experience "rhythm" in paintings, "light and shade" in orchestral "color," the "smell" of decay in a photograph, or "personality" in an abstract painting. (Closely observed, each of these examples would present special features and problems, unique contributory factors, etc., but the general gist of what I'm saying is clear, I hope.) All these parallelisms, whether intuited (felt), inducted, deducted, or constructed, cannot amount to equivalence. In my view any correlation of the different varieties of, for example, "blue" notes with the various shades of the color blue would be arbitrary.

Many such parallelisms boil down to problems of social eytmology: what social conditions, cultural milieu, linguistic confluence gave rise to the expression "feeling blue," for instance? But there are some cases where the idea of the equivalence of qualitatively different phenomena forces itself upon us. One such case is the similarity between acoustic "beats" and visual "moiré."

Acoustic beats are produced when two notes of nearly the same frequency are sounded together. A string producing 440 cycles (vibrations) per second and another producing 441 cps cannot be distinguished by the ear as producing different notes. What the two strings *do* produce sounds like a single note waxing and waning in intensity in cycles of one second (441 minus 440 equals 1). Sound is transmitted through a medium (generally air), with the result that all sounds occurring simultaneously in the same location combine into a single wave form, a single complex shape of disturbance in the air (although this shape will be different in different parts of the room, depending on the proximity of different sound sources, for example). The ear analyzes this wave form back into its components, thus distinguishing the different instruments playing, etc. (Hence the practicability of reproducing music from the single groove of a record.) In our case the nodal points of the two sound waves coincide once every second, so that the resulting wave form repeats itself once a second (rather than 440 times per second as would be the case if both strings were tuned to 440 cps). If the difference between the two frequencies was 2 (440 and 442), the nodes would coincide twice every second. This is a physical phenomenon occurring in the air, independent of any listener.

With moiré effects the situation is different. A simple moiré effect (kinetic art enthusiasts be patient) can be achieved by drawing the same pattern of concentric circles on two transparent plastic sheets and superposing them. If the centers of the circles are made to coincide, the image appears still; if the centers are slightly displaced, the combined image appears to rotate. This is an optical effect, in the sense that it is not the image that moves, but the eye of the beholder that creates the effect of motion. The structure of the combined image obliges the eye to rotate.[1]

So these apparently similar aural/visual effects are not equivalent in fact, and if one were to make a graphic score composed of such moiré patterns, the process of converting them into accurately corresponding patterns of acoustic beats would have to be governed by a complex series of arbitrary rules and conventions.

But such a score can quite easily be converted into sound (or even music) "intuitively" or semi-intuitively. Such intuitive reading of the score is a fundamental aspect of graphic music. Rather than serving as notations, many graphic scores were intended rather as an "inspiration" to the musicians or as an aid to improvisation. In this sense graphic music (or musical graphics) represents a reaction *against* musical notation (although often preserving relics of musical notation) as opposed to graphic notation, which represents a *development* of musical notation.

At this point it is worth looking at the history of musical notation. That will give an idea of what is implied in the term *notation,* and then we can see to what extent graphic music either functions as or departs from musical notation.

---

[1] In acoustics, too, there are effects created in the ear; the ear has its own acoustic properties like everything else. If the ear is overstimulated, it will distort the sound just as a microphone will.

Other phenomena common to both hearing and seeing are the ability to hear and see things "inside your head," both as a result of just listening and looking (as it were at the back of your closed eyelids) and as a result of projecting them in your imagination (thinking through a familiar tune, for instance). Then there are those phenomena where the image you "see" in your head is provoked by a nonvisual stimulus, for example, the stars you see when a policeman's truncheon lands on your head. Again, sounds can be transmitted to the brain through the bone structure of your skull. This accounts for the fact that you can never hear your own voice as others hear it. You hear it simultaneously as vibrations in the air picked up by the ear and as vibrations transmitted through bone, whereas everyone else hears only the vibrations in the air.

Musical notation as schoolchildren learn it today has been in existence broadly unchanged since around 1600, but the fundamental inventions that brought it into existence go back much further. Guido d'Arezzo, a monk born in A.D. 990, is credited with the general introduction of the "staff," a bundle of equally spaced horizontal lines on which notes could be placed so as to indicate their relations to one another in pitch (high/low) and in time (left/right as in our script). It would be interesting to research the whys and wherefores of how the need for notation arose—the social/political/ideological matrix that gave rise to Guido's revolutionary contribution—but it lies outside the scope of this essay. Assuming that notation was designed to *preserve* musical forms by putting them on accurate written record, the actual effect of its introduction was to pave the way for a great *diversification* of musical forms. It was also the chute down which a new-type professional, the composer, the person who designs and manages the musical activity of executant musicians, was catapulted into the arena.

This type of notation—staff notation—shows the shape of the music as it is to be heard. It coexisted and frequently had to compete with systems of notation called *tablatures,* which depicted what the musician was supposed to *do,* rather than showing what was to be *heard.* Such tablatures were prevalent, particularly for keyboard instruments and lutes, from around 1450 to 1800. They consisted usually of a kind of picture of the fingerboard or keyboard of the instrument, with numbers or letters placed on it to show the position of the fingers. New ones are still being invented today: for example, a tablature is often used for teaching the recorder in schools. Their disadvantage is that if the instrument being "tabulated" becomes obsolete, so does the tablature. Guitarists who today unearth old lute music cannot try it out directly because the guitar is built, strung, and tuned differently from the lute. So they have to convert the particular tablature into the general staff notation.

The history of staff notation is a history of increasing differentiation, increasing precision. In the service of this increasing precision a wealth of data accumulated around the basic notational parameters of pitch and rhythm. Tempo indications, at first rough and ready (*andante, vivace,* etc.), were later supplemented by a notation of the precise number of beats per minute, made possible by Johann Nepomuk Mälzel's invention of the metronome in the early nineteenth century. Dynamics, or nuances of loud and soft, were indicated with more and more precision and supplemented by expression marks (*dolce, energico,* etc.). The more differentiated and precise the notation became, the stronger the hegemony of the composer over the art of music. Elements of improvisation and ornamentation, that is, independent contributions from the interpreter, were gradually eliminated.

The main use of this refined and flexible compositional instrument, musical notation, was of course to enable the composer to communicate to the executant musicians what they were to play. With the development of electronic music in the 1950s an area opened up in which notation could not play this main traditional role of providing performance material for the sounding composition. Electronic music was composed once and for all in the studio; thereafter it could be reproduced from tape. Therefore no score and parts for musicians were required; hence no notation was necessary as far as performance was concerned.

But many electronic composers still felt the need to score their works (either before or after composing them), and in the early 1950s many different types of notation on graph paper began to appear. The score of Karlheinz Stockhausen's *Studie II* (1954) serves mainly to elucidate, or at least present in readily surveyable form, the formal characteristics and layout of the piece.

John Cage scored his *Imaginary Landscape No. 5* on graph paper for purely practical reasons, and the notation functions in the traditional way as an intermediary between composer and performer. The instruments in this piece are mechanical reproducers (record players), and to play them is a matter of starting them and stopping them and adjusting the volume controls (it's like an orchestra of DJs). There is no need to notate the sound, for that results automatically if the indicated starts and stops are carried out.

When the technique of combining prerecorded electronic tapes with live performance began to develop, notation again became necessary for the parts of the live performers, and also for the electronic parts, as a point of reference for the players. In cases where the players were expected to synchronize or accurately accommodate their parts to the electronic part, certain modifications of traditional notation were almost unavoidable (were in fact avidly desired[2]), as electronic music of that time tended to be

---

[2] Many composers in the 1950s felt that traditional notation imposed restrictions. It imposed certain rhythmic relationships and certain pitch relationships, and composers exercised their initiative to try and break out of these restrictions (see remarks on proportional notation for time). Electronics was one way, graphics was another. We tried to *simplify,* for the sake of flexibility, and to *complicate,* for the sake of control and precision. It was possible to break out of the established rhythmic and pitch relationships by relaxing the tension between performer and score (graphic music), by saying to the performer: "This is not an obligatory exam paper that you have to fill in but a flexible guide to action." In electronic music the established relationships could be overthrown

measured decimally in seconds rather than in crotchets and quavers, bars and beats, etc. So, for instance, a proportional notation of time became a virtual necessity, with a regular time-span allotted to each line of the score.

In notating the electronic parts, some composers contented themselves with indicating points where the tape should start or stop (as in the Cage example described above), but others developed a shorthand to give the players a rough-and-ready impression of the types of sound they would hear and their relative pitch, loudness, and length. This sketching-in of a rough picture of the sound developed its own conventions, drawing where appropriate on the conventions of traditional notation. An example is Stockhausen's *Kontakte* (1960), where the sketched-in notation of the electronic part is a perfectly adequate guide to the performing musicians.

An approximate notation of this type, which represents music already composed in every detail, is very different from an approximate notation that is intended as a score for musicians to play from. Anestis Logothetis's *Odyssey* (1963) is a piece of graphic music that differs visually very little from the *Kontakte* example, except that it is tangled up into a kind of labyrinth with a superimposed red line running through it to indicate the "path" to be followed by the musicians.

Composers who adopt such approximate graphic indications of what their music is to sound like have lapsed ideologically into the fallacy that music can consist solely of a series of doodles, textures, outbursts, stops, and starts. Never mind how artfully arranged, this amounts to adopting the attitude that your score can be used by anyone, to express any ideas, in any context.

These rough-and-ready graphic composers abandon all musical discipline, and if they are to cover their nakedness at all, it is only by applying a certain amount of graphic discipline to their scores, which then become "aesthetic objects in their own right, regardless of whether or not they are used for making music," that is, they become fully fledged musical graphics.

Such activity is a safe refuge for the musically incompetent, and a fair number of young composers turn to it. About twenty-five percent of the scores I had to read in a recent contest were wholly or partially graphic, and about half of these were of this type, which may be described as the cheapest variety of graphic music. It is a far cry from the type of graphic music established by Earle Brown in his *December 1952.*

---

quite mechanically. Or could they? The "restrictions" referred to did not actually *spring* from notation but from the accumulated practice of centuries of music-making. The notation merely embodied them in a handy conventional form.

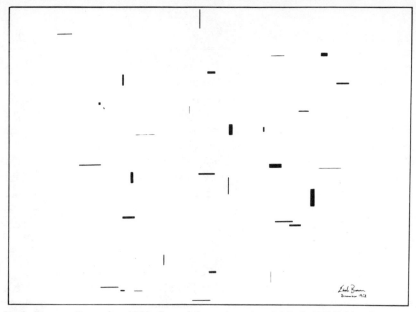

Earle Brown: *December 1952.* Copyright © Associated Music Publishing Inc.

December 1952 is sharp and clear. Brown was fascinated by the Constructivist movement in art, by Alexander Calder's mobiles and action painters such as Jackson Pollock. This score is a single rectangular sheet with black lines and rectangles floating on it. The white space predominates; the impression given is of precise little dashes (horizontal and vertical) of different weights on a white ground. The instrumentalists (any number and kind of instruments) all read from copies of the same sheet, but they may read it any way up. I think that originally interpreters were expected to measure the coordinates of any rectangle and locate a sound correspondingly in the overall ranges of their instruments. This measuring later became softened. Of a 1964 performance in Darmstadt, Erhard Karkoschka says that it was Brown's conducting rather than the score that stimulated the performers, for some of the effects produced were irreconcilable with the appearance of the score. So geometrical and precise in appearance, what the notation of *December 1952* amounts to is an exhortation to be geometrical and precise in your playing. It is a frequent characteristic of graphic music that it seeks to suggest an *attitude* or quality of playing to the performer. In Brown's case this exhortation is generally disregarded. When Brown himself conducts it, one has the impression that the score is merely the starting point of an improvisation that unfolds under Brown's control.

Assuming for the moment, however, that *December 1952* was intended to be a musical score rather than an inspiration to improvise, it raises one of the big problems of graphic music: its two-dimensionality. Whatever the limitations of staff notation, it is an instrument designed to describe and serve the needs of a musical continuum, with its host of interwoven dimensions. In *December 1952* you've got the opposite: the music has to be designed to imitate a two-dimensional black-and-white drawing or diagram. However conscientious your measuring, a score like this uses only a tiny fraction of a trained musician's ability and initiative (which may account for the fact that it is sometimes more rewarding playing this music with untrained people); and the rest is likely to come out in horseplay, improvisation, etc., of a friendly or antagonistic kind depending on the particular social and human relations. When composers and musicians are engaged in harmonious collaboration and share common preoccupations, all goes "well." But when the musicians feel they are being conned or exploited by the composer, you get the type of horseplay that led to the vandalization of electronic equipment by orchestral musicians in Cage's New York performance (1964) of *Atlas Eclipticalis.*

Cage wrote *Atlas* in 1961. It is a good example of that type of graphic music which comes under the proposition: Anything in the universe that has been or can be given a graphic representation is a possible notation for musical activity. Star maps provide the material for the notations of *Atlas.* Cage traced the constellations on tracing paper and then used chance methods to decide some aspects of how they are to be translated into sound. The orchestral parts retain the basic features of staff notation: the five-line staff is used where applicable, and progress from left to right regulates the disposition of the events in time.

A practice that contributed considerably to preparing the way for graphic music was the proportional (as opposed to symbolic) notation of time. The factors leading up to this innovation are outside the scope of this essay, but it can be appreciated how this innovation gave a "graphic" appearance to the musical scores in which it occurred and changed the way the musicians had to "read."

Take a page of an ordinary book: "graphically" it is what a typographer would call a *gray page.* "Literarily" it is the sense of the words in the context of the language and culture that produced it. In reading music, one normally reads the symbols for how long and short the individual notes or chords are supposed to be, but when time is notated proportionally (say 1 cm = 1 second, or some other arbitrary, or even arbitrarily changing unit), you are supposed to "scan" the page with your eye. You let your eye travel from left to right, and when it picks out an obstacle, you play the appropriate note. It is a slightly dehumanizing method, because it aims to replace thought (reading) with an automatic physical reflex (scanning). Normally the speed with which we experience events in the world depends on how much food for thought they provide, or how much attention we decide to devote to them. Of course we do the same when reading graphic music, but not without some feelings of guilt at our failure to reflect accurately in the sound the proportions laid out in the graphic score.

It's true that in normal notation the graphic aspect has a role to play (I've heard that people who select educational music take care to select pieces that are largely in crotchets and quavers, rather than semiquavers and demisemiquavers, in order to avoid the hysteria produced in young learners by a "black page"). But it is not a dominant role. In graphic music the graphic aspect of the notation has become dominant. It's appropriate here to spend some time on graphic notation, as opposed to graphic music. Graphic notation is a perfectly justifiable expansion of normal notation in cases where the composer has an imprecise conception. And I don't mean merely a failure of musical sensibility, because his conception may be quite precise as to its overall characteristics but imprecise as to the minutiae. For example, if a composer wants a string orchestra to sound like a shower of sparks, he can interrupt his five-line staves and scatter a host of dots in the relevant space, give a rough estimate of the proportion of plucked notes to harmonics, and let the players get on with it. This is *graphic* notation in the best sense of the word—vivid and clear. Such methods are used by many relatively established avant-gardists, from Gyorgy Ligeti to David Bedford to Krzysztof Penderecki, and have proved their viability.[3]

Graphic music proper, on the other hand, tends to be conceptual rather than pragmatic. One graphic score I looked at recently consisted of that classic series of split-second photographs that shows a bullet passing through a soap bubble. Such a score obliges the interpreter(s) to make strange decisions: what aspect of the score should one use to determine the type of sound to be used? Bubbling sounds and rim shots (naturalism?) is one possibility. Or you might decide that slow motion is the crucial aspect of the score.

---

[3] I can't hold it against such cultural workers that they battle on in the "struggle for production," even though it's our duty to inform them that every new technique and invention that they come up with will be used against them (against the people, I should say, because the inventors themselves may well come in for some greater or lesser material reward) until the obsolete, fettering social system under which we all labor has been thrown over.

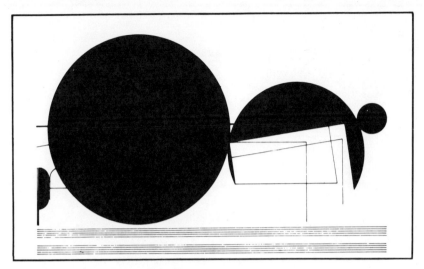

Cornelius Cardew: A page from *Treatise*.

To "compose" such a piece, no musical training or experience is necessary (which may account for the fact that conservatories often take an overresolute stand against it). This is a contradictory phenomenon and has its history. Cage's ideas had a considerable influence on the development of American avant-garde painting of the 1950s and 1960s, particularly Robert Rauschenberg and Jasper Johns. Other visual artists became so interested that they took up composing themselves. George Brecht was one, and he developed a neat kind of conceptual music that often employed musical events in a visual context and vice versa (like piling bricks inside a grand piano). Brecht popularized the expression *intermedia* to denote twilight zones between the various traditionally defined arts. My contribution to intermedia was the graphic score *Treatise* (1963–1967): it's a cross between a novel, a drawing, and a piece of music. In performance it was sometimes more of a happening than a piece of music.

Another visual artist who took up composing was the English painter Tom Phillips. He participated in the Scratch Orchestra; so when I was asked to get a book of Scratch Music together, I wrote to Tom for a contribution. He sent eight picture postcards as examples of his *Postcard Compositions Opus XI*. The idea was to assume that the postcard image depicts the performance of a piece of music. Then you have to deduce the rules of the piece and perform it yourself. There were a number of visual artists in the Scratch Orchestra, and between them they produced a host of compositions of this type, all of which come under the heading of graphic music.

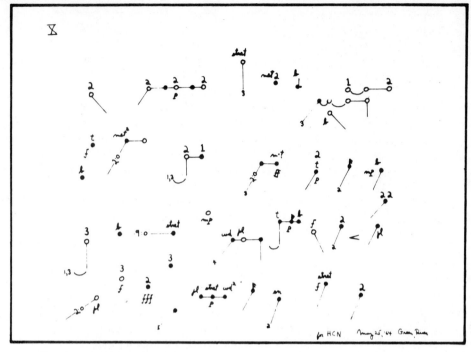

Christian Wolff: Last page from *For 1, 2, or 3 People* (1964).

In the last analysis graphic music *is* part of musical notation, in that it conveys a composer's conception to executant musicians, however loosely defined. But the examples given show how graphic music leaks out into various other areas that have nothing to do with music notation. The type of notation that we call *graphic music* (or *musical graphics*—I've come to the conclusion that these two terms are interchangeable) is characterized by an element of *juggling* with the *concept* of notation, and indeed with other concepts too, such as composing, performing, reading, playing, listening, etc. And in this it shares common ground with a lot of conceptual music, "intuitive" music, and verbal scores, all of which are going to have to fall outside the scope of this essay.

A word on the economics of graphic music. Because the service that composers perform for the bourgeoisie is primarily ideological, we tend to overlook the economic aspect, which although secondary is not negligible. For instance, certain music publishers played a role in consolidating graphic music as a definite genre. Peters Editions brought out works of Cage, Feldman, and Wolff in 1962 (a single part of Cage's *Atlas Eclipti-*

calis—and there are eighty-six in all—now costs over seven pounds). Associated Music Publishers printed Brown's graphic scores. In Europe Universal Editions has dominated the genre, although many smaller publishers have also gotten involved. One of these—Moeck Verlag of West Germany—brought out Erhard Karkoschka's book on *Notation in New Music* (which deals quite thoroughly with graphic music) in 1966. Universal published an English translation in 1972. Something Else Press published Cage's anthology, *Notations,* in 1969. Exhibitions of graphic music have been organized on a number of occasions as a means to publicize avant-garde music in general. Publishers' showrooms are often decorated with enlargements of graphic scores. I don't think a graphic score has yet appeared in a Coca-Cola ad, but at the Venice Biennale this year all the posters and programs for concerts were liberally sprinkled with graphic scores. Almost all of them date from the 1960s. Almost none of them was actually scheduled for performance in the festival.

While it's clear that publishers cannot *create* a genre, they can influence considerably the extent to which it becomes established. They determine whether or not a genre—and this applies particularly to graphic music, where the score, the printed object, has such preeminence—passes into musical history in the sense of becoming a subject for study in colleges and universities.

While researching this essay I was sobered to find that graphic music and related phenomena occur these days in university curricula. Our carefree fancies of the 1960s are now doing a "fine job" wasting the time and confusing the minds of the next generation of composers. Although this is no place for remorse, it does bring home the necessity of revolutionizing music education and throwing out the formalist garbage that has accumulated over the last seventy years or more. It may well take another seventy years to do it, so we should start in right away!

One hears the view that Cage exerted a "liberating" influence on the intellectually musclebound musical avant-garde of the Darmstadt period (the 1950s), which was dominated by the theories and products of Boulez and Stockhausen. Cage's work certainly led to an explosion of irrationalism in the 1960s. But neither of these directions gave any serious thought to the question of the role of new music in Western imperialist society. Certainly a number of people with relatively progressive ideas were swept into the avant-garde and dallied for a shorter or longer time with the manipulative techniques and pseudointellectual ideologies that were currently on show. But where could they go? Their subjective rebellion against the establishment left them in limbo. Today the establishment holds the field, and the avant-garde is in retreat. To be sure it's a slightly updated

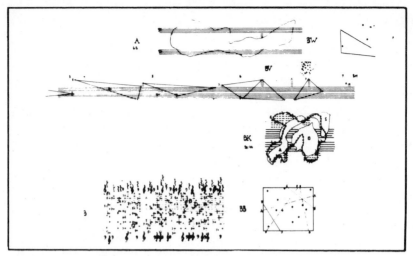

John Cage: A page from the solo piano part of Concert for Piano and Orchestra (for Elaine de Kooning) (1957–1958).

establishment, expanded to include many erstwhile rebels: people like Luigi Nono, Morton Feldman, Sylvano Bussotti, Gyorgy Ligeti, and Iannis Xenakis. However, the body of the new music establishment is composed of people who played a minor role, if any, in the avant-garde: Hans Werner Henze, Luciano Berio, and in England Maxwell Davies, and Harrison Birtwistle. All these and many others make a reputable living out of composing and are well stocked with commissions. Behind them stands the old establishment: Benjamin Britten, Malcolm Arnold, Roger Sessions, Aaron Copland, Goffredo Petrassi, Elisabeth Lutyens, and Alan Bush, many of them veterans of the antifascist movement of the 1930s. Clustering around their skirts are the more traditional minded of the younger genera-tions: Nicholas Maw, Richard Rodney Bennett, and others in this country (and a crowd of university composers). And seated over everything, the mythic heroes on their thrones: Schönberg, Stravinsky, Ives, Webern, Stockhausen, and Cage, who have given their lives (and souls) in the struggle to find, for the bourgeoisie, a way out of the stifling moribundity of bourgeois music.[4]

This is a rough sketch, but it suffices to show the tree and its branches

[4] What is the place of graphic music in this hierarchy? Graphic *notation* is an integral part of it, in the sense that new techniques and new procedures require new notations and these are bound to have a certain "graphic" character as long as they are new. *Graphic music* as a genre is already in its grave, however.

(I haven't touched on the roots this time) and to ask the crucial question: Where in this vast hierarchy is the struggle going on for a new music that genuinely serves the people? Is it where composers are using subject matter that is more "socially relevant"? I suppose Barry Guy's *Songs for Tomorrow* (commissioned for the 1976 Proms) would qualify as socially relevant, with its theme of the pathos of poverty. So would Cage's *HPSCHD* (1969), which, with its fifty-two tracks of electronic tapes and seven amplified harpsichords simultaneously playing music by Mozart and other composers, could be said to reflect the surface anarchy and turbulence of the current political situation. Or is it where composers are trying to write music to appeal to a mass audience? Bernstein is the only example that springs to mind.

Or does the *whole* tree serve the bourgeoisie, regardless of all the skirmishes going on along the branches and twigs? It's possible in fact that the struggle for a new music that serves the people is not actually fought in the field of music at all, but somewhere else (and I don't mean in heaven). It's possible that a new music that serves the people will be a completely new tree, springing from different ideological roots, developing leaves, branches, and a trunk over a long period, while the old tree rots away overburdened with its "cultural heritage," until the people one day come along and cut it down—or leave it standing as a skeletal reminder.

A last example, not strictly graphic music, but its lean and elegant notation justifies its inclusion, and provides a good example of a skirmish on the avant-garde branch of the old tree. Christian Wolff's *Wobbly Music* (1975) is scored for voices and a five-piece instrumental ensemble. Its four sections use texts from U.S. labor history in the period from 1908 through 1913: the first is a setting of the preamble to the Constitution of the Industrial Workers of the World (known as the Wobblies); the second a setting of "John Golden and the Lawrence Strike" (by Joe Hill); the third contains excerpts from Arturo Giovanitti's speech from the dock (an indictment of wage slavery); and the fourth is a setting of part of a speech by Bill Haywood beginning, "It was a wonderful strike." Wolff's settings are sparse and quite monotonous, so that the content of the text determines any dynamism in the work. In the first and last sections words and syllables are passed between different groups of singers creating a sense of sensitive interdependence, like walking with linked arms over stepping-stones, or passing something delicate from hand to hand. The Joe Hill movement takes the form of a bouncy but irregular monodic song. The Giovanitti speech is mostly declaimed against grumpy chords on electric guitar with altered tuning (a tablature notation is given). The whole is preceded by three labor movement songs of the period, presented quite directly in community-sing style.

It's hard to tell what effect all this will have in performance—and how it affects listeners is one of the main criteria for judging whether a piece of music is progressive or not—but certain things can be seen just from the score. First, that Wolff is thinking about *political* subject matter, and it must be considered positive that he has chosen to popularize (never mind to how small an audience) a passage of the working-class history of his own country. Second, that he has striven for complete intelligibility of the texts he has chosen, which wasn't the case in certain other of his recent compositions, for example, *Changing the System*. And third, he alludes, more or less discreetly, to sounds and characteristics of pop music. The question is does all this amount to a struggle against what is reactionary in the avant-garde, or does it merely constitute an "alternative," which implies—because of the relations that prevail among the composers of the avant-garde—that it is simply in *competition* with the rest of the avant-garde on the basis of its "novel" subject matter and certain idiosyncrasies of its style and presentation ("ordinary" singing at the outset, etc.)? Such questions will be discussed when the piece has its first performance in England on November 28 [1976], at the ICA.

One thing seems certain. When we're thinking of progressive/reactionary, new/old in modern music we have to struggle to separate the man from his music. If the new music that serves the people is a completely different tree, we need the *people* from the old tree to help it grow, but they have to leave their bourgeois *music* and outlook on the old tree. Only then can they start to make a new music out of the life and struggle of the people. And the more they participate in that life and struggle the more vivid will be their artistic contribution.

"And graphic music in this context?" I hear an editorial murmur. Graphic music will doubtless curl up and get comfortable in the dustbin of history.

LEFTOVERS

Graphic music is a type of musical notation. But it differs from traditional notation in one very important respect. Whereas a traditional score can be designed to look like anything from Magna Carta to computer printout (given the services of a cunning music typographer/designer), in other words it doesn't matter what it looks like except from a purely practical point of view (legibility), in graphic music the graphic form of the score is fixed by the composer; the way it looks is crucial, hence the term *musical graphics* as opposed to musical notation. But we must keep to the broadest definition of musical notation, as anything used or intended to be used as a directive in the activity of music-making.

One can say of a "free improvising" musician that he uses the world as a directive, however. And of Indian musicians or jazz musicians that they use established, orally transmitted norms or forms such as specific modes or the twelve-bar blues as directives in their music-making. But although these things direct such a musician in his playing, he does not have to *read* them. The *written* directive is the characteristic development that led to the separation out of the composer as a distinct type of musician; as one who works with his head and hence dominant (in bourgeois society) over those who work with their hands (the players).

The composer of graphic music sets himself against this separation, but only succeeds in heightening it. How? By composing graphically he tries to reappropriate a manual role; he no longer just writes, he develops graphic skills. He also tries to remove the reading aspect from playing a score (to a greater or lesser extent). But in liberating the player from the domination of the written score, he liberates (divorces) himself from the activity of music-making.

It's the same with his newly acquired manual (graphic) skill: there is no conventional framework for linking his new skill with the skill of the players. To take two extremes (and such things do actually happen in the arcane world of avant-garde music): enormous playing technique can be deployed in giving a musical rendering of a child's scribble; and conversely, someone who has never before played a violin can nevertheless use it to interpret a highly refined graphic score (assuming certain intellectual predispositions).

The role of idle fancies in the development of notation. A Renaissance monk designs a composition in the shape of the Virgin Mary, or a Valentine card manufacturer bends a melody into the shape of a heart. The one is a devotional meditation and the other a commercial gimmick; neither has anything to do with music. For a composer to lapse into such conceits amounts to an apology, a failure to grasp or recognize music's expressive capacity, how it conveys ideas. What decides whether a notational form or system survives is its viability, its usefulness in the currently developing musical praxis.

It is a quite mistaken view—similar to that which holds that computers make reasoning redundant, or equivalent bullshit—that a highly developed notation (however mechanical in its conception) eliminates the interpretative function of the performers. It's true that the complexity of notation reached intimidating proportions in the avant-garde music of the 1950s, but this did not essentially threaten the interpretative role of the performer. It *reduces* this; and a case can be made out for saying that such reduction in the area of interpretative flexibility makes the area remaining that much more crucial. The whole issue of reducing interpretative "freedom" hinges on whether you see the composer-performer relation as an antagonistic one, in which case each inch of interpretative freedom will be hotly contested. The composer won't rest until he has eliminated the performer completely (for example, through electronic music, or mechanical or self-activating instruments), and the performer won't rest until he has banished the composer (free improvisation). Performers can be found who hated electronic music (it devalued their skills), and others can be found who welcomed it (it relieved them of a burden). Composers can be found who despise improvisation (as a surrender to subjectivism), and others who welcome it (they can use it to put pep in their music). Much depends on what electronic music and what free improvisation are being talked about and who is talking about them. Nothing conclusive is going to emerge from anecdotes.

Since composed music has existed (that is, since there have been composers as a separate type of musician), composers and performers have *collaborated* in the production of music. Within this collaboration there have been all kinds of head-on collisions, ideological and stylistic disagreements, walkouts and sit-downs, but the collaboration is the primary thing. Just as the production of a jet plane is inconceivable without design and management skills, so a complex orchestral form communicating a definite ideology is inconceivable without composition skills. Naturally it doesn't have to be a single, individual composer, or one who is not also a performer, but the act of composition is a necessity.

To compose is to have an overall conception of what is to be communicated combined with the knowledge and experience—and on this base also the searching-out and inventing—of the musical means necessary to convey that. This embodies the fundamental tenet that it is new content that calls new forms into existence and that without new content all formal novelties reduce to trivia and decoration.

Because composers and interpreters primarily collaborate, the division of labor between them is not a hard-and-fast line. In the crisis of extreme formalism that occurred in the postwar avant-garde (the titles are indicative: *Structures, Kontra-Punkte,*etc.) a reaction was inevitable.

Catchwords like *open form* and *indeterminacy* that drifted over from the States in the mid-1950s were eagerly welcomed by young avant-gardists who felt stifled by the dominant determinism of the European scene. Under these catchwords the genre of graphic music flourished. It not only reinstated the interpreter as an active participant in a nonmechanical way in the musical process but also enabled improvising musicians (who often have not learned traditional notation) and amateurs to participate in the production of avant-garde music.

Avant-Garde Issues in Seventies Music*

Thomas DeLio

Basing his observations primarily on a series of concerts called "New Music, New York: A Festival of Composers and Their Music," held at the Kitchen Center for Video and Music in New York, Thomas DeLio discusses several stylistic gestures common to much new music. These include such phenomena as sonic gesture, source pattern, and phase shifting. He relates these concepts to contemporary developments in optical painting and Minimal sculpture.

Among the composers discussed in these notes are Robert Ashley, Charlemagne Palestine, Alvin Lucier, Philip Glass, and Steve Reich. In summarizing his thoughts, DeLio observes, "The music of the 1970s has borne the fruits of some of the richest ideas to emerge during the postwar period, ideas that have challenged many traditional concepts of structure and have revealed an affinity with some of today's most progressive ideas in philosophy, the sciences, and the visual arts."

The musical avant-garde in the 1970s constitutes a complex mosaic whose integrative logic would seem to support a multitude of propositions, each

* Reprinted from *Artforum*, 18, no. 1 (September 1979), pp. 61–67.

with its own unique dialectical thrust. Today, when a composer's sensibility can be dramatically influenced by such diverse musics as those of John Cage, Iannis Xenakis, North Indian improvisation, or African drumming, to trace the various and variable ties among the many fragments of this mosaic becomes a difficult task indeed. This resembles the situation around the turn of the century, when the world of music exploded into a pluralistic universe comprising a myriad of compositional premises. Then

> What the dominant composers [of the early decades of this century] shared in common was a lack of, an avoidance of communality. . . . It was a struggle to create a world of musics, not a struggle between one music and another, serial and non-serial, tonal and a-tonal.[1]

As in the rejection of the a priori conditioning of traditional languages, attention was focused on the absolute uniqueness of each individual creative act.

Later, in the fifteen or twenty years immediately following World War II, one significant concern shared by many musicians and visual artists was the gradual integration of the compositional process into the very form of the artwork. The most striking works of this period had in common their identification of the form of a composition with the processes involved in its construction. This quality appeared in compositions of such diverse origins as Pierre Boulez's *Structures* (1952) and Morton Feldman's *Last Pieces* (1959).

During this period two disparate structural premises in particular—chance and rigorous determinism—seemed to dominate much of Western musical thought and, understandably, have had a profound effect on much of the creative activity of the 1970s. Chance was integrated into the composition in at least two distinct ways, both still widely used. The first was through the involvement of variable performer decisions throughout the composition's unfolding; the second made use of techniques the purpose of which was to eliminate, as much as possible, all bias from the various decision-making processes involved in creating a piece. In either case "chance . . . provide[d] a means for escaping the biases ingrained in our personality by our culture and personal past history, that is, a means of attaining

---

[1] Milton Babbitt, "Edgard Varèse: A Few Observations of His Music," in *Perspectives on American Composers,* Benjamin Boretz and Edward Cone, eds. (New York: W. W. Norton, 1971), p. 45.

greater generality."[2] The second notion, that which involves the use of highly deterministic systems, has, in many respects, addressed these same issues. A rigorous system also tends to minimize the input of personal bias in decision making. In such cases structure is freed from its dependence on specific materials and on any specific compositional style and, as a result, it is opened up to a multitude of different materials and styles. Over time both of these concepts and a resultant pluralism have become crucial, if not necessarily exclusive, methodological bases operating in the world of music.

Significantly, then, these two radical concepts of structure, both of which were watersheds in the history of recent music, complement as much as they contradict one another. "Everything happens as if there were one-to-one oscillations between symmetry, order, rationality and asymmetry, disorder, irrationality in the reactions between epochs and civilizations."[3] In both cases emphasis is taken away from the particular qualities of the end product and shifted onto those processes through which that end product came into being. Hardly a progressive composer now working seems not to have been touched in some way by these two important ideas, which naturally tends to center attention not so much on the end product of the creative act as on the source of that act; more specifically, on the mechanisms of perception and construction guiding that act. Indeed, many composers today recognize this shift in emphasis as they attempt some personal integration of the two approaches.

What the new music typically reveals is not so much the nature of one particular creative act, or of one particular creative methodology, but, rather, the nature of those particular modes of perceiving, transforming, and understanding that constitute each individual creative style. "Reflection reveals that physical analysis is not a decomposition into real elements and that causality in its actual meaning is not a productive operation. The world is the ensemble of objective relations borne by consciousness."[4] In the best new music issues seem to revolve not so much around what one understands when hearing or seeing a particular composition as how one goes about developing an understanding of what is perceived and, ultimately, what it means to be involved in the very act of understanding.

---

[2] George Brecht, "Chance-Imagery," in *The Discontinuous Universe,* Sallie Sears and Georgianna W. Lord, eds. (New York: Basic Books, 1972), p. 93.
[3] Iannis Xenakis, *Formalized Music* (Bloomington, Ind.: Indiana University Press, 1971), p. 25.
[4] Maurice Merleau-Ponty, *The Structure of Behavior* (Boston: Beacon Press, 1963), p. 3.

A recent series of concerts held in New York afforded a unique opportunity to explore the new music at length. From June 8 through June 16 [1979] the Kitchen Center for Video and Music, located at 484 Broome Street, presented "New Music, New York: A Festival of Composers and Their Music." Over the course of nine concerts the works of over fifty composers from around the country were performed. The first evening sampled a fairly heterogeneous group, but each of the remaining evenings presented a generally homogeneous collection of works by artists sharing some common concern or medium. The festival coincided with an Institute on Contemporary Experimental Music, sponsored by the Music Critics Association, at which critics from around the country discussed a variety of issues raised by avant-garde music today. This also coincided with the National Conference of Directors of New Music Centers, which met to discuss and coordinate future activities. As it would be impossible to present a detailed study of all the composers involved in the series, I shall discuss instead a selection of the most original artists represented.

The first and, in general, most interesting concert in the Kitchen's series included the music of two composers whose names are invariably linked, Steve Reich and Philip Glass. While their music does share some superficial similarities they are, in many respects, addressing quite different issues. Both are concerned with gradual processes of change, although in Glass's case this concern is certainly not exclusive. In addition both integrate into their compositions that premise heralded by a number of predecessors that structure and process are one. As Reich himself notes, by music as gradual process "I do not mean the process of composition, but rather, pieces of music that are, literally, processes."[5]

It is, however, the concern with gradualism that is unique in Reich's music and this seems to have specific roots in problems of a perceptual nature. Again, in the composer's own words, "I want to be able to hear the process happening throughout the sounding music. To facilitate close detailed listening, a musical process should happen extremely gradually."[6] Clearly, gradualism is not the only technique available to a composer interested in the projection of compositional processes as formal schemes, as one might note in listening, for instance, to the music of Morton Feldman. As such, the emphasis on gradualism in Reich's music would seem to have more complex origins.

---

[5] Steve Reich, *Writings About Music* (Halifax and New York: Press of the Nova Scotia College of Art and Design, 1974), p. 9.
[6] *Ibid.*

Among the other issues involved is the crystallization of the significant differences distinguishing this music from that of Glass. Reich's music invariably articulates a process the sole purpose of which is to transform some very specific sonic gesture, some pattern, with clearly identifiable pitch, rhythmic, and timbral contours. Such a sonic "object," so to speak, appears typically to precede the unfolding of the compositional process and becomes, in fact, the subject of that process' explorations.

This is most readily heard in Reich's early tape pieces dating from the mid-1960s such as *It's Gonna Rain* or *Come Out,* in which the basic sound gesture of the piece might be considered analogous to a "found object." For *It's Gonna Rain* a tape was made of a minister preaching on the biblical story of the great flood. As the composer tells us:

> I was extremely impressed with the melodic quality of his speech which seemed to be on the verge of singing. Early in 1965 I began making tape loops of his voice which made the musical quality of his speech emerge even more strongly. This is not to say that the meaning of his words on the loop, "it's gonna rain," were forgotten or obliterated. The incessant repetition intensified their meaning and their melody at one and the same time.[7]

Clearly then, the sonic gesture—in this case, the spoken clause "it's gonna rain" as enunciated by this particular speaker—became from the start the single essential element from which the structure evolved.

Specifically, in the finished composition Reich put identical copies of the preacher's voice on two tape loops. These were lined up in such a way that they were first heard precisely in unison but then very gradually moved out of phase with respect to one another. This process, which defined the first section of the composition, completed itself as the two loops gradually moved back into unison with one another. Taken out of context, those passages in which the two tapes are quite far apart seem to have no recognizable relationship to the original spoken clause. It is, however, precisely the gradual nature of the process which preserves this crucial relationship. As such, the exclusive use of gradualism is quite significant. It is through this technique that the composer ensures that all the transforming activities of the piece are heard as rooted in, and growing from, the basic materials of the work. All change is, then, always understood as emerging from one common source. Were the composer to allow sudden or abrupt

---

[7] *Ibid.,* p. 49. These comments originally appeared in an interview with Emily Wasserman, *Artforum* (May 1972), pp. 44–48.

transformations, the crucial connections between those transformations and their source might be lost. As a result the identity of the original sonic gesture—here the clause "it's gonna rain"—is preserved throughout the structure's entire unfolding.

In this regard it might be useful to recall some of the composer's observations concerning another composition from this period—*Slow Motion Sound* (1967). The instructions for this piece read: "Very gradually slow down a recorded sound to many times its original length without changing its pitch or timbre at all."[8] Concerning the genesis of this piece the composer has noted: "Extreme slow motion seemed particularly interesting, since it allowed one to see minute details that were normally impossible to observe. The real moving image was *left intact* with its tempo slowed down."[9]

One of the hallmarks of Reich's style is that the distinction between the act of transforming and the pattern transformed is carefully and consistently preserved. Even as his structures become vastly more complex, as is the case with his most recent pieces, this basic notion remains central to the music's thrust. Object and action are maintained as distinct parameters of structure. As a result each work unfolds an intricate web of overlapped soundings of a single source pattern. One is reminded, say, of Robert Morris's well-known early pieces employing identical L-shaped beams differently oriented, in which the same manner of interaction between object and content is evident. While in Reich's music our perceptions of a single sonic gesture are altered by the shifting over time of relationships between that gesture and various reflections of itself, with Morris the same goal is achieved through the simultaneous presentation of three identical objects in very different spatial relationships to one another and to the room in which they are situated. In both instances the basic shape is understood to be its own frame of reference.[10]

The Steve Reich Ensemble opened the festival at the Kitchen with a performance of the first part of *Drumming* (1971). This section is scored for eight small, tuned drums to be played by four percussionists and consists of one basic twelve-note rhythmic pattern that, in fact, serves as the foundation for all four sections of the piece. The complete pattern is introduced

---

[8] *Ibid.*, p. 14.
[9] *Ibid.*, p. 15.
[10] Kenneth Baker, in "Some Exercises in Slow Perception," *Artforum* (November 1977), pp. 28–31, analyzes Reich's music as it relates to certain questions of intention also raised by recent visual artists.

The performance begins with two, three, or four drummers (usually two), playing in unison at Measure ①. When one drummer moves to the second measure and adds the second drum beat the other drummer(s) may either join him immediately or remain at bar ① for several repeats. This process of gradually substituting notes for rests within the pattern is continued with at least 6 or 8 repeats of each measure until all drummers have reached the fully constructed pattern at measure ⑧.

Steve Reich: Bars 1–8 from *Drumming* (1971).

by the two drummers, who first play in unison but then gradually move out of phase with one another. This process of phase shifting is soon extended as the other two drummers enter. Concurrently the performers introduce derived patterns that they hear resulting from the juxtaposition of the original with itself.

Clearly, the same concerns discussed above are found here. The structure evolves as one fixed pattern is juxtaposed against itself in a variety of ways. In addition, however, two other aspects of this piece add further support to the ideas outlined above. First there is the technique of generating derived patterns. Although these patterns may vary from performance to performance, they are always heard and understood as derived from one basic source, the structural predominance of which is thus further strengthened. Second there is a process of adding and subtracting notes, used quite briefly and only at special moments in the piece, which is first heard at the very beginning of the composition, where it is actually used to construct, gradually, the basic twelve-note pattern mentioned earlier. This procedure begins with two drummers articulating a single beat within a cycle of twelve pulses, eleven of which are, therefore, left silent. Gradually more and more notes are introduced until the complete pattern is heard and the main body of the piece begins. This procedure affords the listener the opportunity to observe the very making of the basic substance of the piece. It is an important gesture, which affirms to the listener the importance of that pattern as the central element of the structure and the subject to which all subsequent activity will be addressed.

The situation with respect to Philip Glass's music seems quite different. The subject of Reich's music is the presentation of multiple views of a single gesture within the context of gradual transformation. Thus, as we have seen, his works typically begin with a fixed pattern, which itself remains unchanged over the course of the entire work. In Glass's music, however, one finds no such fixed pattern but rather a series of constantly changing rhythmic configurations. The processes involved here are those of formation rather than transformation, and the ramifications of this distinction are enormous. Specifically, in this music one finds no real separation between content and process. Here change and the subject of that change are utterly inseparable.

A clear example is found in the early solo violin piece titled *Strung Out* (1967), the same year as Steve Reich's violin piece *Violin Phase*. Comparing the two pieces proves to be quite revealing. The structure of *Violin Phase* is typical of Reich's compositions: one basic pattern is played simultaneously by several violinists in a variety of different phase relationships to one another. In contrast, referring to the structure of *Strung Out,* Glass notes:

> Structurally the piece is, I think, self-revealing. At the outset a first inversion triad is outlined. The upper notes become a point of departure for a series of rhythmic devices. Notes are added one by one to the initial figure finally producing continuous ascending and descending scales. At times the melodic fig-

ures are broken into smaller discontinuous rhythmic fragments contrasting markedly with the more continuous scale passages.[11]

Clearly, the subject of this piece is not so much the exploration of any specific sonic gesture as it is the creation of a rippling surface of change constituting different types and speeds of mutating processes. As such, in this music the transformational techniques employed are not simply tools directed toward the exploration of some specific sound pattern. Instead they become the very substance of the composition. Here the patterns themselves are never static; rather, they create an unstable texture that at every moment of the structure's unfolding reflects the quality and speed of change involved. Indeed, this music is about change and how we perceive change. While listening, interest is focused upon the various qualities distinguishing the many sonic formations that rapidly replace one another throughout the piece. Once again, in the composer's own words:

> Now each figure is related to the next figure, at least in [the] early music, by the addition or subtraction of one musical unit. So that there would be a figure that had five notes in it. And then the next figure would have six, the next would have seven, the next would have eight. . . . Then later in my music I began working with cyclic structures. That is, I would take an additive structure and put that within a recurring larger cycle of notes . . . like a c cycle of eighteen [articulated as] $6+6+6+5+4+5+4+5+4+3+2+1+2+1$.[12]

These simple progressions, however, are used not only to shape the flow of the composition but also to determine different qualities of motion to be felt along the way. "What I found was that the feeling would change very much between the feeling of five, the feeling of six and the feeling of seven."[13]

One may think here of the so-called optical paintings of someone like Bridget Riley, where "our vision . . . is directed to highly mobile and unstable patterns of pictorial space and its fluctuating pulse."[14] There are even more striking analogies. "The movement Riley has been concerned with is twofold; firstly, to do with change in the form of variation in proportion,

[11] Philip Glass, notes from record jacket, *Strung Out* (CP2 Recordings), 1976.
[12] Philip Glass, interview with Walter Zimmerman, in *Desert Plants: Conversations with 23 American Musicians,* Walter Zimmerman, ed. (Vancouver, B.C.: Walter Zimmerman, 1976), p. 111.
[13] *Ibid.* p. 11.
[14] Anton Ehrenzweig, *The Hidden Order of Art* (London: Weidenfeld & Nicolson, 1967), pp. 84–85.

progressions conceived serially as time, and secondly, to do with psycho-physiological sensations (the visual vibrations resulting from a structured canvas conceived as a generator)."[15] Sean Scully's paintings of the last few years, in which a grille of evenly spaced stripes overlays a monochrome ground close in value to the stripes but different in hue, produce an effect closer still to Phil Glass. For the changing visual overtones that touch and optical effects allow depend on only the most subtle variations in an other-wise regular, but distinctly handmade, repetition. These works (by a painter who admires Glass's music) do not depend on shifts in an other-wise Minimal system to make themselves felt clearly as painting. Compare Glass: "It is that one would ... be able to perceive the music as a 'pres-ence,' freed from dramatic structure, a medium of pure sound."[16]

At the Kitchen, Glass premiered one movement of a work in progress. *Dance No. 4,* a solo organ piece, is part of a forthcoming evening-long work titled *Dance,* which is a joint project shared with the composer by the artist Sol LeWitt and the choreographer Lucinda Childs to be premiered in Holland this October. The movement performed is quite different from any of the works already discussed. Among the new and rather striking techniques introduced here is the extensive use of more or less traditional harmonic progressions borrowed from tonal music. The sonic plateaus created through these tonal shifts help define and support multiple levels of activity, which often shift back and forth quite rapidly, acting in various ways as foils to one another. Furthermore, certain changes are given added emphasis through the use of strong harmonic relationships. Writing of an earlier piece, *Music in Twelve Parts,* the composer once noted: "I was care-ful to make the harmonic relationship [between movements] a strong one ... to emphasize the change in harmonic plateau."[17] In the recent piece, however, one finds that certain harmonic relationships employed are much stronger than others. This, coupled with the varying quality and intensity of the rhythmic activity involved, helps to define the hierarchical relation-ships heard among the different plateaus. The effect is analogous to rapid crosscutting between different scenes in film, an idea reflected in music as early as Stravinsky's *Les Noces* (1923). As is often the case in film, the high contrast felt between certain changes adds to the dramatic importance of the scenes involved. Such highly contrasted and rapidly shifting multile-

---

[15] Maurice de Sausmarez, *Bridget Riley* (Greenwich, Conn.: New York Graphic Society, 1970), p. 90.
[16] Philip Glass, notes from record jacket, *Music in Twelve Parts* (Virgin Records Ltd.), 1974.
[17] Glass, interview (note 11), p. 114.

veled activity is new to Glass's music. Unfortunately, this performance seemed a bit uneven. In addition one could sense that this was only one movement of a larger work. For while the piece was complete it still suggested some larger context as its frame of reference. One awaits future opportunities to explore these new developments more fully.

One of the most striking results of Glass's music is that it tends to situate the perceiver rather than the composer in the center of the creative experience. This concept is of paramount importance to the work of another composer represented in the Kitchen's concert series, Robert Ashley, whose works are unique in their approach to this particular problem. Ashley has throughout much of his career been concerned with the understanding of structure as an expression of behavioral tendencies. This seems true even of such earlier works as the quartet, *in memoriam . . . Esteban Gomez,* or the symphony, *in memoriam . . . Crazy Horse,* both dating from the mid-1960s.[18]

In each of these open compositions structure emerges quite differently from one performance to the next. This variability is dependent on both the unique acoustical and mechanical peculiarities of the various instruments involved and the ability of each individual performer to manipulate his or her instrument. The qualities of each particular performer/instrument combination vitally affects the crystallization of each work's structure. In each of these pieces the performers and instruments are tied to one another through an interlocking series of stimulus-response patterns from which the work's very form emerges. Thus, the behavioral characteristics of each individual performer take on a greater importance in the compositional process than had hitherto been the case.

In his more recent speech and conversation pieces this concern is addressed quite directly. In works such as the 1970 composition *Fancy Free or It's There* the performer's activities and the listener's multileveled responses are both brought sharply and equally into the focus of our consciousness. The work is for one male speaker and four cassette-recorder operators. The instructions read, in summary, as follows:

> The cassette-machine players will record [the reader's] speech simultaneously on four tapes, and each of them is obligated to replay various units of the text in which "imperfections" have occurred. Thus if [the reader] stutters or falters

---

[18] Robert Ashley, "in memoriam . . . Esteban Gomez" and "in memoriam . . . Crazy Horse," *Source Magazine* (Davis, Calif., 1967), pp. 41–42.

(*Fancy Free*), or if [he] chooses a version of the text that does not conform to a version they are expecting to hear (*It's There*), one or more players will replay the imperfection while [the reader] is speaking.[19]

In each case the texts are spoken quite deliberately according to specific instructions for enunciation. The result is a fixation on two parallel planes of consciousness, one represented by the actual content of the rather poetic texts involved and the imagery that they evoke—neither of which reflects at all upon the activities of the cassette operators—and the other by the manner and acoustical characteristics of the spoken delivery—which are highlighted by the cassette playbacks. The latter is a level on which one is rarely conscious when listening to someone speak, least of all when such highly evocative texts as these are being heard. In such cases the mechanisms of communication are often overlooked as one concentrates instead on the content of the actual message communicated. In addition, in this particular case, the emphasis placed upon the mechanism involved is highly charged, as it is the human organism itself.

Commenting upon the genesis of such works, Ashley notes:

> During any conversation— . . . but it would be particularly more obvious if you could detach yourself from the immediacy of what's being said; for instance if [the other participant] were insane—there is always imagery in your mind that is only remotely connected to what is being said. But you allow the conversation to dominate that imagery. In that sense the conversation is like the consciousness agreements that characterize western music: the audience submits its consciousness and the composer dominates it for a while.[20]

He continues,

> . . . I began being interested in a personal sense of how . . . self-consciousness works and how it manifests itself from moment to moment. I feel that there must be some sort of similarity or simultaneity between the way the music proceeds and the way the self-consciousness (evolves) in the audience.[21]

Toward this end Ashley "began thinking of kinds of music that would be transparent [so as] to be self-conscious."[22]

---

[19] Robert Ashley, "Fancy Free or It's There," in *Desert Plants*, p. 132.
[20] Robert Ashley, interview with Walter Zimmerman, *Desert Plants,* p. 125.
[21] *Ibid.,* p. 124.
[22] *Ibid.*

To me Ashley's work has always suggested parallels with that of the sculptor Bruce Nauman, with whom he shares this concern for the creation of transparent structures that reveal to the perceiver some aspect of his own personal behavioral style. By raising the listener's activities to a new level of conscious interaction with those of the creator, Ashley forces upon us the recognition that what we perceive in an artwork is as much a reflection of ourselves as it is of that work's creator.

The piece heard last June at the Kitchen is in these respects quite interesting. It was an older piece titled *The Wolfman* (1964), and here performed by the composer. The work began quite gradually and imperceptibly. While the audience was still speaking and shuffling around, the tape began very softly, introducing a wash of sounds many of which seemed to blend quite well with ambient audience noises. As these sounds gradually became louder and louder, the audience began to quiet down. Finally, the tape, now accompanied from the side of the stage by a raucous live organ solo, reached a peak of unbelievable intensity. At this point Ashley entered, paced up and down the stage for a while, and then began to produce vocal sounds. These too began softly and gradually got louder and louder until he finally seemed to be screaming into the microphone. The vocal sounds were produced at regular intervals, separated by approximately ten-to-fifteen-second durations during which he seemed to be preparing himself for his next sound, even the loudest of which was invariably covered up by the other noises. The result was a rather grotesque dialogue that did seem, however, to share some of the same concerns as those works discussed above.

The excruciating noise from the tape and organ, of course, made the audience terribly uncomfortable. Many, in fact, either left or covered their ears. Meanwhile, Ashley rather deliberately and self-consciously acted out their projected responses. As is the case with many of his other pieces, those listening found themselves centered within the middle of the dialogue watching and listening as their responses were ritually exposed from the stage. In *The Wolfman* the composer plays with that very special relationship that exists between an audience and a performer. As the audience became self-conscious, it became very aware of those restrictions under which it functions in any concert situation, where it typically finds itself in the role of the silent observer of actions in which it may never participate. Thus, members of the audience reacting to both this role and to the sounds in the piece found they could respond, as they did, only in certain limited ways—listening in silence, covering their ears, or walking out. Ashley, however, as the performer, became more actively involved in his responses, to a degree ordinarily unacceptable for a concert audience.

Another piece on the festival program, by Charlemagne Palestine, played this same game with the audience and, while rather humorous, was much more obvious and much less interesting than the Ashley. This work, an untitled composition for solo voice (1979), seemed atypical of Palestine's concerns. His most interesting works are striking in their intense identification of each sound quality with the techniques of its production. Several earlier voice pieces and the more recent instrumental pieces employing his innovative "strumming" techniques are clear examples of these interests.[23] Unfortunately, such explorations were absent from the rather idiosyncratic theatre piece heard at the Kitchen in June.

Turning to the music of another innovative composer represented in the Kitchen's series, that of Alvin Lucier, one finds other parallels with recent developments in the visual arts. The best of the sited visual works of the past decade or so are fraught with dialectical implications similar to those discussed above. The roles of the various reciprocal interactions between perceiver and site are crucial to the works of artists such as Carl Andre, Robert Irwin, and Robert Smithson. As was the case with Ashley's music, the most interesting structures created by these artists are also, in a sense, transparent, linking perceiver to site, or perhaps more precisely, to his consciousness of a site. The viewer develops a new awareness of himself as a cognitive being as he discovers his place within the landscape of things.

Unfortunately, many sonic works in this vein seem to have lost this dialectical thrust. For the visual arts the notion of rooting an object to a particular site was a major concern and, indeed, one which the medium itself seemed to demand. Over the past few decades, as questions were raised concerning the central role that context plays in the creation and perception of structure, the integration of an artwork's environment into its structure became a major concern. Sound, however, is a very different medium, and the desire to fix sound to a specific place and determine its meaning within the framework of a composition from the structure of that place arises from different concerns and, of course, involves different problems.

Alvin Lucier is indeed one of the most interesting and successful com-

---

[23] For more extensive discussion of Palestine's earlier works, see Lizzie Borden, "The New Dialectic," *Artforum* (March 1974), pp. 49–50.

posers working with these ideas. A clear example may be found in his composition *I Am Sitting in a Room* (1968). In this piece a reader recites a simple text, which is taped as he speaks. The tape itself is then replayed in the concert hall or some other performance space and retaped on a second recorder. This retaping process is then repeated many times within that same space until a reading many generations old is produced.

> ... you know when you speak in a room certain components of your voice sound strong. That's because those pitches that are in those components reflect off the surface of the room and get amplified. The pitches that don't correspond don't get amplified ... Now you're unable to perceive that under ordinary circumstances, but if you could amplify that in some way, then you could perceive that. The way I amplify it is by recycling the sounds into the room again, again, again and again, until ... those pitches that do correspond to the resonances get amplified and those that don't go away.[24]

As a result, those sonic characteristics of the space to which one's attention is not ordinarily drawn are forced out into the open. The acoustical qualities of the performance space are slowly unveiled and become, simultaneously, the mechanism for structuring the piece and the work's structure itself. What, for music, has been traditionally the most imperceptible of backdrops moves into the foreground and becomes the very subject of the piece: "I decided to use the simplest speech I could find ... because I didn't want the input to be so composed as to take away from the idea of the piece.... What the room does is the content."[25]

Clearly, however, even though Lucier's work is situated in one specific place and draws its structure from the particular acoustical characteristics of that place, the piece is movable. The specific sonic qualities of different spaces may be different, but the fundamental acoustical concept supporting the composition would remain unchanged as it shifted its location. Different spaces reinforce different sounds on the tape and often produce very different results. This situation is quite dissimilar to those found in some of the recent pieces of Robert Irwin, for example, which are conceived and created for only one place and which are meaningful only in that place. Lucier's work, in contrast, is concerned with acknowledging the varieties of acoustical properties found in whatever space is given. Thus, *I Am Sitting in a Room* is truly pluralistic in structure, encompassing and

---

[24] Alvin Lucier, interview with Loren Means, *Composer Magazine* (1977–1978), p. 9.
[25] *Ibid.*

incorporating many different spaces, as is the case with many of this composer's works. Indeed, its full richness is only revealed after it is heard performed in several vastly different acoustical environments, for it always remains dependent upon its variable but particular location for its logic and meaning.

As the critic Kenneth Baker once noted of Carl Andre's work: "In the very best experience of [his] work one gets the sense of being presented with something for the first time, a feeling that I associate with learning the name of something—the thing is there in a new way. . . . In short, I think Andre's best work is about presence to the world as presence to oneself."[26] This same quality of self-reflection is also present in Lucier's best work. He is one of the few composers successfully to have bridged the traditional boundaries separating the composition from its environment, and in so doing he has revealed hidden qualities of each listener's relationship to his acoustical environment.

The work heard at the Kitchen was a work-in-progress for amplified piano, as of that date untitled. The piece was very subtle but, nonetheless, quite impressive. With the aid of an electronic amplification system the composer was able to capture and project the particular spatial configurations determined by a variety of different keyboard tones.

When a key on the piano is struck, the sound does not emanate evenly in all directions from the instrument. Instead, sound waves disperse in an irregular array of patterns determined by the particular disposition of overtones. These patterns create a total sonic configuration unique to each individual tone on each particular instrument. The purpose of Lucier's piece was to delineate this spatial configuration for the audience.

Toward this end two microphones were positioned quite close to the edge of an opened grand piano. The pianist then played an ascending series of tones very slowly and at a moderate dynamic level, allowing each sound to die away completely before beginning the next. As each tone sounded, it was picked up and amplified in such a way that its unique acoustical/spatial flow was perceptibly delineated for the audience. The spatial configuration that each tone produced was, therefore, magnified so that each member of the audience could perceive it as clearly as if he were actually on stage leaning over the piano itself.

As in *I Am Sitting in a Room* the structure of this new piece is simultaneously determined by, and equated with, certain spatial phenomena

---

[26] Kenneth Baker, from a review of a show held in 1971 at the Divan Gallery in New York, *Artforum* (June 1971), p. 81.

that typically, though perhaps imperceptibly, affect the sounds we hear. Sound is made tactile as its spatial qualities are brought into prominence. The space of a sound is the subject here, as new dimensions of our hearing are revealed.

Two areas of importance to contemporary music that did not seem well represented in the Kitchen's series were those of extended exploration into the psychoacoustic properties of traditional instruments and computer-aided composition. The composer-choreographer Meredith Monk, for instance, sang some of her own songs at the opening concert. These were purported to combine various styles from both Western and non-Western music. They seemed, unfortunately, to be rather fortuitous collections of vocal effects, few of which actually explored the enormous timbral and registral potential of the voice as an instrument.

In the hands of certain composers, however, the human voice has proven to be one of the richest sources for psychoacoustic exploration and composition, and this approach, as such, deserved more substantial representation. Much more striking examples would have been found, for instance, among the works of Robert Cogan, a composer and theorist who has been exploring the potential of the human voice for over a decade, integrating the unique sonic qualities of a diverse collection of languages with an extraordinary range of timbral variety. His composition *utterances* ... (1978), for example, would have been a significant addition to the Kitchen's avant-garde series, as it represents one of the most important contributions to the literature of twentieth-century vocal composition.

The situation was quite similar with respect to the quality of computer-aided composition that was presented. Works by Joel Chadabe, Charles Dodge, George Lewis, and David Behrman were heard. The Chadabe and Behrman were innovative in their experimentation with various techniques that permitted live improvisation with the computer. Chadabe, for example, was able to interact with his computer using two theremins to control, simultaneously, the timbre and duration of tones generated by his own composition program. The results, however, were not especially interesting, and one hopes for an opportunity in the near future to sample a more diverse and perhaps more striking collection of computer-oriented projects.

The music of the 1970s has borne the fruits of some of the richest ideas to emerge during the postwar period, ideas that have challenged many traditional concepts of structure and have revealed an affinity with some of today's most progressive ideas in philosophy, the sciences, and the visual arts. In particular, what seems to be central to much of this new music is its reevaluation of those attitudes that support the traditional boundaries separating composer and listener; that is, its desire to remove those barriers distinguishing the creation of an artwork from its experience. Of paramount importance to much of this work are those qualities that lead the perceiver to experience the discovery of relationships, and the emergence of form, from a vantage point once reserved for the composer alone.

The only art that truly recognizes tradition is that art which transforms its content in some way. Over the past ten years the composers discussed above have guided some of the most original explorations witnessed by the music world. Their individuality and intellectual rigor have placed them in the forefront of today's creative activity.

Edgard Varèse:
An Oral History Project*

Ruth Julius

A group of prominent composers were interviewed by Ruth Julius in order to determine their thoughts concerning the influence on contemporary musical composition of Edgard Varèse, the late and complex twentieth-century composer. Among the ideas of Varèse that are touched upon are his concept of spatiality *in music, the composer as a human being, the unique qualities that set Varèse apart from other composers, and his concept of* liberation of sound.

Ruth Julius, pianist and musicologist, helped compile Women in American Music: A Bibliography of Music and Literature *(1979). She is working on an oral history project of contemporary American women composers and teaches at Brooklyn College.*

Edgard Varèse's music and his position in twentieth-century music have not yet been thoroughly examined. Since his death in 1965, there have been several dissertations on and biographies of the composer; the literature, however, is appallingly scanty. Analyses of some of his works have appeared in major music journals, but in many ways are inadequate. The doctoral seminar on Varèse conducted by Professor Sherman Van Sol-

---

* Reprinted from *Current Musicology*, no. 25 (November 25, 1978), p. 39.

kema at the City University of New York, from which this oral history project arose, is the first of its kind to deal with this major musical figure both historically and analytically. By conducting this series of interviews, I hoped to clarify issues and to draw some preliminary conclusions concerning Varèse, his oeuvre, and the world in which he lived and worked.

My data have been culled from fourteen taped interviews with composers living in the New York area. (The one exception was Roger Reynolds from California, who was interviewed while visiting New York.) A list of interviewees and the dates of the interviews is found in table 1.

Table 1: List of interviews

INTERVIEWEE	DATE
Roger Reynolds	November 4, 1976
Henry Weinberg	November 18, 1976
Eric Salzman	November 19, 1976
Henry Brant	November 20, 1976
Vivian Fine	November 21, 1976
Milton Babbitt	November 29, 1976
Earle Brown	December 1, 1976
Otto Luening	December 7, 1976
Robert Starer	December 8, 1976
Harvey Sollberger	December, 10, 1976
John Cage	December 14, 1976
Vladimir Ussachevsky	December 17, 1976
Ross Lee Finney	December 23, 1976
Charles Wuorinen	January 3, 1977

The tapes and transcripts are housed in the Project for the Oral History of Music in America office at the City University of New York for the future use of scholars and researchers. Roger Reynolds and Ross Lee Finney were interviewed as part of the Varèse seminar; after my initial questioning, the discussion was open to all members of the seminar. Professor Van Solkema and I spoke to Robert Starer in a joint interview. The remaining interviews were conducted by me alone. Responses to my requests for interviews were excellent. Of the seventeen composers I approached, fourteen accepted, two declined, and one was unavailable in the United States this year.

This paper is an interpretation of these interviews, which contain a wealth of information on Varèse and other subjects relevant to twentieth-century music. The interviews were structured to include certain topics, but some were more fruitful than others. The quoted material has been edited grammatically, to avoid repetition, and for reasons of space. The broad themes dealt with here are Varèse's concept of *spatiality*, his *liberation of sound*, influences on him, his influence and importance in twentieth-century music, and Varèse, the man.

A clear distinction can be made on the question of the interviewees' first encounters with Varèse's music on the basis of their age. Henry Brant, Vivian Fine, Otto Luening, John Cage, and Vladimir Ussachevsky, all born before 1915 (Finney is in this age group, but he is an exception), first heard Varèse's music in live performances. The world première of *Ionisation*, conducted by Nicholas Slonimsky, took place in New York on March 6, 1933, in what is now Carnegie Recital Hall. Shortly afterward, Slonimsky brought it to the Hollywood Bowl. There were American performances of Varèse's works in the 1920s, but only Brant remembers hearing *Arcana*, conducted by Stokowski.

Those composers born after 1915 first heard Varèse on recordings. *Ionisation* was recorded on a 78 rpm disc in the 1930s on New Music Records, as were *Density 21.5* and *Octandre*. There was also an E.M.S. (Elaine Music Shop) recording made in 1950 of *Octandre, Density, Ionisation,* and *Intègrales* with Frederick Waldman conducting. After the *Ionisation* première in 1933, no Varèse work was heard live in New York (with the exception of the solo flute piece) until 1947, when *Hyperprism* was performed at a memorial service for the critic Paul Rosenfeld. It was not until the 1950s that Varèse began to reappear in the public musical ear, through long-playing recordings and live performances of all the works. Younger and older composers alike attended the New York première of *Déserts* on November 30, 1955, in Town Hall, with Jacques Monod conducting. (The United States première had been held in Bennington, Vermont, on May 17, 1955.)

The composers' initial impression of Varèse's music varied according to which work was heard first, by what medium, and when. Those hearing *Ionisation* live in 1933 were bowled over by the daring qualities of this music; namely, its use of an all-percussion ensemble, and an almost "electronic" concept, as Fine describes it. Cage speaks of the Hollywood Bowl performance as "inspiring, invigorating, and electrifying." Brant was "startled by a piece that didn't seem to need strings, woodwinds, brass, or even much pitched percussion."

From the 1950 E.M.S. recording, Roger Reynolds remembers being struck by the "short-range intensity of the impulse in Varèse, who was willing to achieve tremendous impact in the space of ten seconds, as opposed to a minute and a half." Earle Brown, who listened to the same recording, found his "ears turned around" by Varèse and was impressed by the composer's time sense. In the early 1950s Brown was interested in the works of James Joyce, Gertrude Stein, and Virginia Woolf. He sensed intuitively that Varèse, like these writers, was involved with a new sense of the way time moved.

> By the focus on, or exposition of an area, these artists achieved through words what Varèse achieved through sounds. When I first heard Varèse, the immediate connection was that repetition in Stein, who maintained that there was no such thing as repetition. Woolf slowed up time and Joyce almost stopped time. Joyce was exploring a situation in depth in a density kind of way, rather than horizontally, which was what Varèse was doing by observing the sheer fact of the sonic objects' reality which he constructed. He wanted the sounds to just sit there, and have people listen in to the sounds.

Harvey Sollberger, a flutist who thinks of *Density* in "autobiographical terms," speaks of the "inexorable flow of the music, the very controlled motion from one point to another, and the need to keep going. It almost compelled you, pulled your attention along." Perhaps Charles Wuorinen best sums up his hearing of Varèse, "In a word, world-opening."

One of Varèse's great interests was the concept of *spatiality* in music—spatial projection, sounds moving in space, musical space as being open and unbounded. Although the notion of space in music differs depending on who is asked, those interviewed showed a high degree of concurrence in their feelings regarding Varèse's idea of spatiality. At times, even the same language was used to articulate the idea.

Reynolds referred to his colleague Robert Erickson's term *sound icons"*[1] in discussing spatiality.

> Varèse was talking about the problem of how to describe, metaphorically, the listening to of agglomerations of carefully controlled sound and fused timbres, and understanding that they are significantly different when the entrances and exits are patterned in a different way, and when the dynamic flux is different. These sounds are different entities, rather than differently performed or expressed versions of the same thing. Part of Varèse's use of a spatial analogy was an effort to say that a performance or a realization of a chor-

---

[1] Robert Erickson, *Sound Structure in Music* (Berkeley: University of California Press, 1975), p. 185.

dal sonority could be seen as two distinct phenomena. His sounds are sculptural in terms of their opacity, their density.

Varèse's sculptural quality is alluded to again and again in discussions of spatiality. Sollberger notes the relationship between Varèse's idea of crystalline structure and music in space.

> In *Octandre,* for example, there are certain reference sonorities that assume a physicality which one hears; simultaneously, you have an impression of shifting perspective, as if you were looking at a sculpture from different angles, being different every time, and yet obviously it's the same object rotating and changing its elements. What Ralph Shapey has called the "graven image" (Varèse's term) is a particular configuration of sound, either vertical or horizontal, through repetition and juxtaposition in different phases against each other, forming a network of relations that were changing, yet whose basic elements were always the same.

Like Sollberger, Brown uses the image of sculpture to describe spatiality in Varèse. However, the term *sculpture,* for Brown, has a more static quality: "The movement is there in an acoustic way, not in an aural or kinetic way; you can hear the sounds go across the orchestra." Brown, along with Reynolds and Sollberger, is aware of the variegated perspective in Varèse's music. He compares Varèse's breaking up of chords to the Cubists' fragmentation of painted objects into planes, masses, and volumes. Brown compares Varèse at work to the sculptors Archipenko and Gonzalez, or a metal sculptor. Fine specifically mentions Brancusi, whose simplification and streamlining of materials is similar to that of Varèse.

Milton Babbitt, a more mathematically oriented composer, does not speak of the sculptural analogy regarding spatiality. "Spatiality in Varèse's music involves the degree of total range, his constant varying it with regard to certain kinds of rhythmic ratios, and the placing of instruments within that range."

Varèse's use of metaphorical language and his association with other arts and artists are clearly important factors in his music. His scientific background must not be down-played either, as it, too, affects this language. The image of the crystal structure, which Varèse frequently used, attests to his interest in the physical world. Brown tried to tie the two together: "I thought I knew how he composed by referring what I heard of Varèse back to Schillinger, principles of structuring masses, densities, time spans, and time proportions." It seems possible, thus, that Varèse used metaphors precompositionally as well as postcompositionally.

Unlike the majority of the interviewees, Henry Weinberg and Wuorinen did not connect Varèse's music with other art forms, and they also objected to metaphorical language in discussing the music. Wuorinen asserts that "metaphors are useless, misleading, false, and dangerous, because they are too often used as a substitute for cognitive musical thought, information, and skill."

Varèse referred to sound as living matter and spoke of the *liberation of sound.*[2] Perhaps this term was suggested to Varèse by certain passages in Busoni's 1907 *Sketch for a New Esthetic of Music,* one of the first books to treat electronic music. Busoni had written that "a music score is free, and to win freedom is its destiny."[3] I asked the composers how they thought Varèse liberated sound. It was interesting to discover that most of the composers, whatever their orientation toward music, found the term *liberation of sound* meaningful. Wuorinen and Finney were the only exceptions; Wuorinen felt the phrase itself was, like all metaphorical language, nonsense; while Finney maintained that all composers "liberate sound." Luening felt that "Varèse didn't liberate sound—he liberated himself to work more freely in this area."

Babbitt and Weinberg conceive of Varèse's liberation of sound as an attempt to structure sound elements that were previously unacceptable to the traditional listener. Weinberg commented on Varèse's inclusion of noise elements into a musical composition.

> He spoke of the chromatic scale as a restricting element. Varèse wanted to return sound to nature and to structure the noise element. He wanted not merely two categories of pitch and noise, but a continuum of these. Varèse enlarged the scope of music by taking a realm that was totally unstructured and drawing it into structure, thereby leaving less to chance. One could regard Varèse as a formalist in sound. In order to get away from the clichés of meaning, one must be formalistic about considering the elements aside from their associations.

Babbitt answers the question in similar terms.

> Anything that can be discriminated aurally in context could now be structured. What Varèse meant by the "liberation of sound" was the sense that you

---

[2] Edgard Varèse, "The Liberation of Sound," *Contemporary Composers on Contemporary Music,* Elliot Schwartz and Barney Childs, eds. (New York: Holt, Rinehart, & Winston, 1967), pp. 196–208.
[3] Ferruccio Busoni, *Sketch for a New Esthetic of Music,* trans. Theodore Baker (New York: G. Schirmer, 1911), p. 5. Varèse knew Busoni in Berlin and admired him tremendously.

begin with the human component and you end with the limitations of the human perceptor. Music was liberated because it was no longer the intervention of instruments whose limitations were artificial and fictitious regarding the human's capacity to differentiate musical context.

Reynolds feels that Varèse liberated sound "by providing us with indisputable sonic experiences that had sufficient authority to stand on their own, and by allowing somewhat more untrammeled notions of what is proper into music." Brown states the same view in more concrete terms: "Varèse freed a D-major seventh chord of its necessity of going somewhere; he freed it from the nineteenth-century baggage. Sound could now exist as an object, a physical presence without the consequence of polyphonic or harmonic responsibilities." Starer concurs with Brown, but extends the "liberation" to include rhythm: "any rhythm does not have to be an evolving motive; it needs no reason to exist." Ussachevsky touches on all of the above points, but concludes that "the ultimate liberation, for Varèse, was a machine obedient to his command to produce any possible sound."

The most problematic issue for the composers I interviewed was determining those qualities in Varèse's music that set him apart from his contemporaries. Brant was the most articulate in his response, because of his conviction that Varèse was a highly individual composer. What he finds unique in Varèse is the "absence of protracted horizontal material, its extreme chordal character, and the pyramid nature of the chords."[4] Brant also finds "violent and dissonant harmony in the aggregate as well as in the detail. The amount of highly contrasted material in all the works is an individualistic element." He concludes that Varèse's music is a unique form of vertical, harmonic music.

Indeed, all of the composers were struck by Varèse's combinations of instruments to create block sounds. Weinberg cites Varèse's "unparalleled mastery of integration of tone color with instruments as well as electronically. How he makes and arranges these scales of tone color is fresh and exciting. Not only is the concept of blocks of sound important but the relationships among the elements that make up the blocks are marvelous." Reynolds and Brant mentioned Varèse's unusual use of the piano in its extreme high and low ranges combined with other instruments. Reynolds

---

[4] Brant borrows the term *pyramid* from commercial music, where it is used to describe chords with notes entering and leaving one at a time.

sees Varèse's uniqueness in his "short-term development of force and his capacity to create fusions" and in "his relative lack of dependence upon root progression and harmonic, melodic, or motivic structure in the traditional sense." But perhaps, most important, according to Reynolds, is the "sonorous size of his objects, their frequency or repetitions and the short duration with which he is willing to move over very wide ranges of dynamics of timbre and range."

Fine felt that the source of Varèse's individuality is the unity of his oeuvre. She feels, along with Brant, that all of Varèse's works are really one long work, even though there was a hiatus of eighteen years, from 1936 to 1954, in which no composition was completed. Brant feels that Varèse saw his role and capacity in one way only, and that was to write his music his way, with no digressions. Fine says,

> You sense the search for the realization of this central idea or image that he has. It might be something quite simple, like his knocking on wood with his knuckles and saying, "From this, I can make a whole composition." Varèse was not seduced by sound; his desire to fix things in sound is very strong in his music. He wanted the tone out there, to exist as an object, so you could walk on it, which I sometimes feel I can.

Brant and Brown emphasize the static quality of the music as far as pitch is concerned. "There are so many ways he can vary the pitches to give the effect of an enormous amount of action," says Brant. Perhaps this explains why Fine thinks Varèse's music is "somewhere between static and nonstatic." Even Wuorinen, the only composer interviewed who cannot include Varèse in the "pantheon of great composers because of his relative indifference to pitch relational matters," firmly believes that Varèse's major innovation was in dealing with musical time. He sees Varèse's contribution as "his proposal to mark the passage of musical time by juxtapositional means rather than by developmental ones from the past. The music proceeds according to the juxtaposition of differentiated elements, rather than the interconnection of evolutionarily related elements." Wuorinen cites *Octandre* and *Ionisation* as the most successful pieces in this respect.

All artists are influenced by their backgrounds, their physical surroundings, people with whom they come into contact, and art of the past and present. Certainly Varèse was no exception to this, but in his case it is particularly difficult to trace the origins of and influences on his music. Be-

fore World War I, Varèse lived in Paris and was educated at the Schola
Cantorum under Vincent d'Indy and Albert Roussel. He fled from that
conservative atmosphere to Berlin, where he was befriended by the conductors Karl Muck, Richard Strauss, and Ferruccio Busoni. Varèse's music
was performed in both cities, and he enjoyed quite a career in Europe before coming to the United States in December 1915. His first piece written
here, *Amériques,* is the earliest work that survives. Much was lost in a Berlin warehouse fire, and in 1962 he destroyed *Bourgogne,* a work conducted
by Josef Stransky in Berlin in the 1910s.

Only Brant dissents from the widely held view that *Amériques* was influenced by *The Rite of Spring.* Varèse's treatment of percussion and of
rhythm is very different from Stravinsky's, but one can hear a connection
in sound and large-scale form between the two works. Varèse knew and
admired Debussy; however, the only musical relationships between the
two composers suggested to me were by Salzman and Brown in *Jeux,* and
by Fine and Sollberger in *Syrinx.* In *Jeux* Debussy intimates the idea of
masses, textures, and densities of sound, which Varèse certainly picked up.
Syrinx and *Density* are similar in medium and in use of intervallic structure.

Weinberg believes that all the composers born between 1881 and
1883, including Igor Stravinsky, Béla Bartók, Anton Webern, and Varèse,
share the common base of a "slow rate of harmonic change of pitches."
Brant stands in opposition to this, maintaining that all the aforementioned
composers are highly individual and do not share any traits. Both Brant
and Weinberg feel that Varèse's use of the twelve tones of the octave did
not necessarily come from Schönberg. The unfolding of the chromatic
scale was something that was very much in the air in the 1920s. Weinberg
continues on the Schönberg-Varèse relationship, "In the third piece of *Five
Pieces for Orchestra* opus 16, Schönberg de-linearized the surface of the
piece, which is the aspect that Varèse dwells on at great length." Cage and
Luening share the minority point of view in hearing Varèse as coming
from a Germanic tradition because of his use of a large orchestra.

Brown feels that Varèse was influenced by his early training in mathematics and by the visual arts. "The roots of Varèse's thinking are in Da-
daist books and Futurist manifestoes. His aesthetic was formed largely by
his ruminations about implications of Russolo's and Marinetti's thinking
on noise."

Reynolds mentions New York with its sounds and energies as being
the biggest influence on Varèse. "He processed New York." According to
Reynolds, Varèse's musical and human personality was so forceful that
only the most extraordinarily powerful ideas would get through to him.

One could say that Varèse had three careers: one in Europe before World War I, the second in New York in the 1920s as a composer-conductor and as organizer of the International Composers Guild, and the third as an international composer in the 1950s when Varèse emerged from almost two decades of obscurity. He lectured at Darmstadt in 1949; pieces such as *Ionisation* and *Octandre* were discussed in Olivier Messiaen's master classes, which Pierre Boulez and Karlheinz Stockhausen attended in the late 1940s. A reissue of the Waldman recording appeared on a French label in the 1950s. Varèse's influence only began to be felt in this third stage. The composers interviewed could not name anyone composing in the 1930s in the United States or in Europe on whom Varèse had a profound influence. Although he was friendly with Charles Ruggles and Henry Cowell, they "were doing their own thing," according to Fine. She continues, "Varèse was considered a radical of the twenties who was temporarily put on the shelf in the thirties and forties." She feels that the "eclipse of the avant-garde" in the 1930s deeply affected composers' styles. "Varèse couldn't change and didn't change; perhaps that's why he was so out of phase for so long."

It is the impression of most of the composers interviewed that post–World War II Europe was concerned with following the path marked by Webern. Brown recalled a conversation between himself and Boulez in 1965 in Paris about Webern and Varèse. Boulez said that "what we need now is clean music, constructivist serial plotting of pitches. Varèse is too Beethovenian, too emotional." Brown, at that time, was convinced that "Varèse represented a new way of thnking about sound, in masses, volumes, and densities, whereas Webern was an old polyphonist." Brown speculated that music would go far more in the direction of Varèse than that of Webern, and believes that he is correct today. "There are very few people writing twelve-tone, post-Webern serial music today compared to the number of people working in a more inclusive area, such as Xenakis, Ligeti, and Penderecki." Iannis Xenakis is cited most frequently as a second-generation Varèsian—Xenakis the mathematician, designer, architect, working with planes, masses, proportions, and sculptural objects, seems especially close to Varèse. Brown states that "there could not have been a Ligeti or a Penderecki without a Varèse. The sounds from these three composers are very much like the sounds from *Amériques.*"

Among Americans, Varèse seems to have had more of an attitudinal than a stylistic influence. Varèse did not have many pupils and was not affiliated with a university. There was never a group of composers writing pieces like Varèse, as there was with Stravinsky and Schönberg; however, Brown now sees Varèse in the center of mainstream developments of music. "Varèse was not polemic; he didn't leave us any techniques. He left us a body of works which stands very strongly."

Varèse's influence affected composers differently. Brant says, "Every time I want to write a really sour and dissonant chord with pyramids, I think of Varèse's example, which nobody could beat. I also owe to Varèse the method I use to get the earsplitting results you hear." Wuorinen's interest in loud volumes of sound is acknowledged by him to come partly from Varèse. "My thoughts on form and continuity have been influenced by what I've taken out of Varèse's music; perhaps an orchestrational or instrumental attitude, too."

While Weinberg thinks it is too soon, twelve years after Varèse's death, to detect an influence, Reynolds is firmly convinced of Varèse's influence on contemporary composers: "We're standing on him now." Reynolds cites Varèse's blocks of sound and his short-term intensity as the two most important influences on himself. He also acknowledges that his concept of *timed mixtures,* the idea of not going anywhere within a certain period of time, was influenced by the example set by Varèse.

Babbitt acknowledges a Varèse influence in one of his early pieces, but goes on to say that, more importantly, "all composers have been influenced by the general gesture, the kind of sound, and the liberation of the percussion set by Varèse. Varèse's music has become part of our internalized theory of music." Starer echoes this by saying that Varèse's musical language has become "common parlance" among composers today.

In conversations with the composers, several specific projects for the future were discussed. These include revision of an article, written by Brown twenty years ago, consisting of excerpts from Varèse's writings and lectures on his music. Brown's article was accepted for publication by the British magazine *The Score,* edited by William Glock, but it went out of business before the article was published. Ussachevsky would very much like to restore *Poème Électronique* in the next four or five years. The original components had nine tracks, which were later reduced to three. He wants to reconstruct this masterpiece from the original sources onto nine tracks. Wuorinen has conducted *Déserts* several times in the complete instrumental and tape version and has always been baffled by the relationship between the tape part and the instrumental part. He would like to perform it with only its instrumental sections (a possibility suggested in the score) to see whether the work might not present a more coherent entity without the tape. Perhaps Fine most succinctly expressed her desire for more live performance of Varèse's music, "What we need is a Varèse revival."

Varèse the man cannot be divorced from Varèse the musician. A picture of Varèse as a human being has begun to emerge from this project. All of the composers had some personal contact with him; some more than others. "He was an immense man with an immense concept of sound" is the way Sollberger describes him. Several composers interviewed spoke of the extremes in his personality: he was capable of great rancor and also of great kindness. This may be reflected in the extremes in his music in range, volume of sound, and the use of highly contrasting materials. Salzman associates Varèse's "earthy, proletarian, peasant origins with his earth-rooted, solid, rough-hewn sculptures in sound." Varèse had an intense personality that resulted in music that imposed upon the listener. His sounds were "rich, vibrant, and sensual, close to the experience."

Varèse is described by Wuorinen as "a grand seigneur, a patrician with no pretensions. His gentlemanliness, although he was a rough character at times, made it possible for him to have the most rebellious of musical attitudes without ever seeming to turn against the fabric of civilization itself." Babbitt is fascinated by Varèse's whole personality and the whole "complex of cultural reactions which made him a complicated and volatile man, which, in turn, affected his relationship to music and musicians."

Fine feels very strongly that "Varèse never lost his cast of being a member of the avant-garde. He held onto that idea; that was his stamp. He said to me at the end of his life, 'You know, some people shouldn't have to die.' He wanted very much to go on living and creating. I think he would have continued to be an avant-garde composer always." This point of view is challenged by Starer and Wuorinen who maintain that the term *avant-garde* is meaningless today, because, as Wuorinen says, "the questioning of artistic limits and possibilities has become so complete that there is nothing further that can be done." Starer speaks of the "military function" of the avant-garde, which, when it remains in enemy territory for twenty-five years, ceases to be meaningful. "Avant-garde now simply means one kind of music."

Whether or not we label Varèse "avant-garde" or anything else (Varèse despised labels), the fact remains that Varèse's music clearly stands out in the minds and ears of these composers as a substantial contribution to twentieth-century music. Babbitt seems to speak for all the composers when he says, "There's not one of those pieces which would still not interest me, both to hear in a very good performance and to go over again with a student. I have a very strong feeling that I haven't by any means plumbed Varèse."

Two Tonal Composers*

Richard Kostelanetz

Alan Hovhaness and Philip Glass are two of the most advanced tonal composers working in the West today. In the following essays Richard Kostelanetz traces the musical development and discusses specific compositions by both composers and offers a critical appraisal of their work.

Richard Kostelanetz is the editor of several anthologies, has written for numerous periodicals on the fine arts, and is a well-known critic and poet. He is the author of Music of Today *and edited* John Cage *(1970). His own art with words, numbers, and lines, in several media, has been exhibited around the world.*

ALAN HOVHANESS: THE TRANSCENDENTAL CONTEMPORARY

The composer Alan Hovhaness decided four decades ago to pursue an idiosyncratic path, apart from changing fashions, that he has followed, pro-

* The essay on Alan Hovhaness is reprinted from *Michigan Quarterly Review* (Summer 1979), pp. 365–378, by permission of the author. Copyright © 1979 by Richard Kostelanetz. The Philip Glass essay is reprinted from the liner notes for *Music in Changing Parts* (Tomato Records, 1979) by permission of the author. Copyright © 1979 by Richard Kostelanetz.

lifically, to this day, producing musical compositions that, in my opinion, rank among the best of the past half-century. Essentially, he is a consummate melodist, who uses the modal scales and textures of Eastern music within a framework of Western counterpoint and structure. As his colleague John Cage so acutely observed in 1946, "The use of raga is Oriental; the idea of changing its tones, of letting others appear either at the same time or later is characteristic of Occidental musical thought. The absence of harmony in Hovhaness's music is Eastern. The fact that his compositions are notated and may be played more than once is Western."

No other modern composer has written for as many kinds of musical ensembles and instruments (even, in one piece, the recorded sound of large whales); and few who have worked so totally independent of professional politics are also able to live, as Hovhaness does, entirely off his compositional work. Although tonal music as such is scarcely unfamiliar, he has nonetheless created a musical style that is instantly recognizable as his own, largely because of its personal synthesis of Oriental and Occidental characteristics. Among American tonal composers, only Aaron Copland has created so much uniquely identifiable music. Currently a resident of Seattle, where I met him early in 1977, Hovhaness was on the verge of completing his thirty-first symphony (op. 296). Symphonies 27, 28, 29, and 30 were *all* completed in 1976. He has since completed several more. Symphony no. 36, for one, was performed at Kennedy Center, Washington, D.C., by the National Symphony on January 16, 17, 18 of 1979. Such output is, by itself, an unparalleled achievement for a modern composer.

Actually, Hovhaness has always been a tonal composer. His principal early influences were Mozart and Handel, and then, among the moderns, Bartók and Sibelius. Indeed, the latter he identifies as his single "favorite orchestral composer since Mozart—particularly his Fourth Symphony, "The Swan of Tuonela," *Luonnotar* for soprano and orchestra." Another modern influence, more esoteric than the others, is the Armenian priest Komitas Vartabed (1869–1936), whom Hovhaness calls "the Armenian Bartók." Although Hovhaness is usually generous in his remarks about other living composers, it is not surprising, given these influences, that he strongly objects to atonality in music. "To me, it is against nature. There is a center in everything that exists. The planets have the sun, the moon, the earth. The reason I like Oriental music is that everything has a firm center. All music with a center is tonal. Music without a center is fine for a minute or two, but it soon sounds all the same."

More radically, he objects to the tempered, chromatic scale of the piano, which he finds "efficient only for playing in every key. The string orchestra is the most marvelous instrument in Western music, because it observes just intonation. Human beings will use just intonation unconsciously, because it is the scale of nature; it is what any voice will sing." Hovhaness claims for his own modal music an essential simplicity, which puts off some sophisticated listeners but which he thinks will contribute to its survival. "Things which are very complicated tend to disappear and get lost. Simplicity is difficult, not easy. Beauty is simple. All unnecessary elements are removed—only essence remains." As a conservative who acknowledges definable traditions, rather than a reactionary or a neoclassicist who favors a return to anachronistic forms, Hovhaness characterizes his own music as "giant melodies in simple and complex modes around movable and stationary tonal centers." He pauses for a thought. "I'm most interested in purely melodic forms of music in a timeless sense—without being tied down to any century or any place, I want to write down the best music I hear within myself."

He was born "Alan Vaness Chakmakjian" in Somerville, Massachusetts, March 8, 1911, the son of a chemistry professor at Tufts Medical School, Haroutiun Chakmakjian, himself an immigrant to the United States from Adana, Turkey. (The surname means locksmith or gunsmith in Turkish.) His wife, née Madeleine Scott, was Scottish in ancestry. When their only child was five, the Chakmakjians moved to another Boston suburb, Arlington, where young Alan attended the public schools and was graduated from high school in 1929. He learned to read music when he was seven years old, and immediately began to write his own pieces. An instinctive musician, he taught himself to improvise at the piano before he ever had any lessons on the instrument. So, when he was nine, his parents sent him to a local piano teacher, Adelaide Proctor, who gave him a scholarship and encouraged his composing. By the age of thirteen, young Chakmakjian had written two operas, *Bluebeard* and *Daniel,* in addition to many smaller pieces.

Unlike other Armenian-Americans of his generation, he did not attend the church-sponsored after-school school in which youngsters learned Armenian language and culture. "My mother didn't want me to be too Armenian," the composer recently told me, "but my father did. He taught me secretly." Soon after her death, in 1931, he changed his middle name to 'Hovaness," which is Armenian for John or Johannes, in honor of his grandfather, whose first name it was. Then he decided to add an *H* to his middle name, and completely drop his last name, thus producing his present name, "Alan Hovhaness."

He went to Tufts University for two years, but then transferred to the New England Conservatory of Music in Boston where he studied with Frederick Converse (1871–1940), a now-forgotten American composer whose most noted piece, *The Mystic Trumpeter* (1905), is an orchestral work based on Walt Whitman. In 1936 Hovhaness closely observed the North Indian musician Vishnu Shirali, who had come to Boston with the dancer Ude Shankar (Ravi's older brother). In the summer of 1942 the young composer won a scholarship to the Berkshire Music Center to study with Bohuslav Martinu, but that residency initiated Hovhaness's lifelong quarrel with the neoclassical establishment gathered around Aaron Copland. Unlike other American tonal composers of his generation, Hovhaness never studied in Europe. "I was more interested in Oriental music," he now remembers. "Things like that were very far from Paris." Hovhaness has no academic degrees, other than honorary doctorates. In May 1977 he was inducted into the National Institute of Arts and Letters, joining not only such lifelong friends as Cage and Lou Harrison but also his lifelong nemeses.

In the 1930s he made his living playing the piano, mostly around Boston, for choruses, chamber orchestras, violinists, solo singers, as well as social gatherings of Greeks, Arabs, and Armenians. He also worked as a jazz arranger on the Works Progress Administration and as an organist in an Armenian church, where he acquired a reputation for spectacular improvisations on ancient modes. His first break as a composer came in 1939 when Leslie Heward, director of music for the BBC in Birmingham, England, aired several Hovhaness pieces and, in a public interview, identified the young American as an important new composer; but unfortunately for Hovhaness, Heward died soon afterward. In 1940 the young composer destroyed nearly all the music he had written so far, including an undergraduate, prizewinning 1933 symphony; he wanted to start the new decade afresh. In the early 1940s he met the Boston painter Hyman Bloom, who not only influenced Hovhaness's growing interest in ethnic motifs but also introduced him to Yenouk Der Hagopian, a troubadour folksinger whose music Hovhaness patiently transcribed into conventional (that is, Western) notation. His other important friend during this period was Herman di Giovanno, a "clairvoyant" painter who stimulated Hovhaness's interest in extrasensory phenomena.

This interest in Armenian music led to his organizing a concert of his own compositions in Boston in 1944, for the benefit of an Armenian charitable organization. The successes of this concert led in turn to a series of new compositions, very Armenian in style, such as *Lousadzak* (1944), the opera *Etchmiadzin* (1940), Armenian Rhapsody no. 1 (1944–1945, which incorporates a Der Hagopian melody), among others. With these works he initiated his first technical innovation, which he calls *senza mesura,* or "free rhythm." Essentially, in certain parts of a piece he writes a series of notes without measure bars. The musicians are instructed to repeat these notes, at their own individual speeds, over a fixed period of time. The result is a temporarily chaotic sound or "sound cloud," as Hovhaness calls it; but in his music, unlike that of other chaotic composers, such aural disorganization is nearly always tonally resolved. "I seldom use this anymore," he added. "When everybody copies it, it scarcely belongs to me."

He collaborated with an Armenian student group in cosponsoring annual New York concerts of his music, beginning with one at Town Hall in June 1945. The composer Lou Harrison, then a music critic for the New York *Herald-Tribune,* came to review it. Having an extra ticket, Harrison invited his friend John Cage, also then a young composer, who came backstage after the concert to congratulate Hovhaness. Harrison's review was laudatory, identifying Hovhaness as "a composer of considerable interest and originality." Cage introduced Hovhaness around artistic New York and later wrote favorably about his work in *Modern Music Magazine* (Spring 1946).

In 1946 Hovhaness decided to move to New York, where he lived for a year, mostly composing music for dancers; but unable to survive financially, he returned to Boston. In 1948 he began three years of regular teaching at the Boston Conservatory of Music, the smaller music school in his home city. Aside from three years of Eastman (Rochester) summer school in the mid-1950s, that was his last regular teaching position. In 1951 he moved again to New York to work for Voice of America, making musical programs for broadcast in the Middle East and India. "When Eisenhower came in, in 1952, everyone was fired."

Around 1953 he began finally to collect on his artistic investment. The Guggenheim Foundation awarded him the first of two successive fellowships. Martha Graham commissioned a score for her dance company, and the Louisville Orchestra another piece for its own première concerts series. Hovhaness met the conductor Leopold Stokowski, who had been programming Hovhaness compositions since 1942, and the conductor commissioned the composer to produce his single most famous work, *Mysterious Mountain* (1955), for the conductor's inaugural concert with the Houston Symphony.

It was Stokowski who suggested that Hovhaness ought to observe the classic custom of putting opus numbers after his works. As Hovhaness was prolific, the conductor estimated that the new piece, *Mysterious Mountain,* ought to have the opus number of 132 and advised the composer to count his previous works backward. Unfortunately, Stokowski underestimated Hovhaness's prior output (not including the destroyed works); and as there were already more than 150 pieces in his active catalogue, several different early works were assigned the same single opus number.

The rest of Hovhaness's current catalogue is comparably chaotic. Some works have no opus numbers at all. Many are definitively undated, usually because they were published long after they were first written and sometimes because the dates of composition would not correspond to their opus numbers. The undated *Saint Vartan* Symphony, for instance, was orignally written in 1949–1950, or after Symphony no. 1 but before Symphony no. 2. However, when Hovhaness later decided that *Saint Vartan* was indeed a full symphony, the next available number was 9. As the newly christened Symphony no. 9 already had an opus number (80) that was considerably lower than that of Symphony no. 8 (op. 179), Hovhaness renumbered *Saint Vartan* as opus 180, even though it was composed a decade before no. 8. Then too, when Hovhaness revises an earlier piece that lacks an opus number, he must find one for it. Thus, "opus 80" has since been assigned to another piece from that 1940s period. "This is like Köchel listing," he jokes, "but Köchel was more careful than I was, because Mozart was dead."

In 1959, in his own late forties, Hovhaness began the second phase of his musical education. He received a Fulbright Research fellowship to study Carnatic music in South India. Traveling all over the country for a year, he transcribed ragas (over 300 of them, into a book he would like to publish) and even fulfilled a commission to write a piece for Indian musicians. He visited Japan for the first time, giving well-received concerts of his own works, and returned in 1962/63 to study gagaku music, which he describes as "the earliest orchestral music we know; it came from China and Korea in the 700s." He also learned to play Japanese instruments, such as the oboelike *hichiriki* and the complex mouth organ *Shō* (which he still owns), and even performed with a gagaku group, in addition to transcribing thirteen pieces in Western notation. By 1965 Hovhaness could sharply distinguish himself from his contemporaries by writing that his principal musical preferences were "Seventh Century Armenian religious music, classic music of South India, Chinese orchestra music of the Tang dynasty, Ah-ak music of Korea, gagaku of Japan, and the opera-oratorios of Handel." Typically, one of Hovhaness's favorite modern novelists is Hermann Hesse, a fellow syncretic artist who likewise assimilated Eastern thought to make Western art.

In the middle 1960s Hovhaness lived part of each year in Lucerne,

Switzerland, and part in New York, overseeing the publication of his music and its American performances. In 1972 he moved permanently to Seattle, where he had been composer-in-residence with the Seattle Symphony in 1966/67. I found him living with his present wife, the coloratura singer Hinako Fujihara, in the unfashionable southern section of the city, near the airport. Their apartment is small and anonymous, with no name on the front door that opens onto a concrete courtyard. He works in the living room, mostly on two folding tables. Along one wall is a modest spinet piano; along another, a small television set that he had borrowed from a friend to see a performance of his music. On the floor was a reel-to-reel tape player that did not work. Books filled some shelves, piles of his scores occupied others, and an abstract di Giovanno painting rested on the floor, leaning against a bookcase. There was no record player and no records other than his own. "I never listen to anything more than once," he told me, "except Indian music and Japanese No plays," Next door is a firehouse. "When the alarm goes, the only music I hear is in my head. I can't hear anything else. Varèse would have liked it here." Part Armenian, part Scot, Hovhaness lives frugally. As the composer, like myself, prefers to sleep in the mornings, we met at midnight.

Hovhaness himself is tall and slender, with stooped posture (perhaps from years of music copying) and with deep-set black eyes and a broad dark moustache that caps an easy smile. His appearance reminds his friend Oliver Daniel of figures in El Greco paintings. Hovhaness's face is well-formed, in a long and slender way, and handsome, his mottled skin notwithstanding. His dark wavy hair has begun to gray, especially near his ears; and he wears it long enough to fluff out from the back of his head. The gray beard he has worn these past few years is scraggly. Around his right wrist is a copper bracelet, which, he believes, helps the arthritis that has been plaguing his remarkably long and large fingers (and handicapping his piano playing). He appears physically frail, but when he reveals how many push-ups he does every day, that initial impression passes. Even at home, he wears a suit and a wide tie, with pens in his handkerchief pocket. Although a shy public speaker, he is a bright, fluent conversationalist, never at a loss for answers. "Why Seattle?," I asked. "I like the mountains very much," he replied. "I don't have to go to Switzerland. I expect to stay here."

The principal mystery of Hovhaness's professional career is how he manages to compose so much. One of his several music publishers, C. F. Peters, lists over 240 separate Hovhaness pieces in its catalogue, while other publishers have other compositions, and yet more remains unpublished. "I write every day," he explained over a cup of coffee, rocking back and forth in his dining chair as he spoke. "I have so many beautiful ideas. I must write them down. I can't stop composing. I have more ideas than I can ever use." He writes all the time, wherever he is—on airplanes, in buses or cars, while walking down the street, while sleeping. Always near him is a pencil and a five-inch by eight-inch notebook with music staves. "I don't know how to compose slowly. I correct and revise later, but composing goes in a sweep. Sometimes I just get the beginning idea, but more often the entire score, complete with orchestration, comes into my head at once." The record jacket of Duet for Violin and Harpsichord says that the three-minute piece "was commissioned on May 16, 1954, composed on May 17, and given its first performance two weeks later in Frankfurt, Germany." If a conductor suggests in the composer's presence that, say, the conclusion of a certain piece is weak or inappropriate, Hovhaness, as the supremely obliging professional, has been known to deliver a new one the following day.

His standard procedure, however, is to work every night. "After feeling drowsy in the early evening, I get more and more creative as the night goes on. By dawn, I'm wildly creative; it gets stronger all the time." When inspiration is slow, he scans earlier notebooks and even old manuscripts to get ideas for new pieces. In *Mysterious Mountain*, for instance, is a fugue that Hovhaness found in a 1936 notebook. "Do you meditate?," I asked. "No, I'm too active. I take walks." When these stimulants fail, he spends the night doing mechanical chores, such as copying out previous scores for offset reproduction or publication. Since his regular copyist has recently been ill, he was currently concentrating on his last symphonies. Even at his age, Hovhaness works without eyeglasses but uses a magnifying glass when his eyes get tired. Thoroughly knowlegeable about his work, he never failed to identify the date and place of every composition I asked about. When I inquired about other things, his memory was less sure. Hovhaness is literally a music-making machine who lives for his inexhaustible work. "I really feel that I'm doing my best work now. I'm doing more than I've done in the past few years."

He does not intend his music to be programmatic, unless the piece has a verbal text with a particular subject. Just as most of his program notes are technically descriptive, most titles for his pieces define their instrumentation, and those titles that are evocative, such as *Mysterious Mountain*, are usually coined as an afterthought. (People frequently make the mistake of calling the latter "Magic Mountain," which is the name of a novel by

Thomas Mann.) These descriptive titles usually refer to something religious or natural. "Nature is my great inspiration," he once said, "and I've always regarded Nature as the clothing of God." One could characterize Hovhaness as a transcendental composer whose principal subject is spiritual experience, or, more precisely, musical experience as it approaches spiritual domains. He once wrote, "I have always experienced from earliest childhood the sensation of traveling great distances out into the universe on what seemed like bridges or gossamer threads." That is the kind of experience, I sense, that Hovhaness wants to stimulate in his music.

Like nearly all extremely prolific composers, Hovhaness is also uneven. Typically, he is more interested in creating new works than in publicizing one or another of his previous pieces as a favorite. Nonetheless, his listeners make discriminations, his denigrators exploiting weaker works to dismiss him completely—an unfortunate practice; his advocates, like myself, claiming that *only the good ones count; the others are quickly forgotten.* To my mind, the very best Hovhaness pieces are *Khaldis* (op. 91, 1951); *Mysterious Mountain; Magnificat* (op. 157, 1958); and the *Saint Vartan* Symphony. All but the first are large, encompassing orchestral pieces with dramatic linear forms and rich arrangements. The last is structured like an opera with alternate textures, say, between solo arias by the trumpets and then choruses of brass instruments, as though both were operatic characters. It has marvelous instrumental writing, especially in the canons that get thicker and thicker and then thin out again. "It is like going through the universe," he remarked, "into a thick galaxy and then out the other side." He paused. "The title arose in the course of its composition for an Armenian occasion; the fifteen hundredth anniversary of Saint Vartan's death." One offshoot of his symphony was "an enormous amount of material for four trumpets," and the best of this surplus became the stunning, piano-accompanied canons of *Khaldis* (whose initial recording, now out of print, is superior to the one currently available). Few contemporary composers speak, as Hovhaness unashamedly does, of his own music as "beautiful," and indeed his best pieces are.

On second thought, a definitive critical assessment of Hovhaness is premature now. Some music is still unpublished; too much is rarely performed and never recorded. There is much, too much, that no one except the composer has heard. "He is a major composer in many senses," Lou Harrison told me recently. "He is a great melodist, which may arrive once every few centuries. He has a very fine sense of formal rhythm and exquisite tone color. He can produce sounds for an orchestra that very few composers can approximate. He is like Handel in this respect—an innate sense of the balance and beauty of sound." Harrison paused for breath. "He is one of my favorite composers and always has been." Henry Cowell once characterized Hovhaness's art as "moving, long-breathed music splendidly written and unique in style." John Cage, on the other hand, portrays Hovhaness as "a music tree who, as an orange or lemon tree produces fruit, produces music," which is Cage's way of saying that the music, while predictably sweet, does not confront issues outside itself. Because critical analyses of Hovhaness's music have been scandalously scanty, the most useful writings on the subject are his own, produced largely as program notes for specific compositions. As a professionally independent, awesomely prolific master of a basically traditional style, Hovhaness resembles another Armenian-American artist, the author William Saroyan.

Unlike nearly all composers of his generation, Hovhaness has lived almost entirely off his work. Back in the 1930s and 1940s he budgeted $40 a month and lived in a tiny single room. In New York, in the early 1950s, he began to receive commissions. Around 1959 he started to accumulate royalties from the sales of his sheet music, mostly to churchly amateurs. In his seventeen-page C. F. Peters royalty statement for 1975, nearly all of his 240 pieces sold that year, in amounts ranging from one copy (his Concerto for Accordion) to 5,620 copies of a four-page choral piece, "From the End of the Earth" (op. 187, but actually written in 1951). Since this work costs forty cents in the music stores, and the composer's royalty is ten percent of the list price, Hovhaness earned from his single most popular piece the whopping sum of $224.80, which scarcely pays a month's rent, even in south Seattle. The largest single amount from royalties alone was $311.40 for 1,038 copies of the vocal score of the *Magnificat*. The single piece earning the largest performance fees was *Meditation on Orpheus* (op. 155), which was played by both the New York Philharmonic and the San Francisco Symphony in 1975, thus amassing nearly a thousand dollars for the composer. In other words, Hovhaness's income comes in bits and pieces; but since he has by now produced so many pieces and bits, he is able to live comfortably off his work, or, more precisely, let his income from past music securely finance his present composing.

On the other hand his expenses are considerable. A large portion of his gross income goes to alimony. Much of the money he gets from commissions goes into copying the parts. "Two decades ago I got $500 for doing an hour-length work for chorus and small orchestra," he remembered, as a plane buzzed overhead, "but the copyist got $1,500." In recent years he has spent several thousand dollars annually on travel and roughly an equal amount on studio expenses for recording his own pieces, a few thousand for shipping and storage, and several hundred for postage stamps. Not unlike other serious artists, he spends too little money on himself and too much on his work. So, in addition to collecting royalties and performance fees, Hovhaness must conduct concerts (nearly always of his own music), visit universities, and accept commissions for new pieces, from an unsurpassed variety of patrons, including, in recent years, the International Center for Arid and Semi-Arid Land Studies at Texas Tech University for Symphony no. 24 and the Smithtown Central High School Symphonic Band for Symphony no. 23. Hovhaness has also become the subject of doctoral essays, most notably by Carl Gerbrant, a baritone who teaches at the Peabody Conservatory.

Not unlike other contemporary composers, Hovhaness discovered that most recordings of his work were going out of print and that many of his best pieces were not recorded at all. As his greatest wish is that his music be heard, he took the initiative himself. In the mid 1960s, he and Elizabeth Whittington, his wife at the time, founded Poseidon Records, initially to release tape transcriptions of his own performances, as pianist and/or conductor, that would not otherwise be publicly available. After a trial record in 1963 they began issuing a line that now contains seventeen items, including the best available recordings of both the *Saint Vartan* Symphony (Poseidon's best seller) and the *Magnificat.*

Initially, Poseidon printed 200 copies of each record, then 500, then 1,000; now they do 2,000. The records are manufactured in Allentown, Pennsylvania, by a firm that stores and mails them as well. Orders for the records are mailed to Poseidon Records, 888 Seventh Avenue, New York, New York 10019, and forwarded to Ms. Whittington, who then instructs the Allentown company to fill them. It is a simple operation, with no executives, no salesmen, no receptionists, and no advertising. It is also a persuasive model of what other contemporary composers could do for themselves. "We do not make money on this," she told me. "The main thing is to keep the music available for those who are really interested." Hovhaness is also thinking of forming a comparable company to publish scores of his that are not otherwise available.

I asked Hovhaness if he considered himself religious. "I feel closest to the reality of Shinto," he replied, "but my ancestral gods, or kami, are painters, writers, and musicians. I believe that composers can at times join heaven and earth—can join opposites. At certain times I have been seized by clairvoyance, but that is not a religious talent. I have also been given music suddenly, as in a very vivid dream." The finale of *Mysterious Mountain* was based on a two-stage psychic experience. "I dreamed the music and then woke up to write it down. And then I fell into another dream in which I corrected the parts." He paused. "It was a psychic experience of such strength that I would always leave the hall when it was played."

He then told me about his supernatural mental experiences—visionary, symbolic episodes, one of them drug-induced (under supervision)—which have informed his works. He once had a "vision of Prokofiev on a stage, talking to me. I had this vision just after his death. He predicted that I would write a ballet that would go around the world." And then Martha Graham asked Hovhaness to write one that did. "I once had a vision of Bartók's face on the back of my coat."

Pursuing this interest in his psychic powers, he has frequently consulted professional mediums, one of whom identified Hovhaness's earlier incarnation as "a 14th century Florentine, Atalante Migliorotti, who worked as a musician, perhaps a lute player, in Leonardo's household." He suspects that other past incarnations were Greek and Oriental. I asked if he had any premonition of future reincarnations. "No," he replied. "I have too much music to finish to worry about such things."

PHILIP GLASS

Back in 1970 Philip Glass realized that his music was too advanced for the commercial record companies at the time; so rather than restrict his performances to increasingly popular concerts, he decided to join the art dealer Klaus Kertess in founding a personal record label named Chatham Square, after the principal park in New York's Chinatown. The first record issued by Chatham Square Productions, Inc., was Glass's own *Music in Changing Parts* (1970), which soon became an underground classic that graced the collections of everyone interested in advanced American art and music. This new edition, produced from Glass's own master tapes, makes the exact same work more widely available.

At the time that *Music in Changing Parts* was originally written, Glass was moving out of one phase and into another. His initial music of distinction—a sequence of pieces that included *Strung Out, Music in Similar Motion, Music in Contrary Motion, Music in Fifths*—was monophonic. Like Gregorian chant, it had lines of individual notes, without either harmonies or counterpoint. These pieces were tonal without offering melodies; they were pleasant and accessible, without being seductive.

Such music then seemed unacceptably radical, as it avoided the principal issues that nearly all contemporary composers discussed in the 1960s—issues such as chance and control, serialism and atonality, improvisation and spontaneity. Indeed, given how different this work was, it is scarcely surprising that it was performed largely not in the standard concert halls or in the music conservatories but in art galleries, in art museums, and sometimes in churches.

Initially, the audience for Glass's music consisted largely of people connected to the New York avant-garde art world. Later, especially in Europe, his audience would include pop musicians like David Bowie and Brian Eno and, still later, music students. To this day, music conservatories and university music departments regard Glass as an errant ex-student, and only recently have some of the latter come to sponsor his concerts. "Even then," he mused, "the students come, while the professors stay away." At every step of his career Glass won his own audience of people not prejudiced by fashionable ideas of what should or should not be thought interesting in contemporary music. By now, he has the kind of loyal, expanding following that every advanced artist envies.

With *Music in Changing Parts,* Glass introduced music that moved progressively from monophony, in its opening moments, to a greater polyphonic complexity and then, toward its end, into the kinds of modulations that would inform his next major work, *Music in Twelve Parts* (1974), an exhaustive encyclopedic piece that epitomizes Glass's music in much the same way that *The Well-Tempered Clavier* (1744) epitomizes J. S. Bach's. Glass also remembers that *Music in Changing Parts* was the first piece of his that was long and weighty enough to fill an entire concert program; it was also the first ever to receive a favorable review—from Alan Rich, in *New York Magazine.*

It was also the first Glass work to be recorded, and through it the composer learned about the special advantages of records. "I began to see that it was a completely different medium from a live concert," he says.

> The record doesn't sound like what we were playing. It's a sixteen-track recording, which means that at the end of *Changing Parts* we're listening to eight flutes, five organs, two voices, and a piccolo. We have on the record something which I can never play in public with an ensemble of six or seven musicians. So I decided to exploit the medium and do things that I couldn't have done before. I wrote some new parts that I overdubbed. The tapings took about twenty hours, but three of us spent over two hundred hours mixing. That was the most crucial part, and it took us all winter. When it was finished, I said to a friend, "Maybe someone can do better, but I can't."

The son of a music-store proprietor, Glass was born in Baltimore, Maryland, January 31, 1937, 140 years to the day after Franz Schubert. As a child he studied flute at the local Peabody Conservatory and attended Baltimore City College, a selective, competitive boys high school comparable to Bronx Science in New York and the Boston Latin School. From working part-time in the family store, he can boast, "I grew up in the record business."

At fifteen, he skipped both his junior and senior years of high school by obtaining early admission to the University of Chicago, where he took a liberal arts degree. From there he moved to the Juilliard School, a highly professional New York conservatory, where he studied composition for four years; his classmates included two bright young men who would likewise become famous, if errant, composers—Peter Schickele ("P.D.Q. Bach") and Steve Reich. By most measures, Glass had the most elaborate and rigorous music education America could offer.

After a year as a Ford Foundation–supported composer-in-residence in the Pittsburgh school system, Glass received a Fulbright scholarship that took him to Paris for two years. Here he studied composition with the legendary Nadia Boulanger, who had previously taught a whole stream of American composers, including Aaron Copland, Virgil Thomson, Walter Piston, Roy Harris, and Elliott Carter. While in Paris, he also worked with Ravi Shankar, annotating a score for a film; and this experience prompted him to visit India before returning to the United States.

Once back in New York, Glass decided against pursuing the academic career for which his extended education had prepared him. Instead, he worked initially as an artist's helper and then as a plumber, a furniture mover, and a cab driver. In 1967 he founded the Philip Glass Ensemble with Steve Reich, Arthur Murphy, and himself playing keyboards, and both Jon Gibson and Dickie Landry playing horns. (Reich left in 1970 and Murphy a few years later, while new members have since been added. As the melodies of this music incorporate a strong rhythmic quality, Glass has never felt the need to add a percussionist.) By 1970 or so Glass had become, along with Reich and Terry Riley, a prominent exponent of what can most accurately be called *modular music*—music based upon comparatively elementary musical structures (*modules*) that are repeated and modified into surprisingly complex aural experiences.

The handwritten, photocopied score of *Music in Changing Parts* has eight lines of eighth notes, equally distributed over four staves, two in the treble (G) clef and two in the bass (F) clef. These lines are divided into eighty-eight numbered modules (or "figures" or "phrases"), which vary in length from eight to twenty-four eighth notes. Two parallel vertical lines separate each section from its predecessor and successor. At several points above the vertical lines are the letters *CF,* which indicate that at these points the *f*igures (parts) *c*hange drastically. There are no other markings on the score—nothing about interpretation, nothing about instrumentation, not even any indication about how long each section or the entire piece might be.

"It is an open score," Glass explains, reminding us of Bach's *Art of Fugue:* "I assign the parts." At the beginning of a performance, the group customarily plays only one and then two of the six lines; but as more of the scored lines are incorporated into the playing, the musical texture gets thicker. While the keyboards are playing the notated lines, the horns and the singer either duplicate the keyboards' riffs or improvise harmonically appropriate sustained tones for a long as possible. (That accounts for the long unwavering notes that are almost continually audible.)

Everyone *repeats* his part until Glass as the organist-conductor silently nods his head, which indicates that the current section must be repeated two more times before everyone goes onto the next notated module, which usually differs only slightly from its predecessor. (The exceptions are, of course, those modules following the CF notation.) Because Glass's nods are determined largely by how the piece feels in that performance, *Changing Parts* can vary enormously in total length—from one hour and ten minutes on the record to one hour and forty-five minutes in other performances.

Glass has been known to speak of this early piece as "intentionless music," by which he means that it does not program "a calculated effect. It does not paint a picture." One could also describe it as *pure music*, as abstract painting is pure, in representing nothing other than musical sound itself. As music about music, these pieces exist primarily as sounds in euphonious combination. This explains why this music is more present than symbolic and also why Glass's titles are characteristically more descriptive than evocative.

However, one difference between *Changing Parts* and the earlier monophonic works is that the composer is, as he says, "less interested in the purity of form than in the psychoacoustical experiences that happen while listening to the music. Music is able to create emotional content because of the ways in which the language is built," he continued, rephrasing his idea for emphasis. "Emotional content is built into the language of music. Musical grammar has always been responsive to physiology."

Part of this emotional impact comes from the fact that, in concert, Glass's music is customarily played quite loud, and one member of the ensemble, Kurt Munkasci, sits in front of the group, facing them, much like the conductor in conventional music. Actually, he is "playing" the knobs of his electronic keyboard to ensure that the group's sound is both loud and free of distortion. Glass recommends that his records be played loudly, or be heard over earphones. "It brings out the psychoacoustical phenomena that are part of the content of the music—overtones, undertones, difference tones. These are things you hear—there is no doubt that you are hearing them—even though they may not actually be played."

In the past decade, Glass has since progressed into other music, not only *Music in Twelve Parts,* soon to be issued as a six-record set, but also the music for the great contemporary opera, *Einstein on the Beach* (1976), and more recently the music for an opera titled *Satyagraha* and based upon Mahatma Gandhi's early years. His current major project is a third opera, which he regards as completing the trilogy begun with *Einstein.* Just as the titles of his works are now different in kind, so his latest music is different in style. "I'm now more involved," he explained succinctly, "with dramatic music that paints a picture that is overtly theatrical."

A slender, almost wiry man of medium height, with a familiar face and unusually close-cropped hair, Glass currently lives sparely with his young children Juliette and Zachary in the Gramercy Park area of New York. His living room contains not couches or coffee tables but rugs and a piano, a harpsichord, and an electric organ. Most of his composing is done on the last instrument, played in his stocking feet, and connected to the record-player's amplifier. His house has remarkably few records, fewer books, and even fewer scores. If the truth be known, Glass is not particularly interested in contemporary music and hears little of it, aside from rock. He paused, "The composers I studied with Boulanger are the people I still think about most—Bach and Mozart."

Ear, Heart, and Brain*

Michel P. Philippot
Translated by Geoffrey Smith

In this essay on the music of Milton Babbitt Michel Philippot deals with several aspects of the composer's oeuvre. Babbitt's musical system, his notion of composition, and his critical writings are all considered in an essay written to commemorate the composer's sixtieth birthday.

The author, born in France, is chairman of the music department of the Instituto de Artes do Planalto in São Bernardo do Campo, Brazil, and president of L'Académie Charles Gros. He has written articles for numerous publications and encyclopedias.

I sometimes consider not only music itself, but the position of music in our time as well, from the detached and analytical perspective of an ethnologist recently arrived from Mars, or perhaps even from Sirius, ignorant of all the manners and customs of our planet. The result of this kind of mental abstraction is an astonishment both amused and, shall I say, almost sardonic, for one is confronted with an incoherence so incomprehensible to a rational brain that any attempt at explanation is renounced. But this

* Reprinted from *Perspectives of New Music* (Spring–Summer 1976 and Fall–Winter 1976), pp. 45–60.

amusement is always short-lived, for, inexorably, I return to the awareness that I am a citizen of neither Mars nor Sirius, but indubitably of a planet called Earth. Then astonishment gives way to perplexity and the amusement becomes so sad that rage alone can scarcely divert it.

Nevertheless, the music of the twentieth century (I refer of course to that of the second half, indeed of the last quarter of the century) is alive and well, but, paradoxically, little is said about it. Meanwhile, a great deal is said about certain manifestations that our philosophers and critics persist in calling "music," but what is the point?

I know that in denying the name of *music* to what I have designated as "certain manifestations" I am placing myself immediately in a polemical position. Therefore I am anxious to declare at the outset that the goal of this position is not essentially to stigmatize certain errors or aberrations, but on the contrary to pay homage to those who, against the tide of opinion, persist in maintaining and defending the highest idea and loftiest ambitions of true music—that work of the brain illuminated by the heart that, through the medium of the ear, unites other hearts and brains. *Milton Babbitt* is one of these.

Certainly such a stance can seem proud, perhaps even haughty. It is nonetheless disinterested. Those who adopt it obviously do not refuse success; but their success, when it comes, *can only* be an additional reward, a sort of bonus whose pursuit was not their principal objective. Of course it is an attitude to which the world is sometimes (or even frequently) hostile, compelling those involved to engage in combat on their own behalf, using the weapons of mediocrity. But these weapons wound precisely only the mediocre; they never recoil against the work itself, whose essential value would be degraded by an anxiety to please, surprise, or astonish. History abounds with examples of musicians whose human character was sometimes suspect, Lully or Wagner among others, but this attitude never resulted in the sacrifice, to the public or the ignorant, of the supreme greatness of their work. Thus there exists, in every creator worthy of the name, one of the forms of that sublime detachment which caused the mathematician Jacobi to say that he worked only "for the honor of the human brain." This in itself is enough to disconcert fools, and nothing is more understandable: since they have no brain, what would we be working for?

But before attempting to describe the reasons that make me approve a musical demeanor like that of Milton Babbitt, it seems useful to depict, even briefly, the set of errors that I disapprove. A good part of them appear to me to proceed not from romanticism itself, but from the tendencies it inspired through a facile literature and a dubious philosophy. I should explain, and I shall do so by means of a quotation from a true and great musician, the meaning of which, alas, is apparently forgotten by those who wish to call themselves his followers. "One has a great deal of ear," said Robert Schumann, "when one lacks heart." This was his wise and generous warning to a sterile academicism. But I am tempted to reverse the question and put it in the following terms: could it not be said that one claims to "have heart" simply in order to conceal an obvious lack of ear, to which it is appropriate to add a lack of intelligence and imagination. To give substance to a question of this nature—which, according to humor and temperament, one can find either amusing or distressing—a few descriptions will suffice, in the course of which persons and events, completely concrete and materially existent, will be easily recognized. In other words, resemblances will not be coincidental. The fact that I refrain (only here and for the time being) from citing directly the names of the individuals evoked should be attributed to the fact that I am anxious to combat false ideas, not to wound the persons who indulge in them.

These descriptions could be lengthy; therefore I shall try to abridge them. Moreover I believe that they can be, *grosso modo,* divided into only two categories.

We shall place in the first category everything that seems derived from the vulgarization and misunderstanding of the romantic idea of "inspiration." Although I do not deny the existence of such a phenomenon (as there is a kind of exaltation in creative work), its perversion led rapidly to an almost total rejection of the claims of intelligence and true imagination. Obviously too much time would be required to describe in detail the processes that gradually produced a veritable nihilism in music. It will be enough for us to identify some significant stages.

The adventure begins in an almost amusing manner, by a basic distortion of values whose mathematical justification could have been demonstrated and utilized if those professing them had been less ignorant. I want to speak of a certain capacity of *combinatoriality.* To do so I must cite a specific example that, while not constituting in itself a genuine distortion of values, must be seen as its source: Stockhausen's *Klavierstück* no. 11. We know that in this piano piece nineteen elements, each, in the terms of traditional music, two "measures" long, can be played according to the taste or humor of the interpreter in the order that suits him, with, eventually, certain repetitions. Consequently, *in theory,* the number of possible different versions would be at least 19 factorial (19!), thus: 121,645,100,408,832,-000; which means that should we wish to hear the complete set of possible versions, we should have to allow around 2,313 billion years, or about 193 times the period presumed by the most competent astrophysicists and cosmologists to have elapsed from the primitive "big bang" to the present state of the universe in which we live. But fortunately (or, for the author, unfortunately) the musical reality is there to reassure us: hearing the work three or four times shows us clearly that it always comes to the same thing. The combinatorial richness, poorly understood, is thus reduced to an unquestionable poverty. However, the results of an equally naïve combinatoriality have had much graver consequences.[1]

These consequences were produced by a sort of extrapolation of the romantic view of other people. In effect, when an interpreter could choose any one of the 121,645,100,408,832,000 possible versions of a work, an illusion was fostered making him a sort of coauthor, a "participant" in the creative act. In addition, as the form of the interpretation was *apparently* unpredictable for both composer and listeners, one proceeded to invoke what was falsely taken to be chance, thus giving birth to the notion of "aleatory" music. It is obviously easy to demonstrate that genuine chance did not enter into the result because the latter was still the expression of a *human choice*.[2] But this choice was displaced, transferred from the composer to the interpreter. Then there was a great temptation (too great to be resisted) to pass from an individualist romanticism to a psychosociological one. The dream of this romanticism is a sort of collective spontaneous creation in which the composer no longer intervenes except as a kind of re-agent, a catalytic force stimulating a musical act in others in the guise of a noble invitation to his fellow man to "participate."[3] The logical consequences of such an attitude were easy to predict and the verified results conform to the predictions: tedious and interminable sessions of collective improvisation, the pretentious laziness of the so-called composer who no longer writes anything but a few signs without musical significance merely to "suggest" hypothetical intentions, incantations by gesture and pantomime, the disposition to consider as music any combination of sounds whatever, even fortuitous—and finally, the disappearance of the composer,

---

[1] The example of a naïve combinatoriality has already been given to us by Molière in the seventeenth century. In *Le Bourgeois Gentilhomme* he conceives the following phrase: "Fair lady, your beautiful eyes make me die of love," which would become: "Die fair your beautiful lady make me eyes of love,"...!!!

[2] It has been demonstrated, notably by the mathematician E. Borel, that man is wholly incapable of imitating chance. At most he can "re-create" it by calculation.

[3] I have often met so-called composers who wanted in this way to get performers to "participate" in their pieces. But I have *never* met any who offered to share their copyrights with them.

preceding, naturally, that of music. Indeed, one of the most famous practi-tioners of this type of degeneracy has asserted that, to make a comparison with the art of cinematography, it was his (modest?) ambition not to be the author of a film, but to build the camera with which the film was made![4]

I shall mention only for the sake of memory one other of the ridicu-lous effects of misunderstood romanticism: the composer ceases, ipso facto, to be the conscientious intellectual worker, respectful of his art and ambi-tious for the elevation of his thought, and imagines himself (because, sup-posedly, he provides a musical response in others out of anything) a sort of *deus ex machina* of universal inspiration. An unbearable megalomania proceeds from this, variously garbed but sometimes approaching lunacy. For example, one of these ex-composers seriously affirms that he is blessed by contacts with extraterrestrials and has written a work in which the tele-pathic communications between the players make up—if not happily, at least comically—for the indigence of the rudimentary score.[5]

The second category of errors that I disapprove, because in my view they are detrimental to music itself, is of a less irritating nature but shows itself to be the central impulse of an equally great number of dangers. I wish to examine what I shall call *acoustical illusions.* Here also it is appro-priate that I explain myself.

Since the appearance of the first electronic musics, *concrètes* or elec-troacoustical in general, the attractive and novel sonorities that technology offered composers had a profoundly seductive effect on the musician's ear. Indeed this was normal and understandable, but for various reasons, among which surprise and sensory charm play a great part, purely aural pleasure came to be confused with musical perception. By way of confir-mation I can cite one of the most celebrated theoreticians of musics for tape who declared: "a beautiful sound is already music." It is useless to want to refute such a point of view. To show its inconsistency it is enough to transpose it to another art and say, for example: "a beautiful color is al-ready a painting" or even "a beautiful typographical character is already a novel." What is serious is the fact that a purely acoustical technique could be taken, and is still taken, for a true compositional activity. Not to be misunderstood, I want to make clear that I have the greatest esteem and admiration for all those who, with indisputable skill, advance our knowl-edge in the area of general-, physiological-, and electroacoustics. But if I

---

[4] If one follows closely this kind of person's argument, one wonders why, remaining in his own field rather than seeking a comparison in cinema, he is not satisfied to manu-facture the pencils and paper for music?
[5] I am obviously prepared to cite names and specific instances of these extravagances.

regard their work as useful and even indispensable for the development of music, in no way do I confuse it with that of the composer worthy of the name. Thus I have for these investigators the same respect and admiration I have, for example, for Stradivarius, who was also a sublime creator of sounds. But if it is of the same degree, this admiration is of a wholly different nature from that which I still feel, for example, for Johann Sebastian Bach. Consequently, the danger to which I wish to alert my reader is that of accepting or fostering the illusion that an incoherent sequence of sounds, agreeable in themselves, could be music.

To sum up, we are thus confronted by three perils: the *purely* aural pleasure, which is *not yet* music; the *purely* affective pleasure, or pleasure of the heart,which leads to the most incredible aberrations; and the pleasure *purely* of the brain, which would be nothing but a sterile academicism. These are the perils that Milton Babbitt has managed to avoid.

When, in the 1950s, Milton Babbitt began to work on the Mark II Synthesizer at the David Sarnoff Laboratories in Princeton, he had the wisdom not to indulge in the illusion that the wealth of sonorities offered to him by this new instrument were in themselves solutions to a creative activity that they would automatically renew or even enrich. Being a true composer, he realized that the acquisition of new means for the production and control of sounds certainly provided him with new materials, but that these materials became true values only insofar as they were *organized* toward the *construction* of a musical work. This priority of organization over sensation, of logic and coherence over the empirical and improvisatory, protected him at the outset from one of the perils we have mentioned above—knowing a method of satisfying the ear *alone* which is not and cannot yet be music, although it is indispensable to music's subsequent constitution. In short, Milton Babbitt avoided confusing the whole with one of its parts.

It remains for us to examine the area in which Milton Babbitt's work, both musical and theoretical, is most instructive: the dialectic—not the contradiction—so often evoked by critics of music between the heart and the brain.[6]

Such an examination proceeds by a detour (which will be both slight and brief) where I shall note, without for the moment analyzing, what appears to be one of the constants of Western thought and civilization: the pursuit and existence of what could be called *mathematical models.* Long

---

[6] This subject has been magnificently dealt with by Schönberg in the chapter of his work *Style and Idea* titled "Heart and Brain in Music."

before our present inquiry Charles Lalo (the son of the composer of *Le Roi d'Ys* and *Namouna,* not to mention a famous Concerto for Violoncello), who was at the time professor of aesthetics at the Sorbonne, declared: "Music is, of all human activities, one of the foremost in which mathematics has found its application."[7] Even earlier Leibniz affirmed that "all music is an unconscious calculation"; and earlier still, what would we say of the Pythagorean theories? But it must be said that frequently in the course of music, mathematical models—whose permanence it is possible to demonstrate—were perceived unconsciously by composers, that is, in a form which *seemingly* was not mathematical. Thus, to take an example that should be more well known than it is, the rules of classical and romantic harmony (after the work of the great eighteenth-century theoreticians like Rameau and d'Alembert) were applied by the enormous majority of composers in total ignorance of the physicomathematical bases that produced them and, a fortiori, without suspecting for an instant that these rules could be formalized later to the point of being followed by a computer as well as a student in a harmony or counterpoint class.[8]

Having made this detour, or rather this observation, on the permanence of the idea of the mathematical model, it is easier to describe the essence of what, to Milton Babbitt, constitutes a musical system.

In any period of the history of music (except perhaps our own) one has generally tended to believe that the customary musical system, that is, the set of rules followed by the composer, was a natural and almost permanent feature of music itself. In other words, it seemed impossible, almost inconceivable, to make music by utilizing means markedly different from those that were habitually employed. As our music is evolutionary in nature, however, the means employed changed relatively rapidly; however, these changes were attributed not to the profound nature of music but to the imagination, indeed, to the caprice of innovators who surrendered themselves to an act whose nature was arbitrary and willful. It is well known that such innovators, those whose genius we now recognize, were always violently criticized at the very moment they offered us the most beautiful jewels of their imagination. Among them, the most recent—and one, moreover, who always considered himself an active craftsman rather than a revolutionary, almost the guardian of an evolving tradition—is, obviously, Arnold Schönberg.

---

[7] In Charles Lalo, *Elements d'une Esthétique Musicale Scientifique.*
[8] Which was demonstrated by Hiller and Isaacson in the U.S., P. Barbaud in France, and Zaripov in the U.S.S.R.

It is a body of work like Schönberg's and more generally, the set of possibilities offered by the serial system of twelve-tone composition, that led Milton Babbitt to ponder not only the formal properties of such a method of composition but those that he calls a *musical system*. In any musical system there always exists a set of rules, that is to say, of constraints, more or less cleverly exploited by the composer, by which relations are established between the sonorous elements. These relations always are (or always should be) perceptible by the listener (or a listener), and it is precisely their perception that gives music its logical, coherent character. In the musical system now being considered—that of composition "with twelve tones"—the relations between the sonorous elements (the notes) are of a nature such that, imposed by the "series," they represent a very great potential for coherence. The danger in such a great potential is that of academicism (or perhaps I should say "neo-academicism"), of which one knows numerous examples. But the advantage is the preservation of a *minimum* degree of logic in musical discourse. Establishing, therefore, the permanent existence of relations between the tones, two ideas can be put forward, as was actually done by Milton Babbitt. The first is that musics like those of Schönberg and Webern, seen from a historical point of view, do not appear as negations or contradictions of earlier musics, but rather as points of departure for new musics in a spirit of *continuity,* in the traditional sense of the term. The second is that a musical system does not contain, in and of itself, any kind of universal truth. It involves theories constructed from certain hypotheses whose origins are habitually discovered in the ideas tacitly and almost unanimously admitted by a sociocultural community and whose application constitutes at once an experiment and a proof.

Consequently, for Milton Babbitt, creation, or the invention of a musical system, is already an act of composition. Personally, I should prefer that this creation, or invention, be considered less an *act* of composition than an indispensable preliminary, a condition absolutely necessary though not sufficient for the eventual act of composition. But, before discussing some of Milton Babbitt's ideas, I should at least conclude my examination of their essential characteristics.

Thus, in a spirit totally different from that of Pierre Boulez, Babbitt speaks of *total serialization.*[9] This does not signify that serial combinatoriality must be applied to each one of the components of sound, but that

---

[9] Boulez's idea of *generalized series* consists in applying the serial system not only to the pitches but to all the components of sound, for example, volume, duration, and timbre.

the idea of *series,* even independently from that of the "total chromaticism" it had implied in a recent period of its historical development, was,
if only slightly generalized, one of the constants of the history of music. In
other words, there can be no true musical composition without the existence of rules and constraints, and these rules and constraints, specifying a
degree of invariance in the relations between sonorous events, tacitly imply
the notion of *series.* To repeat that this notion of series becomes independent of that of total chromaticism is to realize, finally, that all music can be
only *serial* or *badly constructed.*

Generalized in this manner the idea of *series* leads naturally to that of
structure. Of course it is proper at first, in order to avoid the most obvious
misconceptions, to define this idea, and an abbreviated account will suffice. The idea of structure implies the existence of a *set* (in the mathematical sense of the term) and the existence of a *relation* applicable to all the
elements of this set, taken in pairs at least, with the existence of an *operation* (or law of internal composition, still in the mathematical sense) by
which one or several elements of the set correspond to two or more of its
elements when they are combined (composed) with each other.

It is easy to show that when Milton Babbitt compares the notion of
composition (musical) to the creation and enactment of a *total structure,* he
is absolutely right. In fact, we do indeed ascertain the existence of a set
(that of the sounds with which one is going to make music) and similarly
the existence of relations between these sounds (for example, a *relation of
degree* from flat to sharp, with regard to pitch) with, furthermore, the existence of operations that enable these sounds to combine with each other.

On the one hand, therefore, we can imagine, or appreciate, how much
the logic and coherence of musical discourse depend on the existence or
nonexistence of a *structure* and, on the other, how many compositional resources depend on the structure's richness, plasticity, and level of complexity. From a purely experimental point of view, Milton Babbitt thus
verifies the existence of a certain number of criteria by which the effectiveness of a musical system could be evaluated, including: (1) the structure
of the given musical system itself, (2) the compositional resources contained in the scope of that structure, and (3) the musical realizations actually produced when the system is applied (although these realizations are
also a function of an immeasurable factor, which is the individual talent of
the composer).

In the course of this discussion (which I have purposely and considerably simplified to avoid lengthy and tedious explication) two notions
emerge that I consider fundamental. The first is the concept of *combina-*

torial power, the second that of *segmental invariance.* The first guarantees richness but does not protect against the danger of incoherence; the second ensures coherence but not security from the poverty of academicism. Only the equilibrium of these two notions, permitting the constitution of a genuine "formal grammar," a *syntactical level of music structure,* can be the source of a genuine music.

If I began this article by castigating a lack of intelligence concealed by the irrational desire exclusively to satisfy the *ear* and the *heart,* it was to contrast these precise excesses with the body of musics worthy of the name and to show that, contrary to the belief resulting from a degenerate romanticism that would wish to oppose the *heart* and *brain,* the first can only be enlivened by the second.

The moment has now come to affirm that, although the word *mathematics* inspires a sort of fear in those who misunderstand its real nature, throughout the history of music mathematical models have been a powerful instrument for the development of the musical imagination, and even a constant resource for the enrichment of intuition.

I should like now to develop certain ideas that, whether they are directly discussed or implicitly suggested in Milton Babbitt's critical writings, appear to me, rightly or wrongly, to be central to his thought and, on the other hand, to belong to what I will call the *common domain* of the various possible theories of music. As Milton Babbitt is also himself a mathematician, I hope he will not be too offended if, carried away by my imagination, I sometimes seem to go beyond his own ideas. In doing so I do not intend any self-aggrandizement but simply wish to make my own contribution to the development of essential research.

Several reflections arise at the outset with regard to the capacity of this notion of combinatoriality. It is evident that any given musical sequence can be regarded and analyzed as one of the possible combinations of elements of a basic set (referential set), which (though this is a simplification), if we take into account only the pitches (or frequencies), will be the set of the notes of the chromatic scale. The most naïve and most commonly held idea is that of limiting this combinatoriality to the set of permutations (factorials) of the twelve elements, thus: $12!=479,001,600$ possible series. This is to commit a slight error of excess and a gigantic error of default. First, the error of excess results from forgetting that each one of the transpositions of a series is musically similar to the original series, and that consequently, because each possible series possesses twelve transpositions, the total number must be divided by twelve; from which the number of possible series is no longer 12! but only 11!; thus "only" 39,916,800. But the error of default is much more considerable, for, following this line of reasoning, it would be necessary to envisage not the number of possible *dodecaphonic series* but the number of possible *melodies* (without taking into account the diverse *harmonic* situations of these melodies). Because, in a melody, a note can be prolonged or repeated as much as one wishes, the problem becomes different: it is no longer that of the number of possible permutations but that of the number of words that it is possible to construct with a given alphabet. The general solution of this problem is well known: the number of words of n letters that it is possible to construct with an alphabet of M letters is equal to M^n (M to the power n); which is to say that the melodies of twelve notes that one can conceive with the chromatic scale (which contains twelve notes as well) is of the order 12^{12}, thus 896,-100,448,000 or 18,614 times more than the number of series envisaged in the most "optimistic" situation, that is, without taking transpositions into account. As no rule in the world forbids, nor could forbid, a composer to conceive melodies of more than twelve notes, it is easy to imagine to what dizzying numbers musical combinatoriality can lead.

Consequently, the crucial problem of such a combinatoriality is not that of its "anarchic" liberation but, very much to the contrary, that of fixing its *limits,* which are the conditions *necessary* (although still not *sufficient*) to promote a minimum of coherence. When, for example, Schönberg expounds the idea by which there are forty-eight possible forms of the series—that is, the original form, the inversion, the retrograde, and the retrograde inversion, each one transposed twelve times from each of the twelve notes of the chromatic scale—he fixes a *limit* to the set of possible permutations. In the same way, when Boulez constructs his theory of *generalized series* he fixes a *limit* to the set of permutations of volumes, durations, and timbres. Therefore, although conceived intuitively by each one of these composers, the idea of *musical system* appears as absolutely primary.

Properly considered then, the idea of *musical system* is equivalent to that of *structure* in the mathematical sense of the term. In effect, like *structure,* the musical system is an *organization* and not a pseudoliberation of the combinatorial richness. From this, the evaluation of the richness or poverty of a musical system, as Milton Babbitt performs it, becomes analogous to the treatment of a logical system in mathematics: it is proportional to the potential results that can be obtained from it.

But as this notion of structure is manifest in the thought of Milton Babbitt, even sometimes only implicitly, I should like to develop it here, not as far as one could extend it, but as far as I can for the time being.

When he declares, for example, that transposition can be compared to the arithmetical operation of addition, he is completely right. To realize this, we need only designate each one of the notes of the chromatic scale by the number of its degree, from *1* to *12* (as Jean-Jacques Rousseau had already conceived), to find that any note thus designated is transposed when any other number is added to it. For example, if by convention we number the notes of the scale from 0 to 11—0 representing C, 1 as C-sharp, 2 as D, and so on in sequence until 11, which would represent B—it is easy to see that the *1*(C-sharp) + 3(the interval of a minor third) yield *4* = E. But it is possible to take this mathematical comparison of transposition and addition a great deal further. In fact if, in conformity with human auditory sensations, we regard the interval of the octave as a similitude much more than a difference, the set of the notes represented by the numbers of their degree can be compared to the set of integers modulo 12. This means that, being congruent to 12, each of the numbers representing notes, whatever the octave in which they occur, can be designated (apart from the index of the octave) by a number between 0 = C and 11 = B. From which it results that we are, mathematically speaking, in the presence of a *group structure:* the group of integers modulo 12, produced by the operation of addition.[10] It is easy to demonstrate this:

1. Every element of the group combined with another yields as a result an element of the set (that of the integers modulo 12); for example, $9 (= A) + 4 (= E =$ a major third$) = 13;$ this 13, congruent to 12, yields $13 - 12 = 1 =$ C-sharp. An *internal* operation is certainly involved.

2. A neutral element exists, which is the unison = 0.

3. Every element possesses its own symmetry; that is, $8 + 4 = 12 = 0;$ or, as well, $5 + 7 = 12 = 0,$ in the set of integers modulo 12.

4. Finally, addition being commutative in this precise case, a *commutative or Abelian* group is certainly involved.

Curiously enough, when one wants to produce this commutative group by an operation other than that of addition, for instance by multiplication, it becomes a subgroup of the preceding one. For example, multiplication by two transforms it into whole-tone scales, by three into diminished-seventh chords, by four into augmented fifths, and so on, until multiplication by eleven, transforming the intervals by their symmetrical elements, yields the exact inversion.

When the commutative group is produced by exponentiation, an in-

---

[10] Pierre Barbaud was the first to have this idea of *group structure.*

teresting phenomenon occurs (although still perfectly explicable, arithmetically speaking): raised to an even power, the set of integers modulo 12 becomes the sequence 0, 1, 4, 9, 4, 1, 0; or the chord C, C-sharp, E, A, which, put in the order C-sharp, E, A, C, is a nontonal chord par excellence and, significantly, one of the chords preferred by Webern and the basic chord of Schönberg's *Ode to Napoleon*. Raised to an odd power, one encounters a "mode of limited transposition" (cf. Messiaen), that is, the chromatic scale without the chord of the augmented fifth (D, F-sharp, B-flat).

Incidentally, the set of notes of the chromatic scale can be redistributed into various subsets, which are modes, scales, and chords. It is easy to show that in the tonal system the set of notes that make up a scale (for example, in C major: 0, 2, 4, 5, 7, 9, 11) is not a subgroup of the group of transpositions, any more than the majority of chords. But here it is important to observe that the only chords that do constitute a subgroup of the group of transpositions are precisely those that Schönberg called "indeterminate chords," that is, those that refer to several tonalities at once, like, for instance, the diminished seventh.

From another point of view if, still in the tonal system, one considers the set of tonalities, either of the major or the minor mode, it is seen that the set of *tonalities* (but no longer the set of *notes*) produced by the operation of addition (transposition) is a group as well. Conversely, prior to the establishment of the tonal system, when music was based on *modes,* the set of modes could not constitute a group.

There are some other interesting observations still to be made on chords or melodic motives in general. These are obviously elements of the set of subsets. It is easy to compare these subsets with each other and to class them according to the force of their intersections when they are taken two by two (the number of notes in common). It would appear then that what would be called "strong or weak progressions" in traditional tonal harmony corresponds to the greater or lesser force of the intersections. When, for example, the intersection is an empty set (meaning there are no notes in common), the progression is particularly "strong," even dangerous from the point of view of harmonic academicism.

Thus the preceding considerations illuminate, in a completely new light, the notion of musical system as Milton Babbitt had conceived it, particularly with the idea of evaluating the different resources of a given system. In effect, everything has happened as if, beginning with the *modes* of medieval and Renaissance counterpoint, then passing through the *tonal* system and its progressive evolution to arrive at the serial system of *twelve-tone composition,* and finally a conception of *total serialization,* we were witnessing a power to generalize systems that would be in a state of constant growth. In particular, we are seeing affirmed and extended, in the technique of mathematically analyzed musical composition, the power of *group structure.* But the richness of such a structure is well known, and with it, the resources of musical systems—their possibilities for supporting a musical coherence and its levels of complexity—would theoretically follow an expanding curve; at least to the extent that the errors and aberrations we spoke of at the beginning of this essay would be avoided.

But if the increased complexity that we have just noted were not rigorously controlled, we should witness the fatal transformation of *complexity* into *complication,*[11] that is to say, that, far from seeing the possibilities of coherence multiply, we should see them diminish, then disappear (which has effectively happened to the musics we described at the outset). Of necessity then, something invariant must exist in the evolution of music, something that would be as common to the first *organa* of the Middle Ages as to the counterpoint of the Renaissance, to romantic symphonies, to the music of Schönberg or Webern . . . or indeed to that of Milton Babbitt.

Apparently, the quest for an invariance throughout the history of music, whose manifestations down the ages have been so varied and different, does not seem an easy thing. Nevertheless it will be sufficient for us to pursue, by the same methods, the type of reasoning we have hitherto employed, which led us to discover the importance of group structure.

Unless the number of elements in a set is very small (which is not the case in music where the number of notes, volumes, timbres, durations, etc., is extensive), a combinatoriality does not enable us to discover sequences of elements that are *orderly* in the broadest sense of the term, that is to say, *coherent.* Combinatoriality enables us only to apprehend the considerable richness, the variety of possible sequences whose number is intuitively inaccessible for the human brain. As we noted above, it is *essential* to limit this combinatoriality. Thus we can declare, a priori, that the rules of a given musical system are precisely the means by which limits are fixed. We

---

[11] The difference between the notion of *complexity* and that of *complication* can be explained with the aid of the following image: let us suppose a certain number of elements in a set (points, for example) distributed in a given space. If these points are distributed at random, a very great quantity of information will be needed to describe the position of each one of them, hence the *complication* of our set. If, on the contrary, relations exist between each of the points, it will be possible for us to deduce the position of one of them by knowing the position of one or several others. We shall need a certain amount of information (perhaps still very great) to describe the relations that will enable us to deduce the positions (without supplementary information). In this second case, our set possesses *complexity.*

have already verified the existence of a progressively appearing group structure, employed constantly but unconsciously by musicians. Such a structure already guarantees a minimum *level of musical organization,* but this is wholly insufficient. In reality the group structure could be compared to a sort of envelope in which could be placed specific rules promoting logic and coherence. To understand this more clearly let us make a comparison with written language, or rather with the set of languages written with the Latin alphabet.

This alphabet, considered as a set of 27 elements (for it must not be forgotten that the inverval between words is itself an element of the set), is equally capable of being produced by an operation that we will name *addition* in the set of integers modulo 27, which will similarly furnish it with a group structure. But supplementary and indispensable rules exist that will provide that the combinations of the elements of this *group* will be words or phrases in English, French, Italian, Latin, etc. Although difficult to define, these supplementary rules can be quantitatively measured. Such a *quantitative* measurement—which one must confess is incapable of yielding any *qualitative* evaluation—is possible using mathematical methods we lack the time to expound here, but which are derived from those employed in information theory. By analogy, this measurement applies itself very well to combinations of musical elements: for example, motives of melody, harmony, volume, duration, timbre, etc. It gives us a quite satisfactory *quantitative* appreciation of the *constraints* that set some precise limits to a combinatoriality that without these limits could be called "lawless."

Thus, one thing appears obvious in the history of music: the quantity of constraints (or rules) remains constant, while the nature of these constraints (or rules) changes according to periods and musical styles. Consequently, the idea of segmental invariance discovered by Milton Babbitt in relation to twelve-tone composition can in reality be applied to any system of composition whatever, as the sole and unique condition that a minimum of coherence be sought. Therefore, the truth of the following postulate (sometimes mistakenly called a theorem) is demonstrated: "the coherence of a given musical system of any kind is proportional to the *quantity* of its *constraints,* but independent of their *natures.*"[12]

In considering the work of Milton Babbitt, we have brought up certain problems and suggested certain reflections that no doubt went beyond his

---

[12] This postulate is known under the name of "Philippot's theorem"; I beg the reader's pardon for citing myself in this way.

own thought. It is my profound wish that in doing so I have not run the risk of betraying that thought, even if I have yielded to the desire, not to surpass it but, to complete it with my own. Therefore I hope that he will pardon me, and would dedicate to him, by way of conclusion, only this quotation from Leonardo da Vinci, in whom, beyond any doubt, the *senses, heart,* and *brain* were combined to realize one of the greatest bodies of human achievement:

> Whoever does not appreciate the sublime certitude of mathematics is repaid with confusion, and will never reduce to silence the chattering of the sophists whose noise is perpetual.

Schönberg—Yesterday, Today, and Tomorrow*

Josef Rufer

Translated by William Drabkin

*Arnold Schönberg is, perhaps, best known for his development of the twelve-tone method of composition. However, as the author of the following essay points out, "Underlying Schönberg's twelve-tone music . . . is a musical in-*spiration, *thus an unconscious act."*

The background for Schönberg's approach, his place in the recent history of music, and his relationship to the masters of the eighteenth and nineteenth centuries are discussed in this essay by the editor of the complete edition of Schönberg's works.

Anyone for whom music is not merely a gourmet's treat, but an art that consists essentially of ideas, will want to provide himself from time to time with an overview of the state and development of the music of our time. And he will probably surrender, at first, to the confusing aspects of mutually contradictory or overlapping tendencies, directions, and opinions with

* Reprinted from *Perspectives of New Music*, 14, no. 1 (Fall–Winter 1977), pp. 125–138.

which we are confronted verbally as well as musically. Tonal music versus nontonal music, polytonal versus twelve tone, serial versus aleatory—or whatever the latest rage is called (although often it is no longer the latest rage by the time it is disseminated): are these concepts reducible in any way to a common denominator: music? Music, which is the resounding of the spirit, the documentation of creative fantasy, and which (as Schönberg profoundly expressed) depicts the unconscious nature of these and other worlds; are we not merely talking around it when we seize it and try to bring ourselves closer with the aid of stylistic and technical terms, when we establish, as criteria for evaluation, such completely external characteristics as style and itemized contents, the recognition of which is certainly not art? Unfortunately, such superficial judgments have become increasingly common. That these remain superficial in nature can be recognized with a minimum of knowledge. And so music is no longer weighed, but labeled and catalogued instead. The newer, the better—this has become the sole criterion. It is the same hectic stampede forward that we have been able to observe for a long time in painting and literature. It destroys the spiritual continuity and organic growth from yesterday to today. It consciously rules out even tradition, and thus the confrontation with tradition that had always been the unquestioned custom in the past, with every master of every era. Hence there follows a paucity of tradition and consequently the loss of all standards of measure. The only standard that remains, then, is the obsession with being modern or ultramodern: originality at any price, even at that of music itself. But are tradition and originality actually incompatible opposites? Before we attempt to find an answer to this question, which might provide a way out of today's dilemma, let me address myself to the other side of this issue of the deterioration of musical culture—the effect on the listener. The present method of labeling music obviates all need to arrive at one's own judgment. Even before hearing a piece the listener knows whether or not he is going to like it, depending on his own attitudes, tastes, and demands—in short, on his own musical education as a prerequisite to these things. This education is the basis of all musical culture per se, and I should not be so presumptuous in speaking of its deterioration had not truly qualified people been warning of it for quite some time. In his *Zeitgemässe Glossen für Erziehung zur Musik* and again in a later communication, *Über das humanistische Gymnasium* (1945), Richard Strauss called for a comprehensive reform of the musical education of our youth, the concert- and operagoers of the future. He wrote: "Wherein consists the so-called artistic enjoyment for the majority of these listeners? In a purely sensuous 'feast for the ears,' in no way impaired by understanding."

Strauss went on to compare the "so-called appreciative audience" with the ten-year-old child who watches a performance of *Wallenstein* in Chinese translation, and then he states clearly what is to be done:

> When the graduate is able to read Homer or Horace in the original, once he is in a position to understand *Wahlverwandtschaften* or *Faust* as an Englishman can understand *Hamlet,* once he also understands a Beethoven symphony, a Mozart quintet, or a *Meistersinger* or *Tristan* prelude in all it profoundness, and has learned to appreciate the architecture of these sound structures in their full magnitude and to read the language of these musical symbols, then will his intellectual preparation have acquired all of the fundamentals that can enable him to accomplish the most, in accordance with his natural abilities. Only then will the humanistic high school have fulfilled its obligations in the shaping of a spiritual, artistic person.

Here in Vienna in 1919, long before Strauss—and encompassing all the arts—the great architect Adolf Loos, in his *Richtlinien für ein Kunstamt,* had already pointed out to the Austrian government its great responsibility in checking the cultural deterioration, which was already evident then. He assigned the task of writing the section on music in this publication to Arnold Schönberg, who began his contribution as follows:

> The most important task of the music faculty is the preservation of the German nation's superiority in music, a superiority rooted in the giftedness of its people. This would seem to be owing to the fact that the German elementary school teacher of earlier times was invariably a music teacher as well: and that even in the smallest village he was active as such, creating a reservoir vast enough to satisfy the needs of the highest strata of society. With the establishment of the modern elementary school, musical training was reduced to a barely sufficient vocal training. And in another hundred years we will have lost our superiority.

These warnings went unheeded, and until now nothing has been done to alter the situation. The consequences began to be felt as early as around 1900, at first with some isolated scandals concerning concert performances of the music of Schönberg and his circle—at that time still tonal music! This must be kept in mind; more than any subsequent resistance to nontonal music, this pins down precisely when and where the rift occurred before the beginnings of current new music, and why it widened: to the extent, namely, that knowledge as well as feeling for tradition was lost. First, among the listeners, the audience. Further—and we have come that far today—among those composers of today's avant-garde for whom tradition was never a vital concept, in other words something productive, which has been for all masters the self-evident point of departure for creative enterprise and not merely an obstacle to that originality at any price, which for them became the sole evaluative criterion. They had not learned it any other way; perhaps they did not want to learn it at all. For had they taken a look at Schönberg's *Harmonielehre* (which is in fact a part of a master's theory of composition), then they might have opened their eyes and ears to the fact that this revolutionary, in 1911, having just realized his first keen visions outside the realm of tonality, wrote a tonal harmony text in which one reads:

> Moreover it is sad that the notion that nowadays one may write anything one pleases prevents so many young people from first learning something worth respecting, and from understanding the classics and acquiring some culture. For in the past one could write whatever one pleased, but it just was not good. Only the masters could never write as they felt like; they had to do the inevitable: the accomplishment of their mission. To prepare for this with all diligence and amid a thousand doubts—whether having a thousand scruples will suffice, whether one has understood correctly what a higher power has commissioned—this is reserved for those who have the courage and the fervor to bear the consequences, like an awesome burden loaded upon their shoulders against their will. This is a far cry from the willfulness of a method—and more courageous.

That was a warning and a confession at the same time, uttered by Schönberg the revolutionary at the very moment when he himself had seemed to throw all tradition overboard, the first step beyond the confines of tonality—note that I use the expression "seemed to"! Because tradition for him was something indispensable, experienced, alive: the sum of everything new in the creative work of the old masters—the link between the new and what had been previously created; the precondition for anything new. For, in his words, "all music is new insofar as it is the product of a truly creative spirit. Bach is as new today as ever—a continuous revelation."

With these words Schönberg destroyed the opposition between tradition and progress. Likewise, I am free of any suspicion of advocating that the future imitate the past—that it take the comfortable path of traditionalism, which must be held in sharp contradistinction to tradition. For the former transmits only the scheme or prescription by which music is *made:* the artistic, which Schönberg abhorred exceedingly and against which he constantly warned his students. He merely taught them at all times to recognize "what music *is*," above all through the works of Bach, Beethoven, Mozart, and Brahms, hence in a continuously self-rejuvenating tradition. On the other hand, he would never have shown anyone how to compose "modern." In this connection it is essential to emphasize this once and for all.

In his lecture "Brahms the Progressive," written in 1947 on the fiftieth anniversary of Brahms's death, Schönberg said:

> Anyone who analyzes my music will realize how much I am personally indebted to Mozart. People who looked at me with disbelief, thinking that I was making a poor joke when I called myself a "pupil of Mozart" will then understand my reasons. This will help them, not to grasp my music but to understand Mozart. And it will show young composers what is essential, what must be learned from the great masters, and how to bear this teaching in mind without sacrificing their own personality.

Can the meaning and function of tradition be outlined more clearly? And the word *personality* here stands for individual style, for being original against one's will, for the unconscious aspect of creative expression.

The musical public was scandalized at Schönberg's originality at the very beginning, during the tonal period (which lasted until 1908), without feeling or recognizing the natural increase of its innate affinity with tradition—this originality *in statu nascendi,* which unfolded unconsciously and imperceptibly from one work to the next. And it is precisely in these tonal works of Schönberg that there lies the key to his later works; to his unbridled unconscious, which represents the roots of an originality that is genuine for this very reason; and to his extremely sensitive feeling for structure [*Formgefühl*], with which his imagination moved resiliently between the Scylla of tradition and the Charybdis of its visions and of its inner compulsion to bring law and freedom, always represented anew in each work, to harmonic resolution. From the first work to the last, this bears the stamp of what we understand and treasure in the concept of *classical*.

At the end of his life, Schönberg deplored his status with the public:

> Those of my works which would have interested them (namely, those which they regarded as atonal and interesting) they did not wish to hear; and those works which are not called atonal, because they are less dissonant, are not interesting enough for these people, who do not know them at all. . . . I am convinced that the works of my last period would at least gain the respect they deserve if the public had the opportunity to do justice to the works of my earlier periods.

Whether yesterday, today, or tomorrow—whether tonal, atonal, or twelve tone—Schönberg remained the same: a composer whose sole endeavor was to make music. The principle by which it is made, the style—these were always questions of secondary importance to him. For this reason he loved and treasured to the end his early tonal works (something we ought to remember with due respect); thus at the high point of his twelve-tone period (after 1934) he returned to composing several significant tonal works (It goes without saying that these are also hardly known.). When news of this reached Europe, after the last war, it was generally reported that "Schönberg had contritely returned to tonality." I recall a telephone call from Furtwängler, who wanted to know more details about this; but anyone knowing Schönberg would have hardly needed to hear his reply:

> Fate directed me along a more difficult road. But there has always been within me a burning desire to return to the earlier style, and from time to time I yield to this desire. And so it happens that at times I write tonal music. For me, stylistic differences of this sort have no special significance. I do not know which of my compositions are better; I like them all, for I liked them as I wrote them.

And so it seems appropriate now to investigate the creative synthesis of originality and tradition which the composer realized ever since his early tonal period; to investigate the New, which still remained hidden here in tonal guise, yet at the time was perceived by the public as new and produced a vehement shock wave; and to trace the tradition that accommodated itself to the New without losing any of its own spiritual identity—indeed, to see itself newly affirmed in its rejuvenation.

The fertile soil in which this grew was Mozart and Beethoven, whose quartets young Schönberg played with his friends in the early 1890s, and Wagner and Brahms, the antipodes about which Viennese families were split. Yet Schönberg at that time sensed the fascination of *Tristan* as much as the constructive forces—the New—that he discerned in the music of Brahms. Both were models to which he dedicated himself, without sacrificing himself to them.

"Schönberg yesterday" conceptually encompasses his entire life and work—which is to say that it includes a yesteryear and a yester-yesteryear. This yester-yesteryear, the first tonal period, began with songs. Strictly tonal, they testify to his schooling in classical models—for example, with the structured bass lines in the counterpoint of Brahms's piano music—as well as in increasingly stronger individual modulations in successive songs.

Germs of a development important for the future are found everywhere, still more or less hidden in conventions dictated by tradition. A striking example of this is *Erwartung* from opus 2. Right at the beginning, the daring chord E-flat-A-D-G-flat-C-flat stands embedded between two E-flat-major triads. But it is not there merely on account of its daring, that is, for it sonic effect. Rather, it is encircled by the voice, which builds it up melodically, thereby illustrating its many facets and establishing an entirely new element of tension in E-flat major. In what follows, freely varied and sequenced, this chord then constitutes the germ cell of the middle section, so that the entire song is built upon and developed from this one chord formation, borne by a stupendous feeling for structure. Already here we can see the compositional foundation upon which he experiences tonality and its carrying capacity, pursuing its subtlest ramifications to the limit. Moreover, it is the same feeling for structure, the same manner of thinking and forming music, that Schönberg applied twenty-five years later to composition with twelve tones that are related only to one another (rather than to a fundamental tone), in which a work is invented and developed from a single underlying construction.

In the melodic aspects of the string sextet *Verklärte Nacht* one can already find Schönberg's characteristic alternation between chromatic passages and those involving wide melodic skips. At the time it made listening more difficult, like constant variations in the repetition of musical ideas, like the rhythmically artful "hamming-up" of the stereotyped metric articulation ("In a given phrase there exists only one strong beat"), or asymmetric melodic construction, that is, the departure from four-bar regularity (which, like the rhyming of "heart" with "part" and "love" with "dove," made understanding and perception easier), and the turning toward something that Schönberg likened to "metrical prose" in contrast to rhyme, a trend in musical development that was already perceivable in Reger.

And of course the rich harmony that was already considered "new" by listeners of the day. The Tonkünstlerverein in Vienna, to which Schönberg had submitted the sextet for performance, rejected it on the grounds that it contained an inversion of the ninth-chord that could not exist, namely one with the ninth in the bass. Schönberg took this in good humor, realizing that one "could not perform what does not exist."

The next composition, the tone poem *Pelleas und Melisande* (1902), represents a further leap forward in the realm of harmony. In one place the basic tonality of D minor is extended by chainlike sequences piled on top of one another in contrary motion, resulting in six-part whole-tone chords. These suspend the tonality momentarily and at the same time prepare the way for the first chords in fourths, which Schönberg created here, independently of Debussy and Scriabin. And this was in 1902! Years later, the composer admitted that he had hesitated to write down these harmonies, but that they had forced themselves on him against his will (!), as a particular expression of a mood, with such clarity that he was unable to reject this inspiration. But if these new harmonies in Debussy and Scriabin are purely impressionistic and motivelike, respectively, in Schönberg they are a means of expression constructively embedded in the tonality. Despite this Schönberg hesitated in the face of such an unusual idea and cautiously probed, in keeping with his deep sense of responsibility.

Schönberg's feeling for structure, which developed from traditional practice, secured him even then and not only in his own musical ventures; but it grew just as the classical models themselves had developed. A page from the composer's *Nachlass* describes how he had fitted content and organization in Maeterlinck's drama into a purely musical four-movement framework. In composing his First String Quartet in D Minor, he followed the formal organization of Beethoven's *Eroica* Symphony, especially in the layout of the development section. The single-movement format of the quartet was retained in his next work, the First Chamber Symphony in E Major, except that now the content and its presentation force an imaginative new formal conception: the first movement, in sonata form, has its reprise only at the end of the work, and thereby frames the middle part, which consists of scherzo, development section, and slow movement. To this is added a new melodic-thematic development: the whole-tone and quartal harmony of *Pelleas* is now linearized as well, opening up entirely new areas that result in new grammatical modes of expression. And one more thing becomes clear: This is not chromatically "softened-up" music. On the contrary, the new harmonies do not explode the tonality, but render it even firmer. Once more, Schönberg tamed the centrifugal forces in a sovereign manner, producing the most extreme concentration of tonality extracted with the greatest harmonic enrichment up until the Second String Quartet in F-sharp Minor. That work—in 1908—marked the end of the tonal period of creativity and, at the same time, the climax; but also, in the last movement, the organically necessitated transition to music without a key signature. The first movement is still clearly in F-sharp minor. In the second and third (the single-movement form is abandoned in favor of the classical separation of movements) the structural cohesiveness of the basic tonality becomes increasingly questionable, and in the last movement Schönberg takes the revolutionary step forward by omitting the key signature altogether—a historic moment in music, which now looks upon new territories and dreams of new worlds. Once again, to be sure, with supreme power the music returns to tonality, as both movement and piece end in F-sharp major. But something truly unheard-of had already occurred—the step beyond the boundaries of tonality was irreversible, and its crisis could no longer be ignored; precisely because Schönberg tried simply everything in his power in order to overcome this crisis.

To this Finale, like the third movement, words are added in the form of a song: Stefan George's poem "Entrückung," which significantly opens with the words, "I sense air from other planets." This is preceded by a brief instrumental introduction, which is also interesting because Schönberg designated it as the first example of what he called *Klangfarbenmelodie* [tone-color melody]. It expresses the feeling of weightless hovering, which the poet utters in words and which is transformed into music here—written in 1908, a glance into the then still utopian future—truly creative vision!

And that was yester-yesteryear. Yesteryear followed immediately and—as we recognize today—entirely organically: the period of free atonality. With a single blow Schönberg opened up new worlds of musical means of expression, inviting boundless freedom and fully unfettered music-making. And here Schönberg's total genius manifested itelf: instinctively, with uncanny sureness, and with the sense of duty of a true artist, he avoided these dangers. Of course he was aware of having exceeded the limits of an aesthetic that had been valid until that time, but he considered himself all the more sure of the language he had built on the foundations of a tradition that was part of his flesh and blood. Very likely he saw himself face to face with sheer, limitless freedom, yet he never let this degenerate into chaos. But that is precisely what he was accused of. He was reviled as the destroyer of tradition—without his accusers recognizing traditions themselves. Professionals and public alike reacted with an outrage of unimaginable vehemence. But Schönberg remained unperturbed. He had arrived at a decision: either to retreat within the confines of tonality, accepting it as an ostensible law of nature and thus sacrificing the veracity of his music; or to believe in the infallibility of the logic of his musical thinking and to fulfill the task assigned to him by fate—despite all the consequences for his bare existence, which for years meant extreme poverty and complete isolation. This posture grew out of a deep religious sense and remained undaunted by the heavy blows from the political and artistic world, which accompanied him until death.

But at that time he replied to his adversaries:

> What I did was neither revolutionary nor anarchical. . . . Never was it the intention or effect of the new art to displace, let alone to destroy, the old. On the contrary, no one loves his predecessors more deeply, intimately, and respectfully than the artist who creates truly new things. For reverence is class-consciousness, and love the sense of belonging together.

What Schönberg composed during the period of free atonality, which lasted about fifteen years, was controlled exclusively by his profound sense of structure, schooled by the models of the old masters. With what sovereignty this occurred is immediately recognizable in the first of the Three Piano Pieces opus 11, which ushered in the new era. It is sixty-four measures long and in strict two-part song form. The eleven-measure theme, itself divisible into three parrts, and its five-measure resolution are followed by a varied repetition, again sixteen measures long. Then, for contrast, a loosely constructed middle section—once more sixteen measures in length—is followed by the fifteen-measure reprise. The sixteenth measure is missing here to compensate for an extra measure inserted before the middle section—an extraordinary structural subtlety!

But his other works of the period are also, in this respect, abundant with links to tradition; in fact, far more than the obvious classical and preclassical forms, as are found in *Pierrot lunaire,* or the artful six-part canons of the choruses in *Die glückliche Hand.* What an abundance of new concepts of form were produced and developed, for example, from the new discoveries and their novel manner of presentation in *Das Buch der hängenden Gärten,* a song cycle on poems of Stefan George; or in the Five Orchestral Pieces opus 16—consider only the third of these, whose musical idea was labeled "changing chord" by the composer; or the Six Little Piano Pieces opus 19, each in the form of a musical aphorism, again a new idea conceived by Schönberg.

I have used the term *originality* several times to mean an apparent contradiction of tradition. Doubtless, there exists from time immemorial a tendency to overrate this term. Its use is especially questionable when it does not refer, spontaneously, to the originality of ideas but to that of workmanlike technique, that is, to purely external ability. Regarding this matter, I found a scrap of paper in Schönberg's *Nachlass* on which some remarks were outlined, dating from the time when *Pierrot lunaire* was composed; and this underscores their importance, because *Pierrot* is to this day regarded among the most original works of the new music: "The originality craze is degenerating into vogue. Artists seek nothing but more newness. And find it!! But surely they are not all geniuses?!? Therefore:

newness (originality) not the decisive factor of genius. Only one of its most common symptoms." From this we can infer that Schönberg never once searched for originality. Rather—recall his assertion regarding the chords in fourths in *Pelleas*—it had intruded "against his will"—unconsciously. The unconscious dominated his creativity everywhere and at all times, and what he produced thereby he esteemed more highly and more profoundly in each case. "When more happens than one can imagine," he said, "then it can only happen unconsciously."

Yesteryear became yesterday; it was fifty years ago that Schönberg, with his "Method of Composition with Twelve Tones Related Only to One Another," succeeded in finding a firm basis on which to construct nontonal music. He was now (as he wrote to J. M. Hauer in 1923) "in a position to compose without hesitation and with imagination, as one does in childhood, and yet work under a precisely defined aesthetic control."

The public's reaction was predictable: Schönberg was now decried as a musical design engineer. He was convicted for all time. The catchword was unsurpassable as an argument. For it relieved everyone of having a personal opinion beyond the slogan "we said it all along" and of the responsibility of listening to these musical designs and coming to grips with them. Had those who had been chosen to be musicians and musical scholars done so at the time, they could have found the path to the music that lay within and behind these designs. Had they but heeded what Schönberg indicated—both orally and in writing—in the way of advice to his students, friends, and anyone who cared to listen: that it was a matter of twelve-tone *compositions,* not *twelve-tone* compositions, that is, of intellectual, sonic, and musical substances; that these were works of a musical conception and not mathematical designs; and that twelve-tone music certainly requires no more design work than is demanded by what is known as "motivic work" in tonal music. Moreover, to what extent is design to be looked upon with such contempt? Surely augmentation and diminution, inversion, and other mirror forms of counterpoint need not be taken entirely as phantoms, especially if the other voices simultaneously contribute to the thematic material. "But," wrote Schönberg to his brother-in-law, violinist Rudolf Kolisch, "although I am not ashamed of a solid design basis in a composition even where I have consciously produced it—where, in other words, it is less valid than in the places where it was conceived instinctively and subconsciously—still, I do not wish to be regarded as a design engineer because of a little serial combination, since that would signify too little reciprocal accomplishment on my part."

"What can be designed with these twelve tones," he stated on another occasion, "depends on the inventive powers of the individual. Expression is limited only by the creative ability and personality of the composer." For Schönberg, the twelve-tone method of composition was "rather a method of a workmanlike nature, which could exercise a decisive influence on neither the structure nor the character of a work. This is a question of the treatment of the material, in the sense of a characteristic refinement of its stipulations, which determines the form. As such, however, it is of a very great importance."

And here, within the scope of our topic "Schönberg yesterday, today, and tomorrow," we must address ourselves to a fundamental misconception concerning his twelve-tone method of composition: the mechanical transfer of the concept of the row [Reihenidee] to all the elements involved in the creation of music—rhythm, dynamics, tone color, and so on—as has been practiced in so-called serial music. Whoever rejects this procedure and denies it the name music is comparable to, and thus apparently branded as, an arch-opponent of Schönberg, in a parallelism as illogical as it is superfluous. In so doing, one forgets or neglects only that the premises in the two cases are fundamentally different. Underlying serial music is a conscious intellectual effort, an artistic manipulation by which an idea—that of Schönberg—is taken over mechanically. Underlying Schönberg's twelve-tone music, however, is a musical *inspiration,* thus an unconscious act. For the tendency toward dodecaphony was intuitive and, long before its recognition and formulation by Schönberg, was clearly recognizable in the music of Reger, Hindemith, Bartók and—last, but not least—Schönberg and Berg. Schönberg did nothing but "hear out" the inspirations of this genre with all their possibilities of development. And he did this not for the sake of effect or of being original but out of a necessity: to compensate for the loss of the supremely structural functions of tonality. He himself used the term *necessity* in this connection. For the transfer of the row concept to all other parameters of music, there was no such necessity; on the other hand, only this necessity legitimizes, in the realm of art, what would otherwise remain arbitrariness, or at best exhibitionistic contrivance.

Hand in hand with this misconception there goes another: the conscious and radical rejection of all tradition on the part of serial composers. In sharp contrast to this, Schönberg's theory demands the complete mastery of classical and preclassical compositional techniques as an unconditional prerequisite for composition with twelve tones. But here the boundaries are clearly drawn, as the incompatibility and, moreover, the contradiction between serial and twelve-tone music are apparent. To this it must be added marginally that the welfare of music is in no way dependent on the use of Schönbergian methods; that these in no way will guarantee the quality of a work; and that most twelve-tone works—written and as yet unwritten all over the world—may be just as dubious as is most tonal music at all times. Value is determined neither by style nor by label, but by whether the music says something; whether we are moved, stirred, or inspired by it. This is the gist of Schönberg's saying that the difference between old and new music is smaller than the difference between good and bad music. And in justifying the necessity of the development toward nontonal music by the richness of its combinations, ideas, and tone pictures, which a priori predestined it to a higher level, he closes with the characteristic sentence: "But everything depends not on material, but on genius, as is always true in Art."

That his genius developed in the fertile soil of the German musical tradition is not only evident in his music but also in numerous self-critical documents. In Schönberg's *Nachlass* I found a penciled remark on a yellowed sheet of paper, probably dating from World War I, at which time German music was boycotted abroad:

> Whenever I think about music, nothing ever comes to mind—whether intentionally or unintentionally—but German music. Whoever is its opponent will often have to take the responsibility for utter starvation before this knowledge becomes natural to him. But German music thrives in times of hunger; deprived of nourishment, its silent power will create and fill banquet halls in eternity. And it will always be reaching toward Heaven, where rampant inferiority boasts artistry.

More than a decade later, during the composing of *Moses und Aron*, Schönberg commented on his deep identification with German music in a paper titled "Nationale Musik":

> The fact that no one has yet recognized this is due not only to the difficulty of my music but also, and to a greater extent, to the laziness and arrogance of those who sit in judgment. For it is quite apparent. But I will say it once more myself: my teachers were Bach and Mozart primarily, and Beethoven, Brahms, and Wagner secondarily.

And then, having summarized what he learned from these masters—it turns unwittingly into an embracing composition method in key words—he continued:

I have never closed my ears to anyone, and therefore can safely say that my originality derives from having imitated immediately whatever good I saw, even when I did not see it in others at first. I might add that, often enough, I saw it first in myself. For I have not stood still with what I perceived: I acquired it in order to possess it; I developed and expanded it, and it led me to new things. I am convinced that people will some day recognize how intimately this New is related to the very best of what was given to us as models. I claim credit for having composed truly new music, which, since it is founded on tradition, is destined to become tradition.

But no one paid any attention to him. That was yesterday, more than forty years ago. His name and his music seemed to fall into oblivion after 1933. In the 1930s the young Dallapiccola, who made an effort to learn something about Schönberg and his twelve-tone music, was advised not to waste his time on something that had been considered passé for a long time. The surprise was all the greater when the free world became accessible to us once again in 1945: Schönberg's ideas, in the meantime, had found resonance everywhere, especially among young people, all over Europe, in all corners of the earth. Today Schönberg has become the center of musical development in twentieth-century music, which does not mean that he is universally understood and accepted. That will still require considerable time, and today nothing is in shorter supply than time. But there exists no composer of yesterday, today, or tomorrow who can avoid coming to grips with Schönberg. It can be said, without exaggeration, that not only Alban Berg and Anton Webern would not be what they are without him, but also Luigi Dallapiccola, Ernst Krenek, Hans Werner Henze, Giselher Klebe, Wolfgang Fortner, Luigi Nono, and Pierre Boulez, the last of whom (as H. H. Stuckenschmidt wrote):

with unsuspecting naïveté wrote his *Schönberg est mort* and then, as a conductor, took ten years to acquaint himself with what he had defamed, as the rebel disciple who had betrayed Schönberg. As once before, namely Hindemith in the 1920s, so the admittedly defenseless Webern, who lost his life in 1945, was crowned a sort of antipope to Schönberg, commensurate with his boundless admiration of the master. The idea that Webern's music, in its essential forms, is thinkable without Schönberg is as absurd for any knowledgeable person as that a pupil could have a formal influence on his teacher. But the power of fanfare, with which nearly every adherent to the Boulez-Stockhausen generation blared out Webern's simple countenance, is leveled, both quantitatively and qualitatively, at their own standard-bearer. It does not diminish Webern's greatness to assert objectively that, in his work and specifically in his adoption of the twelve-tone technique, the elements are a simplification of Schönberg *ad usum delphini.*

This also is part of the picture "Schönberg today," and I could not have expressed it any better. The noise from the fanfare has long since faded away. Perhaps it was needed to chase away the great shadows that lay beneath this generation. Tomorrow and the future will bring new sounds, probably without fanfare. But they will, as before, encircle the focal point called Schönberg and, we hope, understand him as a great living tradition. And out of this recognition, the strength will be drawn for future developments. Until then Schönberg will have the last word, as is the case here and now.

Around 1930 he had an interview with Dr. Eberhard Preussner and Dr. Heinrich Strobel on the Berlin radio network. May his concluding remarks from then be also those of today:

> . . . Herr Strobel, do not underestimate the extent of the circle that has formed around me. It will expand out of the thirst for knowledge of an idealistic younger generation, which feels itself drawn more to the mysterious than to the everyday. But however this may turn out, I can only think and say what my mission prescribes. Gentlemen, do not call that arrogance; I would rather have had greater success. It is in no way my wish to stand on a pedestal as a stylite. As long as I am permitted to consider my thinking and imagination as correct, I will not be able to believe anything except that my ideas must be thought out and expressed, even if they cannot be understood. I personally do not believe that my ideas are so utterly unintelligible. But let us consider: should great incontestable ideas, like those of a Kant, not be permitted to be thought or expressed, simply because to this day honest people must admit that they cannot follow them? To whomever the Lord God has given the mission to say unpopular things, he has lent the power to resign himself to the fact that it is invariably the others who are understood.

Electronic Music and Live Performance*

Elliot Schwartz

In this essay Elliot Schwartz, the distinguished contemporary composer, discusses some of his electronic compositions combined with "live" instrumental sounds. Elliot Schwartz is professor of music and chairman of the music department at Bowdoin College in Brunswick, Maine. He is the author of Electronic Music: A Listeners Guide (*1975*).

There have been many misconceptions about electronic music over the years. Some feel that it "all sounds alike," that it somehow represents "composing by machine," that it is "dehumanized," and so on. One particular fear—widespread among traditionally oriented musicians—is that electronic music will eventually make live human performers obsolete, that our clarinets and violins and pianos will gather dust in future instrument "museums" while all music-making becomes the province of the computer program, tape recorder, synthesizer, and loudspeaker system.

In fact, nothing could be further from the truth. To be sure, electronic studios, loudspeakers, and the like have become important parts of the

---

* Reprinted from *The Instrumentalist*, 31, no. 7 (February 1977), pp. 52–55.

musical scene and they are obviously here to stay. But they certainly haven't supplanted the live performer's role in the music-making process. There has probably been more performance—*live, human* performance—of new chamber music, orchestral music, choral, and band music during the 1960s and 1970s than ever before. A good case could be made for the argument that electronic techniques have actually stimulated interest in a whole new kind of "chamber music" that combines taped sounds with live instrumental ones.

The four works discussed below, which I composed in recent years, all fall into this new category. Each piece presents a different performance problem for the live instrumentalist, a different sort of compositional challenge for me, and (I hope!) a unique aural experience for the listener.

FIVE MOBILES

(flute, harpsichord, organ, and tape) Grade V.

This piece, composed for the 1975 Hartt College Contemporary Organ Festival, was designed to be a rather brilliant-sounding, flashy display piece. Accordingly, I tried to stress synchronization and precision through the interplay of fragments, rhythms, and lines among the four instruments (including the electronic tape part). The three live performers are flexible: they can adjust to one another's lines, pick up on a missed cue when necessary, or hold back and wait for another player's late entrance. The reel of tape, which is always the same from one performance to another, doesn't "respond" in the same flexible ways; therefore, the live performers must learn to respond to *it*. Because the three performers are relatively free and the tape is "fixed," interesting ensemble problems result. The exact coordination of tempos and rhythms, for example, may be particularly challenging.

During the performance of *Five Mobiles* there are extended periods in which I desire *no* tape sound. This can be achieved in either of two ways: by including periods of silence on a continuously playing tape, or by having the tape stopped and started again when various electronic passages are called for. I chose the latter option, which seemed right for the firm rhythmic demands of this particular piece. In real performance, then, the tape operator must follow the score and in effect, functions as a fourth "player" in a true chamber music situation, at least with respect to proper entrances and cutoffs. Note the performing role of the tape operator in illustration 1.

Elliot Schwartz: *Five Mobiles.* Copyright © 1977 by Hinshaw Music, Inc., Chapel Hill, North Carolina. Used with the permission of the publisher.

The sounds on this tape are entirely electronic, and were produced on a voltage-control synthesizer. In composing *Five Mobiles,* I worked out the total fabric (including a general approximation of the tape activity I wanted) and wrote down the entire score, including the tape "part," before I ever entered the electronic studio. My work in the studio in creating the sounds that exist on tape was therefore not really "composition" as much as it was the realization of previously notated concepts.

CYCLES AND GONGS

(*organ, trumpet, and tape*) Grade IV.

This work was also composed for the 1975 Hartt Festival, and I wanted to make it as different from *Five Mobiles* as possible. I chose a single extended movement, rather than the five-movement "suite" format of the *Mobiles.* As a result, the piece developed into a series of quasi variations (highly contrasted and differentiated) against a static, repetitive electronic part—a sort of passacaglia in which the tape functions as the "ground." For this

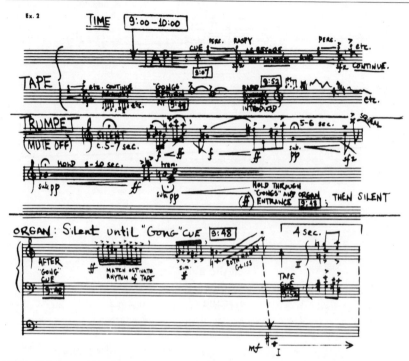

Elliot Schwartz: *Cycles and Gongs.* Copyright © 1977 by Hinshaw Music, Inc., Chapel Hill, North Carolina. Used with the permission of the publisher.

piece the electronic tape part was made *first,* before I ever knew what the live instrumental material would be like. Like the *Mobiles* tape, the electronic part for *Cycles and Gongs* is entirely synthesized; in this case it is a continuously running tape, which does not need to be started and stopped by an assistant, made up of brief rhythmic fragments that repeat, overlap, and change timbre periodically.

The changes of timbre that characterize the tape part are especially important because they function as "cues" for the live players. I decided that the problem of synchronization would be handled by having the live performers relatively *un*synchronized to each other: that is, by having each of them respond independently to the tape. Each page of the music lasts sixty seconds and consists of a tape line (indicating important events and, most importantly, the "cue" that ushers in that particular sixty-second unit), a trumpet part, and an organ part. Within the duration of the page, all of the performing forces are rather "free," as indicated by a typical page from the work (see ill. 2).

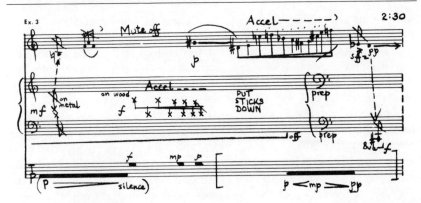

Elliot Schwartz: *Music for Napoleon and Beethoven.* Copyright © 1971 by Hinshaw Music, Inc., Chapel Hill, North Carolina. Used with the permission of the publisher.

The performers know when the next page, or minute unit, begins because they associate this with another "cue" (or timbral change) in the tape part. This new cue is indicated at the top of the next page.

MUSIC FOR NAPOLEON AND BEETHOVEN

(trumpet, piano, and two tapes) Grade IV.

This work, composed in 1969, is quite different from the preceding two in a number of ways, particularly in the sound material on the tapes and in the way the tapes are used in performance. To begin with, the sounds heard on the tapes were not produced by a synthesizer at all, but are representative of *musique concrète:* a collage of natural sounds (laughter, coughing, party noisemakers, whistles), instrumental ones (trumpet and piano sounds that have been distorted and edited into new profiles), and recorded "traditional" fragments of Beethoven, Tchaikovsky, and the like. All of these sounds contribute to the wild, eclectic crazy-quilt effect of the total piece, which was conceived (humorously and rather ironically) as a "birthday offering" for the bicentennials of the two gentlemen named in the title.

The way in which the two tapes are performed is also worth noting. As with the *Five Mobiles* mentioned above, a tape assistant is required, but not just to start and stop the tapes at specified moments. The tape operator also "plays" the tape by turning the playback volume controls up and down (from silence to very loud fortissimo bursts), thus controlling the dynamics of the part and adding a human, "live" kind of synchronization (or free nonsynchronization!) to the total ensemble.

In illustration 3 the tape part is the bottom staff of the system: the staff itself is divided into two areas (top space and bottom space), representing what are called, respectively, "trumpet" and "piano" tapes. The darkened lines of the tape part indicate the duration for which the volume is to be turned up, relative to the fact that each total line or "system" lasts for fifteen seconds. (This particular system runs from the 2:15 mark of the piece to 2:30, the latter number given at the top right corner.) Dotted lines, arrows, and brackets indicate various kinds of synchronization or freedom. Note the variety of activities asked of the pianist, who begins this system playing on the inside of the instrument with drumsticks and then plays notes in the lowest octave, which have previously been "prepared" with coins, screws, pencils, and other objects.

THE HARMONY OF MAINE

(*synthesizer and orchestra*) Grade V.

This composition, composed in 1975, involves no tape at all. It is in fact a completely "live" performance throughout, featuring the age-old concertolike opposition of soloist versus orchestra. The only unusual feature of this relationship is that the soloist's instrument is a portable electronic synthesizer. (I composed the piece to be played on an ARP 2600, but it has also been performed using twin ARP Odysseys and would be equally feasible on a Synthi, ElectroComp, Mini-Moog, or any other prepatched, nonmodular synthesizer designed for live performance.)

The synthesizer part is generally written in traditional notation, as though for any standard "melody" instrument. The vast range of the ARP 2600, though, necessitates writing some passages in treble clef and others in bass. As ninety-nine percent of the part is played upon a pianolike keyboard, I tried to maintain the notion of writing specific pitches, even when it's understood that the resultant *sounds* (perhaps squeals, or percussive rattles, or rapid flurries) would have no relation at all to those "pitches!" As anyone who has ever operated a synthesizer knows, the nature of the sound is determined by a great many factors: filter setting, noise component, wave form of the oscillator, envelope generator setting, and a variety of control voltages applied to any or all of these. All these factors, taken together, might constitute the equivalent of an organist's registration. Accordingly, I

Elliot Schwartz: *The Harmony of Maine.* Copyright © 1977 by Carl Fischer, Inc., New York. Used with the permission of the publisher.

conceived of about eight or nine specific "registrations," indicated the exact settings for each, and then referred to each in the synthesizer part simply as "setting 1," "setting 2," and so on.

The major problem for the soloist is to alter the collection of settings rapidly, so that setting 4, for example, can be changed to setting 5 in a very short span of time—perhaps only a bit longer than the time a trumpet player needs to empty a spit valve, or a cellist to put on a mute, or a clarinetist to switch to a bass clarinet. That's part of the challenge of playing the part, of course, and part of the enjoyment that comes from it (when all goes well!). If the business of rapid "registration" change is under control, then the rest of the part becomes comparatively simple for anyone who already plays a keyboard instrument. A typical line from the score, showing the synthesizer part, is shown in illustration 4.

I have played *The Harmony of Maine* on four different occasions with different orchestras and I find that I learn more about the synthesizer as I continue to perform the piece. Practicing and performing on this instrument, as on any other, bring their own rewards. But in this case I have gained not only a more polished performance of my concerto but also greater experience and flexibility that can be applied when I return to the more private, controlled environment of the electronic studio.

I hope these examples of my music, combining electronic sounds with acoustical "live" instrumental ones, will give a fair picture of the great variety possible with this hybrid medium. There are a great many more works available in this genre, exciting pieces for chamber ensembles, orchestras, and/or choruses with electronic extensions, by such composers as Donald Erb, Morton Subotnick, Richard Felciano, Mario Davidovsky, Milton Babbitt, Larry Austin, Joel Chadabe—the list is very impressive indeed. I hope that more composers, conductors, and performers investigate this growing literature, for its challenges and its great rewards.

Index

Page references for illustrations are in **boldface** type. Musical works are listed under the composer's name.

Adorno, Theodor, 40, 46
Agbadza (dance), 159, **160,** 161
Alembert, Jean Le Rond d', 306
Alorworye, Gideon, 154, 155, 161
Anastasi, William
    Beethoven's Fifth Symphony, see
        gallery
    Broken Jug, see **gallery**
Andersen, Eric, 23–24, 251
    Opus 48, 25
Andre, Carl, 267, 269
Andriessen, Louis, 192
    Flower Song II, A, **192**
Anhalt, István, 192
    Symphony of Modules, **193**
Apple (computer company), 178

Arbus, Diane, 36
Archipenko, Alexander, 276
Arezzo, Guido d', 239
Armstrong, Louis, 205
Arnold, Malcolm, 248
Ashley, Robert, 254, 265, 266, 267
    Fancy Free, 264–265
    in memoriam . . . Crazy Horse,
        264
    in memoriam . . . Esteban Gomez,
        264
    Private Parts, see **gallery**
    Wolfman, The, 266–267
Austin, Larry, 338
Austin, William W., 72, 73
Ay-O, 27

341

Babbitt, Milton, 119n, 202, 204, 255, 273, 276, 277–278, 282, 283, 300–315, 338

Bach, J. S., 6, 7, 47, 50n, 51, 63, 66, 112n, 113, 201, 204, 205, 299, 305, 319, 320, 328
  Art of Fugue, 6, 7, 298
  Vom Himmel hoch, 63n
  Well-Tempered Clavier, 112n, 296

Balla, Giacomo, 81

Barbaud, Pierre, 306n, 311n

Barber, Samuel, xi

Bartók, Bela, 54, 77n, 206, 280, 285, 295, 327
  Bluebeard's Castle, 77n

Barzun, Jacques, 200

Baschet, François and Bernard
  One-Octave Piano, see **gallery**

Baskerville, Charles Read, 45n

Bates, Bob
  Performance on instrument Fuser, see **gallery**

Beatles, 45, 46, 47, 173

Beckett, Samuel, 202

Bedford, David, 244

Beethoven, Ludwig van, 10, 26, 28, 32, 34, 48, 50n, 66, 113, 116n, 117, 201, 207, 320, 321, 328, 335
  Coriolan Overture, 10
  Fifth Symphony, 10, 48
  Ninth Symphony, 26, 50n, 137
  opus 59, 117
  opus 135, 116n
  opus 74, 117
  Third Symphony, 323

Behrman, David, 33–34, 119n, 270

Bell Telephone Laboratories, 184

Belz, Carl, 39, 49

Bennett, Richard Rodney, 248

Berg, Alban, 54, 232, 327, 329

Berger, Arthur, 215–220
  Trio for Violin, Guitar, and Piano, 215, 216, **217-219,** 220

Berio, Luciano, 248

Bernstein, Leonard, 249

Birtwistle, Harrison, 248

Blacking, John, 41n, 51n

Bloom, Hyman, 287

Boccioni, Umberto, 75, 80, 81, 87

Bolcom, William, 60
  Frescoes, 60

Bonzagni, Arnoldo, 81

Boretz, Benjamin, xv, 102, 117–118, 119, 120, 123n
  Meta-Variations, 9

Borges, Jorge Luis, 111, 114

Boulanger, Nadia, 233, 297, 299

Boulez, Pierre, xii, 65, 123n, 202, 204, 234, 247, 281, 307, 310, 329
  Structures, 252, 255
  Third Sonata, 123n

Bowie, David, 276

Brahms, Johannes, 207, 320, 321, 328

Brancusi, Constantin, 276

Brant, Henry, 273, 274, 278, 279, 280, 282

Brecht, George, 15, 16, 17, 22–23, 91, 245, 255–256

Breton, André, 101

Britten, Benjamin, 248

Broonzy, Big Bill, 48

Brown, Earle, 13, 16, 241, 247, 273, 275, 276, 278, 279, 280, 281–282
  December 1952, 241, **242,** 243
  Folio, 16

Brown, Howard, 39, 46–47

Browne, Ray B., 41, 42, 47n, 48n

Bryars, Gavin, 34–35, 137
  Jesus's Blood Never Failed Me Yet, 137, **138-139**

Bryars, Gavin (*Cont.*)
  Sinking of the Titanic, The, 34–35,
    36, 37
Buchla, Donald, 209–210, 211
Burroughs (computer company), 176
Bush, Alan, 248
Busoni, Ferruccio, 74, 202, 277, 280
Bussotti, Sylvano, 248
  Excerpt from composition, **frontispiece**
Byrd, Joseph, 13, 16

Cacioppo, George, 195
  Cassiopeia, **194**
Cage, John, xii, 13, 15, 16, 18, 20, 21,
    22, 36, 55, 90, 91, 92, 97, 102,
    106, 127, **143–149,** 152, 202, 204,
    221, 245, 247, 255, 273, 274, 280,
    284, 285, 287, 288, 293
  Aria with Fontana Mix, 104
  Atlas Eclipticalis, 243, 246–247
  Concert for Piano and Orchestra,
    248
  4'33", 127
  HPSCHD, 123n, 249
  Imaginary Landscape No. 5, 240
  Theatre Piece, 92
Cahill, Thaddeus, 171
Calder, Alexander, 97, 98, 101, 242
Cangiullo, Francesco, 75, 76n
Cantrick, Robert B., 39, 40n, 44n,
    47n, 52
Cardew, Cornelius, 107, 132, 135, 137,
    138
  Great Learning, The, **131,** 132
  Octet '61 for Jasper Johns, 107
  Treatise, 236, **245**
Carlos, Walter, 172, 173
  Switched-On Bach, 172, 173, 205
Carnap, Rudolf, 4, 6, 106

Carrà, Carlo, 75, 80, 81, 87
Carter, Elliott, xi, 55, 102, 122n,
    221–234, 297
  Concerto for Piano, 226, 227–228,
    230n, 231, 234
  Concerto for Orchestra, 226, 228,
    234
  Double Concerto for Harpsichord,
    Piano, and Two Chamber Orchestras, 225–226, 234
  Eight Etudes, 234
  First Symphony, 233
  Holiday Overture, 233
  Minotaur, The, 233, 234
  Pocahontas, 233, 234
  Sonata for Cello and Piano, 224,
    226, 228, **229,** 234
  Sonata for Flute, Oboe, Cello, and
    Harpsichord, 234
  Sonata for Piano, 222, 227, 228,
    233–234
  String Quartet no. 1, 227, 228, 230,
    234
  String Quartet no. 3, 226, 228, 230,
    234
  String Quartet no. 2, 224, 225, 228,
    230, 234
  Variations for Orchestra, 234
  Woodwind Quintet, 234
Casella, Alfredo, 74
Cawelti, John G., 40n, 52
Chadabe, Joel, 270, 338
Chavez, Carlos, 102, 112n
Childs, Lucinda, 263
Clifton, Thomas, 60n, 108, 115n,
    116–117, 124, 126
Cogan, Robert, 270
  utterances, 270
Cohn, Arthur, 230
Coleridge, Samuel Taylor, 231

Commodore (computer company), 178
Control Data (computer company), 176
Converse, Frederick, 287
  Mystic Trumpeter, The, 287
Copland, Aaron, xi, 102, 112, 221, 248, 285, 287, 297
  Appalachian Spring, 233
Corea, Chick, 173
Corner, Philip, 13, 15, 35–36
  Barcelona Cathedral, The, 35–36, 37
Cowell, Henry, 281, 293
Craft, Robert, 75n
Cromemco (computer company), 178

Dallapiccola, Luigi, 329
Daniel, Oliver, 290
Data General (computer company), 176
Davidovsky, Mario, 338
Davies, Peter Maxwell, 60, 248
Debussy, Claude, 56, 65, 280, 323
  Afternoon of a Faun, 202
  Jeux, 65, 202, 280
  Syrinx, 280
De Maria, Walter, 16, 25
Denisoff, Serge, 39, 40n, 41nn, 43n, 44n, 45n, 46n, 48n, 49, 52
Der Hagopian, Yenouk, 287, 288
Diaghilev, Sergei, 75–76
Digital Equipment Corporation (DEC), 176, 179, 188
Dodge, Charles, 270
Donatoni, Franco, 195
  Babai, **195**
Duchamp, Marcel, 18, 101, 102, 106
Dufrêne, François, 194
Dwyer, Terence, 171
Dylan, Bob, 40

Einstein, Albert, 7
Electronic Music Studios, 210
Eliot, T. S., 119
Ellington, Duke, 205
England, Nicholas, 155
Eno, Brian, x, 32, 33, 296
  Discreet Music, 32, 33
Erb, Donald, 338
Erickson, Robert, 275–276
Ernst, Max, 101

Felciano, Richard, 338
Feldman, Morton, 246, 248, 257
  Last Pieces, 255
Fine, Vivian, 273, 274, 279, 280, 281, 282, 283
Finney, Ross Lee, 273, 274, 277
Flynt, Henry, 16
Forti, Simone, 13, 16
Fortner, Wolfgang, 329
Frick, Arthur
  Boat, see **gallery**
Furtwängler, Wilhelm, 321

Gahu (dance), 154–157, **158**, 159, 160
  Hatsyiatsya pattern, 155, **156,** 157–159
Gandhi, Mohandas (the Mahatma), 299
General Electric, 176
George, Stefan, 324, 325
Gerbrant, Carl, 294
Gerhard, Roberto, 55
Gibbons, Orlando, 118
Gibson, Jon, 297
Gillespie, David F., 40n
Giovanno, Herman di, 287, 290
Glass, Philip, xiin, xiii, 254, 257, 258, 261, 263, 264, 284, 295–299
  Dance No. 4, 263–264

Glass, Philip (*Cont.*)
    Einstein on the Beach, 299
    Music in Changing Parts, 295, 296,
       297–299
    Music in Contrary Motion, 295
    Music in Fifths, 295
    Music in Similar Motion, 295
    Music in Twelve Parts, 263, 296,
       299
    Satyagraha, 299
    Strung Out, 261–262, 295
Glassie, Henry, 47
gong-gongs and atokes, **156**
Gonzalez, Julio, 276
Gould, Glenn, 46
Graham, Martha, 288, 295
Guy, Barry, 249
    Songs for Tomorrow, 249

Hancock, Herbie, 173
Handel, George Frederick, 285, 289,
    292
Hansen, Al, 15, 26
Harmon, James E., 46n, 47
Harris, Roy, xi, 297
Harrison, Lou, 287, 288, 292–293
Hauser, Arnold, 68–70
Haydn, Franz Josef, 113, 121
    Violin Sonata in A Major, 121
Heath (computer company), 178,
    188
Heisenberg, Werner, 3, 4, 6, 7, 8, 11
Hellermann, William
    *Experimental Music—A Solid
      Score,* see **gallery**
Helmholtz, Hermann von, 4, 6
Henze, Hans Werner, 55, 248, 329
Heraclitus, 4, 5
Hess, Emil
    Ancient Sounds, see **gallery**
Hesse, Hermann, 289

Hewlett-Packard (computer com-
    pany), 176
Heyworth, Peter, 201
Higgins, Dick, 15, 16, 17, 18, 23
    Danger Musics, 20, 26
    Graphis, 20
    Second Contribution, 23
Hindemith, Paul, 121, 206, 327
    Ludus Tonalis, 121
Holst, Gustav, 233
Honeywell (computer company), 176
Hovhaness, Alan, 284–295
    Armenian Rhapsody no. 1, 288
    Bluebeard, 286
    Concerto for Accordion, 293
    Daniel, 286
    Duet for Violin and Harpsichord,
      291
    Etchmiadzin, 288
    "From the End of the Earth," 293
    Khaldis, 292
    Lousadzak, 287
    Magnificat, 292, 293, 294
    Meditation on Orpheus, 293
    Mysterious Mountain, 288–289,
      291–292, 294–295
    Saint Vartan Symphony, 289, 292,
      294
    symphonies, 289, 294
Howe, Hubert S., Jr., 172

Ichiyanagi, Toshi, 196
    Field, The, **196–197**
Indy, Vincent d', 280
Intel Corporation (computer com-
    pany), 175, 177
Interdata (computer company), 176
International Business Machines
    (IBM), 176, 178
Irwin, Robert, 267, 268

Ives, Charles, 47, 60, 122, 125n, 221, 223, 232, 248
  Fourth Symphony, 60
  Putnam's Camp, 60

Jacobi, Karl G. J., 301
Jasper, Tony, 39–40
John, Elton, 46
Johns, Jasper, 245
Johnson, Ray, 16
Johnson, Robert Sherlaw, 65–66
Johnson, Tom, xii, xiii, 28–29
  Four Note Opera, The, 29
  Imaginary Music, 29
  Nine Bells, see **gallery**
  Private Pieces, 29
Jolivet, André, 192–194
Jones, A. M., 154, 155, 157, 158, 160
Jones, Joe, 90, 91
  Five Pieces for Piano, **198**
  Music Plant, see **gallery**
Joyce, James, 97, 101, 275

Kandinsky, Wassily, 21
Kant, Immanuel, 330
Kaprow, Allan, 15, 21–22
Karkoschka, Erhard, 242, 247
Kiesler, Frederick
  Gong, The, see **gallery**
Kirchner, Leon, 54
Kirstein, Lincoln, 233
Kiss (group), 50
Klebe, Giselher, 329
Klusen, Ernst, 43n
Knowles, Allison, 17
Kolisch, Rudolf, 326
Kosugi, Takehisa, 24
Kotik, Petr, 36
Koussevitzky, Serge, 232

Kramer, Jonathan, xiv, 102, 103n, 104n, 108n, 116, 117n, 120–121, 123n, 125n
Krenek, Ernst, 329
Krosen, Jill
  Original Lour and Walter Story, The, see **gallery**
Kunen, James, 205–206

Ladzepko, Alfred, 155
Lalo, Charles, 306
Landry, Dickie, 297
Lee, Edward, 43n
Leibniz, Gottfried von, 306
Leoncavallo, Ruggiero, 75
Lewis, George, 270
LeWitt, Sol, 263
Ligeti, Gyorgy, 124, 244, 248, 281
  Volumina, 124
Lippard, Lucy, 18
Liverpool (group), 47
Lockwood, Annea, 36
  River Archives, 36
Logothetis, Anestis, 241
  Odyssey, 241
Loos, Adolf, 318
Lucier, Alvin, 254, 267
  I Am Sitting in a Room, 268–269
Luening, Otto, xi, 273, 274, 277, 280
Lully, Jean-Baptiste, 301
Lutyens, Elisabeth, 248
Lynes, Russell, 44

Maciunas, George, 13, 17, 18
  Anthology, An, 17
MacLow, Jackson, 16, 17n, 23, 25n
Maconie, Robin, xi–xii, 57–58, 68n
Maeterlinck, Maurice, 323
Mahler, Gustav, 26
Mallarmé, Stéphane, 97, 99, 101

Mälzel, Johann Nepomuk, 239
Mann, Thomas, 110, 291
Marabini, Claudio, 77n, 78n, 79n, 82n
Marinetti, Filippo Tommaso, 71, 72, 73, 75–82, 83n, 87–88, 280
Martinu, Bohuslav, 287
Massine, Léonide, 75
Masson, André, 101
Maw, Nicholas, 248
Mazza, Amando, 87
McLuhan, Marshall, 203, 206
McPhee, Colin, 163
    Music in Bali, 163
Messiaen, Olivier, 36, 53, 56, 65–68, 281, 312
    Ascension, L', 66
    Cantéjodayâ, 66, 123n
    Catalogue d'Oiseaux, 36
    Chronocromie, 66–68
    Couleurs de la Cité céleste, 66
    Turangalîla-Symphonie, 66
    Visions de l'Amen, 66
Merleau-Ponty, Maurice, 256n
Microsoft (computer company), 184
Minnesota Mining & Manufacturing Co. (3M), 187
MITS (computer company), 178
Molière, 303n
Mondrian, Piet, 99, 204
Monk, Meredith, 270
Moog, Robert, 51, 167, 171, 205, 209, 210, 211
Moore, Douglas, xi
Moorman, Charlotte, xiii, 142, **144–149**
    TV Bra for Living Sculpture, see **gallery**
Morris, Robert, 25, 259
MOS Technology (computer company), 177

Motorola, 177
Mozart, Wolfgang, 28, 34, 113, 118, 127, 206, 207, 249, 285, 289, 290, 320, 321, 328
    Fortieth Symphony, 118n, 123
Mumford, Lewis, 205
Munkasci, Kurt, 299
Murphy, Arthur, 297

Nauman, Bruce, 266
    Tape Recorder with a Tape Loop of a Scream Wrapped in Plastic Bag and Cast into the Center of a Block of Concrete, see **gallery**
Nettl, Bruno, 42
New England Digital Corporation, 187
New York Dolls (group), 50
Nono, Luigi, 248, 329
North Star (computer company), 178
Nye, Russel B., 41n, 42, 48n, 52
Nyman, Michael, 130, 135, 137
    1-100 (Obscure 6), 129, 135, **136**

Offenbach, Jacques, 50n
Ohio Scientific (computer company), 178
Olson, Harry F., 4
Ono, Yoko, 16, 17

Paganini, Niccolò, 50
Paik, Nam June, xiii, 13, 16, 24, 90, 91, 142, 143, **144–149**
    Opera Sextronique, 142
    Symphony for 20 Rooms, 16
    TV Bra for Living Sculpture, see **gallery**
Palestine, Charlemagne, 254, 267
Parmenides, 4

Parsons, Michael, 135, 137
Peckham, Morse, 55n, 102, 107, 111, 141
Penderecki, Krzysztof, 244, 281
Pergolesi, Giovanni Battista, 64n
Petrassi, Goffredo, 248
Peterson, Richard A., 45n
Pfitzner, Hans, 74
Phillips, Tom, 245
   Postcard Compositions Opus XI, 245
Piatti, Ugo, 75, 76, 87
Piston, Walter, xi, 233, 297
Pollock, Jackson, 97, 98, 101, 107, 204, 242
Pound, Ezra, 122
Pousseur, Henri, 126
Pratella, Francesco Balilla, 71–83, 86n, 88, 89
   Aviatore, Dro, L', 74, 75, 82, 88
   Gioia Saggio di Orchestra Mista, 88
   Lilia, 77
   Musica Futurista per Orchestra, 74, 79–80
   Sina d'Vargöun, La, 77, 78
Presley, Elvis, 51
Prokofiev, Serge, 75, 110, 117, 295
   Sixth Symphony, 117
Pythagoras, 4, 306

Quine, Willard, 4

Radio Shack, 178
Rameau, Jean-Philippe, 306
Ratner, Leonard, 102
Rauschenberg, Robert, 21, 245
   Soundings, see **gallery**
Reger, Max, 322, 327
Reich, Steve, 31–33, 55, 150, 254, 257, 297
   Come Out, 258

Drumming, 259, **260,** 261
It's Gonna Rain, 258–259
Music for 18 Musicians, 31–32
Slow Motion Sound, 259
Violin Phase, 261
Reichenbach, Hans, 4
Reynolds, Roger, 273, 274–275, 278–279, 280, 282
Rich, Alan, 296
Riesman, David, 40, 46
Riley, Bridget, 262–263
Riley, Terry, xii, 16, 30, 34, 297
   In C, 30, 34
Rimsky-Korsakov, Nicolai, 77n
   Golden Cockerel, 77n
Roberts, John Storm, 45n
Rochberg, George, 60, 122
   Third Quartet, 60
Romani, Romolo, 81
Roth, Dieter, 16
Rousseau, Jean-Jacques, 311
Roussel, Albert, 280
Ruggles, Charles, 281
Russcol, Herbert, xiv, 172
Russolo, Antonio, 87n
Russolo, Luigi, 71–76, 80–89, 280
   Convegno d'Automobile e d'Aeroplani, 87n, 89
   Rete di Rumori, 87
   Risveglio di Capitale, 87n
   Risveglio di una Città, 87, 89
Rzewski, Frederic, 32, 33, 60
   Coming Together, 32, 33
   Moutons de Panurge, Les, 60
   Opus One, 33

Sahl, Michael, 122
   Mitzvah for the Dead, A, 122
Salzman, Eric, 273, 280, 283

Sanders, Pharoah, 125
Saroyan, William, 293
Satie, Erik, x, 20, 21–23, 31
    Parade, x
    Vexations, 21
    Vieux sequins et Vielles Cuirasses,
    21
Schaeffer, Pierre, 171, 203
Schickele, Peter, 297
Schiller, Friedrich, 318
Schillinger, Joseph, 100, 276
Schmit, Tomas, 24–25
    Zyklus, 24–25
Schönberg, Arnold, ix, xiv, 8, 21, 54,
    73, 127, 201, 204, 206, 232, 248,
    280, 281, 305n, 306–307, 310,
    313, 316–330
    Buch der hängenden Gärten, Das,
    325
    Erwartung, 322
    First Chamber Symphony, 323
    First String Quartet, 323
    Five Pieces for Orchestra, 280, 325
    Glückliche Hand, Die, 325
    Moses und Aron, 328
    Ode to Napoleon, 312
    Pelleas und Melisande, 322–323, 326
    Pierrot lunaire, 325
    Second String Quartet, 323–324
    Six Little Piano Pieces, 325
    Three Piano Pieces, 325
    Verklärte Nacht, 322
Schubert, Franz, 296
Schuller, Gunther, xivn
Schumann, Robert, 302
Schwartz, Elliot, 331–338
    Cycles and Gongs, 333, **334**, 335
    Five Mobiles, 332, **333**, 334, 335
    Harmony of Maine, The, 336, **337**
    Music for Napoleon and Beethoven,
    335, 336

Schwitters, Kurt, 30
Scriabin, Alexander, 47, 73, 323
Scully, Sean, 263
Sear, Walter, 206–207
Sessions, Roger, xi, 54, 55, 221, 248
Shapespeare, William, 119
Shankar, Ravi, 287, 297
Shankar, Ude, 287
Shapey, Ralph, 113
Shiomi, Chieko, 24
Shirali, Vishnu, 287
Shostakovich, Dmitri, 114n
    First Symphony, 114n
Sibelius, Jean, 285
    Fourth Symphony, 285
    Luonnotar, 285
    "Swan of Tuonela, The," 285
Sidgwick, Frank, 47n
Silvestrov, Valentin, 127
Smithson, Robert, 267
Sollberger, Harvey, 273, 275, 276,
    280, 283
Sontag, Susan, 206
Sony Corporation, 187
Souster, Tom, 43n
Southwest Technical Products, 178
Spaeth, Sigmund, 43–44
Starer, Robert, 273, 278, 282, 283
Stein, Gertrude, 275
Stockhausen, Karlheinz, xin, xii,
    53–59, 61, 65–69, 115, 121, 202,
    247, 248, 281, 329
    Adieu, 59
    Carré, 68
    Etüde, 68
    Gesang der Jünglinge, 68
    Hinab-Hinauf, 59
    Klavierstück XI, 123n, 302–303
    Klavierstück IX, 59
    Kontakte, 56, 58, 66, 68, 241

Stockhausen, Karlheinz (*Cont.*)
    Kontra-Punkte, 57, 252
    Mikrophonie I, xin, 68
    Mikrophonie II, 59
    Mixtur, 68
    Momente, 68
    Studie I, 68
    Studie II, 68, 240
    Telemusik, 59
    Zyklus, 121
Stokowski, Leopold, 142, 167, 171,
    203, 274, 288, 289
Storb, Ilse, 44n
Stradivarius, Antonio, 305
Strauss, Richard, 41, 207, 280,
    317–318
Stravinsky, Igor, 53, 54, 56, 58, 61,
    63–65, 69, 73–76, 112n, 201, 205,
    206, 237, 248, 280, 281
    Firebird, The, 77n
    Noces, Les, 263
    Pulcinella, 64n
    Sacre du Printemps, Le, 63, 65, 72,
        232, 280
    Sonata for Two Pianos, 64
    Symphonies of Wind Instruments,
        54, 58, 61, 63–65, 67
Strombom, Tracy, 45n
Subotnick, Morton, 173, 338
    Silver Apples of the Moon, 173
Swanwick, Keith, 43–44, 46

Tchaikovsky, Peter, 335
Tenney, James, 152
Texas Instruments, 176
Thompson, Randall, xi
Thomson, Virgil, 221, 297
Thoreau, Henry David, 36
Tudor, David, 97

Ussachevsky, Vladimir, 273, 274, 278,
    282

Valéry, Paul, 99
Van Solkema, Sherman, 272–273
Varèse, Edgard, x–xiv, 56, 99,
    100, 173, 202, 221, 255n, 272–283,
    290
    Amériques, 280, 281
    Arcana, 274
    Bourgogne, 280
    Density 21.5, 274, 275, 280
    Déserts, 274, 282
    Hyperprism, 274
    Intègrales, 274
    Ionisation, x, 274, 279, 281
    Octandre, 274, 279, 281
    Poème Électronique, 173, 282
Vartabed, Komitas, 285
Verdi, Giuseppe
    Rigoletto, 224

Wagner, Richard, 113, 207, 225, 301,
    321, 328
    Meistersinger von Nürnberg, Die,
        318
    Tristan und Isolde, 202, 318, 321
Waring, James, 16
Watts, Robert, 15, 17
Webern, Anton von, 28, 29, 56,
    99–101, 107, 110, 118, 121, 163,
    222, 231, 232, 248, 280, 281, 307,
    312, 313, 329
    opus 21, 121
Weinberg, Henry, 273, 277, 278, 280
Whitehead, Alfred North, 233
Whitman, Robert, 26
Williams, Emmett, 17, 23–24
Winsor, Phil, 122
    Melted Ears, 122
Wolf, Hugo, 41
Wolff, Christian, 125, 246
    Changing the System, 250

Wolff, Christian (*Cont.*)
   For 1, 2, or 3 People, **246**
   Wobbly Music, 249–250
Woolf, Virginia, 275
Wronski, Hoene, 201
Wuorinen, Charles, 173, 273, 275,
   277, 279, 282, 283
   Time's Encomium, 197

Xenakis, Iannis, ix, 60, 202, 204, 248,
   255, 256n, 281
   Bohor I, 60

Pithoprakta, 204
Xerox Corporation, 176

Young, La Monte, 13, 16, 17, 23, 25n,
   53, 59, 90, 91, 124
   Composition 1960, 17, 59
   Piano Piece for David Tudor, 17
Yuasa, Jōji, 198
   Cosmos Haptic, **198**

Zilog (computer company), 177–179

GREGORY BATTCOCK was editor of several anthologies of criticism in the fine arts, including *The New American Cinema, The New Art, Minimal Art, New Artists Video, New Ideas in Art Education, Super Realism,* and the author of *Why Art,* all published in the Dutton Paperbacks series. He taught art history at both The William Paterson College of New Jersey and New York University. Dr. Battcock died December 25, 1980.